WHY ME, GOD?

WHY ME, GOD?

A Jewish Guide for
Coping with Suffering

Lisa Aiken

JASON ARONSON INC.
Northvale, New Jersey
London

The Halachic Living Will is reprinted with permission from Agudath Israel of America, 84 Williams Street, New York, NY 10038.

The Appointment of a Health Care Agent/Advanced Directive is reprinted with permission from the Rabbinical Council of America.

This book was set in 10 pt. Times by AeroType, Inc., Amherst, NH.

Library of Congress Cataloging-in-Publication Data

Aiken, Lisa.
  Why me, God? : a Jewish guide for coping with suffering / by Lisa Aiken.
    p. cm.
  Includes bibliographical references and index.
  ISBN 1-56821-535-5 (alk. paper)
    1. Suffering—Religious aspects—Judaism. 2. Judaism—Doctrines. I. Title.
  BM645.S9A37 1996
  296.7′4—dc20

                                                                    95-19572

Manufactured in the United States of America. Jason Aronson Inc. offers books and cassettes. For information and catalog write to Jason Aronson Inc., 230 Livingston Street, Northvale, New Jersey 07647.

This book is dedicated to the memory of

Rabbi Yitzchok Kirzner, *zt"l*

whose compassion, warmth, and love of God

touched thousands.

May this book be a merit for his soul.

Contents

Foreword

Dr. Lisa Aiken has authored a meaningful book, *Why Me, God?,* which combines the Torah tradition with deep psychological insight. The book is permeated with the words and ideas of our sages. Dr. Aiken has taken these ideas and, by virtue of her experience in the field of psychology, has given them a contemporary context. This book should serve as a source of inspiration for people looking for answers for themselves, or for those looking to help others experiencing pain. Additionally the book serves as a monument to the life of an exemplary *talmid chacham*, Rabbi Yitzchok Kirzner ל"צז.

"אין עושים נפשות לצדיקים, דבריהם הן הן זכרונן" (ירושלמי שקלים ה:ה)

May Dr. Aiken merit to write many more books, and may her books serve as a conduit to bring our people back to their Father in heaven.

Rabbi Noah Weinberg
Rosh HaYeshiva
Aish HaTorah College of Jewish Studies

Preface

I was privileged in 1989 to have had the opportunity to collaborate with Rabbi Yitzchok Kirzner, *zt"l*, on our book *The Art of Jewish Prayer*. What a rare individual he was! Totally dedicated to serving God, he had tremendous warmth and an extraordinary ability to relate to people. His precious pearls of Torah were always peppered with psychological insights, and tailor-made for his diverse listeners. He was equally able to touch the hearts and souls of Yiddish-speaking grandmothers and American-born yeshiva students; unaffiliated Yuppie women and middle-aged secular businessmen. As we worked together, I was impressed by his concern and love for everyone who crossed his path. He spent countless hours helping people with their personal problems, and his role as a teacher encompassed being an adviser, counselor, and friend.

As our first of many planned manuscripts neared completion, we approached each other with an idea. Each of us, unbeknownst to the other, had wanted years earlier to write the present book when Harold Kushner's *When Bad Things Happen to Good People* became a best-seller. Kushner misled many Jews into thinking that Judaism proposes that bad things happen because random forces cause tragedy to everyone, and God is powerless to intervene. Rabbi Kirzner and I felt it imperative to write a book that expresses what our beautiful tradition has to say about the topic of suffering, but it was not until we met in 1989 that our present collaboration began.

Tragically, less than a month after we decided to write this book, Rabbi Kirzner was diagnosed with cancer. Undaunted, he continued his heavy teaching schedule, including lectures about suffering so that I could incorporate his ideas into the present work. Although he had given similar lectures many years earlier in Los

Angeles, his personal ordeals gave him a different perspective on suffering that he had understood only theoretically before.

Unfortunately, Rabbi Kirzner passed away before I completed this book, but it incorporates many thoughts that he shared with me during its initial stages.

As I finished this book, memories of Rabbi Kirzner came back to me. Soon after he moved back to New York from Los Angeles, we waited patiently one night for women to come to his lecture. After twenty minutes, only five women had shown up. A scant three years later, approximately 6,000 mourners attended his funeral in Brooklyn, and thousands more attended services in Los Angeles and Jerusalem.

He was an amazing man who made an extraordinary impact on Jews. In his forty-one short years, he founded the Jewish Learning Exchange in Los Angeles and Congregation Kol Yehuda in Brooklyn. He cofounded and taught at the Jewish Renaissance Center in Manhattan. He was the spiritual adviser and teacher at a *yeshivah* in Edison, New Jersey. He also taught weekly classes in Manhattan, Brooklyn, and Long Island. He left a legacy of some 850 taped lectures that Jews around the world now enjoy.

When I lecture in the United States, Canada, or Israel, someone often approaches me after a talk and says, "I was a student of Rabbi Kirzner's. There's such a void in my life now that he is gone. I've never met anyone who could replace him." Even two years after his passing, students still talk about him with tears in their eyes.

"A good name is better than good oil," says Ecclesiastes. Rabbi Kirzner explained that oil gives light to others with no effort of its own, but a person achieves a good name by toiling constantly to work on himself, to give to others, to spread the light of Torah, and to make the world a better place. Oil eventually burns out, while the deeds of someone who creates a good name for himself live on eternally in the souls of those whom he leaves behind.

Rabbi Kirzner had many beautiful qualities. His good name lives on for all of us who knew him.

* * * * *

Sooner or later, tragedy strikes each of us, and we try to come to terms with it. This is the first English-language book that melds traditional Jewish perspectives about suffering with practical suggestions for coping. The first part of this book describes the purpose of life and the role of suffering in it. The second part discusses how to cope with specific crises and problems, and how to help others do the same. For the sake of completeness, the last part of this book discusses national suffering and the Holocaust.

Some of the listed resource organizations and readings espouse non-Jewish philosophies, because Jewish resources were not always available. Readers will have to glean the useful information from the irrelevant ideas.

When no resource agencies are listed for a locale, readers should call a listed agency and ask for information and/or referrals nearby.

I don't necessarily endorse the listed resource books or agencies, but I recognize that different people will find solace or help through different avenues. I take no responsibility for the quality or appropriateness of services or information provided.

Names and personal details in the stories have been altered to protect the anonymity of the people concerned. It is purely coincidental if any names or situations correspond exactly to those of real people.

I hope this book will help readers find comfort and meaning in their suffering and encourage others to do the same.

Acknowledgments

I am indebted to Rabbi Yitzchok Kirzner, *zt" l,* for collaborating with me on this book. His philosophical insights are an integral part of it.

I would also like to express my appreciation to Diane Laderman for her help in organizing and editing this manuscript, and her hugs over the telephone when I reached my wits' end with it.

I wish to thank Rabbi Dovid Gottlieb for reviewing this manuscript and making suggestions for its improvement. I am also grateful to Rabbis Noah Weinberg, Moshe Weinberger, Ari Kahn, and Dr. Ira Michaels for doing the same.

Finally, I would like to thank Sharon Friedman, my agent, for her wisdom, encouragement, patience, and hard work in getting this book published.

Last but not least, I would like to thank the Almighty for granting me the wherewithal to publish this book after four years of painstaking effort.

Introduction

Everyone . . . views God as just and fair when they are comfortable and successful. . . . But when they lose their fortunes, their children, or suffer physical torment, some reject their faith and believe the world is misgoverned."[1]

We tend to believe that life should be fair, and that good people should have easy lives, be happy, and get what they want. But sooner or later, tragedies and crises make us realize that life doesn't work that way. When we see terrible suffering and injustice, we question God. Does He exist? And if He does, does He really care about us? When good people suffer and bad people have easy lives, can life have any real meaning? Some people conclude that a caring God couldn't possibly allow the apparent injustices that we see every day and assume that random forces, nature, or bad luck cause pain and hardship.

Our lives have little meaning or purpose if we believe that we are governed by random forces. Judaism teaches that the objective value of any experience depends upon how much it spiritually rectifies our souls and the world, and allows us greater closeness with God in the present and future. If unpleasant events are mere accidents, we are but helpless pawns in a cosmic game. Misfortunes can't be meaningful if they happen randomly.

Judaism teaches that there *is* meaning in every crisis and tragedy, even if we aren't *responsible* for them. Our Torah and Jewish teachings help us to find this meaning.

When we wonder why "bad" things happen to people who don't "deserve" it, we assume that pleasant events are good and that unpleasant ones are bad. But it is more accurate to say that purposeful events are good and that meaningless ones are bad. Both tragedy and pleasure can give our lives meaning, and it is often the difficulties and challenges that help us to grow the most.

Only meaningless occurrences are bad. Painful situations are always good if they serve a useful purpose; pleasures that interfere with our spiritual growth are always bad, no matter how good they feel. Pleasure and pain, then, aren't reliable indices of what is truly good or bad. Eating a lot of junk food or abusing drugs can feel great, but the long-term effects are disastrous. The pain that a woman undergoes in labor results in her bringing a baby into the world. How pleasurable something is says nothing of its consequences later, and how painful something is now tells us nothing of its real value in the future.

When we wonder why bad things happen, we often let our emotions judge who and what are bad and good, instead of using objective standards to evaluate what happened. Meanwhile God judges us according to how well we fulfill His purpose in putting us here,[2] in addition to making purposeful things happen regardless of whether or not we deserve them.

We can't understand suffering if we use our criteria for deciding how God should run the world, instead of learning how He actually runs it. If we insist that God run the world our way, intellectual explanations of why unpleasant things happen will never satisfy us.

Since God gave us life and sustains us, He defines what makes life meaningful. He designs events according to how they fit into His plan, not ours. Death, illness, poverty, and other forms of suffering are totally good and fair in God's game plan for the world. As we learn more about that game plan, sad and tragic events make a lot more sense.

Our Creator wants us to see His hand in every facet of life, to serve Him and draw ever closer to Him. When we don't do that, He makes things happen that encourage us to live up to our spiritual potentials. He sometimes uses unpleasant situations to that end.

We often want to feel close to God, yet not live up to His expectations of us. Rather than let us comfortably live our way, He may steer us in a direction that feels unpleasant that He knows will benefit us. For instance, a young Jewish woman had aspirations of becoming a dancer. She rehearsed for many hours with her Gentile dance partner until they had their routine down pat. Three days before their first contest, she suddenly felt feverish and lethargic and couldn't stop coughing. The night of the contest, she was too sick and exhausted to get out of bed. Her partner managed to get a seasoned partner on a moment's notice, and they won the contest without her. By the time the woman recovered from a three-month bout of pneumonia, her partner had moved to another city.

She resumed dancing, but this time decided to try her luck as a jazz dancer. Shortly before auditioning to join a small company, she started experiencing severe knee pain that made it hard to walk. She required intensive rehabilitation for months and missed the auditions.

When she recovered, she resumed rehearsing again in hopes of joining a regional dance company. Within two months, she contracted debilitating pneumonia again. When she recovered, she moved to New York where she resumed taking dance classes. But she had so much pain after every lesson that she had no choice but to give up dancing forever.

At that time, it was one of the worst tragedies of her life, and she was not open to hearing that there might be anything positive or redemptive in it. She only felt angry that this had happened to her. It took her five years to come to terms with her shattered dream and acknowledge that it might be for the best. She *felt* that it was good only years later when she saw the negative effects that a dance lifestyle had on her spirituality. She has not danced in years, but today that woman teaches Judaism and is the author of the present book. She has brought Judaism instead of dance to thousands of people.

Some people can't relate to the pain of losing a career dream, but they can appreciate the devastation of losing a loved one. That type of pain is so overwhelming that no words can describe it. Survivors may feel they will never be happy again. Waking up without their loved one next to them is unbearable. They feel an ache in the pit of their stomach that won't go away. They may even wish that they were dead so that they wouldn't have to continue facing life alone.

This is exactly how a man felt after losing his wife in a drowning accident at the age of thirty-six. He and his wife had been happily married for ten years, and he struggled to get through one day at a time without her. After five years of being a lonely widower, he met a religious Jewish woman who turned his life around. He had always been a secular Jew, and Sarah showed him the treasures of traditional Judaism. He found a richness and meaning in life that he had never known before.

After being remarried for several years, he confided, "After my wife died, I never thought that I'd be happy again. Life seemed so dark, empty, and meaningless without her. We'd had a seemingly perfect marriage and had been very close. I loved her so much that I really felt that part of me had died when she did.

"But then Sarah came into my life. She is warm, loving, funny, and smart, and she makes me feel whole again. I am happier with her than I ever imagined was possible. She is an observant Jew and showed me the beauty of Judaism that I missed my whole life. I am so indebted to her for opening up vistas to me. I love learning Torah, I love spirituality, I love being her partner when we invite guests to our home for *Shabbat* and holidays. My life has so much more depth and meaning now, thanks to her. She's the best thing that ever happened to me. It was terrible when my first wife drowned. I loved her so much that I'll probably carry a void deep inside me for the rest of my life. I think about her when I go places that we once went together, or I look at our photos. And of course, it hurts when I think about her on our wedding anniversary, or on the anniversary of her death. But along with those twinges of pain, I am comforted by the fulfilling life I have now. I would never have found those treasures if my first wife hadn't been taken away.

We may not always appreciate it, but nothing happens randomly.[3] "Everything that the Lord made testifies about Himself, even the wicked man for the day of evil."[4] All of our experiences—pleasant, unpleasant, painful, and enjoyable—are engineered by a Supreme Being who continually watches us and responds to everything that we do.[5] He even sends us sad experiences and tragedies when they will ultimately benefit us.

We can hear these philosophical ideas yet not believe that a loving God could allow so much suffering. We see so much pain around us that we question His ways, just as our ancestors did. Abraham asked how a perfect Judge could destroy the people of Sodom and Gomorrah.[6] Our foremother Rebecca questioned why God gave her an evil son.[7] Our forefather Jacob wanted to have an easy life, and felt bitter that he had to endure one tragedy after another.[8] Even Moses asked God why He let the wicked prosper and the righteous suffer.[9] In turn, each ancestor resolved his or her conflicts about God's ways, and so can we.

Having questions about God doesn't mean that we can't believe in Him. When King David suffered, as he did throughout his life, he felt like complaining against God,[10] yet did not stop believing in Him. He had many questions about the Lord's ways, but didn't resolve them by estranging himself from his Creator. He knew that not believing in a God who runs the world offered even fewer solutions to his questions than believing did.

God knows that it is not easy for us to feel close to Him when we face tragedy. Our grief at those times is so all-consuming that we can do no more than express our faith in God's ways of running the world. We do this by saying, "Blessed are You, God, Ruler of the universe, who is a true Judge."[11]

Judaism teaches that God is totally benevolent and that everything He does is good. If so, we might think that we should thank Him for being good to us regardless of how terribly we suffer. But we can't always relate emotionally to the idea that God never does anything bad. When our feelings contradict our philosophy we bless God by expressing how we *feel,* not what we *think.* When we suffer because of God's ways of running the world, we can truthfully say only that we have *faith* in His ability to judge. We might *believe* that His judgment is good when we stare tragedy in the face, but we can't honestly *feel* that it is.

At such times, it is important for us to know that God is sensitive to our religious tensions. One way that He showed this in ancient times was by requiring Jewish women to bring Temple sacrifices after they gave birth. These offerings atoned for their having sworn, in the midst of excruciating labor pains, that they would never again have sexual relations with their husbands.[12] Since God knew that women in labor would say things that they would later regret, He gave them a way to rectify their actions.[13]

Similarly, He accepts that we may act one way when we are in pain and another way when we feel better. This is why the Talmud says that we are not held accountable for what we say in the throes of pain.[14]

We cope with sorrow and tragedy by first acknowledging and reacting to our pain. Once it subsides, we can try to find meaning in the ordeal, provided we don't misinterpret it as a sign that God doesn't care about us or our loved ones. Feeling rejected by God makes our emotional pain worse and leaves us feeling depressed and alone.

When we suffer, we should ask ourselves, "Is this a divine message to change my life, my attitudes, or the way I relate to others? How can I grow from this? Can I feel God 'holding my hand' through this challenge and helping me spiritually?"

We can share our upset feelings with God by saying, "It's not that I don't believe in You, but You've made my life so painful. Help me understand what this is all about."

The Talmud expresses the idea that God empathizes with our pain, and so to speak, suffers with us. Even when a man is condemned to death for committing a capital crime, the Almighty "feels" for him, as it says:

Rabbi Meir said, "When a person suffers, what does the divine Presence say? 'My head is weak, my arm is weak.' If this is how the Omnipresent suffers over the blood of the wicked that is spilled (when he must be hanged for his capital crime) how much more does this apply to the blood of the righteous?"[16]

In order to allow us to earn maximal reward in the afterlife, the Almighty does not tamper with a system that allows pain and suffering to occur in meaningful ways. Yet the fact that He "feels" for us when we suffer is expressed by the concept that the divine Presence went into exile with the Jewish people some 1,900 years ago. He "suffers" with His people until the time of redemption from all pain and suffering occurs. At that time, both He and we will be redeemed from exile.

When Job suffered, he never stopped believing in God. He said, "Behold, fear of the Lord is wisdom, and turning away from evil is understanding."[15] In other words, when God hurts us terribly, our only opportunity to fathom His ways is to observe His commandments and study His Torah, not assume that He doesn't exist or care about us.

We don't have to squash our pain or make believe that it isn't there. But instead of walking away from our Heavenly Father or being paralyzed with rage, we can and should take our pain to Him. We can ask Him to help us deal with our tragedy and give us insight into what it means. If we don't even get that, we can still turn to Him and ask for His companionship to comfort and soothe us.

We should be willing to share our distress with God, even though our first inclination may be to turn away from Him and share our anger and pain with the rest of the world. It is obviously more productive to share our feelings with the One who brought us the suffering in the first place. When we pose questions to God, we will not always get answers. Sometimes, we may partly understand why our suffering was necessary, while at other times we may never find satisfying answers. Either way, once we engage God in our pain and suffering, we can at least grow from the encounter. Once we invite Him to share in our distress, He becomes a greater Presence in our lives. That alone can keep suffering from immobilizing us.

We can find meaning in suffering only by going beyond what we see and feel, using the Torah and Judaism as our guides. Our emotions and intellects will always limit how much we can fathom the Lord's ways. When He does things that are beyond our comprehension, we must sometimes stretch ourselves to trust that He knows what He is doing.

We need to be honest enough to realize when we want emotional balms, not intellectual answers to questions about why we suffer. Some people who have been very traumatized won't accept philosophical explanations as to why God acts as He does. This is why the Talmud says, "Don't try to appease a person while his dead [loved one] lies in front of him."[17] Explanations can help us find meaning only when we're not shattered by pain. We need a respite from suffering, along with understanding and caring, before we can look for meaning in an ordeal.

A book can satisfy intellectual questions about why God lets us suffer, but emotional questions need to be taken to a supportive and insightful spiritual adviser. This book cannot substitute for the emotional comfort that many people seek when they ask, "Why me, God?"

NOTES

1. Moses Maimonides, *Guide for the Perplexed*, 3:22.
2. Jews are required to observe as many of the 613 laws of the Torah as currently apply. A righteous Jew is someone who properly observes these laws, and an evil Jew is someone who knows how and why to observe the Torah but willfully violates it. Few secular Jews today know how God requires them to live. They are not evil for violating Jewish law, but neither can they be totally righteous, even if they are kind and moral by secular standards. Between these two extremes are Jews who are essentially good but who sometimes act improperly, and Jews who are essentially evil but who occasionally act meritoriously.

Gentiles are required only to observe seven moral principles that were commanded to the descendants of Noah. These laws include not murdering, not stealing, not being sexually immoral, not worshiping idols, not cursing God, not eating a limb from a living animal, and the requirement to set up an effective legal system (*Sanhedrin* 56a-b).
3. *Shabbat* 77b.
4. Proverbs 16:4.
5. For example, Isaiah 45:6-7 tells us that God creates everything, even evil. Although He does not actually cause evil, He does allow it to exist so that we can create true goodness by rejecting evil.
6. Genesis 18:23-32.
7. Genesis 25:22.
8. Rashi on Genesis 37:2. The One Above then told him that a righteous person could not have it easy in this world and in the next. See also Genesis 47:9. Shortly before Jacob died, he finally saw how all of his tragedies helped make his twelve sons into the tribes of the future Jewish nation.
9. Based on Exodus 33:18. God told Moses that human beings cannot fathom His ways as long as they are alive.

10. Psalms 39:2: "I will guard my mouth, not to sin with it, and I'll muzzle my mouth when the wicked person passes by."
11. *Brachot* 46b.
12. Leviticus 12:6–8.
13. *Me'am Lo'ez* on Leviticus 12:6–8.
14. *Bava Batra* 16b.
15. Job 29:28.
16. *Sanhedrin* 46b.
17. *Pirkei Avot* 4:23.

1

The Purpose of Life

A man only hurts his little finger in this world if it has been decreed Above."[1]

"Everything that God does is for a good purpose."[2]

Traditional Judaism teaches that God is a totally good and powerful Being who knows and controls everything except for our moral choices.[3] He planned and created a purposeful world for us to live in and put each of us here to fulfill a spiritual mission. He constantly oversees and directs the details of our lives so that we can live meaningfully.[4] Suffering is an important part of this plan.[5]

That's not to say that we should make ourselves suffer by being negligent, self-destructive, or reckless.[6] We are supposed to avoid dangerous situations and take care of ourselves as best we can.[7] But if we are reasonably cautious and misfortunes still happen, we can know that they carry divine messages that await our discovery.

God made the world only in order to give of His goodness to people.[8] His greatest good is letting us attach ourselves to Him as fully as possible so that we can enjoy His perfection and closeness.[9] The greatest pleasure that we can possibly feel is closeness to Him in this world and the next.[10]

God made us a world so that we would search for and find Him behind its trappings. The Hebrew word *olam* means "world," but it comes from the root *he'elem,* meaning hidden. God made the physical world a place where His Presence would be hidden, but we can find Him if we only look. When we see a beautiful landscape or vivid sunset, feel the delicious coolness of fresh water on a hot summer day, or see deer grazing in a meadow, God is hoping that we will realize that this is His handiwork. When we have health, a family, possessions, or accomplishments, He hopes that we will realize that they all come from Him. He doesn't want us to think that Mother Nature or fate run the world while He has more important things to do. God is the One who gives us good fortune, talents, and every pleasure that we enjoy. Since He also directs the unpleasant events of our lives, we should look for His signature in them as well.

When a famous chasidic rabbi was a young boy, he played hide-and-seek with his friends. He found a terrific hiding spot and waited a very long time to be discovered. When it didn't happen, he ran home crying.

When his father saw him, he asked, "What's the matter?"

The boy wiped his face and replied, "When my friends and I played hide-and-seek, I found a great hiding spot. I waited a very long time for them to find me, but they didn't. So I came out of hiding and saw that all of my friends had left long before.

"It wasn't so terrible that my friends didn't find me. What really hurt was that they didn't even care about me enough to look."

He paused and added, "Now I know how God must feel."

God spends every day by our side, so to speak. Imagine His "pain" when we don't even make the effort to look for Him and respond to His presence.

Even if we do search for Him behind the scenes, it can be difficult to find Him because He is totally spiritual. We know how to find only objects that we can see, touch, hear, smell, or feel. How do we find a Being whom we can't perceive with our five senses?

The answer is that we can't find God using our physical senses, but we can find Him using our heart, mind, and soul. For instance, we can see the complexity, awesomeness, and beauty of nature and know that a Creator must have designed it. We can study Jewish history and see God's hand throughout. We can study biology, physiology, or physics and see God's Presence revealed in the grandeur of science and its lack of randomness.

God helps us find Him in other ways, too, such as by putting a divine spark in each of us. Our similarity to Him, then, makes it easier to relate.

We can't imagine how a frog thinks and feels (if it does either!) because we don't have enough in common with it to relate to it. A mother, on the other hand, has a very good idea of what her child thinks and feels because they are so alike.

We can relate to God because He put some of His "spiritual genes" into us. That is what a soul is. The divine spark in each of us lets us bridge the gap between our physicality and God's total spirituality. The more we tune into and develop our inner divinity, the more we fulfill our soul and grow closer to God.

The entire purpose of life is to have a meaningful relationship with our Creator. We can do that only by acting like Him and using the world as He intended. To that end, He made the world a place where we would be challenged to choose what's right over what's wrong and thereby earn the constant opportunity to feel His Presence.[11]

God could have given us spiritual pleasure without any effort on our part, but He chose not to. Receiving rewards without doing anything to deserve them would make us feel like welfare recipients who get undignifying handouts. Our Creator knew that gifts are most meaningful when we work hard to earn them, and He wanted us to feel accomplished by doing that.[12] We earn our Creator's gifts by choosing right over wrong, according to His definitions of both. The harder it is for us to make the right choices, the more reward we earn for overcoming challenges.

God did not want us to be robots who mindlessly follow orders. He wanted us to choose to do what He wants, so He gave us free will in the hope that we would use it to serve Him and thereby rectify the world and our souls.

Free will is meaningless if all choices are equally good, or if we don't know which choices are best. Free will is meaningful only if we are tempted to make bad choices instead of good ones.

In order to give us a lifelong moral challenge, God created the *yetzer hara,* or negative inclination, and the possibility of doing evil. He also created the good inclination (the *yetzer hatov*) and the option to choose good. The *yetzer hara* (the id) constantly urges us to go against God's will and do what makes us happy at the moment. It battles the good inclination that urges us to do what God wants us to do. This is the entire reason why the possibility of doing evil exists. Without the potential to choose evil, we could not truly choose to be good.[13]

As an example, imagine that someone gave you $100. You know that an impoverished friend desperately needs money to buy food and medicine for her very sick child. You, however, are tempted to keep the money to buy a new outfit for yourself. Because you are tempted not to do what's morally best, you do a virtuous act by giving the money away. You also become a better person in the process. If you lived in a world where money had no value and you had everything you could possibly want, giving the money away would show no virtue.

God gave us free will so that we would choose to express our divinity and sanctify our daily lives. At the same time, He gave us animalistic, materialistic, and self-centered instincts as competing forces. The Torah tells us which choices dignify or degrade us, which develop our soul's potentials or create distance from God and urges us to choose wisely.

The Torah is our soul's instruction manual. By following it, we show that we accept and appreciate God's will.[14] The more we study and live by it, the more we refine our souls, earn spiritual blessing, and draw ever closer to God.[15]

All of our life experiences are designed to help us properly receive the Almighty's bounty and appreciate His closeness. They allow our souls to develop fully and spiritually rectify the world so that we can be rewarded with maximal pleasure in an afterlife.

We can understand this idea better by picturing a father who wants to give a lucrative business to his son. The nineteen-year-old will appreciate it some day, but now he knows more than his "old man" and wants nothing more than to listen to rock music and hang out with his friends. His father loves him and is determined to train him to receive the business properly so he won't run it into the ground when he gets it.

It takes a few years, but the father gradually draws his son away from childish pleasures, ignoring his son's initial boredom, complaints, and exasperation. The son eventually gets interested in knowing how the business works. He learns the art of dealing skillfully with suppliers and customers, and enjoys the challenges of solving problems and troubleshooting. The father and son have a lot of differences of opinion, and matters get tense when the son insists on doing things his way. But no matter what happens, the father is always behind his child, giving love and support.

When the son matures, he realizes how good and wise his father was. When his father gives him the gift of the business, the son can finally appreciate it. The son feels good about what he has learned and achieved, and he feels worthy of his father's gift.

More importantly, though, the son realizes that his father's greatest gift was not the business. It was giving himself. The son values his father's insights, concern, and even rebukes once he sees that everything his father did stemmed from love and was for the son's benefit. By becoming a businessman himself, and seeing life from his father's perspective, the son learns to appreciate how wonderful his father was and that everything his father did was only for the child's benefit.

God, too, gives us many wonderful gifts to encourage us to grow close to Him and appreciate Him. Yet we often want to relate more to the trappings that He gives us, or relate to Him only when we feel like it. Instead of letting us stay estranged from Him while we pursue temporary pleasures, God keeps bringing us circumstances that will help us feel close to Him and live a truly meaningful life.[16] We may suffer when He takes away our health, money, jobs, loved ones, or dreams, but He knows that we can gain much more from this in the long run. Every tragedy can benefit our souls, but we can appreciate this only by knowing more about them.

THE SOUL

A soul is the part of God in each of us.[17] Even though we can't see, touch, or measure it, it is the highest form of life there is, besides God. Our soul is our essence, and it keeps us alive.[18] Every soul is unique and has an indispensable role to play in God's plan for spiritually perfecting the world. When put into a body, a soul is supposed to help us find God, do His will, and live in a way that reveals His Presence to others.

Some Jews think that Judaism is not a "spiritual" religion. Yet the existence of souls, and their importance, are at its core. When God created the first person, the Torah says that He "formed Adam from dust of the earth, and He blew into his nose a soul of life."[19] When we die, Scripture tells us, "And the dust shall return to the earth as it once was, and the spirit shall return to God who gave it."[20]

Souls are immortal, and they go to a spiritual afterlife when we die. While the Five Books of Moses do not specifically refer to the immortality of the soul or the afterlife, they repeatedly allude to them. For example, God tells Cain after he kills Abel, "The voice of your brother's blood is screaming to Me from the earth."[21] This means that Abel's tortured soul screamed to God because it had not accomplished what it was put in the world to do.[22]

Another example of the soul's immortality is implied by the Torah's statement that anyone who commits suicide will have to answer to God for his crime.[23] How can someone who is dead in every sense of the word defend his actions? Obviously, God calls the immortal part of us to task for our deeds.[24]

The Torah says, "Then Abraham expired and died in a good, old age, and he was gathered to his people."[25] Similarly, it says, "And (Jacob) expired, and he was gathered to his people."[26] Being gathered to one's people means the soul joins its predecessors in a heavenly realm.

The Torah refers to the future resurrection of souls in the verse, "See . . . I kill and I make alive."[27]

The soul is directly mentioned in a scriptural story about King Saul. He went to a witch in order to have her contact the soul of the deceased prophet Samuel.[28]

The books of the Prophets and Writings refer to our immortal souls and the afterlife in very explicit terms. For example, Abigail told King David, "A man has risen up to pursue you and to seek your soul, and your soul will be bound in the bundle of life with the Lord your God."[29] The "bundle of life" was David's eternal afterlife. In Psalms, David said to God, "You will not abandon my soul to the pit."[30] "The pit" is the realm where souls are punished in the next world.

God made the world so that all people would recognize Him as its Ruler and do His will. Our purpose in life is not to have a good time enjoying sensual, material, or emotional pleasures as ends in themselves. It is to channel our desires only in ways that spiritually complete and elevate our souls and the world. To this end, the Almighty decides when and where to send each soul into this world by considering the world's entire history, from the dawn of humanity until the time of the Messiah. He is constantly mindful of billions of souls and what each needs to accomplish at a given place and time. Because of this awesome complexity, we can't know why any of us were put here when we were, with our unique set of life circumstances. What we can know is that if we are here, we have an important job to do in terms of spiritually perfecting ourselves and the world.

God deliberately made our world incomplete so that we would appreciate our importance in helping Him perfect it. We do this every time we make spiritually meaningful choices that use the world in ways that God directed. For instance, male babies are born with a foreskin, and we spiritually perfect their bodies by removing it during a *brit milah* (ritual circumcision). We do this because God commanded us to make bodies holy this way, not because of any hygienic considerations.[31] We spiritually perfect food by eating only what is kosher, and by saying blessings before and after eating. Following God's will with respect to food makes it so holy that our tables are likened to sacrificial altars. We perfect raw materials like wool, flax, and cotton by making them into modest clothing and ritual objects like prayer shawls (*tallitot*), *yarmulkas*, and Torah coverings. We perfect wood and stone by making them into furniture, homes, and buildings that are used by people who serve the Almighty. Every time we use the physical world to find and serve God, we redeem its potential holiness.

God helps us yearn to do His will by telling each soul, before it is put into a body, what its mission is and how to fulfill it.[32] He commands each soul to go into the physical world because only souls can spiritually elevate physical existence. They come here to reveal God's Presence and constant involvement with us as we see Him in our daily activities.[33]

Every soul knows about its awesome potential and responsibility. This idea is expressed by saying that an angel takes the soul of every fetus on a tour of heaven and hell. In heaven, it asks the soul, "Do you recognize anyone here?"

"No," the soul replies.

"All of these souls were your neighbors in the soul-repository before they were sent into the physical world. (Souls are eternal, and they stay in a spiritual realm before they are sent into the physical world.) They are here now because they used their time on earth well," the angel explains. "They developed so beautifully that you can't recognize them now."

The soul then goes on a tour of the place of punishment (hell) and is asked, "Do you recognize anyone here?"

Again, the soul recognizes no one. The angel remarks, "These souls were all with you before, but they look unfamiliar now because they misused the physical world. Make sure that when you go into the world you become unrecognizable for good reasons, not for bad ones."

Each soul has a critical task with respect to bringing the physical world into perfect harmony with God's will.[34] By studying Torah and having a spiritual mentor we get a sense of how to actualize our soul's potential. Each time that we use the world in ways that God intended, we help perfect the world and our soul.[35] The more we do this, the greater our future spiritual reward will be, and the closer the world will be to its spiritual destination.

Souls come here because they can grow only by overcoming challenges that they confront in a body.[36] Our souls are supposed to motivate us to live up to our spiritual missions and follow a path of truth, not one of ease and comfort.[37] God often thwarts our attempts to live comfortably, because resting on our laurels doesn't help us, or the world, to grow spiritually.

When we die, our souls leave this world and can no longer grow by overcoming physical temptations. They go to a realm where they are eternally rewarded with the pleasure of their spiritual achievements and the closeness to God that they developed.[38]

It is a lifelong challenge to believe that our souls should be our life's focus, and to live up to that belief. This is especially hard when we are constantly bombarded with secular messages that a good life is about having money, possessions, good looks, and a good time.

Some people believe that if God had really wanted us to develop our souls, He would not have made worldly pleasures so enticing and delicious. But the fact that they feel wonderful proves nothing about how God wants us to use them. He deliberately made forbidden pleasures alluring because He wants to challenge our commitment to obeying Him. At the same time, He wants us to overcome this challenge and develop our souls' inner beauty and greatness. Every time we sanctify permitted pleasures and reject forbidden ones, we show that we value our souls more than worldly pleasures. Our ongoing struggles for spiritual growth allow us truly to own our souls when we die instead of feeling alienated from spiritual pleasure in our eternal afterlife.

Physical pleasures are always short-lived, but our spiritual strivings always affect us forever because they develop our eternal souls. We can nurture our souls by doing God's will, even when it doesn't feel good physically or emotionally. We can never nourish our souls by going against what He wants, no matter how good or sensible it seems.

This world has been likened to a corridor, and the next world to a palace. We were meant to prepare ourselves in this corridor so that we can enter the palace when the time comes.[39] That does not mean that we should ignore this world because we'll enter a better one after we die. Rather, the whole purpose of this physical world is to give us opportunities to bring out our souls' qualities.

The palace that we eventually enter is our soul. When we die, the corridor to the palace (the physical world) will be taken away, and all that will be left will be our spiritual essence.

Many people dislike paying rent for a house or apartment because the place will always belong to someone else. We'd rather put the same money into a mortgage so that we can own our home and develop equity in it.

Pursuing bodily pleasures or materialism as goals, instead of using them to elevate us spiritually, is like paying rent. When we die, we can't take our bodies, money, or physical pleasures with us. But we always take our soul-investments with us.

It pains our souls every time we squander our spiritual potentials by indulging in physical pleasures at the expense of our souls. We have the mortgage (our soul), so we may as well pay it off so that we will own it when we die.

Many people think that the afterlife is a paradise that has nothing to do with how we live. They try to create a paradise in this world, and don't think that they need a different one later. But the real paradise is the spiritual achievement we take with us into our eternal afterlife.

When we die, our souls go to a spiritual realm where they are punished and rewarded according to how we lived.[40] If we used the physical world to elevate our soul, and our life circumstances to grow closer to God, we go into a spiritual paradise that is more pleasurable than anything that we can imagine in this world of toil.

THE AFTERLIFE

"Better one hour of tranquility of spirit in the World-to-Come than all of the life in this world."[41]

The afterlife is a spiritual realm where souls experience pleasure or pain that is proportional to how much they developed on earth.[42] God judges souls,[43] then cleanses them in hell from the spiritual damage that we caused. Hell (*gehinnom*) is a realm where souls stay for up to a year,[44] experiencing as much pain and suffering as they need to be spiritually purified for their misdeeds.[45] When this process is complete, they go to heaven, where they enjoy pleasure from the spiritual potentials that they developed by learning Torah and doing God's commandments.[46] The greatest pleasure they can experience is a closeness to God, and the worst punishment is distance from Him.[47]

While our souls are being purified in the next world, our bodies are purified from the spiritual damage that we inflicted on them by decomposing in the earth.[48]

We can believe in an afterlife even though it is hard to imagine what it will be like. "No one has ever heard it, no ear perceived it, no eye has seen it, other than God—what He will do for those who hope in Him."[49] Trying to imagine what the afterlife is like is akin to describing nature's beauty to a blind person, or a fragrance to someone who can't smell.

Yet we know that we will take with us into the next world the spiritual sensitivities that we develop here, and see clearly what we could have been and what we could have achieved. One way of conceptualizing hell is feeling the utter humiliation of knowing what we could have been, but weren't. We will feel the enormity of the damage that we caused by every one of our misdeeds.

The idea of taking our "spiritual personality" with us into the next world is expressed in the following story:

A man asked to see heaven and hell. An angel first took him to hell, where people who deserved punishment sat at huge tables laden with every imaginable delicacy. The fragrances and aromas were mouthwatering, and the fruits and vegetables were palettes of color. Unfortunately, everyone had his hands tied so that he could touch the delicious food but couldn't possibly get it into his mouth. Each suffered the constant torment of seeing and smelling delectable dishes while he starved.

The angel then took the man to heaven, where worthy people enjoyed their rewards. Amazingly, the scene was almost identical. The tables overflowed with gourmet food, and the residents sat with their arms tied, just like the people in hell. But unlike hell's tortured residents, people in heaven were happy and well nourished.

The confused man turned to the angel and asked, "How is it that the people here are so happy and well fed, while those in hell are emaciated and tortured?"

The angel smiled. "In hell, everyone tries to feed himself, but it's not possible. In heaven, everyone feeds the person next to him."

Sooner or later, who we are catches up with us — for better or worse.

RESURRECTION

"Everyone who is born is destined to die, and the dead will come to life, and the living will be judged."[50]

"From the fact that You renew our lives every morning, we know that You will be faithful to resurrect the dead."[51]

God gave each of us a body and soul so that the soul would elevate both during their time on earth. While we are alive, our bodies suffer because they can't fully make use of everything that the soul has to offer. The soul suffers because the body limits the soul's actualization. God relieves their mutual anguish through death.[52]

As long as we live, our bodies can't receive the spiritual reward we deserve for our good deeds because bodies have physical limitations and imperfections.[53] After we die, though, both souls and bodies are fully rewarded for their efforts to develop the soul.

God rewards and punishes us with perfect precision, and resurrection is an underpinning of His system of justice. A body that worked hard to develop its soul deserves to be rewarded. It would be unfair to reward only the soul and neglect the body. That is why God will resurrect our bodies without their former taints of spiritual damage and will reunite them with their respective souls.[54] At that time, He will change the world to accommodate purified bodies so that they can absorb perfect spirituality.[55]

Our resurrected body-soul will form an awesome entity that will live forever.[56] The body will no longer have impurities, nor will the body and soul be separated by barriers that once made death possible. We will enjoy an eternal pleasure that is proportional to how hard we worked to achieve spiritual growth.[57]

The Bible makes many explicit references to resurrection.[58] For instance, God told the Israelites, "Now see that I . . . am He [who] puts to death, and I will bring to life. . . ."[59] The prophet Isaiah said, "Your dead will live [and] my corpse will rise up. Wake up and sing, those who sleep in the dust . . . and the earth will cast out the dead."[60] Ezekiel saw God resurrect a valley of dry bones, and God instructed the prophet to tell the Jewish people, "I will open your graves, and raise you from the graves of My people, and bring you to the land of Israel."[61]

Daniel received a prophecy about what the era of resurrection would be like: "Many of those who sleep in the dust of the earth will wake up. These people will [go] to everlasting life, and these [people will experience] shame and everlasting contempt."[62] Daniel was told that he would die, then rise up at the end of days.[63]

FULFILLING OUR SOULS

"And now, Israel, what does the Lord your God require of you, but to fear Him, to walk in all of His ways, to love Him, and to serve Him with all of your heart and soul. Keep His commandments and statutes that I command you today for your good."[64]

"The end of the matter, when all is said and done: Fear God and observe His commandments, because this is the entire purpose of man."[65]

God revealed Himself to approximately three million Jews when He gave us the Torah 3,300 years ago. He told us to follow it so that we would prepare our souls for the afterlife and fulfill ourselves spiritually.[66] We can know how to grow close to our Creator only by studying His Torah, and we can accomplish what He put us here to do only by observing His commandments.[67]

Since souls are spiritual, our actions affect them spiritually, but we can't see how. Since only God knows how we can spiritually elevate ourselves, we need Him to tell us how to live. Yet many people dismiss biblical commandments as outdated and assume that life is no more than what they can see and understand. They reduce God to their level by using human logic to determine what ultimate reality is.

A rabbi wanted his son to learn a lesson about ultimate reality. The son planned to take his children to Los Angeles. The rabbi insisted, "While you're there, make sure to see Universal Studios."

When his son and grandchildren returned, the rabbi asked how their trip was.

"It was very nice," the son answered.

"What did you see?" the father inquired.

"Everything—Hollywood, Disneyland, Venice, Marineland, and Universal Studios."

"What was Universal Studios like?" the father prodded.

"Oh, it was amazing. In the middle of the California desert, they had models of towns from around the world. One area looked like eighteenth-century London. Another block looked like Wall Street. Around the corner was a Western ghost town. Then we crossed what looked like the Red Sea and an 'ocean' where 'battleships' waged war. The entire place was a world of illusions."

The son thought for a moment and then smiled, realizing why his father had wanted him to go there. "Universal Studios was just like our world. We think that what we see here is absolute reality. It's not until we look behind the scenes that we realize that it's all a bunch of facades and illusions."

Some people think that the physical world is all there is, and that what they can't see isn't real. Universal Studios reminds us that the world is simply a facade for a powerful spiritual reality. Ultimate reality is the Supreme Being that runs the show behind the scenes, and the spiritual afterlife that we create by how we live.

God designed Judaism as a system for living that draws us into a relationship with Him. It uses the same techniques (such as communication) and creates the same feelings (such as love, trust, and appreciation) that help us forge and nurture human relationships. Just as mistrust stops us from furthering a relationship with people, so does it hinder a relationship with the Almighty.

Our minds have limited ability to create a relationship with God. To learn more about the Ruler of the Universe and how He runs the world, we allow our hearts to go beyond our mind's limits, to trust what our minds don't comprehend. To do otherwise is to shortchange the depth of our relationship with Him. We will never fully understand His ways, so we have to trust Him when He asks us to obey divine laws that seem illogical.[68]

Adam, the first human being, was extremely spiritual and wise. He was supposed to obey his Creator's command to enjoy the entire world, but not eat the fruit of one tree. Adam thought it illogical that God made anything off limits to him, so he ate the forbidden fruit. His "logical" reasoning cost him (and his descendants) immortality and a life in Paradise.

This teaches us that no matter who we are, we need to trust God in order to have a relationship with Him and fulfill ourselves.

In order to help us trust Him, God revealed Himself to the entire Jewish people when He gave us the Torah. For almost 2,000 years, He predicted many specific events to our ancestors that came true.[69] They learned from experience that the Almighty is trustworthy and lives up to His word. He asked Jews to believe in Him after we learned that we could trust Him, not because He expected blind faith from us.

In the Torah, He commanded us to do many things that are obviously logical and good, such as practicing social justice, observing business ethics, and respecting our parents. He forbade us to steal, murder, commit adultery, and give false testimony. He told us to act lovingly to each other, to respect our elders and rabbis, and to treat animals humanely.

He also commanded us to do a few things that don't make sense, such as undergoing rites of spiritual purification, and refraining from cooking or eating dairy and meat foods together. Some laws seem "irrational" because we mostly see how our behavior affects our bodies, other people, and our environment. But our actions affect our godly soul and our spiritual afterlife much more than our life on earth. Since it's hard to relate to pure spirituality, it's also hard to appreciate how keeping God's commandments affects our souls. The fact that every commandment affects us spiritually is why the Torah's "illogical" commandments are as important as its "reasonable" ones.

Even "logical" laws have ramifications we cannot grasp. These laws do more than merely protect our society or our individual rights. Every divine law, even those of "social justice," affects our souls.

Since "the reward for doing a commandment isn't given in this world,"[70] we can't know what we accomplish or destroy by observing or neglecting any commandment. This is one reason Maimonides advises us not to tamper with what God has told us to do.[71] We defer to His judgment about how to live, even when it doesn't make sense to us. Since souls are immortal and not bound by time, the Torah is as valid a system for developing our inner divinity now as it was long ago.

NOTES

1. *Chullin* 7b.
2. *Brachot* 60b.
3. *Brachot* 33b.
4. Rabbi Moshe Chaim Luzzatto, *The Way of God* (New York: Feldheim, 1983), p. 385.
5. Among other things, suffering was created as an antidote and atonement for sin. *The Way of God* 2:2:5, 2:3:9.
6. Ibn Pakuda, *Duties of the Heart* 4:4, Moses Maimonides, *Guide for the Perplexed* 3:12.
7. Deuteronomy 4:15.
8. *The Way of God* 1:2:1.
9. See Psalms 73:28.
10. *The Way of God* 1:2:1.
11. *The Way of God* 1:2:5.
12. The Talmud (*Bava Metzia* 38a) expresses this by saying that a person would rather have one portion of his own than nine portions of his neighbor's. See also *The Way of God* 1:2:2.
13. See Aryeh Kaplan, *Handbook of Jewish Thought,* vol. 2 (New York: Moznaim, 1992), p. 206.
14. *The Way of God* 1:4:7.
15. *The Way of God* 1:3:1.
16. *The Way of God* p. 385.
17. *Sanhedrin* 91b; *Nefesh HaChaim* 2:17; *Zohar* 3:25a.
18. *Brachot* 10a.
19. Genesis 2:7.
20. Ecclesiastes 12:7.
21. Genesis 4:10.
22. See Rabbi Israel Lipschitz, *Zera Israel,* at the end of Tractate *Sanhedrin.*
23. Genesis 9:5.
24. There are also many references in the Five Books of Moses to punishments that will affect our souls if we sin. For example, it says of a male Jew who remains uncircumcised, "that soul will be cut off from its people" (Genesis 17:14), and that Jews "who spurned the Lord's word and abrogated His commandment, their souls will surely be cut off" (Numbers 15:30–31).
25. Genesis 25:8.
26. Genesis 49:33.
27. Deuteronomy 32:39.
28. 1 Samuel 7–17 says (paraphrased): "And the woman saw Samuel ['s spirit]. . . . And she said to Saul, 'I see a godlike [man] coming up from the earth.'

"And Saul said to her, 'What do you see?'

"And she said, 'An old man is coming up, and he is covered with a cloak.' And Saul knew that it was Samuel. . . .

"And Samuel said to Saul, 'Why have you disturbed me, to bring me up?'

"Saul replied, 'I am very distressed. The Philistines are warring against me, and God has turned away from me, and has not answered me. . . . I called you to tell me what to do.'

"And Samuel replied, 'Why do you ask me? God has turned away from you and is now your enemy. He has done what I told you: He has torn the kingdom out of your hand and has given it to David. . . .' "

29. 1 Samuel 25:29.

30. Psalms 16:10.

31. *Genesis Rabbah* 11:6; see also the *Aleinu* prayer.

32. The Talmud expresses this by saying that an angel teaches every fetus the wisdom of the entire Torah (*Niddah* 30b).

33. The Jewish perspective about the physical world is unique among the world's religions. For example, Krishnas believe that souls who are inappropriately tantalized by the physical world beg God to let them come to earth. This is a terrible mistake, caused by the soul's attraction to the wrong things. Therefore, Krishnas believe that the sooner people reject the physical world and live ascetic lives, the better off their souls will be. Christians view the body as the enemy of the soul. They believe that physical desires and indulgences are concessions to the flesh and inherently sinful. Only Judaism says that the physical world and its pleasures are spiritually neutral. We are supposed to enjoy and elevate those that can be sanctified and reject those that cannot. Bodies are sinful only when we misuse them by indulging our animalistic desires at the expense of following God's desires for us.

34. A soul does not want to leave the comfort of its totally spiritual home. When God first tells it to go into the material world, the soul refuses. God finally tells it, "I'm not asking you. I decree upon you, 'Enter the physical world.' " This implies that souls are sent here not because they inappropriately lusted for pleasure but because their interactions with this world are needed to serve a vital purpose.

35. *The Way of God* 2:2:1.

36. *The Way of God* 1:3:12. The purpose of having bodies and a physical world is to create opportunities for us to channel our physical, emotional, and material drives in ways that perfect our souls (*The Way of God* 1:2:5).

37. When a baby takes its first breath, its soul loses its clarity about what it is here to do. The Talmud expresses this by saying that at birth, an angel presses every baby on the mouth and causes it to forget all of the Torah (*Niddah* 30b). Our mission is to spend our lives relearning what is right and wrong, and to do only what is right (*The Way of God* 1:4:2).

38. *The Way of God* 1:3:11–12.

39. *Pirkei Avot* 4:21.

40. *The Way of God* 1:3:11–12.

41. *Pirkei Avot* 4:22.

42. Our spiritual level and closeness to God in the next world depends upon how much we sanctified our souls in this world by cleaving to Torah and doing its commandments (Chofetz Chaim, *Torat Or,* chapter 7).

43. A talmudic story illustrates how this is done:

"Antoninus said to Rabbi Judah the Prince: 'The body and soul can make themselves immune from judgment. The body can plead, "The soul sinned, the proof being that I have been like a lifeless stone in the grave (unable to do anything) since it left." The soul can say, "The body sinned, since I fly in the air like a bird (and don't sin) since the day that I left." '

"Rabbi Judah replied, 'I will tell you a parable. We can compare this to a human king who owned a beautiful orchard with appealing figs. He set two watchmen to guard it. One was lame and the other was blind. The lame one said to the blind one, "I see beautiful figs in this orchard. Come and carry me and we will go there and eat them."

" 'The lame one got on the blind man's back, and they went to the figs and ate them.'

" 'Some days later, the owner of the orchard asked them, "Where are those beautiful figs?" The lame man answered, "Do I have feet to walk with?" The blind man replied, "Do I have eyes to see with?" '

" 'What did the king do? He set the lame man on the blind man's back and judged them together.'

" 'The Holy One, blessed is He, will do the same. He will bring the soul, replace it in the body, and judge them together (at the time of resurrection).' " (*Sanhedrin* 91a–b)

44. *Rosh HaShanah* 17a. The rabbis described the afterlife using symbols and codes that were not meant to be taken literally. They correctly assumed that other religions would misappropriate and distort the truth, so they expressed them in terms that only someone steeped in Judaism could properly understand.

45. Rabbi Moshe Chaim Luzzatto, *Maamar HaIkkarim,* "Paradise and Gehenom."

46. *The Way of God* 1:3:12.

47. *Torat Or,* Chapter 7; see *Maamar HaIkkarim,* "Paradise and Gehenom."

48. *The Way of God* 1:3:9.

49. When God made Adam, He wanted him to make choices that would always nourish his soul. Had he done this, Adam would have fully infused his body with soul-like qualities, including immortality (*The Way of God* 1:3:6). By sinning, Adam let his physical desires (instead of his soul) rule his body. That automatically disrupted his soul's total control over his body. Once that happened, the soul could no longer fully share its immortality with the body. Since Adam had within him the souls of all humanity, all subsequent generations were affected by his actions. Since that time, bodies subsequently succumb to their physical limitations instead of becoming immortal from the soul's influence (*The Way of God* 1:3:9).

50. *The Way of God* 1:3:8.

51. *The Way of God* 1:3:9–13. Maimonides' Thirteenth Principle of the Faith states that it is a cardinal Jewish belief to "believe, with complete faith, that there will be a resurrection of the dead, at the time that the Creator, blessed is His name, wills it. . . ." Although traditional Jewish philosophers disagreed about the details of the afterlife and resurrection, they all agreed that both occur. Most traditional Jewish Sages believed that resurrected bodies will live eternally with their respective souls. *Sanhedrin* 92a–b discusses this. Rabbi Saadiah Gaon in *Emunot VeDeot* 7:8; the Raavad on the *Mishneh Torah, Teshuvah* 8:2; Nachmanides on *Torat HaAdam,* at the end of *Shaar HaGemul;* and all of the Kabbalists (*Avodat HaKodesh,* 2:42–43; *Shnei Luchot HaBrit,* Bet David [Jerusalem, 5720], 1:31b; *The Way of God* 1:3:9; and *Derech Mitzvotecha* [Chabad], p. 14b) share this opinion. Others held that resurrection of the dead is only a transient state that will be followed by the death of the body and the soul's return to the world of souls. See Maimonides, *Mishneh Torah, Teshuvah* 8:2; *Guide of the Perplexed* 2:27; and Treatise on Resurrection of the Dead; Rabbi Judah Halevi in *Kuzari* 1:115; and Ibn Pakuda in *Duties of the Heart* 4:4 for opinions about this latter view.

52. *Pesachim* 68a.

53. Deuteronomy 32:39.

54. *The Way of God* 1:3:9.

55. *The Way of God* 1:3:9; *Sanhedrin* 97a. We do not know what kind of bodies we will have then nor what kind of world will exist at that time.

56. *The Way of God* 1:3:3; *Genesis Rabbah* 76.

57. *The Way of God* 1:3:10.

58. Isaiah 64:3.

59. *Pirkei Avot* 4:29.

60. Isaiah 26:19.

61. Ezekiel 37:12.

62. Daniel 12:2.

63. Daniel 12:13. *Sanhedrin* 91b–92a brings additional scriptural sources for resurrection.

64. Paraphrased from Deuteronomy 10:12–13.

65. Paraphrased from Ecclesiastes 12:13.

66. *The Way of God* 1:4:5.

67. *The Way of God* 1:4:6–9.

68. When the Jewish nation began, God took care of all of their material needs for forty years while they wandered in a desert (Deuteronomy 2:7). He fed them manna, made sure their clothes never wore out, and protected them from the sun's scorching heat, the night's freezing cold, dangerous animals, snakes, and scorpions (Deuteronomy 8:4, 15–16). Meanwhile, He commanded the Israelites and all of their descendants to observe some seemingly illogical rules, without explaining their rationales. These laws are known as *chukim,* and include prohibitions against wearing clothes made of linen and wool (Deuteronomy 22:11), eating dairy and meat products together (Exodus 34:26), and planting wheat with grapes (Deuteronomy 22:9). Although God could have explained their significance in ways we could understand, He gave these laws without explanation so that we would obey and trust Him.

69. In ancient times, God told Abraham that his Jewish descendants would be slaves in a foreign land for hundreds of years, then they would be redeemed and would conquer the land of Israel (Genesis 15). The Lord fulfilled this promise, which we commemorate on the holiday of Passover (Exodus 3:16–22). He foretold the ten plagues that He subsequently brought upon the Egyptian oppressors, including killing the Egyptian firstborn (Exodus, chapters 7–12). He fulfilled His promise to part the Reed Sea and save the Jews in the same waters (Exodus 14). He promised the Jews that He would reward them for observing the Torah and punish them with national calamities if they didn't live up to their spiritual responsibilities (Deuteronomy 28). He foretold their exile from the land of Israel because they would worship idols and neglect the Sabbatical laws (Deuteronomy 28). See also Joshua 23.

70. *Kiddushin* 39b.

71. Maimonides, *Mishneh Torah,* end of *Hilchot Meilah.*

2

Types of Suffering

T he person who despises God's word will be punished, and the one who fears the commandment will be rewarded."[1]

"The person whom God loves He corrects, as a father does to a son who pleases him."[2]

One way that souls develop their qualities is by suffering. People may suffer for many different reasons, one of which is that God is punishing them for their misdeeds. (Numerous other reasons will also be discussed.) We never know at any given time exactly why we are suffering, but we can try to find meaning in it by knowing what might be causing it.

PUNISHMENT

God rewards us for doing what He asks and punishes us for disobeying Him. These rewards and punishments primarily affect our souls, although they often affect our bodies as well. Punishment can remove spiritual insensitivities that we create by acting improperly,[3] atone for our sins by weakening the grasp of our physical drives on our soul, and free the soul to reconnect more closely with its spiritual Source.[4] When we need to be cleansed from sin, it is much better when it happens in this world rather than in the next.

God does not make us suffer as an end in itself because our physical selves don't deserve that much attention. Even the most painful experiences are designed to improve our souls and help us experience the Almighty's essence.[5]

Since the Almighty created the world only in order to give to us, His love for us demands that He punish us.[6] His system of justice is His way of showing interest and investment in us, not a way of getting even with us when we misbehave. Punishment encourages us to continually review our actions and make ourselves worthy recipients of what God wants to give us.

The true purpose of divine punishment is to allow us to receive more, so God usually punishes us in ways that help us receive what we reject by acting improperly. Still, we don't like being punished, even when we know that it is for our own good. We tend to feel angry, hurt, or rejected when it happens, and may retreat into our hurts or indignation instead of rectifying what led to the punishment in the first place.

God wants us to be close to Him, so He created a system of reward and punishment that lets us deserve this intimacy. The system reminds us that He's constantly interacting with us and responding to our choices.[7]

When the All-Powerful One does miracles that show His Presence, we think that He is wonderful. He is no less wonderful when He makes His Presence known by disciplining us in ways that feel unpleasant. Our challenge is to improve our behavior so that we can enjoy His Presence and love, not go through life resenting His chastisements.

A couple who grew up as observant Jews faced this challenge. They both decided in college that a Torah lifestyle wasn't for them. They started eating nonkosher food, went out on the Sabbath, and felt liberated from the restrictions of a religious way of life. They rationalized that it was enough to be Jewish "in their hearts." Their major link with Judaism was driving to the synagogue on the Sabbath and holidays (which they knew the Torah forbade) in order to attend services and see their friends.

One night, a fire burned their house down. Miraculously, no one was hurt, but everything in the house burned beyond recognition. Everything, that is, except for four items that survived intact: The man's *tallit* (prayer shawl), *shofar* (ram's horn that is blown on the Jewish New Year), Hebrew prayer book, and *tefillin* (phylacteries), none of which he had used for years.

The couple resented the message that came through loud and clear—that they should return to Jewish observance. When they bought a new home, though, they moved within walking distance of the synagogue.

People often misinterpret biblical references to God's becoming "angry." They think His anger is divine outrage over our disrespecting Him and hurting His ego,[8] rather than a sign that He cares about us. He gets angry when we violate His will because we prevent ourselves from taking from Him.

Some people need help but reject it. They squander their lives drinking, using drugs, or creating problems for themselves. When we give them help or good advice, they waste the money and ignore our suggestions. We then get angry because they don't appreciate what we've done for them.

Likewise, nothing "frustrates" and "angers" God more than our self-destruction. If He didn't care about us, He would never become "angry." He gets "angry" only because He wants us to benefit fully from life, and we don't let that happen.

An orthopedic-surgery resident once asked me to evaluate a patient's mental status. John had been shot in the leg during a fight, and his medical condition had to stabilize before the doctors could operate. He had strict instructions not to leave his bed for any reason, but he tried to walk to the bathroom anyway. As soon as he stood on his fractured leg, the bone shattered and he collapsed.

After determining that John had a major machismo disorder, I asked the resident, "Doesn't John's self-destructiveness make you angry?"

The doctor casually replied, "No. Why should I care more about someone than he cares about himself?"

We can be indifferent to someone's self-destruction only if we really don't care about him. When we love someone, we naturally feel angry when he harms himself. God's love for us means that He also feels "angry" with us when we are self-destructive. He can't let it be "our problem" when we frustrate His plans for us. He constantly prods us to do what we must to properly receive His gifts.

God notices and responds to everything that we do. We would prefer, however, that He reward us for our good deeds and overlook our bad ones. And yet, accepting responsibility for what we create, both the good and the bad, helps make us great. If nothing we do is bad, then nothing can be good, either. If everything that we do is automatically good, achievement and excellence lose their meaning.

God gave us enormous power insofar as He allows most of what we do to affect the world metaphysically. Very few acts are morally neutral. Every time that we do a godly act, we bring a little more spiritual light into the world. And when others see how we live, we can affect them more than just metaphysically. For example, if we use only refined language and don't gossip, people around us will emulate us when they talk. If we observe the Sabbath and invite others to join us for meals, they will be impressed by the beauty of Judaism. If we are honest and ethical in business, our business associates will respect us and the religion that guides us.

On the other hand, if we react impatiently and angrily to others, they will think, "Jews are such pushy and nasty people." If we boast about our homes, our cars, our incomes, and the like, others will be jealous of us. If we are rude to people, we discredit Judaism as a religion that makes people godly. If we disdain the Torah's ritual laws, others will see nothing holy about us.

Accepting responsibility for what we create or destroy, such as our character traits, the atmosphere at work and at home, and our laxity or scrupulousness in fulfilling the commandments, helps us realize the incredible impact that we have on the world every day. This realization helps us to grow into a mature relationship with God as we try to live up to His expectations of us.

We have a covenant with God to bring His plan for the world to completion. The more we do this, the more He rewards us. Yet many of us expect God to act benevolently with us regardless of how we act.

We wouldn't say to a friend, "Let's have a relationship. I can do whatever I want and you will do whatever I want." The same applies to our relationship with God. The more we do what pleases Him, the more He is likely to give us blessings that will help us continue to do so. The more we defy His plans for us, the more He will try to get us back on track by punishing us.

When God sends us harsh punishments, He's not only punishing us because of what we did; He's also giving us what we need to build a future. He does this by sending tailor-made punishments to help each of us develop spiritually.

In talmudic times, Jewish courts meted out corporal punishments for certain crimes.[9] The man who administered punishments had to be a scholar with a broad range of knowledge, who was also physically weak.[10] The latter requirement was because the humiliation of the lashes was supposed to be more distressing than the physical pain. But the man also had to be a scholar because of what punishment is supposed to accomplish. Anyone who sees only a criminal's bad points will want to destroy him. But if we also see his inner beauty, we can punish him with the desire to remove impediments to his goodness. The lashes will feel the same to him either way, but what motivates the hitting will be very different. Lashes with constructive intentions can bring out positive qualities and encourage a former sinner's spiritual expression.

A disciplinarian's motivations, then, affect a sinner. Destructive motivations lead to destructive punishments, and constructive ones help the person grow. This is why the person giving the lashes had to be a scholar. He had to see the sinner's inner potential and hit with the desire of bringing it to the fore.

When we punish others, we tend only to see the person's bad points. God never does this. He mostly punishes us so that our shortcomings will stop tarnishing our overwhelming beauty and goodness. He then sends us situations that will help our positive traits emerge.

We tend to think that God imposes punishments on us, and that we would be fine if He would leave us alone. But punishment is intrinsic to sin, so God "can't" ignore our negative deeds' real and lasting effects.[11]

Punishment is not God's way of saying, "You disobeyed Me, so here's a slap in the face," even though it sometimes feels that way. Rather, punishment is a direct result of our erecting blockages between our body and soul. When we disobey God, we prevent our body from fully benefiting from the soul's bounty. That automatically results in spiritual, and often physical, pain.

We can conceptualize this better by imagining that someone has drunk poison. He can't simply regret it and hope that the poison will magically vanish, or ask God to magically make him recover as if nothing had happened. He needs to get the poison out of his system by having his stomach pumped or by vomiting. Even though it is unpleasant, he needs it to survive.

The same happens spiritually. Just as vomiting gets physical poison out of our bodies, punishment helps rid us of spiritual poisons.

Our Sages tell us to worry if nothing unpleasant happens to us for forty days[12] because we continually bring spiritual toxins into our systems that need to be removed. Just as someone without kidneys could not stay healthy for forty days without dialysis, we can't tolerate forty days of spiritual toxins building up in us.

These ideas seem ludicrous to people who think that spirituality and religion are forms of magic. They want God to do magical things to make spiritual problems disappear instead of accepting that souls are every bit as real as bodies are.

Because every negative deed has real effects that need to be reckoned with, we should never think that we are too wonderful to need cleansing. Even if we do one hundred good things, and one negative one, that one deed still needs to be addressed. God doesn't subtract our negative deeds from our positive ones and respond to our bottom line. No good deed is ever erased, nor is any negative one ever forgotten or cancelled.[13] God rewards us fully for every good deed and punishes us for each negative one.[14] This is to our advantage because the reward for doing even one good act is so enormous that we would not want to lose it. Spiritual rewards last forever, while all punishments are relatively short-lived.

The accomplishment and reward of doing even one *mitzvah* (divine commandment) is so tremendous that nothing in this world can fully compensate us for it.[15] Our good actions can be justly rewarded and enjoyed only in a wholly good and spiritual realm.[16]

Another reason why God does not fully reward us in this world is that He wants the world to be a place where we are challenged to choose good over evil. We would lose our free will if He rewarded or punished us immediately every time we made our choices. If the real consequences of choosing good or bad were totally obvious, no one would be challenged to do what's right. Everyone would do God's will simply as a matter of self-preservation.

For example, if every Jew who kept kosher became wealthy, and those who didn't died of food poisoning, everyone would keep kosher. If our tongues caught fire every time we slandered others, or if lightning struck us every time we violated the Sabbath, who wouldn't be observant? Doing the right thing under these circumstances would not show our commitment to morality, only our wish to stay alive!

Maimonides said that if we dismiss communal punishment as merely coincidental, or as a natural phenomenon, we are terribly cruel to ourselves.[17] Individually, we should consider suffering as a way that God tries to get our attention. As long as we deny the Source of our suffering, it accomplishes nothing except to make us miserable.

We cause most of our suffering by living in physically or spiritually destructive ways. When we damage our spirituality, discomfort or suffering act as spiritual drain cleaner to unclog the spiritual pipelines to our soul and God.[18] But suffering from disasters and tragedies is not the only way to do this. Experiencing any kind of discomfort, even the most minor type, can do it. According to the Talmud, reaching into a pocket to take out three coins, and instead pulling out only two, or accidentally putting on a shirt inside out, can cleanse us![19]

All suffering that is brought as punishment helps us spiritually, even if our inappropriate behavior made it necessary in the first place. We can also pray to get the benefits of suffering, but in other ways. For example, once we improve our behavior, we can ask God to cleanse us without pain and suffering. We can spend extra time doing kind deeds for others, or give extra money to charity, above and beyond what is required.[20] We can sleep less, or have fewer luxuries, and devote our time, energy, and/or money to serving God more intensively. We can also take on extra religious responsibilities to substitute for the painful cleansing that we might otherwise need.

We may not need cleansing all at once, either. We can ask God to refine us over a period of time, or in a less intense way than He otherwise might.

We have to let God pull us close when He sends us punishment. Then we have to be willing to grow in our encounter with Him. Only then can punishment feel redemptive and serve its highest purpose.

WAKE-UP CALLS

"Don't despise your father's chastisement, my son, and don't grow weary of his correction."[21]

When we pull away from our Father in heaven by ignoring Him, He tugs us back. When we try to run and hide, He takes incredible measures to draw us back into His embrace. He sometimes sends us a "wake-up call"—a jolting and unusual experience—that leads us back to a more meaningful life, as the following story illustrates:

"My husband and I were assimilated Jews who lived fairy-tale lives. Ben had a terrific job that he loved, and I was a busy and happy housewife. Two years after we got married, we were blessed with a daughter, and we were ecstatic. Two years later, I was pregnant again, and life was uneventful until I went into labor.

"My obstetrician thought that I would be in labor for a long time, so he went to play tennis. A short while later, somebody gave me a drug that made me unconscious, and the doctors ended up delivering my son by cesarean section. Thank God, he was normal, but I was not.

"When I woke up, I had bizarre symptoms that no one had ever heard of. I stayed in the hospital for months, until my doctors finally admitted that there was nothing more they could do to help me. For the next four years, I was exhausted and had symptoms that no one could explain or cure. I went to several renowned medical centers and underwent hundreds of tests, all to no avail. No one had a clue what was wrong.

"I was usually too weak to get out of bed for more than a few hours each day, but I did my best to read medical journals that might discuss my condition. My perseverance paid off, and I finally found a relevant article. I contacted the author, and he suggested that I come to his hospital 1,500 miles away. I stayed there for a few months while he treated me and I slowly recovered. Meanwhile, a group of observant Jewish women visited me every day.[22] Their wholesomeness, faith in God, and compassion impressed me. They exposed me to my religious heritage and modeled how I should have been living. My husband and I decided to learn about Judaism and we found it very meaningful.

"Had I not been ill, we would never have known about traditional Judaism. We became observant as a result of my ordeal, and we now send our children to a Jewish school and have a Jewish home.

"I still suffer from muscle weakness and fatigue, and I would never have chosen to undergo what I've been through these past six years. But it was worth it, since it helped me discover my Jewishness and convinced me to raise my children as Jews. As difficult as my ordeal has been, I am thankful that it happened because my whole family is now living more meaningfully than we would have otherwise."

Unlike this woman, some people keep running away from God's messages. They attribute tragedies or painful events to "natural forces," bad luck, or "coincidences." Their experiences would be so much more productive if they would only search for spiritual meaning in their financial crises, family tragedies, sicknesses, and the like.

Once we stop running away, our heavenly Father can catch up with us so that we can have a productive encounter. But if we keep wrestling ourselves out of His hold, we will feel the pain of His tugs without benefiting from them. We can bear suffering once we make peace with the idea that our Creator will tug at us and push us. When we consider Who is sending us messages and why, He needs to do less to get our attention, and we can take comfort in His Presence.

Some kinds of suffering sensitize us to how precious life is and make us want to live more meaningfully. They help us become less preoccupied with nonsense and take life more seriously.

Carl was a twenty-six-year-old heroin addict who stole cars to support his decade-long habit. When he was hospitalized for a drug-related heart infection, his only concern was being discharged as soon as possible so that he could resume taking drugs.

Two weeks after his admission, a stroke suddenly paralyzed half of his body and left him with slurred speech. The resulting medical complications prolonged his hospital stay another six months, during which time he had to learn to walk, speak, and write again.

Before his stroke, Carl cared about nothing but using heroin. Only after he was paralyzed and lost his abilities did he realize how precious life was and decide never to touch drugs again. Had his ordeal not forced him away from his drug-infested environment for such a long time, he probably would have died of a drug overdose by the age of thirty.

During his ordeal, strangers who knew nothing about Carl saw a suffering young man who was hospitalized for a stroke. They felt angry with God for treating such a good person so shabbily. People who heard the whole story, though, quickly changed their reactions. How often are we uninformed observers who judge God without knowing the details of someone else's life?

There are countless people who neglect their families and their spirituality in order to pursue money. It's not until they have bypass surgery, a heart attack, stroke, or family crisis that they wonder if there is more to life than making money. Tragedies remind us not to take life for granted and to appreciate what we have before we lose it. If we are smart, we'll take advantage of every day and make the most of it now.

SUFFERING WE BRING ON OURSELVES

"God made man upright, but people made many inventions."[23]

Although we often assume that God makes us suffer, we bring most suffering on ourselves. Maimonides said that most suffering comes about because of what we do to each other and to ourselves.[24] People start wars, oppress each other, kill, rob, rape, cheat, and the like. God doesn't directly create evil. We do, though, when we act as if He is absent. He then withholds obvious punishments so that we don't feel always compelled to do what's right.

The Almighty wants us to preserve our health, but He doesn't force us to do it. And in fact, most Americans don't live healthfully. The overwhelming majority of sickness today happens because people don't take proper care of themselves. The main causes of adult death (heart, lung, and liver disease, cancer, and strokes) are largely preventable. For example, cigarette smoking is the single largest preventable cause of death, lung cancer, and chronic lung disease. It is responsible for one in six American deaths and has left millions of damaged lungs and hearts.[25] The Surgeon General estimates that smoking kills 434,000 Americans *every year,*[26] more than the number of Americans who died in World War II and Vietnam *combined!*[27]

Seventeen million Americans drink excessively.[28] In 1988, 107,800 American deaths were alcohol related.[29] Of these, over 17,000 deaths resulted from drunk driving accidents.[30]

It has been well established that eating refined foods, chemical additives, pesticide residues, and high-fat diets promotes cancer and heart disease. Eating refined sugar promotes diabetes and tooth decay and weakens the immune system. Feeding children cow's milk has been linked to asthma and allergies. Untold misery could be prevented by eating healthfully, exercising regularly, and avoiding alcohol, drugs, and smoking.

Developing good character traits such as patience, self-discipline, a pleasant demeanor, and a sense of balance also minimizes our suffering. A person who values money and work above all else is likely to make himself very stressed by working too hard and worrying too much. He is likely to suffer from heart disease, ulcers, high blood pressure, and the like, and may well become a heavy smoker and drinker. In the process of devoting himself to making money, he will also neglect his family and cause them to suffer.

Someone who does not constructively deal with anger will vent his or her rage on others and cause untold suffering to those in his life. Others eat themselves up with their anger and suffer physically and emotionally in the process.

People who don't develop the right character traits or priorities cause untold suffering by squandering and misappropriating resources that could be used to alleviate much suffering. Their greed and jealousy causes untold harm. For instance, there is more than enough food to feed all of the world's inhabitants, but it is not distributed properly. Cures for many illnesses and diseases have been found, but are barred by physicians' lobbies and pharmaceutical companies whose profits would be reduced were these alternative therapies widely used. Dangerous pesticides and chemicals are dumped onto fields and in water supplies, and harmful drugs and other substances are readily available because business people are more concerned with profits than with health and morality. Money and energy that should be available for alleviating misery often find their way into politicians' and bureaucrats' pockets and personal disposal, instead of going where they belong.

Maimonides said that most bad things happen because of what we do to ourselves. "Many times patients come to me and I tell them to avoid certain foods in order to protect their health and prevent their sickness from getting worse. Later I find that they have disregarded my advice and thereby made themselves very sick. I am very surprised when I hear these people complain, 'Why has God brought this sickness upon me?' They don't understand that they can't hold God responsible for their own folly."[31] He said that most of the world's misery is due to poor eating habits, too much alcohol, excessive sexual indulgence, and wasting energy trying to acquire unnecessary things instead of reserving it for important and meaningful pursuits.[32] Things haven't changed much during the past thousand years!

He also said that most sickness is due to people's poor diets and eating habits. He recommended that we not eat unless we are hungry, nor drink if we are not thirsty. We should eat only until we are three-quarters full, not until we feel stuffed. (Sage words of advice for the next bar mitzvah or wedding!) He advised us not to drink during meals, and to wait until food has left the stomach before quenching our thirst so as not to dilute our digestive juices. He said, "Excessive eating is like a deadly poison to the body and is a principal cause of all illness. . . . A person [will wane in strength] if he does not exercise and he lives a sedentary life . . . even if he eats good food."[33] If we only took his sage words of advice, one-third of Americans would not be overweight and there would be a lot less sickness.[34]

Our Sages advised us to chew food well, to sit down while eating and drinking, and to eat slowly and leisurely.[35] What sound suggestions in today's fast-food world!

Maimonides also warned about the dangers of breathing polluted air. "The concern for clean air is the foremost rule in preserving the health of one's body and soul," he said.[36]

If we smoke, eat irresponsibly, don't exercise, have risky sex, make ourselves stressed, and the like, we shouldn't blame God when we get sick. We are responsible for taking care of ourselves and it's not our Maker's fault when we neglect our health.

When we don't know how to take care of ourselves, God may protect us, even when we are reckless. But we should take responsibility for learning how to stay healthy and then doing it.

When we bring suffering on ourselves that might not have occurred otherwise, it can still serve a spiritual purpose by cleansing us spiritually and motivating us to develop our potentials.

WHY "GOOD" PEOPLE SUFFER

"Rabbi Yanai said, 'It is not up to us to understand why wicked people prosper and righteous people suffer."[37]

Not only don't we know with certainty in any specific situation why good or bad things occur, we don't even know who is truly righteous or wicked according to God's system of judgment. To do that we would have to know how well people are fulfilling their godly mission here, and what goes on in the inner recesses of their hearts, minds, and homes. We are rarely in a position to do that. A man with a long, white beard who spends hours poring over holy books is not necessarily righteous, nor is someone whom we see doing negative things necessarily wicked by God's standards.

For example, King David was a generally righteous man, but he deserved to suffer for having acted improperly in a specific situation. At various times, King Saul ordered his men to kill David because he saw David as a threat. David was afraid that Israelites who saw him running from Saul would think that God was unjustly punishing him, so he fled to a mountain with a pagan temple on it. Anyone who saw him would then think that God was punishing him for worshiping idols, rather than wrongly conclude that God was unjust.[38]

Even when we think we know people well, we can't know the inner workings of their lives. We can judge people only by what they choose to reveal to us. Some philanthropists are highly esteemed, yet their money comes from embezzled funds and fraud. Some men and women are regarded as pillars of their community, yet their personal behavior leaves much to be desired. Some people publicly present themselves as ideal parents and spouses, and they are adored by neighbors and coworkers. Only their families know how monstrous they are at home, because only there do they reveal their true selves.

There are countless stories about respectable teachers, day care workers, and youth leaders who turned out to be child molesters. Likable politicians and sports figures do the most despicable things privately, yet the public adores them as heroes. Supposedly reputable doctors sometimes abuse their patients and perpetrate massive insurance fraud. "Religious" men are now in jail for convictions from racketeering to murder.

We can be just as mistaken in thinking we know who is "bad." A young woman was rumored to be a drug addict and alcoholic because she "spaced out" in public, often reeked of alcohol, and was secretive about her private life. Neighbors even found syringes and needles in her trash. Few people knew that she was a brittle diabetic who didn't disclose her condition for fear of unpleasant social and career consequences.

Another case: An elderly man and his wife owned a very profitable business. When charity collectors visited him, he gruffly refused one and all until he got a reputation as a self-centered miser. What people didn't know was that he was a generous donor to many Jewish causes but had to do so anonymously because his wife strenuously objected to his giving away their money.

When people inaccurately present themselves as upright and innocent, God will eventually deal with them as they truly are. When that happens, observers get angry with Him instead of with the people who created the misleading impressions.

God judges people according to what He expects of them, taking into account their potentials and motivations. Someone who seems righteous to us may not be living up to God's expectations, and someone who seems to be a sinner may be doing very well in the Lord's eyes. This is why we should leave judgments about who is good or bad up to the One who is truly qualified to make them.

AFFLICTIONS OF LOVE

"If the Holy One, blessed is He, is pleased with a person, he crushes him with painful sufferings."[39]

"Our father Abraham was tried with ten tests, and he withstood them all. This was done to show how great Abraham's love [of God] was."[40]

"The greater one's [spiritual] wisdom, the more grief he has."[41]

Even though people tend to equate suffering with punishment, they are not one and the same. Suffering happens for many different reasons, and one of these is "afflictions of love."[42] These don't result from our having done anything wrong. To the contrary, we undergo them because we have hidden potentials such as fortitude, courage, and faith that God wants us to develop more. We may not know that we have these qualities until we are put to certain tests.

Only going through certain experiences makes us grow. For example, it's easy to say that we would never buy stolen goods, or take part in a profitable but illegal business deal. However, if push came to shove, would we really keep our integrity?

We need to consider how we would face spiritual challenges if we had to, but we grow infinitely more by actually going through them. Our choices and actions make us who we are more than our thoughts and wishes do. Or, to put it differently, we grow more through difficulties and challenges than we do through comfort and ease.

We each have so many hidden potentials that God constantly challenges us to make sure that we use them. Some challenges come through sad or even tragic events because their intensity catalyzes us to plumb our depths, use our potentials, and internalize tremendous strength and fortitude.

We may not "deserve" to suffer by undergoing crises that are designed to help us. But God sends them anyway because He knows that without these challenges we can never develop our greatness.

When we wish that the Almighty would spare us His challenges and let us breeze through easy, painless lives, we lose sight of how temporary pain here is as compared with what we will ultimately enjoy in the afterlife. Suffering that cleanses us, or helps us actualize our spiritual potentials, is an investment that will allow us to receive infinitely more in the future.

King David had a terribly painful life. God killed his first child with Batsheva as a punishment for his inappropriate behavior with her. King Saul frequently pursued David and jeopardized his life so that David had to hide in fields and caves and face starvation and capture. He was humiliated by his enemies, and his own son tried to usurp his crown by spearheading a revolt to overthrow him in his old age. In short, he suffered throughout his life.

Still, David wrote the Book of Psalms in which He constantly praises God. He said, "God's wrath is momentary, because His desire is for people to live."[43] David viewed his seventy years of earthly life as momentary compared to his soul's eternity. He was willing to suffer here in order to improve his immortal life. Like David, our suffering is momentary compared to the eternity for which it prepares us.

Judy was a religious woman who once had tremendous faith in God, yet questioned His "feelings" about her when she had terrible tribulations. Her parents had been so poor that she had to work a part-time job in high school. When she was accepted to medical school, she could not go because she could not afford the tuition. She started a potentially lucrative career, but had to stop when a hereditary illness disabled her. A decade later, she had undergone forty-eight hospitalizations and was living alone on disability insurance. She felt like a failure because she had no tangible achievements or possessions to "show" for her life. She assumed that God must be deeply disappointed with her to have sent her so many misfortunes.

Afflictions of love have nothing to do with our failings. To the contrary, they reflect God's faith that we can develop our abilities to the utmost through painful challenges.

People who are especially religious often suffer more than others. This is because God sends us increasingly intense trials as we grow spiritually. While no one wants to be tested, this kind of suffering can bring us especially close to our Maker.

Abraham was a classic example of someone who was sent afflictions of love, and he showed us how to face them. He believed in God, despite living in a pagan world, and tried to convince others of his beliefs. But instead of bringing tribulations to the sinful idol worshipers, the One Above subjected Abraham to ten tests that all involved tremendous self-sacrifice and emotional pain.[44]

Abraham did not "deserve" to undergo terrible ordeals, yet he was tested anyway. The Almighty wanted him to internalize a belief in God as the ultimate reality. Abraham could do this only by making choices that valued God over everything else—including loyalty to his nation and family, and even over life itself. The way that Abraham rose to these challenges created spiritual accomplishments so magnificent, they still benefit us today.

Abraham's most difficult test was being asked to sacrifice his son Isaac. Abraham was a hundred years old when Sarah finally gave birth to their son. Only Isaac would be able to carry on his parents' moral teachings, but God asked Abraham to offer his son to Him.[45] The father and son traveled for three days, during which Abraham had plenty of time to reconsider his path. But he didn't. They finally came to the place where the Binding of Isaac was to take place. Abraham prepared his son as a sacrifice and was poised to slaughter his beloved child. Just then, an angel told him to stop. God had only wanted Abraham to show his total dedication and obedience to Him. He had not wanted him actually to kill Isaac.[46]

A moment before the angel called out, Abraham cried so bitterly that tears flowed down his face, yet his heart was full of joy.[47] The test felt terrible and he cried bitterly at the thought of killing his beloved son. At the same time, he felt tremendous joy that he could express absolute love for God. He celebrated his newfound spiritual greatness while his heart was torn by the pain of his terrible ordeal.

Like Abraham, we often cry tears of deep sadness and bitterness. At some point, we can console ourselves that developing our deepest qualities will benefit us, and possibly others, in this world and the next.

Many of our ancestors went through afflictions of love. For example, Moses told Pharaoh to free the Israelites, but Pharaoh retaliated by oppressing the Jews more. Moses was so upset that he asked God, "Why have You harmed this people and sent me here? Since *(me'az)* I came to Pharaoh to speak in Your Name, he has wronged them [the Jews] and You have not rescued Your people."[48]

The Israelites did not leave Egypt for almost another year. But when they safely crossed the Red Sea, Moses sang a song of salvation to God, using the same word that he had previously used to complain to Him *(az)*.[49] This showed Moses' understanding that the previous year's crisis was meant to facilitate the Jews' faith in God. Moses celebrated his people's salvation, as well as the crisis that preceded it.

King David expressed a similar idea by saying, "I will exalt you, God, because You have lowered me."[50] David knew that had he not been forced into many "low places," he would not have developed his unique relationship with his Creator, nor would he have become spiritually great.

At some point, most of us find ourselves in low places. When that happens, it may be difficult to see anything good in our situation. With distance, we might be surprised at how much we grew from the experience.

Sandra was a perfect example of this. She had abused drugs for a decade before she got married, but then she turned her life around. Although she raised two children, she still viewed herself as an emotional cripple who needed her husband to take care of her.

When she was nine months pregnant with their third child, a blood vessel suddenly burst in her brain. Emergency surgery stopped the bleeding and she delivered a healthy baby boy, but she suffered brain damage that paralyzed her arm and leg and affected her speech.

Her rehabilitation was difficult. She cried a lot, and often refused to do physical therapy unless her husband Robert was by her side. Meanwhile, he was over-whelmed by taking care of their three children, running a small grocery store, and visiting her in the hospital every morning when she had physical therapy. Finally, he couldn't take the stress anymore and refused to visit her until his work day was over.

Sandra was devastated. She initially refused to do any exercises unless Robert was there, and she wouldn't leave her wheelchair. When he refused to give in to her, she gradually realized that she had to stop depending on him so much and start taking care of herself. She mustered every ounce of determination that she had and forged ahead with the massive rehabilitation that lay ahead. A few months later, her speech was back to normal, she had limited use of her affected arm and leg, but still spent most of her time in a wheelchair.

As her day of discharge neared, she spoke constantly about how she would soon walk and take care of her infant without any help. Her doctors and therapists were pleased with her recovery, but they knew that she would never walk or hold her son unaided. One doctor confronted her and made it clear that she should not antici-pate a rosy future. This hit Sandra like a ton of bricks. Her emotional reaction was so severe that the doctor had no choice but to retract his discouraging words.

When she left the hospital she proclaimed, "You mark my words. I'll be back in three months, and I'll walk into this place without even using a cane." The day of her follow-up visit, the staff was amazed that Sandra made good on her vow. She sat down, more self-assured than ever, and told the staff, "My whole life I thought that I was a nobody who couldn't cope with life. I never finished high school, and I never had a decent job, so I saw myself as a failure. I let people take advantage of me for so many years that I believed I was garbage.

"When I had my stroke, I was sure that I was going to die. When I realized that I wasn't, I assumed that my husband would take care of me for the rest of my life. It was very painful at first when he refused. I felt like I had no one in the whole world to rely on, and even he betrayed me. But after thinking about it, I finally decided that I'm an adult, and it's time that I act like one.

"Depending on others felt good in one way, but they also told me how to live and how capable I am. These past nine months, I found out that no one knows what I can or can't accomplish. The only way that even I know is to put all of my effort into something and see what happens.

"No one believed that I would ever walk again or take care of my baby. I can do both, even though they are very hard and I sometimes need help. But it's given me a lot of self-esteem to see how much I can accomplish.

"I always saw myself as a weak person. Now I know that I'm even stronger than most people. I would never have known that if I hadn't been forced to find out."

Sandra's terrible ordeal helped her discover an inner fortitude that no one knew existed, least of all herself. Thanks to her tragedy, she ended up much better equipped to face life.

BEING ROLE MODELS

God makes some people suffer so that they will be role models to others who face tragedy. For instance, Abraham developed an extremely close and intense relationship with God as a result of the tests he faced. But he also modeled to the world, by sustaining his trials with perfect faith, that everyone is capable of deep spiritual fortitude.

Our life missions are not only to grow personally but also to help others who need strength and support. God needs us to be role models who act as His partners. We do this partly by bringing others to an awareness of Him and dedication to His service. His role models grow tremendously and receive an eternal reward for their efforts that is indescribable.

Such people may have no idea as to why God is causing them such pain, although they may eventually find out. By keeping their faith despite suffering, they model their religious fortitude to others who might want to abandon their belief in God and/or who might see no point in living amid terrible suffering. Role models can inspire others to make it through their trying times, especially when both are in similar straits.

Jack was an idealistic, religious man who spent his life trying to place Russian Jewish children in religious schools. As he drove to a solicitation meeting with a potential financial sponsor, a speeding car smashed into him and killed him. Jack's young widow Miriam and their small children were left financially destitute and emotionally bereft. They could not believe that they had a loving father and husband one minute and an emptiness beyond description the next.

Miriam adored her husband, and was dazed by her loss for a long time. How could she begin to put her life back together? She had not imagined in her wildest nightmares that something so terrible might happen to her and her family. But she had little time for self-indulgence. She had to start working full-time and go to night school to earn a marketable degree. Jack had no life insurance, and he had never made enough money to save any. She felt guilty that she rarely saw her children except on weekends, and they felt deprived of both a father and a mother.

Two years after the incident, Miriam still missed her husband terribly but was not angry with God for taking him away. She accepted her loss and gracefully went on with her life. She had no answers as to why the Almighty took Jack, just as he was on the verge of bringing spiritual and emotional life to hundreds of children. But she accepted that He must have had His reasons for not wanting her husband's plans to come to fruition. Despite her personal suffering, she comforted other women whose parents, husbands, and children died, and encouraged them to find solace in Judaism, in prayer, and in a religious community. The fact that she was a widow made her more credible in helping others who had been similarly hurt.

Our Creator tests us so that we will develop and express our qualities. A different way of saying this is that He wants some people to get multiple Ph.D.s. in spiritual growth. Those He tests less may get only high school diplomas. In this regard, He is like a pottery merchant who has some well-made wares and others that are fragile. In order to sell his high-quality merchandise, he shows his customers how the pottery sounds when it is hit. We may also show our true qualities only when we are struck by tragedy and suffering.

We were put here to develop our hidden spiritual qualities. The pottery analogy suggests that we sometimes suffer so that we will model our qualities to others, not only because of what we personally must go through. Just as people hear a pot's quality when it is struck, the same happens when we stay spiritually strong while enduring suffering. Others learn to weather their trials and tribulations and are inspired by our reactions.

Alyssa was a good-natured, funny, devoutly religious woman who studied the Bible and prayed for hours every day. She generously shared her money with friends in dire financial straits and selflessly gave a listening ear and comfort to those who needed it. She was afflicted with a rare, painful, and poorly understood muscle disease that caused her to be hospitalized repeatedly. She needed enormous doses of painkiller to withstand the torture of intense and chronic muscle spasms that would make most people want to die.

To make matters worse, few nurses were sympathetic to her plight. They humiliated her by calling her a "quack," "psycho," and drug addict, and berated her for coming to the hospital to get drugs. Her emotional pain from being constantly judged and condemned made her suffering almost unbearable. Nevertheless, instead of wallowing in self-pity, she left her hospital room on her better days and comforted other patients.

Her doctors, friends, family, and other patients marveled at her fortitude. She was an extraordinary role model who inspired them by her unshakable belief in God's goodness, despite her horrible suffering.

Alyssa had a wonderful sense of humor and rarely complained. Her conversation normally centered around others, until a series of setbacks lasted for months. At that point, she asked to see me. During the previous years of sickness, she had never lost her composure or fortitude. Finally, though, she wept with utter resignation and defeat. Through her tears she said, "Dr. Aiken, you know how much I've suffered from my illness. I've had twelve long hospitalizations during the past five years. I lost my job because of my health. My fiancé died of leukemia a few years ago, and now I'm too old to have children. I doubt any man will ever marry me because I'm so sick.

"As if that weren't enough, my father had a heart attack last week, and my brother treated me as if I'm a junkie. My life has been so much harder than most people's, but I never questioned God's ways. I've always been grateful for all of my blessings. I have loving parents, wonderful friends, and good disability insurance that allows me to survive financially. I've always had faith in the Lord, and I'm lucky that He always gives me the strength to keep on going.

"But now I've reached the end of my rope. I just can't see the point of fighting this anymore. I can't understand why God is making me suffer so terribly. I've reconciled myself to the fact that I will never get married or have children. I've even come to terms with the fact that I will probably die in a few more years. What I can't understand is why God would want me to be so sick. How can I serve Him when I spend every day trying to get through another twenty-four hours of pain?"

It was heartrending to see her so broken. I struggled to find answers to her questions. She was so moral, so good, so kind to others. Why *had* God done this to her? What could anyone say to her without being presumptuous or trivializing her suffering? What *was* the point of anyone going through such terrible and seemingly endless ordeals?

Her suffering reminded me of the biblical character Job. He was a righteous man who suffered for no apparent reason. He lost all of his children and all of his wealth, and was then covered with boils from head to toe.[51] His best friends admonished him to repent for whatever sins he must have committed. They insisted that a just God would make him suffer only if he were being punished for his sins, and they chided him for not admitting his religious failings and rectifying his deeds.[52]

Job believed that he hadn't done anything wrong. He thought that God had let random forces afflict him for no reason. He felt insignificant, helpless, and manipulated by an all-powerful deity who was acting unjustly.

Meanwhile, Job's worst pain came from feeling that God had abandoned him. He cried out, "What I would give for someone to hear me! I desire the Almighty to answer me. . . ."[53]

After being tormented for a year, God finally gave Job his much sought-after response by appearing to him in an unexpected and powerful encounter:

"The Lord answered Job from the whirlwind and said, 'Who darkens advice with ignorant words? Prepare yourself like a man, because I will ask you, and you will let Me know. Where were you when I set down the foundations of the earth? Tell me, if you have understanding. . . . Have the gates of death been revealed to you? . . . Do you know the laws of the heavens, can you set orderly rules on the earth? . . . Who prepares food for the raven when his young cry out to God and they wander for lack of food? . . . Do you wait for the deer to give birth? . . . Did you give the horse his strength? . . . Is it by your order that the eagle flies high?' "[54]

God's message to Job was that He watches over and is concerned with every being that He created. Nothing happens without purpose, and He constantly supervises His world, down to the most minute detail. People are privy to only a tiny fragment of His universe, and to actions that occur in a minuscule frame of time. We can never know how every event from the dawn of humanity until the Messianic era fits together to eventually bring the world to the Lord's intended goals for it.

The Creator told Job to accept that He runs the world in ways that don't make sense to the human mind. The Lord also told Job that everything happens for a reason. No one and nothing is too insignificant for God's watchful eye to monitor. Moreover, He promised Job that He has a system of justice where He will ultimately give the wicked their due and the righteous their just desserts.

We can't know why specific innocent people suffer, and must have faith that the One who designed a purposeful world knows what He is doing. Although Job did not know why God caused him to suffer, the fact that the Almighty responded to him taught Job that tragedies don't happen in His absence. The Lord is always present when He sends people suffering, and it is never pointless, unjust, or a sign of rejection or abandonment. Only the Master of the Universe knew why He wanted Job to be a role model of how to react to suffering. However, once Job realized that an omnipotent and omniscient deity was aware of his plight, he could accept his calamities without further questions.

Could God have chosen Alyssa for a similar purpose? I suggested the following to her: "Alyssa, we never know why God acts as He does. His ways are beyond our comprehension. What we do know is that you have inspired many people with your fortitude. All of the doctors who have treated you, the patients you've visited, your friends and some of your family have all been touched and inspired by your faith and courage. Your attitude has helped scores of other troubled people put their problems in perspective. You have supported them in their crises and have shown all of us how much we have to be grateful for.

"When God tested Job by stripping away what he had, he responded, 'God gave and God took away. Blessed is the Name of God.'[55] Reading a story about a biblical character who suffered terribly while keeping his faith was nice, but I don't know many people who could respond as Job did. Having the privilege to know you—a real, live person who loves God despite the terrible suffering that you've been through—has impacted me in ways that reading could not. I don't know if I could be as strong as you are if I were put to the test, but at least I know what the ideal is that I should strive for."

Alyssa wiped away her tears and felt comforted. Like Job, she still did not know why she had been sent such terrible suffering, but it no longer mattered. Her suffering was bearable as long as she could find spiritual meaning in it. We can endure the worst types of pain if only we know that it is serving some worthwhile purpose.

Alyssa demonstrated how deeply we can love and serve our Creator without even leaving our beds. Knowing such people helps us fathom how pain and incapacitation can serve important purposes.

After Rabbi Kirzner, *z"tl,* died, many people were moved and inspired by how remarkably he confronted his terminal illness. On one occasion, he got an absolutely devastating biopsy report. Minutes later, he taught a class about how unshakable our trust in God should be. "For instance," he told an audience who had no idea that he was sick, "let's say you go to the doctor and he tells you that you are going to die. And you pour out your heart to the One Above, day after day, week after week for months, knowing that He controls nature and can make miracles happen. And after none of your prayers are answered the way that you would like, what can you do? You have to throw yourself on God and trust that He will do what's best for you."

Throughout his three-year ordeal, he and his wife were incredible role models of how to face suffering. They focused on the All-Merciful One's many kindnesses to them. They were so grateful that he lived to attend a son's bar mitzvah long after his cancer was diagnosed. They were so appreciative that God allowed him to be so prolific during his last three years of life. The All-Merciful One did not make his hair fall out when he had chemotherapy, allowing his students to think that he was healthy enough to continue his intense teaching and counseling schedule. (Had they known he was sick, they might have encouraged him to take it easy.) He had been privileged to teach hundreds of lectures and personally counsel hundreds, if not thousands, of Jews during the years of his illness.

Many people would hate God for taking their life or a loved one's life away at such a young age. This remarkable couple looked for, and found, God's goodness in every one of their ordeals. Those who had the opportunity to see and hear their reactions were very moved and inspired.

No book knowledge can touch us as intensely as actual experiences do. It is one thing to read about how people face adversity with dignity; it is quite another to *see* how they do it, especially when they die maintaining their faith in God and expressing their spiritual vibrancy. Some people are role models of how to live with dignity, even under harsh circumstances. Others teach us how to die with a full belief in God and the justice of His ways.

We never know who will be touched by our responses to tragedy. God sometimes sends us difficulties so that we will model to future generations how to undergo similar experiences. These people may not even personally know us or see what we accomplish. For example, Abraham and Isaac were role models of how to sacrifice ourselves for our Creator. Their actions enabled Jews from all walks of life to die as martyrs during the past 2,000 years, rather than renounce their belief in God.

When Abraham's wife Sarah heard that he had offered their son as a sacrifice, she realized that her family had to undergo such a test in order to set precedents for future generations of Jews. She had a mental flash of what Jewish history would be like and saw the tremendous self-sacrifice that God would ask of her descendants. She understood that He wanted her husband and son to be role models so that future Jews would be willing to give up their lives for belief in God.

Sarah cried when she realized how terrible the Jews' trials and ultimate sacrifices would be for millenia to come. At the same time, she took solace in the fact that she had raised a son with the spiritual fortitude to pass a divine test requiring total dedication to their Creator's will.[56]

Many of our parents, grandparents, and great-grandparents lived and died in ways that inspired us to follow in their spiritual footsteps. Each of us can be role models to our descendants in the same way.

FINDING MEANING IN SUFFERING

"And God saw everything that He had made, and behold, it was very good."[57] Rabbi Meir said, "God saw all that He had made, and behold, death was good."[58]

"The Holy One, blessed is He, gave the Jews three precious gifts. Each was given only through suffering. They are: the Torah, the land of Israel, and the World-to-Come."[59]

Suffering feels terrible, but it can help us appreciate what we have. The death of loved ones is devastating, but it makes us aware of how precious life is. We truly appreciate material possessions only by knowing what it means to lose them. We value our health only when we know how easily sickness can take its place. Illness humbles us and erodes our sense of invulnerability.

There are many levels on which we can find meaning in our painful experiences. For example, we can appreciate being spiritually cleansed in this world or developing our faith and character through afflictions of love. We can develop deeper levels of empathy when we know what it's like to be in someone else's shoes. Firsthand experience can sensitize us to others in ways that living an easy life cannot, and it makes us more credible when we give hope and reassurance to others.

Life is like a wheel of fortune. When we are on top, we should help those who are on the bottom. And when we are on the bottom, we need to allow ourselves to be comforted by friends and a Creator who will help pull us up again.

God sometimes expresses His love for us in pleasant ways; at other times, He does it by sending us difficulties and tragedies. Finding meaning in our suffering helps elevate us above it so that we can transcend it.

Even in our worst tragedies, God is not absent.[60] We have to know that He is especially close to us at those times when we seek Him the most. The more we want to relate to Him, the more intense our relationship can be.

To enhance our intimacy, He sometimes reminds us how artificial the security of worldly props is. Our health, money, friends, family, homes, and possessions can disappear in a moment. The only thing that is permanent and can truly take care of us is the Almighty.

A beautiful story illustrates this idea:

A man died and went to heaven. There, he and God watched a videotape. One side of the frames showed the events of the man's life, while the other half showed God's and the man's footprints side by side in the sand on a beach.

As the film showed every crisis that the man had gone through, the two sets of footprints symbolized that God had stayed steadfastly by his side. But as they viewed the man's most painful tragedies, only one set of footprints remained.

The man felt devastated and began to cry. "God," he plaintively asked, "I always had such faith in You. How could You have abandoned me in my time of greatest need?"

God gently replied, "My beloved child, I would never abandon you. Where you see only one set of footprints is where I picked you up and carried you."

NOTES

1. Proverbs 13:13.
2. Proverbs 3:12.
3. Rabbi Moshe Chaim Luzzatto, *The Way of God* (New York: Feldheim, 1983) 2:2:5.
4. *Brachot* 5a; Maharal, *Netivot Olam, Netivot HaTeshuvah* 3 (156b) and *Netiv HaYissurin* 1 (174a).
5. *The Way of God* 2:8:1.
6. *The Way of God* 2:8:1.
7. Every Rosh HaShanah (Jewish New Year) we actually *ask* God to judge us! This is because mature people know that taking an inventory of our strengths and shortcomings can foster growth. Even though analyzing our misdeeds is uncomfortable, it can motivate us to live better. (Every twelve-step program incorporates this idea.)
8. The Torah uses anthropomorphisms to give us a way to understand divine responses. When it says that God became "angry" (such as in Exodus 32:1–9), the Torah speaks in human language so that we can conceptualize what happened. God doesn't have human emotions, a body, nor any human characteristics. He has no failings and doesn't get "upset" when people disrespect Him.
9. Deuteronomy 25:2.
10. *Makkot* 23a.
11. *Midrash Tehillim* 62:13 and 30:4; *Tomer Devorah* on Micah 7:19.
Adam was created to be immortal, but he brought death into the world by disconnecting his body from his soul when he sinned. This prevented his soul from infusing his body with immortality and subjected him to physical limitations. Since everything physical has to decay and die, Adam lost his immortality by putting a spiritual barrier between his soul and his body. We likewise erect barriers between our body and soul every time we do things that are spiritually negative. See *The Way of God* 1:3:5–8.
12. *Arachin* 16b.
13. *Midrash Tehillim* 62:13. However, proper repentance for misdeeds can erase them wholly or partly. See also Proverbs 14:23, "In all labor there is profit."
14. Psalms 18:25–26; Ovadiah 1:15; *Chaqiqah* 5a; *Sotah* 9b; "According to the pain is the reward" (*Pirkei Avot* 5:23).

15. *Kiddushin* 39b.

16. See Aryeh Kaplan, *Handbook of Jewish Thought*, vol. 2 (New York: Moznaim, 1992), p. 266.

17. Maimonides, *Mishneh Torah, Hilchot Taanit* 1:3.

18. *Brachot* 5b.

19. *Arachin* 16b.

20. *Emunot VeDeot* 9:1

21. Proverbs 3:11

22. Most communities with a substantial observant Jewish population have *"Bikur Cholim"* organizations. These consist of volunteers who visit hospital patients on a regular basis.

23. Ecclesiastes 7:29.

24. Maimonides, *Guide for the Perplexed*, part 3, chapter 12.

25. David Larson, ed., *Mayo Clinic Family Health Book* (New York: Morrow, 1990), p. 409.

26. *Morbidity and Mortality Weekly Report*, March 11, 1994, Volume 43/No. RR-4, iii.

27. *Mayo Clinic Family Health Book*, p. 409.

28. *Mayo Clinic Family Health Book*, p. 418.

29. *Alcohol Health and Research World* 17:4 (1993): 266.

30. *Accident Facts* (Ithaca, IL: National Safety Council, 1994), p. 59. More than 1.6 million drivers were arrested in 1992 for driving while intoxicated or under the influence of narcotics.

31. *Guide for the Perplexed*, part 3, chapter 12. A midrash says, "God brings suffering on only one in 1,000 people. The rest bring it upon themselves." Quoted in Aryeh Kaplan, *Facets and Faces* (Brooklyn, NY: Moznaim, 1993), pp. 27–28.

32. *Guide for the Perplexed*, part 3, chapter 12.

33. *Mishneh Torah*, Laws of Moral Dispositions, chapter 4. Quoted by Fred Rosner in *Medicine in the Mishneh Torah of Maimonides* (New York: Ktav 1984), pp. 81–85.

34. "Rise in Obesity in U.S. Is Explored by Experts," *New York Times*, December 6, 1994, p. C11.

35. *Shabbat* 152a; *Brachot* 54b; *Gittin* 70a.

36. Final chapter of Maimonides' Treatise on Asthma, quoted by Fred Rosner in *Medicine in the Mishneh Torah of Maimonides*, p. 9.

37. *Pirkei Avot* 4:19.

38. 2 Samuel 15:32; *Sanhedrin* 107a.

39. *Brachot* 5a.

40. *Pirkei Avot* 5:4.

41. Ecclesiastes 1:18.

42. *Brachot* 5a.

43. Psalms 30:6.

44. *Me'am Lo'ez* on Pirkei Avot 5:4. Abraham was thrown into a blazing furnace by King Nimrod in order to discredit Abraham's belief in God (*Genesis Rabbah* 38:13). His second test was being asked to leave his family and homeland and go to a foreign country. He was forced to move to Egypt when a famine struck; his wife was abducted and held in Pharaoh's palace. Some time later, kings who hoped to kill Abraham drew him into battle by kidnapping his nephew Lot, and Abraham risked his life to save Lot. When he was

seventy-five, God told Abraham that his children would be slaves in exile for hundreds of years. When he was ninety-nine, God commanded Abraham to circumcise himself (Genesis 17:24). Sarah was abducted again when they went to the land of the Philistines. After Isaac was born, Abraham had to evict his son Ishmael because he was a terrible influence on Isaac. Finally, God asked Abraham to offer his son Isaac as a sacrifice.

45. Contrary to popular belief, mostly promoted by Christians and their religious paintings, Isaac was not a little boy when this event happened. He was thirty-seven years old, and he married his wife Rebecca three years later.

46. Genesis 22:10–12.
47. *Genesis Rabbah* 56:8.
48. Exodus 5:22–23.
49. Exodus 15:1.
50. Psalms 30:2.
51. Job 1–2:7.
52. Job 4, 5, 8, 11.
53. Job 31:35.
54. Job 38:1–9.
55. Job 1:21.
56. *Shem MiShmuel* on *Chayei Sarah*.
57. Genesis 1:31.
58. *Genesis Rabbah* 9:5.
59. *Brachot* 5a.
60. *Nedarim* 40a. This expresses the idea that God's Presence hovers over the bed of a sick person, staying very close to him.

FOR FURTHER READING

Kaplan, Aryeh. *The Handbook of Jewish Thought.* Vol. 1. New York: Moznaim, 1979.
——. *The Handbook of Jewish Thought.* Vol. 2. New York: Moznaim, 1992.
Luzzatto, Moshe Chaim. *The Way of God.* Trans. Aryeh Kaplan. New York: Feldheim, 1983.

3

Poverty and Financial Loss

Poverty in one's home is harder [to bear] than fifty plagues."[1]

"Who is wealthy? The person who is happy with his portion."[2]

"This is what God says: Let the wise man not glory in his wisdom, let the strong man not glory in his strength, and let the rich man not glory in his wealth. But if one will glory, let him glory in this: that he has intelligence and knows Me, because I am the Lord who does loving-kindness, justice and righteousness in the land, because I desire these things."[3]

One way that God challenges and tests us is by how He provides for us financially.[4] While having money brings only transient happiness, poverty can cause abject misery to those who live in cramped, decrepit quarters with broken furniture, without heat or hot water, and with too little nourishing food. The Talmud recognizes how ruinous poverty is by saying that a person who lives with crushing poverty is like the dead.[5]

While money allows bare survival for some people, it is a yardstick of success for those who think that their possessions or savings reflect their importance. Asking "How much is he worth?" or calling someone a "self-made man" reflects this idea.

People like to give money and possessions imaginary powers in order to feel secure and worthy. But when they lose their jobs or have a financial setback, their enjoyment of life and self-esteem plummet.

Money can buy only some forms of comfort. It cannot buy real security or happiness. Donald Trumps go bankrupt, stock markets crash, and "unthinkable" calamities wipe out lifetime savings. People who are rich today may lose their businesses and homes tomorrow in fires, floods, storms, or economic reversals. Huge banks, real estate holders, businesses, and investors went bankrupt during the 1980s and 1990s. Even successful multibillion-dollar companies suddenly found themselves in overwhelming debt. Wall Street bankers and traders who were wealthy one day contemplated personal bankruptcy the next.

The fact that money is here one day and gone the next reminds us not to think that it can really make us happy. Material possessions can give only temporary happiness because our excitement with them wanes as we get used to them. We have to keep buying more and newer things to keep up the excitement.

Some people think that if they really struck it rich, they would always be happy. A pollster checked this out by asking lottery winners if they were happier before or after they won. Contrary to popular belief, most said they were happier before. One lottery winner even robbed a bank a few years after he won his fortune! Obviously, true happiness comes from inner self-esteem and a feeling of achievement, not from external props.

Just as having money doesn't keep people happy, not having it doesn't make everyone miserable. Those who reconcile themselves to living with bare necessities are often more resilient than those who lose their luxuries and comforts. It is hard to live with less than what we are used to having. This means that people of modest means can be satisfied with less than people who are used to a higher standard of living, and our attachment to comforts and possessions determines our devastation when they are taken away.

For example, Harry was a commodities trader who developed anxiety attacks from the stress of his $750,000 a year job. When it was suggested that he apply for a less stressful job that paid $100,000 a year, he was incredulous.

"Nobody in New York can live on that kind of income," he snorted. He was a single man with a full-time housekeeper, two homes, and two expensive cars. He considered living on less than six figures a year akin to being on welfare.

A woman with similar ideas complained about her husband. "I really want to start a family," Ellen lamented, "but Tim can't earn enough to support us."

"Are you willing to work while Tim takes care of the children and the household responsibilities?" her therapist asked. "He seems very interested in and capable of doing that."

Ellen replied, "I wouldn't mind if Tim were a househusband while I worked, except that we couldn't live on my salary."

"How much do you make?" the therapist inquired.

"Only eighty-five thousand dollars a year," she admitted, "and I can't see how we can afford to raise a child on less than a hundred thousand dollars a year."

At the extreme was Eugene, a computer programmer who was always satisfied with his lot in life. He described himself to a friend as a very rich man. When asked how, since he made less than $40,000 a year, he explained, "If I have one dollar more than I need, I'm rich. If I have one dollar less than I need, I'm poor. Most of the time I'm rich."

We can't always change how much we earn or have, but we can feel better by changing our perspectives about it.

Traditional Judaism views money and material possessions as tools that God gives us to serve Him. He tests the faith of destitute people every day, and they grow closer to Him every day that they believe that He will provide for them. He makes some people poor so that prosperity will not estrange them from Him.[6] He also makes many righteous people poor because their poverty in this world saves them from judgment in the next one.[7]

When the Almighty gives people more money than they minimally need, He hopes that they will further His plans for the world by giving charity, supporting Jewish institutions of learning, and spending their money on worthwhile Jewish pursuits. Money is a blessing only if we spend it properly; otherwise, it can cause emotional and spiritual ruin.[8] Making and spending money as ends in themselves encourages us to seek gifts from God instead of a relationship with the Giver.

God rewards some good people by giving them wealth. For example, Abraham, Isaac, Jacob, and Moses were all blessed with tremendous material wealth, as were the Jewish kings and many prophets.[9] This was a reward for their righteousness, as well as a way to increase the Jews' respect for their leaders.

While having money is sometimes a reward for being righteous, it is not inherently better than being poor. God wants us to serve Him with whatever resources He gives us. No matter how much or how little we have, we are equally important to our Creator. Wealth and poverty are inherently neutral; they become good or bad depending upon how we use them.

Rabbi Judah the Prince, the compiler of the Mishnah and one of the greatest Jewish Sages, knew this well. He was extraordinarily wealthy, yet asserted on his deathbed that he never personally benefited from his wealth. He hosted frequent and opulent banquets, but ate and enjoyed only in order to study Torah and serve God. He used his money to help others do the same.[10]

We learn more about the Jewish view of wealth by understanding biblical Hebrew. There are no words meaning "to have." We can't say that something is "mine," "yours," or "his" in Hebrew. We must say that something "is to me," or "is to him." Since biblical Hebrew expresses theological concepts, it tells us that whatever we own or have isn't really ours. We only get loans from the Ruler of the World so that we will use what we have to do His will. It's not "ours" to do with as we please.

Unlike other religions, though, Judaism frowns on asceticism or avoiding pleasure and possessions. God wants us to enjoy what money can buy, but in ways that elevate us spiritually. In fact, every Jewish soul will have to give an accounting in the next world for every legitimate pleasure that it avoided![11]

King Solomon, the wisest of men, told us how to spend money. He said, "Honor God with your wealth."[12] This means that if we decorate or furnish a home, we should do it in a way that draws God's Presence into it and helps our families serve Him. We do this by furnishing it with Jewish books and beautiful religious articles such as *mezuzot* (scrolls of parchment inscribed with Torah selections), *kiddush* cups, *challah* covers, ritual handwashing cups, and the like. Visitors should be impressed by the holiness of our homes, not by the sophistication of our VCRs or the completeness of our video-game library. A beautiful home with material comforts is good if it helps us feel better so that we can serve the Almighty with greater devotion and equanimity. Homes that look inviting to guests help us fulfill the commandment of offering hospitality. We should spend money for good food to enhance our enjoyment of the Sabbath and holidays. Our homes should create an atmosphere that allows us to study Torah and talk to others in a calm state of mind.

When we buy clothes, we should be concerned that they be modest and not have wool and linen together,[13] rather than insuring that they have designer labels. Men should own properly made ritual objects such as a prayer shawl *(tallit)*, fringed undershirt *(tallit katan)*, and *tefillin*.[14] If we spend a lot of money on our clothes, we should be willing to spend a premium for our ritual items, too. If we are concerned with dining out, we should give charity liberally so that poor people can also eat well.

Jews who have more than enough money to pay for basic shelter, food, and clothing needs are required to give at least 10 percent of their after-tax incomes to Jewish charities.[15] We honor God by saving or spending the rest of our money in ways that enhance our service to Him. Money should be more than a way to afford a "good life" that is disconnected from God.

God is "pleased" when we use our material possessions and wealth to bring His Presence into the world. But He may reallocate them if we misuse His gifts.

Affluence is a tremendous responsibility, and it can easily draw us away from a godly life. Moses recognized its potential dangers when the Israelites were about to enter the Promised Land. The Almighty had said that He would bless the land of Israel with agricultural abundance and mineral wealth if the Jews would observe the Torah. But Moses worried that the Jews' material abundance and self-sufficiency would weaken their motivation to rely on their Provider, and they would become "fat and rebel against God."[16]

King Solomon tried to find a balance between wealth and destitution, because either extreme can lead to spiritual corruption. He said, "Give me neither poverty nor riches, just feed me my allotted bread. Otherwise, I might get full and deny and say, 'Who is God?' or be so poor that I steal and profane the name of my God.' "[17]

Ironically, affluence has led unparalleled numbers of Jews to assimilate since the 1800s. Those who "make it" financially are prone to be arrogant and ostentatious instead of becoming humble and showing unbounded appreciation for their good fortune.

People are tempted to deify money and worship the god of Mammon. Some resort to illegal or unethical methods to amass wealth, rather than trust the Almighty to provide for them when they work hard and honestly.

When we think that work and money will give us security, our Creator sometimes takes them away to remind us who is the true Source of security and Director of resources. In other words, financial setbacks and insecurity remind us to depend on God and not make work and wealth more than they are.

After Adam sinned in the Garden of Eden, the Almighty told Him, "The earth will [now] sprout thorns and thistles for you . . . and you will eat bread by the sweat of your brow."[18] Adam sinned because he didn't want to depend on God. He then had to work to grow food instead of receiving everything without effort. This reminded him that nothing grows without God's daily help. Like Adam, our work should remind us that without divine assistance, we can't survive.

Adam didn't appreciate the food that he freely received in Paradise. Making an uncertain livelihood helped him, as it helps us, to recognize the Lord's daily kindnesses and our dependence on Him.[19]

The Almighty allows us to think that He doesn't constantly take care of us. We must see beyond this illusion and appreciate that He gives us our jobs and our incomes. We forget this when we attribute them solely to our skills, hard work, smart investments, and the like. Do we think about what role God plays? Do we realize that our homes, clothes, and food are due to divine benevolence?

It is easy to become enamored of what we have. Losing it, or not having everything we want, reminds us not to view the material world as more significant than it really is.

PERSPECTIVES ABOUT MONEY

Judaism has some unique perspectives about money. For example, every Rosh HaShanah (Jewish New Year), God determines how much money each Jew will get during the coming year.[20] Once those amounts are determined, we cannot earn a penny more by year's end than what was allotted.

Joe, for instance, normally earns $40,000 a year. He decides to work overtime in order to make extra money, but the One Above decided that he will earn only $40,000 this year. Joe does earn $60,000, but he spends the extra $20,000 on some unexpected medical and legal expenses.

Even though God decides how much we will earn, we still have to work hard to get it. This is because we are supposed to act normally and not expect God to make miracles for us.[21] If we don't work, we don't normally get a paycheck. But no matter how hard we work, we still can't earn a penny more than what God determined we should.[22] This is why some people will never earn much money no matter what they do. They can change jobs, work overtime, generate new ideas, and so on, but their bottom line will stay the same.

Rabbi Elazar ben Pedas experienced the futility of trying to change his financial destiny. He was extremely poor, and dreamt that he asked the Master of the World how much longer he would have to suffer. The Lord replied, "Elazar, My son, should I re-create the world anew? Perhaps you would like to be born at a time of abundant food?"[23] After hearing that he was destined to be poor, he accepted his lot. God then promised him a tremendous reward in the next world for sustaining his challenge of poverty so beautifully.

A medieval Jewish philosopher and writer discovered that every business venture he entered invariably failed. After years of crushing poverty he once quipped, "I have such terrible luck making a living that if I were to become a shroud-maker, people would stop dying. If I were to become a candle-maker, it would stop being dark."[24]

For four generations now, rabbis have advised the women in one family not to work because each one's income has been reduced by unusual expenses. One of these women sold vitamins for a year, when her car suddenly needed repairs. They cost exactly what she had earned. A few years later, she got an office job. After working for six months, her house became infested with termites. The cost of extermination exactly equalled her income. The third time she tried to make money, her father became ill. Not surprisingly, her travel expenses to see him neutralized her income again. At that point, she accepted that she could not augment her husband's income so she may as well do volunteer work.

God decides how much money we make, but we decide how to use it, and how satisfying it feels. How well we appreciate and use it is more important than how much we earn. Many Jews lived in abject poverty, yet felt grateful for whatever they had. Most poor Americans today live in affluence compared with the poor of other countries or of previous generations. Yet how many of us who are blessed financially really appreciate what we have?

A very poor Eastern European man was always happy. He said that he could feel this way despite his oppressive poverty because "every morning I ask God to give me what I need, and I never get much. Obviously, the Lord believes that I need poverty. If so, I have everything I need, so why shouldn't I be happy?"

People who lived during the Depression, as well as many elderly and religious Jews today, know what it is to live in poverty. They must walk long distances because they can't afford a car, or wait outdoors for public transportation in the rain and bitter cold. Some make their own food, clothes, toys, and gifts because they have no money to buy them. Their children wear hand-me-down clothes, and they furnish their apartments in "early attic and late relative." They learn to do without and become masters of invention and creativity.

Life isn't easy for them, but they can have happy and meaningful lives. Their poverty may help them appreciate the simplest things—the luxury of a glass of regular milk instead of reconstituted powder; getting a ride to work instead of taking two buses or walking several miles; having boots, gloves, hot water, and heat during the winter; and eating a small amount of chicken on the Sabbath that more affluent Jews would disdain.

A lecturer asked a group of poor, religious, Jewish sixth graders what they had to be grateful for. The children wore hand-me-down, torn clothes, their parents barely had money for necessities, and they had difficult lives. Yet, every child had something to say: "I am grateful that we have food to eat." "I am grateful that I have clothes to wear." "I am grateful that everyone in my family is healthy," and so on.

This lecturer posed the same question to a group of wealthy Jewish children at a private school. Several minutes passed, but none could think of anything to be grateful for. They took for granted the latest designer clothes and shoes that they wore. They expected to live in their expensive homes, many of which had swimming pools. They didn't appreciate having personal computers, color TVs, and video libraries in their bedrooms. They all had traveled to Europe, Israel, and the Caribbean on vacation. Their housekeepers relieved them of all domestic responsibilities and chores, and a cook prepared any food that they did not eat out in restaurants. Yet none of these children appreciated what they had because they felt entitled to it.

We should train ourselves to appreciate what we have and not take anything for granted. Instead of *expecting* God to give us what we want, and valuing most what we lack, we can learn to receive with a proper attitude. That makes it is easier to gracefully relinquish what we lose.

Job said, "The Lord gave, and the Lord took, may God's Name be blessed."[25] Most people don't believe that God gave them what they have in the first place, so they resent it when He takes anything away. When pleasant things happen to us, we often feel that we deserve it. On the other hand, when we lose our comforts, we tend to think that God unfairly robs us. If we have the attitude that everything we have is a loan, then we are prepared to cope with disappointments or losses when, and if, they happen.

Poverty can help motivate us to develop abilities that we didn't know we had. In my case, years of poverty forced me to write letters to family and friends because long-distance phone calls were unaffordable. The skills that I developed during those years turned out to be a boon when I became an author. Poverty also motivated me to become resourceful and creative. I could not afford to buy gifts, so I made them for my hosts for Sabbath and holiday meals. I traveled all around the world on a shoe-string budget and met fascinating people that way. But most importantly, I learned to trust that God would give me whatever I needed, even when it defied logic.

Many other poor people have learned the same. When God determines what we will earn, it does not include what we spend in honor of the Sabbath and holidays. Families who host guests for these meals often find that the leftovers somehow tide them over for much of the rest of the week. It makes no sense that people who barely have enough for themselves should have enough to share with others. Yet this is exactly what happens.

Rather than wanting to be wealthy, we should want to be proper "servants of God." We can fulfill this role no matter what challenges, losses, or financial resources we have.

Mary had a psychiatric illness that prevented her from working. She lived on disability checks that weren't always enough to support her, and she depended on God to survive.

She once told her therapist that she could not afford sessions for a month. Then she reconsidered and said, "Give me an appointment for next week. The Lord always takes care of me, and I'm sure that He wants me to take care of myself by coming here. He'll find a way to help me see you."

She began her next appointment by saying, "Do you remember my saying that God always provides for me? The day after my last session I got a letter from my mother. We haven't spoken to each other for two months, but for some reason she sent me a check for one hundred dollars. . . . I told you that God always takes care of me."

That winter, she said that she needed to suspend therapy so that she could save enough money to buy a warm coat. She reconsidered a few minutes later and decided to schedule herself for the following week's appointment.

"I must have faith that God will provide for me. I'm going to pray when I leave here and I'm sure that He will answer me."

Mary walked into her next session wearing an old fur coat. She smiled and said, "You know what happened to me last week? When I left here, I went to pray across the street. After I finished, the rabbi came over and told me that a rich lady came there the night before and gave him an old fur coat that she didn't wear any more. She asked him to give it to someone who could use it, and he gave it to me. . . . As you can see, God doesn't necessarily give us what we want, but He always gives us what we need!"

God constantly takes care of us. We only need to notice and feel grateful for it.

THE CHALLENGE OF POVERTY

God wants some people to develop their potentials through having money, and others to do so through the challenges of being poor.[26] Throughout Jewish history, some of our most illustrious Sages lived in abject poverty. Rabbi Akiva was a woodcutter, even though his wife Rachel was from an extraordinarily wealthy family. Her family disowned her for marrying him because he was ignorant of even the rudiments of Judaism at that time. Akiva and Rachel were so poor that she once sold her hair to get money for food.

The Sage Hillel was so poor that he hired himself out for a dime every day. He spent half of his meager earnings on his family's living expenses and the other half on the daily entrance fee to the main Torah academy. One freezing winter day he couldn't even earn a dime, so he couldn't pay to enter the academy. He decided to listen to the study hall classes through a window on the roof, and nearly froze to death in the bitter cold and snow. (This prompted the rabbis to stop charging money for classes.) Hillel eventually became a very wealthy man.[27]

Rabbi Chanina ben Dosa's trials of poverty were legendary. He was a very righteous man, and God sustained the entire world in his merit, yet he personally lived a hand-to-mouth existence.[28] He subsisted on bare necessities, and survived on carob when he didn't even have bread to eat. He totally trusted the Almighty to provide for his family, even when they had no food or firewood moments before the Sabbath.

The Master of the World performed miracles for him and his family because of his unshakable faith in divine providence. For example, his wife burned a smoke-producing substance in the oven every Friday so that neighbors would see chimney smoke and think that she was preparing food for the Sabbath. She didn't want them to know that the kitchen was bare until food miraculously appeared moments before the Sabbath.[29]

One Friday, a rude neighbor tried to uncover her ruse by barging in on Dosa's wife. His wife was terribly embarrassed that there was no food in the house, and she disappeared into another room. Meanwhile, a miracle happened, and the neighbor found the oven full of baked bread and the kneading trough filled with dough.[30]

On another occasion, their daughter lit vinegar when they couldn't afford oil for the Sabbath lamps. When she told her father that she was afraid that the lights would soon burn out, he declared, "The One who determined that oil should burn will make vinegar burn." And it did, until the next evening.[31]

Eventually, Dosa's wife couldn't stand living this way. She pleaded with her husband, "How much more do we have to suffer from such dire poverty?"

He asked what they should do, and she begged him to ask God to send them something of value. The rabbi did as she requested, and the Almighty responded by giving them a golden table leg. Its sale would support them for the rest of their lives.

The next day, the rabbi told his wife that he had dreamed that righteous people sat at tables in the World-to-Come. The Dosa family's table had only two legs, while the others all had three. She told him to ask God to take back His gift, and that is what happened. They understood that their financial security in this world would reduce their reward in the next world, and they weren't willing to make the trade. They accepted their challenge of financial insecurity in order to benefit their souls.[32]

Instead of equating our worthiness with what we own or earn, we should view our wealth as a God-given responsibility and poverty as a divinely given challenge. We should do our best to live morally, earn a decent living, and pray for financial success, remembering that God, not we, ultimately determines our bottom line.

This is not to say that we can spend money irresponsibly or expect to earn a living without working. But if we use our money to serve God, then lose it, we should not feel worthless or guilty.

God sends us only challenges that we can overcome. When He brings us financial struggles, we can use them to deepen our faith and gain a spiritual perspective about the true value of money.

There is a wonderful saying, "Don't pray to have an easy life. Pray to be a strong person." When we spend our lives learning to trust that everything the One Above does is for our good, we can cope with any adversity. We should not spend our lives building sand castles to protect us. We should develop the coping skills to overcome the many challenges that our Creator sends us.

Some people believe that the Almighty gave us life to do with as we please, as long as we occasionally thank Him and do a few reasonable things that He asks of us. But the One Above gave us life so that we will address a spiritual calling with it. We are not private citizens who are here to do as we please. We are all His emissaries and delegates, sent here to accomplish a task for the world.[33]

When we work for an employer, we don't eat whenever we want, take breaks whenever we feel like it, ignore job assignments that don't interest us, and so on. An employee's time belongs to the employer who decides what needs to be done, and the employer decides how to allocate resources among his employees.

The same applies to us. Our time belongs to the One who gave us life, and He knows best how to allocate the world's resources. This belief helps us have minimal concerns about having, taking, and living for ourselves. Knowing that we are here to serve our Creator helps us face life. When we suffer because we don't get what we want, or because what we want is taken away, we find meaning in the fact that God gave us these challenges for a reason.

We set ourselves up for disappointment when we think that our Sponsor has no right to interfere with our lives, especially if we think that we are already living the way that He wants. We need to know that our greatest fulfillment can come by accepting whatever missions God gives us. When we suffer, we can tell Him, "I don't know what You're doing, but You obviously think that I need this to fulfill my mission in life."

Being tied to our personal wants makes it difficult to accept losing what we value, or never having what we want. When we believe that our sole purpose here is to serve the One Above, challenges and suffering continue this service. We suffer most when we hurt only for ourselves and see no greater purpose in it.

When we know that everything in our lives serves God's purposes, not our personal wishes, we can accept that what happens is exactly what we need to fulfill ourselves. No deprivations and pain can conquer our spirit if our mission is to serve our Creator. On the other hand, any deprivation can defeat us if we are here only to take.

A man invited his friend to a formal dinner party. The host stressed that the friend should wear his tuxedo and arrive on time. The friend did as he was told, only to discover upon his arrival that he was invited to be a waiter! Instead of being at the party to take, he was brought there to serve. He became furious at his former friend.

Had he expected to help out, he would have graciously done whatever was needed. He would have felt good about being there, and would have feasted on the delicacies when the party ended.

This is analogous to how Judaism views the world. We come here thinking that we are supposed to have a good time. When life doesn't go our way, we feel outraged or hurt. If, instead, we believe that we are here to serve, we react much better to adversity. Instead of feeling violated and rejected when we don't get what we think we deserve, we serve God with different resources, depending upon what the Almighty lends us.

JOB LOSS

Many people feel angry, bereft, or worthless when they lose their job. Having a spiritual appreciation for why these events occur can make coping easier.

People who lose their jobs often chalk it up to bad luck, the boss having it in for them, or being the junior person at work during a reorganization. While these explanations may be true, attributing major events to nothing more than chance or bad luck obscures God's hand in our lives.

We can't know whether specific tragedies or difficulties were intended to wake us up spiritually or to cleanse us. Either way, we can benefit from them by recognizing that our crises have a spiritual message to convey.

For instance, Al was a department chief in a hospital for twenty years. Soon after health care reform started, he got a pink slip and had to leave. His excellent work as a physician was completely ignored by the hospital administrators, and he felt devastated to lose his job in this drastic and humiliating way.

He could easily have shrugged this off as being due to upheavals in the medical care system. Instead, he wondered what he might have done to cause God to send him this misfortune. When he reflected honestly on his work behavior, he realized that it left a lot to be desired.

Al knew that the Almighty punishes people "measure for measure."[34] This means that He tends to punish us by doing to us what we did inappropriately. For example, Jews who slandered others were once punished with a skin disease that resembled psoriasis *(tzaraat)*. They had to live outside the mainstream community until their condition improved.[35] The punishment fit the crime because the slanderer encouraged people to shun the "slanderee." The slanderer then experienced what it was like to be shunned.

Al wondered if he got fired because he had once fired an employee abruptly, without giving him a chance to improve. When Al had a similar experience, he felt such anguish over losing his job and not being able to find another one that he had anxiety attacks, lost weight, and felt terrible about himself. He learned firsthand how devastating and calamitous it was to be fired. His newfound sensitivity made him realize how terrible his employee must have felt, and taught him to be more sensitive with unemployed patients and friends.

As his introspection continued, Al recalled that he had also slandered other doctors. Other staff members did the same, yet that did not justify his doing it. Now he felt the same humiliation that those he slandered must have felt when he damaged their reputations.

Al felt especially humiliated when other hospitals ignored his impressive resume. He had no choice but to go into private practice with a young doctor who was just starting out.

While losing his job was traumatic, it reminded him that financial security comes from God, and that "what goes around comes around." A year after learning from the school of hard knocks, he reaped some unexpected benefits: he earned more money from private practice than he had at the hospital and no longer felt compelled to compromise his integrity by playing politics.

When Al was fired, he initially felt very hurt, angry, and depressed, and he couldn't imagine any good coming of it. It was only with time that he felt grateful that God gave him a chance to improve his life, become more sensitive, rectify his mistakes, and learn a lesson about trust.

Today, job and business losses are common, especially with recessions, mergers, employee cutbacks, health care reform, and bankruptcies. Many people who lose their jobs are initially devastated, but most find reasonable, or even better, jobs elsewhere. This gives some people a chance to admit that they were never happy at their jobs, and they have a welcome opportunity to reassess their careers. When a lawyer couldn't earn a living and a fur dealer went out of business, both became psychologists. A woman whose bad knees ruined her dance career became a lawyer. An artist who was usually out of work and a man whose business burned down both became social workers, a singer who couldn't find work started a bed-and-breakfast in her home, a fired commodities trader started his own company, and a "burned-out" nurse became a drug research coordinator. Had they not lost their jobs, they would never have left their unfulfilling work for better positions elsewhere.

One man discovered that losing his job was the best thing that could possibly have happened to him. Arnie was a hardworking, driven yuppie. He gauged his self-worth by his success at work, and his primary goal was to see how high he could climb the corporate ladder and how much money he could earn. After five years of neglect, his wife Ellen decided that it was time to have a baby. Arnie had no interest in raising a child because it would disrupt his life. He decided to go along with Ellen's plan because he thought that she would raise the baby. He could hire help if she couldn't manage on her own.

Arnie was working sixty to seventy hours a week as a company vice president when Ellen got pregnant. Ellen had medical problems and needed to stay in bed, so Arnie hired a housekeeper to take care of her. A month later, he got the shock of his life. He was dismissed because his company was being taken over and his services were no longer needed. He flew into a panic about finding a new job and busying himself until he did. Although he had enough savings to support his family for a few years, it never occurred to him to take time off to care for his wife or bond with his new baby.

When Robin was born, Arnie's plans were wrecked again. The housekeeper quit, and they could not quickly find a replacement. Ellen had had a debilitating pregnancy and labor and needed a month to recuperate, so Arnie was forced to take care of his daughter and his wife.

He initially resented this. He was a businessman, not a cook, maid, or nanny. But the more he woke up in the middle of the night to feed and soothe Robin, and the more he held her during the day, the more attached he grew to her. He felt that she needed him, and he fell in love with her, even though he had never wanted children. He also learned to appreciate how hard his wife had worked as a mother and homemaker. By the time Arnie got a new job, he actually looked forward to coming home to his two new careers—being a husband and a father.

CHARITY

"Giving charity saves one from death."[36]

The Torah says that God will send us what we need if we follow His will. But a man named Korah tried to convince the Israelites that Moses had made up the Torah and that following it would cause financial ruin.[37] To bolster his point, he told a tale of woe about a widow and her two daughters: The women toiled as farmers and harvested a bountiful crop. Moses then told them to give tithes to the priests and Levites.[38] They did as they were told, but little was left for themselves.

The widow didn't believe that she could eke out a future living from her field, so she sold it and bought sheep. When she sheared them, Moses told her that the first wool belonged to the priests.[39] She was so disgusted that she slaughtered her livestock, only to be told that certain parts of them also belonged to the priests.[40] The story ended with the unfortunate widow becoming destitute and dying of hunger.[41]

Korach used this story to illustrate how illogical tithing was, and that God could not have promised that it wouldn't diminish our assets.

On the surface, Korach seemed to be right. Logic says that if we have $1,000 and give away $100, we will have only $900 left. Tithing apparently makes us poorer. This is why we must trust that the Almighty will somehow give us back what we give away. We need to transcend our intellects to understand how this can happen.

Tithing did not destroy the widow's prosperity. She did. She lost her wealth because she did not trust that God would replenish what she gave away. That led her to sell her capital, which ruined her financial solvency. Had she only trusted God to somehow replace what she gave away she would have held onto her field, and it would have produced more and more. Her reactions destroyed her, not her observance of God's commandments.

Our Sages made a play on the biblical verse that commands us to tithe produce. It says, "You shall surely tithe all of the produce of your sowing."[42] The Hebrew word for "tithe" can also be read to mean "rich." Thus, "You shall surely tithe" is homiletically interpreted to mean, "Tithe your produce so that you will become rich."[43]

A scriptural verse even allows us to test God to see if He will reimburse us for giving charity. It says, "Bring all the tithes . . . and test Me with this, says the Lord of Hosts. See if I open the windows of heaven for you and pour out an overflowing blessing for you."[44]

A man who owned a small company discovered how true God's promise was. He started tithing his income when he became observant, and found that he earned more money than ever before. Each year, he continued making appropriate charitable contributions and the company earned more and more. A large food conglomerate noticed how profitable his business was and offered to buy him out. They figured that they would make the company even more profitable by eliminating his sizable charitable deductions.

The owner set them straight. "My company is profitable *because* of my charitable contributions. I will sell it to you only if you agree to continue tithing its profits and give that money to charity."

The buyers thought that he was crazy, but the books spoke for themselves. They bought the company on his terms.

Trusting God to provide, directly or indirectly, has never been easy. In order to help us do this, God sent the Israelites manna from heaven during their many years in the wilderness. (It fell every day except for the Sabbath, when the double portion that fell on Fridays sufficed for both days.)[45] When the Jews went to sleep each night, they had no guarantee that they would get food the next morning. They couldn't even hoard manna from one day to the next because it became wormy! They learned to trust their Creator to provide for them as they spent forty years in a desert with only enough food for one day at a time.

This general lesson of trust was also individualized. The less someone trusted the Almighty, the further he had to walk in order to find his daily food. Someone who totally trusted God found his daily manna at his doorstep. Those who didn't trust Him had to learn a lesson by walking far away to find food.[46]

Some people ask how we can trust God to provide when there are millions of people, including innocent children, who starve every day. One answer is that the Lord made the world imperfect, and we help perfect it by taking care of His needy children. The Lord provides more than enough food for everyone, but He wants us to earn merit by distributing what we have to those who don't.[47] He gives humanity more than enough resources to feed the poor, clothe the naked, and take care of the needy. We have only ourselves to blame when people go hungry because we haven't distributed the blessing that He gave us, or because cruel and selfish people hoard what is supposed to be given away.

We are supposed to serve the Lord with all of our resources; as we say in the *Shema* prayer, "You should love the Lord your God with all your heart, with all your soul, and with all of your resources."[48] This means that we are supposed to serve our Creator with our feelings, with our lives, and with our money.

At first blush, this order seems very peculiar. We might think that it is harder to die as martyrs, if need be, than to serve the Almighty with our money. But the *Shema* tells us that serving the Lord with our money and possessions can be more of a challenge than dying for belief in Him. How could that be?

A joke helps explain the answer. The devil offers a chief executive officer the deal of a lifetime. "Roy," he says, "I will make you the richest man on the face of the earth. All you have to do is to sell me your soul."

Roy ponders the proposition for a few minutes, then asks, "What's the catch?"

Sadly, money is more important to many people than life itself.[49] Some compromise their morality for money, while others get killed during robberies because they refuse to relinquish their wallets or jewelry. Wars are fought and innumerable lives destroyed in the quest for wealth. Even today, people die working at hazardous jobs, unsafe factories, dangerous oil rigs, mines, and the like, and workaholics shorten their lives amassing more and more money.

Once people make money, few willingly give 10 percent or more to charity.[50] They don't want to give away what they think belongs to them. If only they understood how important giving charity is for our self-actualization, not only for the poor people we benefit. We can fully develop our divine qualities only by sharing what we have. We think that we do poor people a favor by giving to them, but they actually do more for us than we do for them.[51] God rewards us with six blessings when we give away even a small coin, and eleven blessings when we verbally console and comfort a needy person.[52] Being charitable also helps us grow close to God and brings redemption to the world.[53]

WHY BAD PEOPLE PROSPER

"Woe to the wicked man who does evil, for what he does will be done to him."[54]

While God sometimes makes good people poor, He also gives wealth to some undeserving people. This is because He rewards us in the currency that we value.[55] This is expressed in the saying, "The reward for doing a commandment is the opportunity to do another commandment, and the reward for a transgression is doing another transgression."[56]

Immoral people think that this world is the ultimate good, and they don't relate to spiritual rewards. So God fully rewards their few good deeds in this temporary world by giving them wealth and honor.[57] They are then punished severely in the next world for their misdeeds.[58] They are spiritually bankrupt and humiliated there because they already enjoyed their rewards. They have totally severed their souls from their spiritual Source by the time they die, so they can't receive spiritual pleasure.[59] Their material prosperity in this world is a poor trade-off for the eternal blessing they forfeit later. Wicked people don't believe in an afterlife, so they are content to have a "good life" now. But when they die, the money and objects they valued are meaningless.

Spiritually sensitive people know that the greatest earthly reward is having opportunities to do good deeds and feel close to God.[60] They want to improve their spirituality and moral shortcomings here, even if it means suffering, because they will earn a greater eternal reward that way. They know that one moment of spiritual pleasure in the afterlife is more enjoyable than all of our earthly pleasures combined. When righteous people are cleansed here, they can enjoy spiritual bliss in the next world without any further suffering. They leave a world of physical pain and toil and enter a world of unimaginable spiritual delights.[61]

We express our essence through our behavior. If we mostly act properly, God cleanses us of our misdeeds here. Since wicked people's good deeds don't reflect their essence, they may have easy lives now and receive punishment later. This is one of many reasons why we can't evaluate the Almighty's justice by how miserable or easy someone's life is. One person may enjoy temporary pleasure now, while another's rewards are deferred for the afterlife. The eternity of future pleasure or pain becomes a major factor in why "bad" things happen to good people, and why "good" things happen to bad ones.

The Lord not only rewards people with wealth but also gives it as a spiritual test. A prosperous, unworthy person may retroactively earn God's gifts by improving himself spiritually and/or by helping others.[62] The following stories illustrate how:

Sam was a very wealthy, assimilated Jew who had everything that money could buy. His happy marriage ended when his wife died in her fifties. When he stopped grieving for her, he had to decide what to do with his life. His children were already grown, so he moved to southern France and spent his days cavorting around the Mediterranean on a yacht. He enjoying his bachelorhood as he hobnobbed with the rich and famous.

Meanwhile, his son Dennis enrolled in an Israeli *yeshivah* (institute of higher Jewish education) and became an observant Jew. Sam immediately flew to Israel to rescue Dennis from what Sam perceived to be a "cult." Rather than leave the *yeshivah,* Dennis convinced Sam to attend classes with him for a week. They agreed that if Sam believed that Dennis was being brainwashed, Dennis would consider leaving.

Sam prided himself on his open-mindedness and agreed to his son's suggestion. Instead of leaving after a week, Sam continued studying. He and his second wife now live in Jerusalem, where he studies Torah and she does volunteer work. They support themselves, as well as many Jewish charities, on the interest from his wealth.

Another remarkable story took place in a country that has a small, highly assimilated Jewish community. A Jewish man married a Catholic woman and "converted" to Christianity. (A Jew may become an apostate or idol worshiper but can never relinquish his Jewish identity.) He became very wealthy and supported the Catholic Church his entire life.

As he lay on his deathbed, two priests hovered nearby to make sure that he ceded his estate to the Church. He was so outraged that he declared, "As you stand here, I am calling in my attorney and rewriting my will."

When he died, he left the Jewish community a million dollars to build a synagogue, but only on condition that they also build a religious day school. He knew from experience that a Jewish community has no future without intensive, traditional Jewish education. Today, that school has 500 students.

These stories show that God sometimes gives undeserving people riches while He patiently waits for them to repent and use their wealth properly.

Peter and his wife were also assimilated Jews, although Peter's grandparents had been traditional. He opened a business that became wildly successful, allowing his family to buy anything and do anything they wanted.

After ten years of unimaginable affluence, Peter and Sarita took stock of their lives. They were grateful for their affluence, yet realized that so much money could easily destroy them as it had so many other assimilated Jews in their neighborhood. Their neighbors were largely self-involved snobs who spent their days shopping, gossiping, eating out, and running to social functions and cultural events. Their children could not appreciate what they had because they had everything that money could buy. They were bored with life by the time they were fourteen and fifteen and experimented with drugs and sex for thrills. Their parents gave them $100 bills instead of love and discipline.

With the realization of how easily money can destroy people, Peter and Sarita became *baalei teshuvah* (returnees to observant Judaism). They enrolled their children in religious schools and used their wealth to support Jewish charities and to host nonobservant Jews in their home for Sabbath and holiday meals.

As Peter and Sarita realized, financial prosperity is not always a blessing; it can also cause people's downfall[63] if it's not used in spiritually meaningful ways.[64]

Many people who amass money do it for egocentric reasons. They could share what they have with the needy, sponsor community projects, and humbly thank God for their blessings. Instead, they often become conceited, use people, and think that they are above the law. Their arrogance may lead them to make risky or illegal investments that catch up with them and exposes their personal and financial bankruptcy.

The 1980s showed how money lured yuppies and businesspeople into a false sense of security. Instead of using their good fortunes to serve God, the "Me Generation" felt entitled to what they had. Their prosperity destroyed them when they lost their fortunes in the stock market crash and subsequent recession. Many ended up in worse straits than before they had much money.

Wealth can undo people who become obsessed with losing it, who spend their free time maintaining their extravagant lifestyle, or whose friends and family care only about their money, not them. Obsessions with money often destroy personal relationships and ruin people's health. Having too much, then, can be as ruinous as having too little.

God also makes unworthy people prosper if they will leave money as a financial trust for children who will use the inheritance properly.[65] The children retroactively justify their parents' undeserved wealth. Also, the Almighty rewards some righteous parents by giving their children material security.[66] The children may not deserve it, but their parents did.

Sometimes immoral people prosper so that we will see how comfortable they are and wonder if being virtuous is really worth it.[67] We'd all act morally if we saw that good actions were rewarded and bad ones were immediately punished. But if the opposite happens, we end up acting properly only if we commit ourselves to truth.

Some wicked people appear righteous because they want others to think that they are good. When these hypocrites see evil people prospering without even pretending to be virtuous, the hypocrites abandon their disguises and show their true colors to the world.

A final reason why God lets undeserving people prosper is so that we will see how bountifully He rewards them for the few good things they do.[68] We can then imagine how enormously moral people will be rewarded in the next world.[69]

SELF-HELP: HOW TO COPE WITH MONEY OR JOB LOSS

Don't "beat yourself up" if you have financial problems or lose a job. Learn what you can from the situation and apply it to the future. Be realistic about your job qualifications and try to improve your marketability. Consider getting more training, or look for a job in a different field. Find a good vocational counselor or headhunter to help you.

Review your resume and rehearse mock interviews with an objective friend who can give you constructive criticism. Network with people who may have contacts for a (better) job.

If you have been fired from more than one job, or have altercations with coworkers or superiors, you may behave improperly or have unrealistic expectations at work. Discuss this with a therapist or objective confidant.

If you have financial or job problems because of illegal actions (such as being robbed, swindled, or inappropriately fired), consider reporting it to the proper authorities. Pressing charges or standing up for yourself may help you feel empowered and less victimized, anxious, and depressed.

Many people feel humiliated or guilty about causing their financial misfortune. No matter how bright and successful we are, almost everyone has been conned, swindled, or robbed, has lost money in bad investments, gone bankrupt, lost a job, and so on. Share your distress with sympathetic friends or family. Many of them have already been through similar experiences and know how you feel.

People with financial or job problems often lose their self-confidence and feel overwhelmed, helpless, angry, anxious, and so on. These distressing feelings may come and go, even after getting a new job or improving financially. Getting support, reassurance, and practical suggestions from friends or relatives can help you feel better.

Misusing credit cards has caused millions of people to be choked by debts that they can't pay off. If you overspend or gamble too much, go to a Debtors Anonymous or Gamblers Anonymous free self-help meeting. Get financial and legal advice if necessary.

Losing money or a job shatters many people, especially those who think that financial and job security depends upon their efforts and skills. If you feel immobilized for longer than a month, a psychotherapist can help you regain your self-esteem and sense of control and put your life back in order. If necessary, a doctor can prescribe medication for depression and anxiety.

Traditional Judaism tells us that we can sometimes improve our destinies. For example, we can adopt new Hebrew names,[70] which represents changing our identities. We can change where we live.[71] We can also pray,[72] give charity,[73] and repent.[74] This means that we might possibly improve our financial situations by being nicer, changing our career path, moving to a place with better financial opportunities, and praying for the Almighty's help. The following is a prayer for financial blessing that may be added to the fifteenth prayer of the daily *Shemoneh Esrai* (the Eighteen Benedictions):

> You are the Lord God who feeds, provides for, and sustains (everything), from the horns of the buffalo to the eggs of lice. Give me my allotted bread, and give me and all of my household our food before we need it, contentedly and not in pain, in a permissible way and not in a forbidden one, with honor and not in disgrace. (Give it) for life and for peace, from Your wellspring of blessing and success, and from the flow of Your wellspring on High, so that I may be able to do Your will, immerse myself in Your Torah, and keep Your commandments. May I not need human gifts, and may the verse be fulfilled through me: "God opens His hand and satisfies the desire of all living things." As it is written, "Cast your burden on the Lord and He will sustain you."

When God challenges us financially, He might want us to grow spiritually, improve our lives, and/or pray. If we do these things, yet our situation doesn't get better, we may feel disappointed, angry, and rejected. Once we react emotionally to our pain, we can refocus on what we still have. In any crisis or tragedy, we have to stop feeling that nothing else is meaningful except for what we have lost.

HELPING OTHERS

Most people appreciate a listening ear and concrete help when they first lose a job, money, or possessions. Don't offer pearls of wisdom like "It's only money," or "Obviously, this was meant to be," or "What a learning experience this will be for you." These remarks are trivializing to someone who is devastated and feels that his or her world is coming apart. Express empathy and compassion if you know what it feels like to be in your friend's shoes. ("It's so hard to feel good about yourself when you lose your job." "I once lost a lot of money in the stock market and I took it as hard as you are.") If you don't know what it's like, ask the person to tell you, then validate how he or she feels. ("It must be so hard to face your friends in the synagogue, feeling the way you do.")

Let the person know if you, or anyone you know, has gone through a similar experience. We are comforted knowing that we all make mistakes, including those whom we like and respect. Knowing others who have recovered emotionally and financially can give us hope of doing the same.

It was once common for men to get their first full-time job in their teens or early twenties. They then kept that same job for life. Today, however, changing jobs or careers a number of times is more the rule than the exception. Lifetime job security is a thing of the past. That alone is reason enough not to identify too closely with our jobs.

The same goes for identifying with what we have financially. It is easier today than ever to make fortunes—and lose them. I once lost a great deal of money in a humiliating way, and was amazed at how many people whom I respected had done the same. Virtually everyone whom I assumed was too smart to do "stupid" things had comparable experiences. One colleague lost her life savings when her financial adviser absconded with her money instead of investing it. An employer gave a friend $20,000 to invest for him and never saw it again. A good friend—a bright, successful attorney—and his closest friends lost $80,000 in a business venture that never existed. The list went on and on. Anybody can lose money to good con men, sound investments that turn out to be risky, and poor choices.

Many people feel depressed or have anxiety attacks (panicky feelings accompanied by a sense of choking, faintness, and/or heart palpitations) when they are plagued by financial problems or have lost their jobs. Reassure them that that is normal and they are not going crazy. Encourage them to talk about their losses, sense of worthlessness and helplessness, and fears. After hearing them out, reassure them that you will help in any way you can until things get better. If need be, recommend a physician or therapist or consult a professional about what to do if they need such help but refuse it. A good doctor can prescribe nonaddictive medications that alleviate anxiety and depression and can monitor their symptoms.

A listening ear is important, but some people need financial and concrete help. Try to channel them into business, employ them, or recommend them for a job. If need be, collect money and leave it anonymously. Drop off needed food, clothes, supplies, and so forth to the person's doorstep. It is important to maintain the person's dignity.

Before taking up a collection, find out if the person needs it. If so, see if he or she is eligible for government or organizational aid. For example, many people who anticipate staggering medical bills for pregnancy, birth, or surgery expenses are eligible for Medicaid or Medicare. There are also excellent doctors at clinics who, if asked to do so, will reduce their fees or donate their services for exceptional cases. (See Resources section.) Many families can be spared financial devastation by making sure that they have health insurance and that the breadwinner has disability and life insurance. Neglecting insurance because someone "can't afford it" is being penny-wise and pound-foolish, and has been disastrous for many families.

Needy people should avail themselves of resources such as food stamps and unemployment insurance, victims' assistance boards, Red Cross disaster aid, veteran's aid, and synagogue community funds before private donations are collected for them.

Most Jewish communities have a Hebrew Free Loan Society (a *gmach*) that gives interest-free loans to qualified individuals. Other organizations *(Tomchei Shabbos)* provide weekly Sabbath or holiday meals for indigent Jews, while *Hachnassat Kallah* ("dowering the bride") groups give money, dishes, linens, appliances, and home furnishings to poor brides who can't afford them. Consider starting these organizations if your community does not have them.

There is a beautiful custom at *bar mitzvahs,* weddings, and celebrations to donate the leftover food to poor people, and to give 3 percent of the cost of the affair to charity.

If someone you know needs help but is too disorganized to get it, call a local hospital social work department. Someone there may be helpful in sorting out what resources are available and how to obtain them.

NOTES

1. *Bava Batra* 116a.
2. *Pirkei Avot* 4:1.
3. Jeremiah 9:22–23.
4. *Me'am Lo'ez* on *Pirkei Avot* 4:11; Moshe Chaim Luzzatto, *The Way of God* (New York: Feldheim, 1983) 2:3:1.
5. *Nedarim* 7b.
6. Rashi on *Yevamot* 47b.
7. *Eruvin* 41b.
8. *The Way of God* 2:3:1.
9. Genesis 24:1; 26:12–14; 33:11; *Shabbat* 92a; *Nedarim* 38a.
10. *Ketuvot* 104a.
11. Yerushalmi, *Kiddushin* 4:12: "Man will have to give an accounting for all of the fruits that he saw but did not partake of."
12. Proverbs 3:9.
13. The Torah prohibits wearing garments made of both linen and wool, known as *shaatnez.*
14. These are leather straps attached to boxes with Torah verses written on parchment inside. A man ties them to his arm and forehead every morning to symbolize dedicating his mind, heart, and actions to God.
15. Based on Deuteronomy 15:7–8, 11 and 14:22. Many authorities say that we tithe after-tax income. See also footnote 50.
16. Deuteronomy 32:15.
17. Proverbs 30:8–9.
18. Genesis 3:18–19.
19. Genesis 3:18–19.
20. *Bava Batra* 10a. God determines our earnings and losses for the entire year between the New Year and the Day of Atonement. This amount does not include what we spend for the Sabbath, festivals, and teaching our children Torah. If we spend little to celebrate the Sabbath and holidays we get little more; if we spend more, we get more.
21. See Deuteronomy 2:7.

22. Proverbs 10:22, "God's blessing is what makes a person rich, and toil adds nothing to it."

23. *Taanit* 25a.

24. Written in a poem by Abraham ibn Ezra.

25. Job 1:21.

26. *The Way of God* 2:3:1.

27. *Yoma* 35b.

28. *Taanit* 24b.

29. Rashi as explained by Maharsha on *Taanit* 25a.

30. *Taanit* 25a.

31. *Taanit* 25a.

32. *Taanit* 25a.

33. *The Way of God* 2:2:2.

34. For example, see Deuteronomy 19:19.

35. Leviticus 13.

36. Proverbs 10:2.

37. *Bamidbar Rabbah* 18:3.

38. Based on Leviticus 27:30 and Deuteronomy 18:4.

39. Based on Deuteronomy 18:4.

40. Based on Deuteronomy 18:3.

41. *Me'am Lo'ez* on Numbers 16:1.

42. Deuteronomy 14:22.

43. *Taanit* 9a; *Midrash Tanchuma* on *Parshat Re'eh*.

44. Malachi 3:10.

45. Exodus 16:14–26.

46. Quoted by Eliyahu Kitov, *The Book of Our Heritage,* vol. 3 (New York: Feldheim, 1978), p. 234.

47. *Bava Batra* 10a.

48. Deuteronomy 6:5.

49. *Brachot* 61b.

50. Contributing to scientific research, arts and cultural foundations, colleges, American hospitals, or similar nonprofit institutions does not normally constitute tithing. Tithes include money given to poor people and/or to support Jewish education. See the Chofetz Chaim, *Ahavath Chesed* (New York: Feldheim, 1976), chapters 18–20 for a discussion about how much money to give, to whom, in what priority, and so forth.

51. *Vayikra Rabbah* 34:8.

52. *Bava Batra* 9b.

53. *Bava Batra* 10a.

54. Isaiah 3:11.

55. Eliyahu Dessler, *Strive for Truth* (Jerusalem: Feldheim, 1988), p. 72.

56. *Pirkei Avot* 4:2.

57. *Strive for Truth,* p. 72.

58. *The Way of God* 2:2:3.

59. *The Way of God* 2:2:3, 6.

60. *The Way of God* 2:2:8.

61. *The Way of God* 2:2:3.

62. *Ikkarim* 4:12; *Duties of the Heart* 4:3.
63. *The Way of God* 2:3:4, 6.
64. *The Way of God* 2:3:1.
65. *Ikkarim* 4:12.
66. *Ikkarim* 4:12.
67. *Ikkarim* 4:12.
68. *Emunot VeDeot* 5:1.
69. *Makkot* 24b.
70. *Brachot* 7b states that one's name determines one's destiny.
71. *Genesis Rabbah* 44:12, based on Genesis 12:1–2.
72. *Genesis Rabbah* 44:12, based on 2 Chronicles 7:14.
73. *Genesis Rabbah* 44:12.
74. *Genesis Rabbah* 44:12, based on 2 Chronicles 7:14.

RESOURCES

Hebrew Free Loan Society
Local Orthodox synagogues or Jewish outreach centers
Jewish Association for Services for the Aged
Jewish Board of Family and Children's Services
Jewish Community Center, Social Work Department
Jewish Poverty Coordinating Council, (212) 267–9500
Victim Services Agency, (212) 577–7777
    Provides emergency financial aid and counseling to crime victims.

4

Coping with the Challenges of Being Single

A man who has no wife lives without joy, without blessing, without goodness . . . without a protecting wall . . . without peace. . . . Any man who has no wife is not a proper man."[1]

God designed everything in the physical world to teach us spiritual concepts. To that end, He wanted marriage to let us experience true love and giving so that we would have a model for appreciating how much He loves us and how deeply we can love Him.

Yet, getting married is not easy for many singles. And instead of feeling the joy of love and companionship, they feel pain and loneliness. Many question their self-worth, while others feel depressed and hopeless about the future. They can't imagine that they will never find a soul mate with whom to share their lives and raise a family, but the dating scene offers no glimmers of hope, either.

One quarter of adult, American Jews have never been married, and 38 percent are currently single.[2] In 1970, most Jewish women between twenty-two and twenty-four were married. In 1990, only 10 percent were.

The older single women become, the less likely they are to marry. The ticking of their biological clocks catapults some women into panic and others into despair. Singles of both sexes often put their lives "on hold" for a decade or more, as they waste their free time dating, going to singles' events, meeting matchmakers, and feeling depressed or angry about their predicament.

Many singles have accomplished other goals, such as graduating from college and graduate or professional schools. They have achieved financial and career success. They own homes or apartments and have done many of the "finer" things in life. Yet no matter what, some singles can't find a suitable mate. This is so devastating that their other achievements often seem meaningless in the face of their loneliness and pain.

At some point, many singles feel angry with God (if they still believe in Him) for making their lives so difficult. They resent the opposite sex for being "messed up" and feel jealous of friends or peers who got happily married long ago. Some take stock of themselves and conclude that they are no less attractive, desirable, or successful than their married friends. They are baffled as to why, despite all of their efforts, they have been "singled out" for their terrible situation.

Although this problem is more prevalent now than ever, even our ancestors had a hard time finding the right mate. For example, Isaac was a forty-year-old bachelor when he married Rebecca, and his father had to send a servant to a neighboring country to find her. There was nothing spiritually, morally, or psychologically wrong with Isaac, so why did his Maker allow him to be single for so many years?

The answer is that the Almighty had destined a wonderful wife for him, but Isaac simply had to wait until the right time to meet her.

Traditional Judaism proposes that the Lord destines two people to marry each other before conception even occurs.[3] The man's and the woman's souls were once united before they came into this world, and these halves reunite when the couple marries. Although God wants us to choose who we marry, and our deeds and prayers can change our destiny, a successful marriage depends upon divine providence.[4]

When singles wonder why marriage keeps eluding them, they rarely think that a divine plan has anything to do with it. Yet God has a hand in that as much as in every other part of our lives.

Sue was a wonderful woman who was divorced twice. During the many years that followed, she kept wondering why she never met Mr. Right. She went to a psychotherapist to discuss what was wrong with her. She assessed and reassessed her marriages and relationships to try to understand what mistakes she had made.

When she was thirty-five, Sue's recently divorced employer asked her out. By the time they got engaged, she understood that her flaws had not kept her from meeting her soul mate earlier. Her appropriate husband had simply been married to the wrong woman, and Sue had to wait for him to get divorced before he was available for her to marry. Meanwhile, both of them had needed to go through certain life experiences that prepared them to marry each other. When Sue thought about this, she saw how carefully God had engineered the events of her personal life.

In our generation, many people discover authentic Judaism only later in life, at which point they meet their intended spouses. Some people need to develop emotionally or spiritually by going through divorce or widowhood before they can marry. Others are ready for marriage but must wait for a partner to be ready. It is only in retrospect that many couples realize why they didn't get married earlier.

A Roman matron once asked a rabbi, "What has your God been doing since He created the world?"

The rabbi answered, "He sits and makes matches, assigning this man to that woman, and this woman to that man."

"That's not so hard," she replied. "I can do the same." She then went and matched her slaves to each other.

Some time later, the spouses beat each other up. The wives said, "I don't want this man," and the men protested, "I don't want this woman."

After the matron admitted that the rabbi was right, he replied, "Making matches is as difficult before the Holy One, blessed is He, as was dividing the Reed Sea."[5]

This illustrates how difficult making compatible matches has always been. Still, one wonders why there are unprecedented numbers of Jewish singles today.

Sociologists say that it is because many Jews delay marrying in order to establish careers, and then many of them get divorced. Those for whom marriage is not a priority deliberately put professional or financial success first. They finish four years of college, then three to eight years of graduate, law, medical, or postgraduate training, and only then start dating seriously.

This has more than sociological ramifications. The pool of available singles is much larger when one is twenty than when one is thirty-five or forty. In addition, people who have stunted their emotional growth for twenty years while trying to establish a career will have very little to offer in marriage, other than money.

One man complained, "I'm forty years old now, and I've never been married. All of the women I meet are divorced and have kids." Another man in his late thirties lamented, "I have nothing to offer most single Jewish women. My best asset is my ability to provide financially, and the women I meet make good livings themselves. They own their own co-ops, they have good pension plans, they buy everything they need and are very self-sufficient. They don't need a husband to take care of them."

While it is certainly not true that all women over thirty are either financially independent or divorced with children, singles in their twenties have different needs and characteristics than those in their thirties or forties. Those who are still looking for the same kind of partner at thirty or forty that they sought at twenty are likely to stay single.

Life is supposed to be a process of change and growth. If we channel most of our time, energy, and emotions into school, training, or work, it will usually be at the expense of our social, emotional, and spiritual growth. This is especially true of men. It is very difficult to excel in many areas at the same time. Those who dedicate themselves to one area of life automatically have less time to spend elsewhere.

Singles who make marriage a priority are more likely to get married than those who hide behind their careers to avoid intimacy and marital responsibilities. While it is hard to work on a career and a marriage at the same time, it is possible to find a healthy balance. The two don't need to be mutually exclusive.

Psychologists say that many singles have unconscious barriers to marriage. They are afraid that committing to one person will reduce their options with others. Some fear being controlled by a spouse or losing their identity and freedom. Many have a detailed wish list about how a date should look, think, and act—a combination that has never been found in any mortal being. It may include a model's looks, Rockefeller's wealth, Hillel's compassion, Sarah's hospitality, and Moses' spirituality, all in the same person.

Some people approach marriage as an entitlement program where they unrealistically expect a mate to take care of them. Some date only unavailable men or women, while others enjoy the thrill of the chase, then get bored when the object of their desire finally shows interest.

Others "fall in love" with someone's superficial, or even imagined, qualities. Women who "love" a man because of his generosity will lose these feelings once he stops wining and dining them. When love is based on getting material things, people feel empty or bored with the person soon after they get what they want. They like the gifts, not the giver.

Deep and stable love comes from giving, not taking.[6] Love can endure as long as a partner will receive what we give, just as a mother's love for her child is sustained by giving her time, emotions, and energy. The more she gives, the more she loves her baby.

Relationships don't survive when people date in order to take. If, instead, they seek someone who can receive what they have to give, they have a chance to develop deep and permanent love.[7]

Singles with unsatisfying relationships should consider the possibility that they have emotional barriers to marriage. These need to be worked out, usually in psychotherapy, before they damage a marriage.

People with self-defeating or unproductive dating patterns can change them as long as they stop blaming their past and ruing their raw deal in life. They may as well use the same energy to work on themselves and make the present better instead of regretting the past.

We can overcome challenges only when we accept life as it is, not by imagining how we would like it to be. Singles who can't improve their situations with the help of supportive and insightful friends or spiritual leaders should seek professional help. A good therapist can objectively point out how to change self-defeating behavior, feelings, and attitudes, and help work through barriers to growth.

Singles need to view themselves realistically. We must know what our strengths and weaknesses are before we can find a marriage partner to bring out the best in us. We should also know that the people who attract us the most might not be good spouses for us.

For example, an introverted man might like extroverted women and appreciate their having social skills that he lacks. But when he marries a woman who invites house guests every weekend and goes out to social functions once a week, he may regret his choice. Extroverted women might also expect him to be a good conversationalist and be disappointed that he has little to contribute verbally. In similar fashion, women who seek ambitious husbands because they like wealth may regret how little time and energy they have for a wife.

Many singles from dysfunctional homes seek partners like their parents, hoping that a mate will miraculously be as wonderful as they wanted their parents to be. They exaggerate a date's positive qualities and delude themselves that glimmers of goodness will become major traits. Unfortunately, that rarely happens outside of movies and romance novels.

Some singles seek troubled people whom they can "rescue" and can thereby feel needed and earn a spouse's eternal gratitude. What happens instead is that the rescuer gets frustrated when the "helpee" neither gets better nor appreciates the rescue efforts.

Singles would do better to focus on who *they* should be rather than focus on finding Mr. or Miss Right. Some singles with poor self-esteem try to get it by marrying someone who is respected or makes a lot of money. Others expect a spouse to make them feel whole and make up for their childhood hurts and losses. It is healthier, as well as less risky, to become whole ourselves, rather than seek a spouse to magically heal us.

One patient expressed the futility of seeking a man to give her what she had been unwilling to do for herself: "Some women spend their whole lives trying to make men strong enough to take care of them. If they would only use that same energy to nurture themselves and become healthy, their relationships would be much more rewarding." If women with poor self-esteem and mediocre education, jobs, or salaries would only develop themselves, they would not spend years looking for a rich husband who is unlikely to give them the emotional support they want.

Some singles attribute their predicament to bad luck, and feel helpless, victimized, jaded, and bitter. They are tired of wasting their lives dating, and they stop appreciating what they have and what they have to offer. Religious singles especially feel empty and unimportant because they don't realize how productive and meaningful life can be if they aren't married.

The tribulations of being single can help people refine their souls, just as any form of suffering does. Singles need to continue to grow and make life meaningful, not live in dread of never getting married. They are supposed to perfect the world every day, just like everyone else, and need to find ways to deepen their relationship with God despite their difficulties. Being married is no prerequisite for making spiritual or personal contributions to the world.

Married people serve God while raising a family, and singles serve Him in a different but equally important way. Each has challenges to overcome and difficulties to face, and each must find ways to make life worthwhile. When singles realize that they can't find a spouse without God's help, it can motivate them to have a close relationship with Him and remind them of the critical role that He plays in every part of their lives.

Some singles think that being married is always easier than being single, but even a good marriage is often more challenging than being single. It is said that married life is not as wonderful as singles imagine it will be, nor is it as bad as married people claim it is.

Beth always assumed that no matter how difficult married life was, it had to be better than being single. Beth had dated for eleven years by the time she was thirty, and her friends had all married long before. She spent many evenings lamenting her fate, then finally decided to start living instead of waiting for life to start with Mr. Right. She found a satisfying job instead of hoping that marriage would rescue her from the stressful, dead-end one where she worked. She went to concerts, plays, restaurants, and museums by herself or with female friends. She took classes in Judaism one night a week and made new friends there. She furnished her apartment nicely and invited guests to share Sabbath meals with her. Instead of waiting to see the world with a husband, she started visiting interesting cities on long weekends. In short, she started living.

While vacationing in San Francisco, Beth impulsively called a former room-mate, Miriam, whom she had not seen in years. When they met for lunch, Beth was surprised that Miriam was not nearly as beautiful as she once was. Miriam looked worn, and her face had lost its glow. Beth asked Miriam to catch her up with events since they last spoke.

Miriam did not know where to begin. "As you know, I married a wonderful man. Steve has been a great provider and a caring husband, but I'm lucky to see him an hour a day. He's a very busy surgeon, and he's been on call every third or fourth night since I've known him. It's like a day off when he works only twelve hours.

"That's it for the good news. I had three miscarriages before I had Claire, who is now three. She was very premature, and spent the first three months of life in the intensive care unit. She seems to be out of the woods now, but worrying about keeping her alive has really aged me. She needed a transfusion every week, then stopped breathing off and on during her first six months home. She's been a sickly child, and I've rushed her to the hospital for one emergency or another more times than I can remember.

"When David was born, he had severe muscular problems. He's a year old now, and it's unclear how long he will survive. He has spent more than half his life in the hospital, and he could choke and die at any time.

"I guess you thought when I got married that I would have a fairy-tale life. I thought that, too. I never imagined that my life would end up like this. It's been so depressing, I really don't want to spend our time together talking about it. Why don't you tell me about your life? I'm sure it's been more interesting and pleasant than mine."

Beth had never imagined that two people who loved each other could have these kinds of problems. For the first time, she felt grateful that she had her challenges and not somebody else's.

That conversation convinced Beth to stop lamenting her fate. Whether she got married soon was not in her hands, so she focused on what she could control. She worked on refining her spirituality, eliminating her character flaws and negative attitudes. Miriam's comments also convinced Beth to think about whether potential mates would weather difficulties well, instead of evaluating primarily how enjoyable they were to be with.

Singles typically expect marriage to make them happy and give them more of what they want. The Bible tells us that our forefather Isaac met Rebecca just as he finished saying the afternoon prayers.[8] That prayer reminds us not to pursue personal goals like career advancement, making money, or getting married as ends in themselves. Instead, everything we do should be used to serve God. That Isaac met Rebecca after saying the afternoon prayers may suggest that we should want to get married so that we will be able to serve God better, not simply feel happier.

It is easy for singles to become self-centered the longer they live alone. Some stagnate, others become hedonistic, yet others rue their misfortune. It takes a lot of emotional and spiritual work to transcend the frequent disappointment and loneliness of being single. One way of avoiding destructive self-absorption is by taking care of others instead of thinking only about ourselves.

Being single for a long time can motivate people to search for greater meaning in life and help others who are suffering. They can visit the sick and elderly, do good deeds for others, and support charities.

We prefer to invest our time and emotions with people who make us feel good and with whom we can build lasting relationships. When singles channel their energy into temporary relationships with those who don't give them immediate gratification, they can give in a godly way, even though it may not feel as satisfying as giving to a spouse.

Jon and Rina joined a group of Jews who visited local hospital patients every Sabbath afternoon. They had met each other at many singles events but never considered each other "dating material." One day, they both visited an elderly widow who was recuperating from a broken hip. She told them about the wonderful life she had had with her husband, and Jon and Rina were very touched. When they left, they agreed that they would like to love a spouse as much as she did. This was their first serious discussion together, and they continued talking throughout the evening. They got engaged a few months later.

Singles can transcend their self-absorption by helping each other, not only the sick or poor. They can pray for one another, introduce friends to potential mates, invite them for Sabbath meals, and host singles parties.

A Jew's hallmarks are compassion, humility, and acting kindly.[9] The more singles express these qualities, the better prepared they will be to continue doing the same in marriage.

Instead of being a waste of time, dating can be a learning experience if singles notice traits that they admire in others and develop those qualities in themselves.

They can also modify unattractive habits when they realize how unappealing they are in a date.

Since the Almighty sends us what we need, not necessarily what we want, He may arrange for us to meet people who model our best or our worst traits. For example, I once went on an absolutely terrible date. When I thought about why I disliked this man so intensely, I realized that he had two of my worst traits. Although others had criticized these to me before, it was not until I saw them in someone else that I appreciated why I needed to change. Had I never dated this man, I might never have accepted the criticism. On the other hand, when I dated men with tremendous empathy, warmth, and moral strength, I realized how much further I could develop those qualities in myself.

Singles who view dating and marriage as opportunities to give and grow usually find it more tolerable than those who expect it to make them feel good. We can grow by treating a date kindly and respectfully, even if we don't like the person. That fulfills the commandment to love our neighbor as ourselves.[10] Even when a date is someone you would never set up with your worst enemy, acting sensitively is still valuable in its own right.

Singles often think that the only purpose of dating is to enjoy it and find a spouse. But God may have other reasons for arranging dates between certain individuals. He may want us to impact or help them, to learn how people think and feel, or to glean information that we will eventually use. Since nothing happens by accident, every date can have meaning, even if it is not the meaning that we wanted it to have.

Few singles would choose to stay single in order to influence others. But if God is not enabling them to marry, this is yet one more way of serving Him.

Some years ago, I spent the Sabbath with a friend named Sandy. As we chatted, Lydia, the dinner hostess, asked me if I wanted to get married.

"Of course," I answered.

"Do you date?" she inquired.

"More than I care to think about," I grimly replied. "I've gone out with hundreds of men."

Lydia said, "How exciting! You must meet a lot of interesting people."

"It's hardly exciting," I countered. "It only makes me feel jaded."

Later that night Sandy said, "Lisa, I'm very upset about what you told Lydia. You shouldn't feel that way about dating."

"How would you feel if you were in my shoes?" I asked defensively.

She replied, "Don't focus on what you haven't gotten from dating. Think about how many people you've influenced. Maybe you are single because God wants you to teach or influence men. If you weren't single you wouldn't date them and wouldn't affect them. Think about all of the men whose lives you've touched."

After she said this, I realized how right she was. I did help some dates feel better about themselves, and had encouraged others to become more religious. In subsequent years, I re-encountered men whom I once dated and was able to give them practical help. Sandy's perspective gave new meaning to my many years of dating, and for the first time, it didn't seem like a colossal waste of time.

Had it had been up to me, I would never have chosen to stay single. But since God didn't give me that choice, I tried to make the best of my circumstances and live meaningfully.

A month after my conversation with Sandy, I encountered a man I had once dated. We discussed Sandy's comment and he replied, "Of course your friend is right. I have shared so many of your insights and ideas with my new wife. It's really enriched the spiritual side of our marriage."

People rarely tell us how much we affect them, but we all have something to offer others. Knowing that we are here to contribute instead of to take can make spending time with strangers more purposeful.

We sometimes find out, years later, why we had to date certain people. In my case, men I dated ten years earlier changed my views of Judaism and promoted my Jewish outreach. In other cases, I did marital counseling with them, gave them medical or Jewish-legal information they couldn't find on their own, or helped them find a path to greater spirituality.

Shortly before I wrote this chapter, I was a scholar-in-residence at a synagogue. The sponsor introduced himself as someone I had met in Boston fifteen years earlier, in an encounter that changed his life. I did not remember meeting him, so he told me that he had asked why I wanted to be a psychologist. I replied that a prayer caught my attention one morning:

"These are the things whose fruits we enjoy in this world, but the capital remains for us to enjoy in the world to come: Honoring one's father and mother, doing deeds of loving-kindness, rising early to go to the house of study every morning and evening, being hospitable to guests, visiting the sick, dowering the bride, accompanying the dead to their burial place, praying intensively, and *bringing peace between a person and his friend, and between a man and his wife. . . ."*[11]

I decided to spend my life bringing peace between people by being a psychologist who would help individuals and couples. This man had thought about that conversation almost every day since and had incorporated it into his life by bringing harmony between people as a management consultant. Prior to that conversation, he had never thought that God could be brought into the workplace. He assumed that Judaism was relevant only to the synagogue and the home.

FULFILLING OUR MISSIONS

We each have souls that were here in a previous lifetime, and they have unfinished business to complete. (This idea will be discussed further in the chapter on handicapped children.) This may cause singles to go through circumstances that seem unpleasant or unfair, but allow them to rectify their souls and the world.

Every Jew needs to make his or her contributions to the world before the Messiah can come. By focusing on making contributions, on giving instead of taking, on being sensitive to others, and on finding ways to grow spiritually, singles can help fulfill their missions. Our marital status does not prevent us from bringing the world closer to where God wants it to be.

It is helpful to pray for God to help singles meet their soul mates. He hears all heartfelt prayers, but here is a formal prayer that some men say:

> May it be Your will, my Lord God and God of my fathers, that in Your great mercy and abundant kindness, You send me a mate who is appropriate for all of my needs and hopes. Let us meet at the right time. Let her be a mate with whom I will have righteous and truthful children who will grow into upright adults. Just as You sent Adam, Isaac, Jacob, and Moses proper partners at the right time, send me a partner who is a good woman, pleasant in deeds and appearance, who does good deeds. Let her be charming, discerning and God-fearing, righteous, loving, and kind to others. Let her have no disqualifying blemishes or defects, and may she not be an angry person. Let her be a humble woman who is healthy and strong.
>
> May others' cruelty, hatred, trickery, and bad advice not prevent me from marrying my intended mate. May the scriptural verses be fulfilled in me, "The staff of the wicked will not rest on the lot of the righteous," and "Your wife will be like a fruitful vine on the walls of your house, your children shall be like olive trees planted around your table." You are the One who brings singles home, and frees prisoners (!) May the words of my mouth and the counsel of my heart please You, Lord, my Rock and my Redeemer. May my prayer to You, Lord, be at a pleasing time. God, in Your tremendous loving-kindness, answer me with the truth of Your salvation.[12]

It is customary for Jewish singles to pray at Rabbi Yonasan ben Uzziel's grave (located in Amuka, near Safed in northern Israel). He promised singles who do this that they will marry within a year, and many have. (It doesn't happen to everyone. I confess that I had to go twice.) At least it couldn't hurt.

USING MATCHMAKERS

Observant Jews have traditionally used matchmakers to find their mates. In some circles, it is still the usual way to find a marriage partner. It can be helpful for recently observant Jews to know how this system works:

While some matchmakers (*shadchanim*) are professionals and charge a fee, others do it for free. Those who charge may collect a "registration" fee, then get a larger, agreed-upon amount when an introduction leads to marriage. This fee may be a few hundred to a few thousand dollars and is sometimes negotiable.

Jewish matchmakers operate wherever there are substantial numbers of Jewish singles, but they differ widely in their approaches, expertise, contacts, and fees. Some matchmakers work only with specific types of people, such as *yeshivah* students (former or current); female graduates of religious schools; "*baalei teshuvah*" who grew up in nonobservant homes and became religious later;

divorcees; singles over thirty; or handicapped singles. Conservative Jews should not go to a matchmaker who knows only Bais Yaakov graduates. Someone older than thirty-five shouldn't go to a matchmaker who works primarily with eighteen-to twenty-year-olds, and so on.

Find out a *shadchan*'s fees, what kinds of people have been set up, and how many successful matches have been made before giving personal information. Some *shadchans* and matchmaking organizations have interviewed (and collected fees from) hundreds of singles with almost no resulting marriages.

A *shadchan* who is willing to set you up without first meeting you, or after knowing only a little about you, is likely to have only superficial knowledge of others. You should give a matchmaker a realistic picture of who you are and what kind of mate you are looking for, but don't expect magic.

Do not expect a *shadchan* to do a background search on anyone he or she sets you up with. You are responsible for finding out about a date's background, his or her personality problems, and any medical, psychiatric, financial, or legal problems.

Shadchans will learn a lot about you from your appearance. Any time that you circulate in Jewish circles you could potentially meet a spouse, or someone who will set you up. Most *shadchans* will ask for personal references and will want to speak to your friends, acquaintances, or rabbi about you. The impressions you make on others at a *Shabbat* table, on dates, in the synagogue, or at singles' events are likely to be shared with people you hardly know. That's one reason always to dress and act in ways that will make a good impression on others.

A New Yorker vacationed in Israel, where she met a reputedly excellent *shadchan* who had made seventy matches. The young woman was taken aback that the *shadchan* would not meet her unless she showed her passport. Apparently, so many singles lied about their ages that this was the only way to guarantee someone's true birth date. The *shadchan* asked for a five-minute synopsis of her life, religious background, personality, and what she was looking for in a husband. The *shadchan* then informed the woman that she would get back to her after checking out the information with her own sources.

Two days later, the *shadchan*'s investigation turned up some very unflattering data. The woman was amazed at how this *shadchan* had managed to find out so much about her—some true and some not. The woman realized for the first time how negatively she had impressed others by "being herself" in public and not showing her positive qualities in a stronger way.

When a *shadchan* sets up a couple, each reports back to the *shadchan* how the first date went. Having an intermediary spares many singles embarrassment. If both are interested, they continue dating. If not, the *shadchan* tells them that the other party does not wish to continue dating. What they say to the *shadchan* may also affect who the *shadchan* sets them up with in the future.

"Religious" dating is much more serious than secular dating. Observant couples date to see how compatible they are for marriage and try to get to know each other in a short time. They may ask each other pointed questions about their religious perspectives and life goals on a first date. Couples with little potential for marriage rarely go out after the first date. Dating four or five times implies that two people see real potential for marriage. If they continue dating for three months, they are likely to get engaged and be married a few months later.

This kind of dating is too intense for people who are indecisive, who have intimacy problems, or who have no idea what kind of spouse they are looking for. Those who like it appreciate not having to play games or waste time dating for fun. People who are interested in this kind of dating can learn more about it from a friend, rabbi, or *shadchan* who is familiar with the process.

Young couples often go to a hotel lobby or bar for a soda, or to an inexpensive restaurant on a first date. Older singles may go for a lunch date, a drink, or a meal at a pricier restaurant. Some couples converse in airports, stroll through a park, or meet at a friend's Sabbath table. Newcomers should find out how to conduct themselves on a date so that they don't make *faux pas*.

RECOMMENDATIONS FOR SINGLES

Be emotionally available and circulate among eligible singles or matchmakers. Go to singles events, network with friends and acquaintances, relocate to a city with good social opportunities, and contact reputable matchmakers. Be as serious about getting married as you would about getting a good job.

Be as attractive as possible. Lose weight if you are chubby, dress and groom yourself well, and improve your conversational skills. Don't think that others should accept you as you are if you aren't packaged attractively. Most people won't bother looking to discover your contents if they don't like the trappings.

Ask yourself honestly: what is it like going on a date with me? Do I attract the kind of person that I am looking for? What can I do differently to attract that kind of person? See a qualified psychotherapist if you repeatedly attract the "wrong" people, have unsatisfying relationships, or hear people criticizing flaws that you fail to see.

Show your best side at the beginning of a relationship, and let a date appreciate what you have to offer. Don't pour out your life story in the first few dates, or try to scare people away by showing your worst liabilities. Dissuading people by showing skeletons in your closet does not prove that they would eventually leave, anyway. People are much more accepting of someone they already like than they are of a stranger.

Decide what kind of husband or wife you want to be and become that person. Look for a mate who will complement your qualities, bring out the best in you, and receive what you have to give.

Don't love someone until you know who he or she is, and that the person sincerely cares about you and could be a reasonable mate.

Observe the individual's preferred lifestyle and how that might affect you. Don't gauge people only by what they say. See if their actions are consistent with their thoughts and words.

Don't decide who someone is based on who you want him or her to be. Know the family and cultural background, the strengths and character flaws, and with whom the person does and doesn't get along. Is there a stable work history? A drug or alcohol problem? Find out what emotional baggage will be brought into a marriage. Are you interested and able to adapt to it?

We tend to repeat with others the kinds of interactions that we had with our parents. Men who had good relationships with their mothers are likely to have the same with a wife, and women who had good relationships with their fathers are likely to relate well to a husband. People who had bad relationships with their parents are likely to repeat these conflicts in marriage.

It is always risky to assume that a potential mate will change. It is more accurate to gauge people by how they act now, not by how they say they will be. The Talmud says that we can evaluate a person by how he handles alcohol, anger, and money.[13] Take this good advice to heart.

Instead of putting your life on hold or viewing it as a waste, live productively. Work on skills that will help you be a good marriage partner, such as communicating, appreciating others, bringing out their good qualities, dealing constructively with anger and disappointment, responding to others' needs, developing spiritually, and asking God for help. Being single may not always be pleasant, but it can always be productive.

RECOMMENDATIONS FOR HELPING SINGLES

Treat singles with dignity. Put yourself in their shoes and imagine how you would want to be treated. Help singles feel desirable and welcome by inviting them for the Sabbath and holidays, by spending time together, and by calling them periodically to see how they are.

Don't tell singles that you know why they aren't married, and don't give unsolicited advice. ("You're too picky, you wear the wrong clothes, you choose the wrong kinds of dates . . .") Unless someone asks for more, offer only a listening ear and support.

If someone close to you is receptive to your ideas, and is frustrated by being single, ask what he or she feels is the difficulty in finding a mate. If something helped you when you were single, mention it and see if your friend appreciates it. If not, giving other suggestions is not likely to be productive. If the person is receptive, try offering concrete suggestions like where your friends met their spouses, where to get a new hairstyle, or where to find bargains on more appropriate clothes.

Ask singles if they would like to be introduced to other singles before assuming that they would. Don't give them a hard time if they aren't interested. Ask those who would like your help what kind of person they would like to meet instead of deciding for them. If they tell you that certain traits or shortcomings are absolutely unaccept-able, don't insult them by introducing them to dates with those characteristics.

For example, if a woman says that she does not want to date men who are fat, don't set her up with a man who is twenty-five pounds overweight and tell her that if she really likes him they'll work it out. It is difficult enough being single—don't humiliate singles by implying that they should be grateful if anyone of the opposite sex is interested in them.

Don't assume that singles over thirty will jump at the opportunity to go out with anyone who is alive. If you wouldn't marry someone who is physically unappeal-ing, has serious emotional problems, or lacks basic social skills, why should others with similar standards do it?

It is extremely painful when well-meaning friends or acquaintances play the catch-22 dating game with singles. It goes something like this: Mary is thirty-two and single, and would like her friend Roz to be supportive. Roz is the same age, but has been married for six years and has two children. Roz asks Mary what kind of man she's looking for, and Mary replies, "He should be my height or taller, be attractive, caring, a college graduate who makes a good living, and be under forty."

Roz can appropriately respond, "It sounds like you're looking for something reasonable, and I looked for the same things when I was single. I was just a bit luckier than you. If I hear about anyone like that, I'll let you know. In the meantime, would you like to join us for a barbecue this Sunday?"

The catch-22 game begins when Roz asks Mary what she's looking for, yet Roz rarely introduces singles to each other. She is just trying to make conversation, or ease her own helplessness and anxiety about Mary's desperation and emotional pain. Rather than admit her discomfort and empathize with Mary's plight, Roz implies that something is wrong with Mary.

Roz says, "You know, Mary, at your age you shouldn't be so choosy. What if the guy is terrific, but forty-four?"

If Mary says that that's a bit too old for her, Roz replies, "No wonder you're not married. You're not flexible enough."

If Mary allows that she might consider it, Roz persists, "And what if he's also bald and on the stout side but has a great personality?"

If at any stage Mary turns down the hypothetical offer, Roz will criticize Mary for being too picky. If Mary agrees that she will consider dating a man with additional liabilities, Roz eventually tells her, "No wonder you're not married. You're not looking for the right kind of man."

If you do this, please stop.

Some married people judge or interrogate their single friends, and the singles allow it because they want the interrogator to introduce them to appropriate people. Hope springs eternal, but the typical outcome of these interactions is that the singles end up humiliated.

Another version of this game is to tell singles, "You should have told me what you were looking for two months ago. I just introduced Jane to a great guy who's exactly what you're looking for. She's been dating him ever since."

Other versions of the "If only" game are: "If only you were (check one) ten years younger, never married, without children, less educated, more educated, less religious, more religious, taller, shorter, blonde (and so on, ad nauseum) . . . I could have introduced you to the perfect mate."

Dangling "prizes" in front of singles, especially when you have no intentions or ability to help them, is devastating. Be sensitive enough not to discourage singles from trying to get married, and don't dampen their spirits. Their lives are difficult enough as it is.

Don't belittle singles and make them feel like damaged goods by throwing two people together simply because they have the same handicaps or superficial traits in common. It is very painful to be set up with a date only because both parties are short, tall, physically handicapped, unattractive, overweight, responsible for children, and so forth. Don't add to singles' anguish by reinforcing their feelings of undesirability or desperation.

A little support can go a long way. One who has an obvious disability probably needs even more encouragement than others do. Bear in mind that every pot has its cover.

Before I wrote this chapter, I took a bus tour with a group of senior citizens. One couple looked like newlyweds who were obviously enthralled with one another. She was a fifty-five-year-old grandmother who had been widowed for fifteen years. He was a seventy-year-old grandfather who had lost his wife a few years before. They met when she went apartment hunting in his neighborhood, and they got engaged a few weeks later.

A man with ten young children was widowed, yet he married a woman who had never been married before and lived thousands of miles away. A young widow with eight small children had a similar predicament, yet she married a man in his early thirties who had never been married. Many severely handicapped or medically ill people are happily married to able-bodied spouses. Just because someone has what you consider to be a liability (age, looks, medical problems, financial difficulties, many children), don't assume that everyone else will feel the same way about him or her.

It is hard enough for singles to keep their spirits up. If you can't find it in your heart to encourage their optimism, at least don't add to their sense of defeat.

NOTES

1. *Yevamot* 62b.

2. North American Jewish Data Bank, quoted in *The Jewish Women's Journal,* February, 1993, p. 6.

3. *Sotah* 2a. This destiny is not absolute, and may be changed by one's deeds, among other things.
4. Yerushalmi, *Kiddushin* 3:12, 40a.
5. *Genesis Rabbah* 68:4.
6. Eliyahu Dessler, *Strive for Truth* (Jerusalem: Feldheim, 1988), p. 130.
7. *Strive for Truth,* p. 133.
8. Genesis 24:63–67.
9. *Yevamot* 79a.
10. Leviticus 19:18.
11. Based on *Shabbat* 127a.
12. Formulated by the Shelah, and found in *Sefer Chasanim.* This is a free translation.
13. *Eruvin* 65b.

FOR FURTHER READING

Aiken, Lisa. *Beyond Bashert: A Jewish Guide to a Better Marriage.* Northvale, NJ: Jason Aronson, 1996.
   A detailed guide to finding and being the right marriage partner.
Cowan, Connell, and Kinder, Melvyn. *Smart Women, Foolish Choices: Finding the Right Men and Avoiding the Wrong Ones.* New York: Crown, 1985.
Hendrix, Harville. *Getting the Love You Want.* New York: Harper & Row, 1990.
Rich, Hilary. *Get Married Now: The Definitive Guide to Finding and Marrying the Best Mate for You.* Boston: Bob Adams, 1993.

RESOURCES

Chupa Helper (for the Jewish population at large), and Frumfile (for observant Jews), c/o Bert Miller, P.O. Box 32426, Baltimore, MD 21208
   Has a "dater base" consisting of religious Jews' resumes, their likes and dislikes. Interested singles can peruse profiles of hundreds of registrants. Client names are confidential. Six months' membership is $12.
Brenda Goldbrenner, (914) 426-0692, 8–10 P.M., Mondays through Thursdays
   Runs free matchmaking service for nonreligious Jews.
The Jewish Press—advertisements of singles events and personals column.
Ketuba, (212) 563-4000 ext. 153 or 154
   The matchmaking service of the Orthodox Union, serving observant and traditional Conservative Jews.
Local Singles Jewish Week newspapers—advertisements of singles events and personals columns.
Mosaic Outdoor Mountain Club, (215) 568-1043 or (212) 696-8666
   Jewish hiking group, primarily for singles. Has independent affiliates in Denver, Baltimore, and Boston.
National Singles Torah Network, (404) 321-4085
   Organizes singles' weekends with a maximum of 100 participants.
Perspectives; R.S.V.P., (416) 636-7530
   Aish HaTorah-sponsored singles evenings in the Toronto area.

Table Talk, (212) 643-8800
  Aish HaTorah-sponsored singles evenings, centered around discussion groups in the New York area.
Twenty-Something; The Life-Love Encounter, (310) 278-8672
  Singles evenings in Los Angeles, sponsored by Aish HaTorah. Small groups of singles discuss issues designed to provoke controversy and encourage meeting.
20 Something, 30 Something, and 40 Something
  Aish HaTorah-sponsored singles programs for people in these respective age groups in St. Louis, Missouri. Contact the local Aish HaTorah office for information.

Singles with Children

Young Orthodox Single Parents, 2169 85 Street, Brooklyn, NY, (718) 313-2984
Orthodox Single Parent Center
Parents without Partners—check your local Jewish community center to see if they have a chapter
Jewish Unmarried Mothers Service, (212) 876-3050
Jewish Big Brothers-Big Sisters, (212) 582-9100
Services to the Widowed, (212) 582-9100

5

Coping with Infertility

Τ he Holy One, blessed is He, has three keys in His hand that are not given to a messenger. . . . [One is] the key to childbirth, as it is written, 'And God remembered Rachel, and listened to her, and opened her womb.' "[1]

"Let the eunuch not say, 'Behold, I am a dry tree.' For thus says the Lord, 'To the eunuchs who observe My Sabbaths, and who choose to please Me, and who hold fast to My covenant—I will give them, in My house and in My walls, a place and a name that is better than sons and daughters; I will give him an everlasting name that will not be cut off.' "[2]

Most people want to create a sense of immortality by having children who share their genes and live by their values. Most women yearn for the chance to carry a child, give birth, and nurse a baby. Most people take for granted that they will have children when they want it to happen and don't think that they might be among the one in six couples who are infertile.

Couples are considered infertile if they can't have a pregnancy that leads to a live birth after a year of ongoing marital relations.[3] Although women were automatically the suspect partner for ages, it is now known that they are responsible for infertility only about half of the time. Husbands' problems are responsible another 40 percent of the time, and 10 percent of the time there is unexplained infertility, or both partners are infertile.

Infertility is practically an epidemic today, but it has existed since ancient times. For example, our forefather Abraham and his wife Sarah were childless for decades. When he was seventy-five years old, God promised to give him a tremendous reward, to which Abraham poignantly responded, "Lord, God, what will You give me, since I am childless? . . . You have not given me seed."[4]

God told him to stand outdoors and "count the stars, and see if you can do it. So shall your descendants be."[5]

Neither Abraham nor Sarah could initially have children, but they changed their destinies by trusting God to override the laws of nature.[6] Their faith was against all logic, because it was not until Abraham was one hundred years old and Sarah was ninety that she gave birth to their son Isaac.

Rebecca, Isaac's wife, was unable to conceive for twenty years. After he prayed for her, she became pregnant with their twin sons, Jacob and Esau.[7]

The last two Matriarchs were sisters. Rachel was Jacob's favorite wife, and "when the Lord saw that Leah was hated, He opened her womb, but Rachel was [still] barren."[8]

Infertility affected even the most pious people in biblical times, as it does today, yet some individuals consider it a sign that God has rejected or abandoned them. They feel like failures and find it hard to come to terms with shattered dreams of having biological children. Most have intense feelings about their predicament, going from helplessness and devastation one day to anger or sadness the next. They can't imagine filling their emptiness as they yearn for a child that, for some, will never be. Rachel expressed this pain vividly when she pleaded with her husband, "Give me children, for if not, I am dead."[9]

Some childless people think that they caused their infertility by their lack of piety. Others believe that God is punishing them for their moral failures or sins, and that they are unworthy of having a child. They may feel jealous of couples who are blessed with offspring, then feel guilty when those couples are friends or relatives whom they love. Even the barren Rachel felt jealous when her sister Leah had four sons. She assumed that Leah had children because Leah was more righteous.[10]

The crushing pain of infertility has typically been compounded by outsiders' insensitive comments and questions. For example, after years of childlessness with Sarah, Abraham took a concubine named Hagar. Hagar became pregnant immediately, then taunted Sarah, "You pretend to be righteous in public, but you aren't that way in private. You haven't had children throughout the years that you have been married to Abraham, yet I conceived from my first union with him."[11] People also insulted Abraham when Sarah finally became pregnant, by insisting that Isaac must have been fathered by someone else.[12]

Things are much the same today. Infertile couples are asked why they haven't started a family, and if they plan to do so; why they are putting their careers ahead of having a family; why they have only one, two, or three children; or—at every baby naming and *bris* (ritual circumcision)—when they will have a *simchah* (celebration) of their own. Nosy intruders cannot imagine how hard it is for infertile couples to even attend celebrations that reinforce their heartbreak and humiliation at being left out.

Rookie thought that it would be nice to attend a woman's community function, so she went to a membership luncheon of a local Bikur Cholim. She was the only woman at her table who was childless, and the other nine ladies happily chatted about their children and grandchildren throughout the meal. Several women whom she hardly knew were even so callous as to show her pictures of their children and grandchildren without considering that she might not want to see them. The same thing happened when she went to a sisterhood meeting, the annual synagogue dinner, and a lecture-brunch. On several occasions, she pointed out to those near her how painful it was to be excluded from the conversation, and they felt bad for her. Unfortunately, they did not know what else to talk about. Rookie decided to find friends who had careers or who were single.

Yaakov became a religious Jew in his early thirties, a year before he married Bracha. Unfortunately, he had had a vasectomy during college because he believed that the world was too overcrowded. He regretted his decision after he became religious, but there was little he could do about it. Six months after he got married, friends and relatives gave broad hints at every family gathering and synagogue celebration that Yaakov and Bracha should soon start their own family. Others spent hours chatting insensitively about their children, unaware of the singles and childless couples who were completely left out of their conversations.

Three years later, Yaakov and Bracha avoided all communal and family celebrations because someone inevitably made insensitive remarks to them. For ten years, they periodically stopped going to the synagogue because people were bound to make humiliating comments or tell them about the latest birth or *bris*.

Meanwhile, Yaakov underwent seven operations to try to restore his fertility, but each failed. They also spent years trying to adopt a healthy, white baby from agencies, but that also failed. They couldn't afford a private adoption, so they sadly reconciled themselves to a life without children.

THE POWER OF PRAYER

Judaism does not teach that infertility is a form of divine punishment.[13] Rather, our tradition teaches that God made our ancestors infertile so that they would pray with greater fervor and develop their spiritual potentials.[14]

Today, as in ancient times, infertility can motivate people to pray intently with the realization that each child is a divine gift. It can challenge people to be angry with, and distant from, God, or to draw close to Him by feeling their utter dependence on Him. Infertility can also motivate people to observe Judaism with greater devotion and refine their character traits in attempts to be the best possible spiritual mentors for a child.

The Bible relates many poignant, relevant stories about infertile people. One involved a pious, childless woman named Hannah who was married for many years to a man named Elkanah.[15] Despite his being a prophet, his prayers for her to have children went unanswered. With her permission, he took a second wife named Peninah so that he could father children. Imagine Hannah's anguish as she watched Peninah give birth to ten children and raise them in Hannah's house![16]

Elkanah, his wives, and children made annual pilgrimages to the Jewish Sanctuary. As many modern couples do at holiday time, Hannah found this devastating because she had no children with whom to celebrate.[17] Her husband tried to comfort her by telling and showing her how much he loved her, but she stayed inconsolable. She couldn't endure the constant reminders of her childlessness and lack of fulfillment.

Finally, Hannah went into the Sanctuary and stormed the gates of Heaven with her prayers.[18] She wept bitterly as she confronted the Almighty: "Master of the world, You made all of the heavenly constellations. Is it too hard for You to grant me just one son?"[19]

She was like a poor person who came to the king's doorway when he made a feast for his servants. Since she was ignored when she asked for a morsel of bread, she forced her way in front of the king and said, "My Lord, the king, is it so hard to give me but one bite from this huge banquet that you've made?"[20]

Hannah continued, beseeching, "Lord, You created two kinds of beings in Your world. Heavenly beings do not reproduce, nor do they die, but earthly beings do. If I am an earthly being, let me multiply, and if I am a heavenly being, let me be immortal!"[21]

She continued, "Master of the world, no part of a woman is superfluous. You gave her eyes with which to see, ears with which to hear, a nose with which to smell, a mouth with which to speak, hands with which to work, feet with which to walk, and breasts with which to suckle a child. These breasts that You put over my heart, are they not here so that I may nurse with them? Give me a child, and I will nurse!"[22]

She concluded her supplication with a vow: "Lord of Hosts, if You notice Your servant's pain, and remember Your servant by giving me a child, I will give him to the Lord all the days of his life."[23]

Hannah's prayers were answered the following year when she gave birth to the prophet Samuel. She subsequently had four more children as well.

Her touching story reminds us that the ultimate purpose of having a child is to enable us to fulfill our godly purpose here. She channeled her maternal yearnings into service to her Creator, and so should we.

Infertility can be a catalyst for strengthening our faith in God and growing closer to Him through prayer. Otherwise, we end up putting our trust in doctors, medications, technology, and the like. That denies God's role in giving us this challenge and in helping us overcome it.

Susan and Mark believed very strongly that God, not fate or nature, controls our destiny. They married in their late twenties and expected to have a baby the following year. Much to their shock, however, Susan had still not conceived four years later. Both she and Mark underwent many fertility tests, all of which were normal. Finally, Susan's doctor suggested that she have exploratory surgery to see if her Fallopian tubes were blocked. He also warned her that the procedure might cause scarring that could prevent her from ever conceiving.

Susan discussed this with Mark. She decided to have surgery if she did not conceive after praying for a child at the Western Wall in Jerusalem. They didn't have much money, but they agreed to spend $2,000 on a five-day trip to Israel. His only concern was that Susan not regret doing this if their prayers were not answered. She assured him that she would have no regrets, so they flew to Israel as planned.

A month after they returned, Susan went to her gynecologist. He couldn't contain either his amazement or his delight when he discovered that she was pregnant.

"What do you attribute this to?" he asked. "Did you change your diet or try some kind of relaxation exercises?"

Susan initially felt too embarrassed to tell her Catholic doctor what she had done, but she also wanted him to know that God had answered her prayers. She replied, "There is one place in the world that is holier to Jews than all others. That place is the site of the Temple in Jerusalem. Jews have prayed there for thousands of years, and prayers there go directly to God. My husband and I went to pray at the Western Wall last month and we begged God to give us a child. That night, on the Sabbath, I conceived."

The doctor told her, "Thank you for sharing your story with me. I am also religious, and my patients often think that I have the ability to give them a child. They don't realize that I'm only God's agent. He gives me the tools to help, but it's entirely up to Him whether or not a couple is blessed with a child.

"The next time a patient tells me that she wants me to help her conceive, I will tell her your story, and suggest that she pray for God to help both of us."

Infertile people sometimes give up their relationship with God because they think that He doesn't hear their prayers. Stuart was such a man. He and his wife had spent three years trying, unsuccessfully, to have a child. They had been subjected to every imaginable fertility test. He had had surgery, they had both taken medications, and they had even tried in vitro fertilization. Still, Jill wasn't pregnant.

When his friends discussed where they were going to pray for the High Holidays, he announced that he was staying home. "God doesn't do what I want, so I'm not doing what He wants."

Two years later, after his son was born, Stuart reconsidered his position. He had worked through his feelings to a point where he believed that God always hears sincere prayers, but sometimes His answer is, "No," or "Not yet."

Prayer has helped many infertile couples conceive, as Asher related in the following story:

"I had the mumps when I was fifteen, but my parents didn't tell me that until my wife and I had been childless for five years. I went to two of the top male fertility specialists, and they both told me that it was completely impossible for me to father children. When I went to a third specialist, he told me that my chances of getting my wife pregnant were one in a million.

"When the first doctors gave me no hope, I figured that there was nothing that I could do. When the last doctor told me I had one chance in a million, I figured that at least I had something to work with.

"I prayed a lot for myself and my wife, and I asked everyone I knew to pray for us. I got a blessing from a special rabbi in Israel, too. Three weeks later, my wife was pregnant. As you can see, we are now blessed with four children."

An especially good time for women to pray for children is when they light the Sabbath candles eighteen minutes before sundown on Friday evenings. The following is excerpted from a prayer that includes Hannah's plea for a child:

> You are our God and the God of our forefathers. Compassionate One, please remember me, your servant [the woman says her Hebrew name] with Your holy Name of Hosts. Lord of all creation, grant my request when I turn to You, just as You granted the prayer of our mother Hannah, peace be upon her. She was barren and prayed to You, and You heard her prayer. You gave her the righteous prophet Samuel, who lived up to his worthy mission here.
>
> Please hear my prayer with mercy and compassion, and always grace me with Your free gifts. May the merit of my keeping the three holy, beloved commandments that You gave women — the commandments concerning family holiness, to separate a piece of dough for the priests when we bake bread, and the lighting of the Sabbath candles — defend me in front of Your holy throne. May I be worthy to raise good and observant children who will be Torah scholars, whose hearts will be open to understanding the mysteries of Your Torah and who will learn it for Your sake.
>
> May I have children who are entirely healthy, and who have no bodily defects. May they not be too tall nor too short, not too white nor too black, not overly smart nor big fools. But they should be appropriately wise, and find grace and mercy in Your eyes and in the eyes of people.
>
> May my husband and I merit to raise them in dignity for many years, and let none of our children die during our lifetimes. . . . May we give charity and do good deeds for others, and be worthy of seeing grandchildren who are committed to learning Torah and to doing good deeds.
>
> May the words of Isaiah the prophet be fulfilled, that words of Torah will always be present in our mouths, and in our children's mouths. Amen, so may it be.[24]

Some recommend saying the following prayer for forty consecutive days if a couple wants to conceive:

> May it be Your will, my God, and God of my forefathers, Rock of the worlds . . . Bless me with a child who is pleasing, proper, good and beautiful, acceptable and worthy of life. Give me a righteous child and bless me and my house, and let me know that my tent is full of peace. Give my child a body, spirit, and soul that are hewn from a pure mold. Let him be complete and healthy, full of pleasantness, grace, loving-kindness, and mercy, courageous, vigorous, and full of fortitude.

Have mercy on him when you form his body, spirit, and soul. May none of his limbs be damaged or missing, and let him be without disease or sickness. May he never lack every good thing all of the days of his life.

May he be born with a good constitution and at an auspicious time. May he live a good, long, and peaceful life, be blessed spiritually and materially, with wealth, riches, and honor in the midst of Your nation Israel.

Bless me, my children, and my grandchildren with everything that will allow us to know, comprehend, and fathom Your will.

Bless me with the heavenly blessings from above and with the blessings of the deep below, with blessings of the breasts and the womb.

Please, Lord of Hosts, God of Israel, hear my supplications. Consider me from Your holy dwelling place in a good way, and grant me a child, imbued with a holy soul, who will immerse himself in Torah and in observing Your commandments.

Bless me from Your bounty, and may the house of Your servant be blessed together with the entire Jewish people forever. Hear my prayer, Lord, and let me fulfill Your intention in creating human beings because You wanted Your world to be inhabited.

Give me a child who is holy and pure, with a new soul that is holy and pure, drawn from the celestial chamber, and attached to souls in the holiest heights.

You, holy souls that were in this world, entreat God for me. Let Him fulfill my request in your merits, and in the merit of my yearning to bring a child into this world who desires to do God's will, who immerses himself in Torah, and who is fit for prophecy. Hear my voice, Lord God, and accept my prayer with mercy and compassion.

Please don't refuse me empty handed, but fulfill my request for good. If You do this, I will raise him, and his children, to be God-fearing all of their days, as they live among the Jewish people. Amen.[25]

Some people add the following Psalm:

A song of ascents. Happy is the person who fears God, who walks in His ways. You will eat the [fruits of] your labor, you will be happy, and things shall go well for you. Your wife will be like a fruitful vine by the sides of your house, your children like olive plants around your table. This is how a person who fears the Lord is blessed. May the Lord bless you from Zion, and may you see the goodness of Jerusalem all of the days of your life. You will see your children's children, with peace upon Israel.[26]

People who pray for themselves should also pray for others. We learn this from a biblical incident where Avimelech, the king of Gerar, abducted Sarah. God told the king to return her to her husband and punished Avimelech by making his wives infertile.[27]

After Avimelech released Sarah and apologized for the incident, Abraham prayed that the royal wives be healed. Soon afterward, Sarah conceived.[28] This illustrates that when we pray for someone else to get what we ourselves need, our prayers for our needs are answered first.[29]

FINDING MEANING IN INFERTILITY

"He who teaches his neighbor's child Torah is as if he had begotten him himself."[30]

Infertility reminds us that children are a miracle, given to us to fulfill more than just emotional or physical hopes and dreams. The Talmud says that there are three partners in the creation of a child—the father, the mother, and God.[31] Each parent contributes certain physical attributes to the fetus, while the Almighty contributes the soul. This reminds parents of their enormous responsibility as God's partners in the creation of life. Every child is a link in a vast spiritual chain to which God contributes part of Himself. People are entrusted with the task of preserving children's spiritual purity and raising them in ways that will help them accomplish their spiritual missions here.

Infertility makes people think about why they want children. Instead of wanting them only for emotional reasons, people should want children so that they can further God's spiritual plans for the world.

Many couples feel worthless if they don't have biological children. They need to realize that they have spiritual contributions to make to the world whether or not they have children who share their genes. Our self-esteem should depend upon how well we serve God with the challenges that He gives us, not on what we produce biologically. Sometimes our greatest service to the Almighty is accepting that what He wants for us is not what we want for ourselves.

While we never know God's precise reasons for challenging specific individuals with infertility, their ordeals often help them see God in the most intimate part of their lives:

A nonobservant Jewish couple used birth control until they were "ready" to have a child. After unsuccessfully trying to conceive for a year, Harold was found to be infertile. A year after he had surgery and took medication, Ellen was still not pregnant. She took fertility drugs to help her ovulate, but she still didn't conceive. Next, they tried in vitro fertilization (for a "test tube baby") four times without success. After giving up hope of having a biological child, they decided to adopt one.

After hiring an adoption lawyer and placing ads in newspapers across the country, Ellen got pregnant without any medical intervention. She had a healthy baby boy.

During their three-year ordeal, Harold and Ellen went through many metamorphoses. They were both scientists who initially viewed pregnancy as a biological accident. Their ordeal taught them that pregnancy is a miracle.

Until Ellen got pregnant, neither Harold nor she thought that God involved Himself in people's lives. Infertility, followed by having a baby, taught them how much God interacts with His children. When their son was born, they raised him with a consciousness of God's Presence and a sense of gratitude that they didn't have before.

Their tribulations also affected people beyond themselves. Harold's mother Sylvia had been a devout agnostic her entire life. As she watched what her son and daughter-in-law went through in their quest to have a child, she understood that only God could overcome the laws of nature and make pregnancy possible for them. When David was born, Sylvia knew that she had witnessed a true miracle. For the first time in her life, she believed that God involves Himself in our lives and cares about what happens to us.

Another outgrowth of infertility is that it encourages couples to develop patience, give each other support, and grow closer to one another. Because infertility is so traumatic, couples' intense emotions can either break them apart or help cement their bonds with love, support, and appreciation for one another. Growing closer during their trying and often heartrending times can give them the strength to weather other tragedies and crises together. They can also develop the sensitivity to empathize with and support others.

While few people would ever choose to be infertile, those who finally have children (biological or adopted) are different parents and spouses than they would have been without their ordeals.

Infertility often motivates couples to be more observant, and it has prompted many nonobservant Jews to learn about traditional Judaism. For example, many Jewish couples never knew that Judaism has laws that sanctify marital relations. These laws require couples to abstain from sex from the time a wife gets her period until a week after it stops. After this twelve- to fourteen-day separation, she cleanses herself physically, then sanctifies herself spiritually by immersing in a ritual bath (known as a *mikvah*). That evening, she and her husband may resume having marital relations.

Some nonobservant, childless couples are so desperate to have a baby that they turn to God for help. They hear stories about previously childless women conceiving after going to the *mikvah* and also decide to try it. In the process, they discover the beauty and depth of traditional Judaism and learn how to make marriage, and the rest of life, holy. Some moderately observant couples also become more scrupulous in their performance of commandments in the hope that this will remove spiritual impediments to their having a child.

Miriam was a secular Jew in her late thirties when she married, but she became observant soon afterward. Her doctor told her that due to a medical condition, she had less than a 10 percent chance of ever having a child. She conceived after going to the *mikvah* for the first time, and gave birth to healthy twins. The next time that she went to the *mikvah* she conceived again! Her husband was initially skeptical about her spiritual journey in Judaism, but he ultimately joined her.

Zelda was so assimilated that her sister had to drag her to the temple once a year, on Yom Kippur. Although she happened to have married a Jewish man, she never prayed. She believed that the Torah was written by men and that Jewish rituals were anachronistic. When she turned forty, after being childless for more than ten years, a more desperate woman could not be found.

Meanwhile, a few of her relatives had become *baalei teshuvah* (returnees to observant Judaism). She approached one of them and shared her plight. "Does Judaism have any suggestions for me?" she pleaded.

Her cousin suggested that she go to the *mikvah* and referred her to a woman who taught her how to do this properly. Zelda went to the *mikvah* for the first time at the age of forty-one. That night, she conceived.

Thirteen months later, Zelda went again, and conceived again. She is now the proud mother of two daughters.

While praying and strengthening one's ritual observances helps many couples conceive, it obviously doesn't alleviate infertility for everyone. We should not believe in God only if He does miracles when we want them. Instead, we should feel that it is wonderful in and of itself to come close to God, talk to Him, and benefit our souls by serving Him better. People shouldn't regret their spiritual growth and intimacy with their Creator when they don't get what they want in the short run.

CAUSES AND TREATMENTS OF INFERTILITY

The fact that some infertile couples conceive after growing closer to the Almighty does not imply that infertility is caused only by moral failings and spiritual shortcomings. A twenty-three-year-old woman expressed a common misconception (no pun intended) by saying, "My husband and I became religious shortly before our marriage four months ago. I have gone to the *mikvah* every month since our wedding, but I'm still not pregnant. Am I doing something wrong? All of my friends who go to the *mikvah* got pregnant within the first month they were married."

Although it sometimes happens, her friends' experiences were exceptional. Eighty percent of women who don't use birth control become pregnant within a year, but only a small number get pregnant on their wedding night. Since her gynecologist had no reason to believe that she would have difficulty conceiving, there was no reason to think that she was either infertile or morally deficient.

Infertility affects both righteous and immoral people, but not necessarily for the same reasons. For example, millions of women who enjoyed sexual "freedom" contracted sexually transmitted diseases and pelvic inflammations that caused infertility. On the other hand, many people did nothing to "cause" their infertility. When mothers took DES (diethylstilbestrol) in the 1950s to aid their pregnancies, many of the resulting children subsequently had fertility problems. Some infertile men and women were unknowingly exposed to hazardous chemicals and radiation. Men who are treated for some forms of cancer or who have varicoceles are subfertile, as are 25 percent of men who had the mumps as adults.

Infertile couples should be evaluated and treated by fertility specialists in ways that follow Jewish law. While advances in technology now help approximately 80 percent of infertile couples to have children, doctors and medicine can do only what God allows. He "holds the keys" to the miracle of childbirth,[32] and doctors are only His agents. Infertile couples should strengthen their spirituality and connection to God *in addition to* using medical expertise to diagnose and treat their problem.

Couples may benefit from improving their diets, refraining from recreational drugs or alcohol, and avoiding situations that expose them to chemicals or radiation. Men who sit for prolonged periods, take hot baths, or wear very tight clothing may be advised to change their habits. Reducing stress may be helpful, but that is often easier said than done.

Generally, both the husband and wife need a thorough examination by competent fertility specialists. General gynecologists and urologists may perform preliminary evaluations, but some sophisticated tests are best done by specialists who perform them frequently and with state-of-the-art laboratories. While most preliminary fertility tests are not physically uncomfortable, they can be humiliating and stressful.

Preliminary tests for men usually include semen analyses, blood tests, and physical examinations. Women usually have a gynecological exam, blood tests, and a postcoital test, and they are asked to chart their basal body temperatures and use ovulation kits for several months. Sperm antibody tests are often done on both partners as well. Further testing might include an endometrial biopsy and hysterosalpingogram (X ray of a woman's reproductive tract after dye is injected), which most women find uncomfortable but only mildly painful. Laparoscopy or hysteroscopy may be recommended for a smaller number of women.

Fertility tests and treatments should be done in ways that conform to Jewish law and interfere as little as possible with one's marriage. A qualified rabbi can recommend how to do both.

Diagnostic procedures and treatments usually intrude into and regulate a couple's sex life more than is already required by Jewish law. This enforced abstinence adds even more stress to already trying circumstances.

There are many ways to treat infertility and, thank God, treatment efficacy keeps improving. Some couples need only make simple changes, such as improving the timing of their marital relations, while others will need medication, assisted insemination, and/or surgery. The various procedures are discussed in current books about infertility.

The nature of infertility makes it highly stressful. Tests and treatments intrude into the most intimate parts of the couple's bodies and lives. They repeatedly violate their sense of modesty, privacy, and closeness. Instead of creating a baby through a union of love, it may be a calculated, manipulated, and regulated procedure that is engineered by strangers in a cold, clinical setting. The husband is not even present when his wife becomes pregnant through assisted fertilization—a doctor or laboratory technician is!

Infertility treatments cause constant stress, starting with decisions that couples must make every few days or weeks. They must first choose a doctor or treatment center. Then, they must decide if they want to switch when the doctor is too inflexible, inept, expensive, insensitive, or arrogant. Most couples hope to find the "best" doctor in their quest to have a baby, yet many doctors in their locale may be equally qualified (or unqualified) to treat them.

In 1992, there were 235 in vitro fertilization (IVF) clinics in the United States, plus thousands of doctors and laboratories performing other fertility-related procedures. Some report higher success rates than others, although these numbers may be inflated due to unethical reporting or accepting only patients with good prognoses. Some places with the best results may have waiting lists as long as a year and a half. Each couple must decide which procedures to try, considering the pain, expense, time, disruption, risks, and benefits involved. A woman in her twenties may want conservative and noninvasive procedures, while a forty-year-old woman may be more desperate and consequently want more aggressive techniques.

The emotional toll of infertility is enormous. Once couples choose a doctor and decide on a course of treatment, they have seemingly endless waits with each test or treatment. One writer quipped that the term "infinitime" should describe the time span between any fertility procedure and the time couples get the results. By contrast, "instantime" should refer to the time span between any medical procedure and the time the couple is expected to pay for it.[33]

Some fertility tests can be done only on a specific day of a woman's cycle. If that day falls on a holiday or weekend, when she is out of town, or when she cannot get to the doctor for any reason, she must wait another month to do the test. If the husband cannot produce needed specimens during specific hours, the couple may also need to wait indefinitely to complete the procedure or test.

Having to wait until the end of the day to get test results can seem like weeks. Waiting two weeks every month to know if the wife is pregnant can seem like years. And when the couple must wait three to six months to find out if a husband's surgery improved his fertility, or nine months to be taken off a waiting list and get into a treatment program, time can seem endless.

Infertility tests and treatments also have physical effects. Surgeries, daily drug injections, and frequent blood tests give some women black-and-blue arms, sore insides, and painful buttocks. It is easy for them to feel like human pincushions. It is also common for women on fertility drugs to have mood swings, hot flashes, fatigue, back and abdominal pain, and bloating. Many get temporary ovarian cysts, gain weight, and feel depressed. All in all, not a pretty picture.

Infertility also tends to be enormously expensive. Basic fertility evaluations, including doctors' visits and diagnostic procedures, can cost thousands of dollars. While intrauterine insemination with a husband's sperm may cost "only" $200–$500, a few days of fertility medications can cost $2,000, and a try at in vitro fertilization typically costs $8,000–$15,000. Couples who must travel out of town to a clinic can spend up to $20,000 for one chance at a pregnancy. Some couples spend $50,000–$80,000 trying to have a baby and still not get one (usually four failures at IVF are the maximum). Unfortunately, even the best of the expensive procedures has less than a 30 percent chance of success per trial, although nearly half of "good candidates" may end up pregnant after a few tries.

Some couples go into lifetime debt trying, and failing, to get pregnant as few insurance companies fully reimburse fertility expenses. Some policies specifically exclude fertility reimbursement.[34] When insurance does cover some expenses, filling out forms and resolving billing disputes can become a full-time job.

Many fertility treatments require people to completely rearrange their lives. Some women who get fertility drugs need frequent sonograms and/or blood tests, and the husbands must inject them with hormones at roughly the same time every night. If the wife or husband needs to go out of town, she must hire a nurse or find someone else to give her injections. Many women who are undergoing fertility treatments find it impossible to keep working full time, go on business trips or vacation, or plan more than a few days ahead.

Susie was typical of many women who try to get pregnant. She was a teacher who had to be at school every morning at 7:30, but her doctor's office didn't open until 8:00. She had to get blood tests and sonograms several mornings a week, and asked her principal if he would rearrange her classes to accommodate her. He refused. She ended up waiting four months until summer vacation to start an IVF cycle. Had she not had a summer vacation, she would have had to give up her job. As things turned out, Susie didn't respond well to fertility drugs, and she was not even able to undergo an IVF cycle. She and her husband are now trying to adopt.

Paula was a secretary who was overwhelmed by the constant disruptions caused by fertility evaluations and treatments. She missed a lot of work because of her many doctor appointments and couldn't predict in advance when she would need to see him. She finally told her boss about her plight. He was sympathetic, but the office couldn't run when she came in late day after day. She finally quit her job and worked as a temporary secretary. That allowed her to make her own hours and have a flexible schedule. She earned less money and lost her health insurance, but her husband's job still provided some coverage. The trade-off of less money for less stress was worth it for Paula. It took a few months, but Paula got pregnant on IVF and delivered healthy twins.

Women may need to give up jobs that require travel or advance planning, and some men will have to occasionally miss work. One surgeon who had to be in the hospital at 5:30 every day had to call in sick every time his wife was inseminated because the fertility lab did not open until 8 A.M. A man who needed varicocele surgery took a week off from work for "hernia surgery." Another man took off a vacation day whenever his wife needed insemination.

A business executive was not so lucky. His company had a tendency to send him out of town when his wife's fertile time came. It happened more than once that he was in Los Angeles when she needed to be inseminated in New York. While some men can keep their jobs and have their sperm frozen for such occasions, Don's sperm count was not high enough to do this.

A female consultant was scheduled to chair an all-day business meeting for her company. Her doctor told her a few days before the meeting that her eggs were ripening more quickly than they expected, and that she must come in for egg retrieval the morning of the meeting. There was no one else to chair the meeting, and it was critical that she be there. She agonized about what to do while thinking that these kinds of stresses did not make getting pregnant easy.

Few fertile couples can imagine what infertile couples go through in their nightmarish journey with no end in sight. They build up their hopes, then are defeated every month. Worse, some feel ecstatic when the wife gets pregnant, only to be devastated a few weeks or months later when she loses the pregnancy in the first trimester. The emotional roller coaster only begins once a diagnosis is made and a couple attempts to do something about it.

Ed and Nancy got married in their twenties, expecting to have a child within a year or two. When that didn't happen, she went to her gynecologist. Nancy was fine, so the doctor recommended that Ed be evaluated. When he was found to have almost no sperm, they were shocked. It never occurred to them that this might happen. His urologist recommended surgery to correct his infertility, and the couple decided to seek a second opinion. The second urologist agreed with the first diagnosis and recommendation, but told Ed that the first doctor was a poor surgeon using antiquated techniques.

Nancy consulted her doctor, who told her that the first doctor had an excellent reputation. After agonizing about what to do, Ed scheduled surgery with the first doctor. The surgeon was booked for the next two months, so Nancy and Ed waited patiently.

After surgery, it took three months to know if the operation was successful. They waited with bated breath, only to find out that his fertility was unimproved. The doctor recommended that Ed get injections three times a week for a few months, then get a retest. Ed dutifully did this, then took a few more tests, with equally dismal results. Instead of admitting that he could do nothing more to help Ed, the doctor continued suggesting more tests and useless treatments. Ed had the good sense to realize that the doctor was unwilling to admit that he had nothing more to offer. Ed then consulted the second urologist.

That doctor recommended some experimental medication. After Ed took this for a few months, he was tested again. The doctor had forgotten to tell Ed that 10 percent of the men who took the drugs got worse. Ed was one of those 10 percent.

Ed and Nancy had now spent a year and a half, fervently praying every day for a miracle and agonizing over scores of decisions. They felt desperate, demoralized, exploited by doctors, and angry with God for making their lives so difficult.

They decided to try a vitamin regimen after getting on a six-month waiting list for IVF. When the fateful day arrived, Nancy was evaluated by the IVF program director. He gave her a gynecological exam as nine nurse trainees, doctors, staff nurses, and residents poked, prodded, and examined her private parts as if she were a lab specimen. Nancy had never felt so violated in her life.

The director told Nancy to get $800 worth of blood and invasive diagnostic tests before they could consider her for the IVF program. After dutifully complying, she was told to wait another two weeks for the program director to get back to her.

He never did. She tried calling him several times, but he never returned her phone calls.

After waiting another two weeks, Nancy pleaded with a nurse to tell her what was going on, and the nurse relayed the following message:

"I'm sorry, Nancy, but the doctor says that you should wait another six months until a new researcher joins our staff. That doctor specializes in treating men like your husband, and only he can tell you if IVF can help you. We can't accept you at the present time because your husband's infertility is too severe."

They waited another nine months while Ed tried acupuncture and meditation. After spending four years hoping to have a child, and paying $8,000 for surgery, tests, injections, and medications, Nancy and Ed were rejected for IVF. They gave up trying to have a biological child and started exploring adoption.

Some couples try indefinitely to have a child. They go through cycles of hope and devastation almost every month for five to ten years until they either have a baby or decide to stop trying. Sometimes the most important decision they make is to reconcile themselves to childlessness and/or prepare for adoption.

MISCARRIAGE AND STILLBIRTH

At least one in three pregnancies ends in a miscarriage.[35] Despite its frequency, few parents who lose unborn or young children get the support and empathy they need. Friends and relatives tend to get annoyed that they have such intense feelings about unborn or extremely young babies. Many people cannot appreciate how attached mothers are to a fetus, and the terrible loss they feel when it dies.

Doctors or hospital staff often compound the mothers' pain by minimizing their loss or by preventing women who want to see their stillborn infants from doing so. Not all mothers want to do this, but those who do should ask to be prepared for what they will see and be told why the baby died. The hospital staff should drape the baby with a blanket if necessary, and provide a private room where the mother (and father) can be alone.

Some fathers grieve over a miscarriage, but may not feel or express the pain as strongly as their wives do. Women may wonder why their husbands don't feel devastated about losing a baby, while their husbands wonder why their wives are so pained about losing "only" a fetus. Some men feel less upset than their wives because they mostly bond with children after they are born. While mothers often feel the loss of part of themselves when a fetus dies, fathers tend to feel this way only after loving a live child.

Women who miscarry often wonder what they did or did not do to cause it, and they sometimes carry strong feelings about their loss even years later. They commonly feel guilty and sad, angry and bitter. As one woman put it, "After going through all of the pain and trauma of morning sickness, fatigue, bleeding, and having my baby kick me until I felt bruised all over, God pulled a mean trick on me by making my baby die."

When a woman miscarries, doctors, friends, and relatives may try to convince her to forget about it and get on with her life. This invalidates her feelings about what may be the worst catastrophe of her life. Others, husbands included, may want her to forget about the "incident" and may discourage her from sharing her loss, anger, and regrets. This only reinforces her sense of isolation.

Parents who lose unborn children need to grieve their loss just as if they'd lost an older child. Their pain is just as real, and they have the same unfulfilled dreams as do other bereaved parents. They fantasize about what they wanted to give to a baby and wonder what their relationship would have been like.

As painful as it is to listen to parents pouring out their tears, regrets, sadness, and anger, this is how they heal their wounds. When husbands are sad, but think that they have to be "strong" instead of feeling their loss and tragedy, they feel cheated and resentful, while their wives think that their husbands don't share their grief. Both partners need a lot of support and love but may instead share anger and tension.

Bereaved parents need to avoid and ignore insensitive people who make inappropriate remarks about letting go of the past. Otherwise, they may end up mourning a miscarriage a lot longer than is necessary. Bereaved parents need to talk about their turmoil and pain until they work it through, and that takes different lengths of time for different people.

ADOPTION

"He who brings up a child is called 'father,' not the one who gives birth to the child."[36]

"Rachel said [to Jacob], 'Here is my maid Bilhah. Have relations with her and she will give birth to a child on my knees, and I will be built through her.' "[37]

Infertility can prompt couples to adopt children that God wants them to raise. For example, our foremother Sarah could not have children, so she asked Abraham to marry her servant Hagar so that Sarah could help raise their offspring.[38] Rachel did the same by giving her maidservant Bilhah to her husband Jacob. Rachel wanted to help raise Bilhah's children.[39]

God sometimes grants a couple a biological child once they extend themselves to adopt someone else's child. A couple's relief at knowing that they will be able to raise an adopted child can reduce their tension to a point where some conceive. However, couples should not assume that this will happen. The numbers of adoptive parents who spontaneously conceive are the same as for infertile couples who do not adopt (roughly 5 percent).

Adoption helps many couples transcend their pain and disappointment at not having biological children. There are several ways to adopt, depending upon how long a couple is willing to wait, how much money they are willing to spend, and where they live. Couples who can afford to pay $10,000–$20,000 for fees and expenses often adopt privately and typically get a healthy baby within a year. State laws govern how couples find adoptable babies. Lawyers in some states locate expectant mothers, while adoptive parents do so in others.

Some couples prefer to adopt through an agency. This generally costs less but takes longer than private adoption if a healthy, white baby is desired. (Some agencies currently have five- to seven-year waiting lists; some no longer have white babies for adoption.) Special-needs children are usually adopted through agencies, and waiting times tend to be shorter for them.

Marsha and Andy decided to adopt their first child after only two years of diagnosed infertility. By the time they were married for eight years, they had adopted three children and were glad that they had a family. The stresses and poor success rates of infertility treatments, given Marsha's condition, were not for them.

Unlike Marsha, Barbara wanted a biological child more than anything in the world. When she did not conceive after a year of marriage, she went through a battery of inconclusive fertility tests. She decided that she wanted to try using fertility drugs, and was delighted when she became pregnant a few months later. Her joy was short-lived, though, and she miscarried in her fourth month of pregnancy.

For the next nine years, Barbara took fertility drugs almost every other month, and she had fourteen pregnancies. None of them went beyond her sixth month, and most spontaneously ended within the first three. She finally decided that enough was enough, and she stopped trying to get pregnant. By the time she adopted, she was thrilled to have a healthy child, even though it didn't share her genes.

It is beyond the scope of this book to detail how to adopt. The interested reader should speak to adoptive parents and knowledgeable professionals who can inform them about local adoption lawyers, agencies, support groups, and the process of adoption.

RECOMMENDATIONS FOR INFERTILE COUPLES

Get a good fertility evaluation from a competent andrologist/urologist and reproductive endocrinologist. If you feel intimidated or patronized by your doctor, consider seeing a different specialist. Many doctors are too busy to give much emotional support, but they should be informative and respectful. If they aren't readily available to answer your questions, they should have nurses on staff who are. They should also be able to refer you to a psychotherapist who can give extra emotional support if you need it.

Be an educated consumer. The better informed you are, the easier it will be to find an appropriate doctor and make decisions about what to do. It will also help you know when your doctor is not treating you well.

If your fertility problems are not covered by your insurance, consider switching to or adding a policy that will cover you *before* you are diagnosed and treated. Otherwise, individual and group policies may exclude coverage for preexisting conditions. It can pay to postpone an evaluation or treatment until you have adequate insurance. If you expect to need IVF or fertility drugs, buying insurance that covers medication and treatment may quickly pay for itself.

Couples need to share their feelings and support each other, or the pressures of trying to have a baby can ruin their marriage. Don't displace your anger and frustrations about doctors and infertility onto one another. Be understanding of each other and let your ordeals enhance your love and commitment to each other.

Find supportive friends, relatives, and/or strangers, including those who are infertile themselves. People you meet through RESOLVE or fertility clinics are often the best informed about which doctors to see, what to expect from various procedures, problems to anticipate and how to get around them. They also tend to be most understanding and can direct you to support groups, therapists, or adoption lawyers.

Don't feel that you have to be stoic. Some people fall apart for a week after going to a baby naming or a family gathering where everyone else has children. If you feel like taking antidepressants after these events, don't feel obligated to go. Explain to family or friends that you would love to share their joy but would prefer to do it another time.

Be prepared for insensitive and stupid remarks and do your best to ignore them. People who say inappropriate things need to be diplomatically educated about how hurtful their words are and how to be more constructive. There's nothing wrong with responding to an insensitive comment, "I'm sure that you don't realize that it's not easy for every couple to have children. It hurts terribly when you ask, 'So when are you going to start a family?' The answer is, 'As soon as God wills it.' "

If you ask more than one doctor what treatments or diagnostic procedures they recommend, expect to get different answers. One doctor insists that the wife try one medication while a second says that it is contraindicated and she should use a different drug. One lab says that a husband's fertility is normal, while a second says that the first is unreliable and the man indeed has a poor count. Some doctors treat couples aggressively, while others take a much more conservative approach.

There may not be one "right" or "best" solution to a specific couple's infertility, and no doctor has "magic." You will be the ultimate judge of which medical procedures you want to try, and for how long. Some patients have a gut feeling that a procedure will or won't work for them. Don't be intimidated into acquiescing to procedures that you don't want, and try to find a doctor who will nondefensively discuss and consider your ideas and suggestions.

Don't assume that doctors will tell you everything that you need to know about infertility, or that they always know what's best for you. Your choices will depend upon what you can tolerate physically, psychologically, and financially. You will make the best choices by doing your own research and knowing the risks, benefits, emotional stresses, and financial costs of your options.

Doctors also tend to recommend tests or procedures that may violate Jewish law or unduly interfere with an observant couple's sex life. A knowledgeable rabbi can tell you what methods are halachically preferred and medically acceptable. Your fertility doctor should be sensitive to and accommodate your needs as an observant Jew.

If you have not had a child by a certain point, you may want to explore adoption and/or put off trying to have a biological child for a while.

Adoption lawyers and agencies may not tell you everything you need to know about a particular child. For example, some lawyers offer children whose mothers were drug users and alcoholics, or children who are handicapped, without telling this to adoptive parents. Learn what questions to ask a birth mother, agency, or attorney, and don't take anything for granted, even if an agency or lawyer is well regarded. Anyone can be less than thorough in getting and giving information.

If you plan to adopt, consult a competent rabbi about issues such as naming and converting a child.

Finally, don't let infertility overwhelm you to a point where nothing else seems meaningful. Having a loving marriage should not be less important when you are trying to have a baby. Make time to go out for a relaxed evening, movie, concert, or dinner where you and your spouse can think about something besides pregnancy. Make time to share enjoyable activities, and spend time with friends without discussing fertility or adoption.

BEING HELPFUL

The best way to help someone who is infertile is by first "doing no harm." If you are a parent of an infertile adult, don't be intrusive or expect that he or she will want to share feelings with you. Some children do, but many don't. Parents should ask their sons or daughters if they would like support, financial assistance, or advice, and accept that they may want to keep this part of their lives private. If it pains you that you don't have grandchildren, don't lay that guilt trip on your children. Find a therapist or supportive friend with whom to discuss your disappointment. You can't protect your children from the pain of infertility, and they need to make their own choices about what to do without unsolicited advice.

If an infertile person discusses his or her dilemma with you, listen supportively. It may be hard for you to appreciate their emotional, physical, and financial ordeals if you have no firsthand experience with these matters. You can always say, "I'm so sorry that you are going through this. My heart goes out to you, and I'll include you in my prayers."

Naomi tried to have a child for several years, and was chatting with Leah, who had six children. Leah asked how she was, and Naomi replied, "I've been better. I just had another miscarriage this *Shabbos.*"

Leah's eyes welled with tears, and she took Naomi's hand in hers. "I'm so sorry. I think about you all the time, and I wish that there was something that I could do to ease your pain."

Naomi was touched and comforted by Leah's reaction. No response could have been better than Leah's heartfelt empathy.

When a woman has a miscarriage or loses a baby, don't say, "You're lucky you're young, you can have more children," "It's a good thing you lost only a fetus—it was probably defective anyway," "What month was it in? At least you weren't further along," or "At least you have other children." Every loss for a mother is real and painful. A fetus was part of her at one time, and she felt that child growing inside her. The above comments are like telling someone whose legs were amputated that he should be happy that he still has his arms! Before responding, ask yourself if you would be comforted by your remarks.

Couples who lose a fetus or infant often feel better when they have another child. Still, they lost a baby that they wanted very much. It is inappropriate to tell people that at least they know that they can get pregnant, that they can have more children, that their child is with God, or that they are overreacting. It is normal for them to feel angry, sad, and guilty. If you can't understand why, you cannot possibly help them, and it would be better not to try. Above all, don't add insult to injury by talking about your or other people's pregnancies or children when someone is trying to deal with a loss.

Never ask childless couples if they plan to have children. Don't tell them that it is obvious that they put their careers first or must not like children very much. And don't offer unsolicited advice about how to get pregnant.

Tobi was aware that her friend Shelly was still not pregnant after a year of marriage. She didn't know if this bothered Shelly, and didn't want to pry, so she found an opportune time to say, "I don't know if you and Ricky are trying to get pregnant, but Shimon and I had a hard time and needed help. If you'd like me to share what I know about infertility and where to get help, feel free to ask."

Don't assume that you know why a couple is childless or how they feel about it. You can't tell what kind of fertility problems people have by looking at them. Infertility is painful enough. Don't add insult to injury by judging people and offering lay opinions.

If you have personal experience with infertility, let people who might be infertile know it. Most of them will be relieved to share their burden with you, and you might both benefit from sharing information and experiences.

Don't be offended if your supportive offers are rejected by people who don't want to discuss their private life with you. To each his own.

If you are blessed with children, be sensitive to the fact that some childless couples don't want to socialize around your offspring or discuss children. Don't judge them as being heartless, cold, aloof, or self-centered. It may be too painful for them to rejoice over your latest birth, ritual circumcision, baby naming, or family gathering. If you want them to attend an affair, explain that you would like to see them, but not if they will be uncomfortable. They might appreciate your suggesting an alternate time and place to meet.

Don't talk about your children or grandchildren, or show photographs of them, to people who don't have children, unless they ask. Be patient with infertile couples who seem to be consumed with visiting doctors, adoption lawyers, infertility seminars, and support groups. It takes many infertile couples five years or more to have or adopt a baby, and their medical or legal situations may make it impossible to plan more than a few days ahead. Be gracious if they can't make plans until the last minute or if they cancel on a moment's notice. The greatest kindness that you can do for many infertile couples is to be understanding and compassionate.

NOTES

1. *Taanit* 2a–b.
2. Isaiah 56:3–5. This is the verse from which the Holocaust Memorial in Israel, Yad Vashem, draws its name.
3. J. J. Stangel, *The New Fertility and Conception* (New York: New American Library, 1988), p. 4. When women age thirty or older have not conceived after six months of trying, some doctors recommend that they have a fertility evaluation. It is now known that women who have elevated estradiol or follicle-stimulating hormone (FSH) levels in their blood on day 2 or day 3 of their cycle are unlikely to have a successful pregnancy those months, even with fertility interventions. Infertile women over age 35 should have this checked so that they don't waste their time and money getting ineffective treatments and other unnecessary tests.
4. Genesis 15:2–3.
5. Genesis 15:5.
6. Rashi on Genesis 15:5.
7. Genesis 25:21.
8. Genesis 29:30–31.
9. Genesis 30:1.
10. Rashi on Genesis 30:1.
11. *Genesis Rabbah* 45.
12. Rashi on Genesis 21:7; *Bava Metzia* 87a; Rashi on Genesis 25:19.
13. A rare exception was King Saul's daughter Michal, who was punished with infertility for humiliating King David. See 2 Samuel 6:23.
14. "Rabbi Isaac stated, 'Why were our ancestors barren? Because the Holy One, blessed is He, longs to hear the prayers of the righteous" (*Yevamot* 64a).
15. 1 Samuel 1.
16. 1 Samuel 1:1–2.
17. 1 Samuel 1:7–8.
18. 1 Samuel 1:10.
19. *Brachot* 31b.
20. *Brachot* 31b.
21. *Aggadah* of Rabbi Jose the Galilean.
22. Brachot 31b.
23. 1 Samuel 1:11.
24. *Techinah.*
25. Kabbalistic prayer, condensed and loosely translated.
26. Psalm 128, loosely translated.
27. Genesis 20:2, 7, 18.
28. Genesis 20:17–21:2.
29. Rashi on Genesis 21:1.

30. *Sanhedrin* 9a.

31. *Kiddushin* 30b.

32. *Taanit* 2a.

33. Rich Hall, "Laugh a Little." Reprinted from RESOLVE of Dallas/Fort Worth in "Pathways," Fall 1994, a publication of Boghen Pharmacy.

34. Ellen Hopkins, "Tales from the Baby Factory," *New York Times Magazine,* March 15, 1992, p. 40.

35. Arlene Eisenberg, Heidi Murkoff, and Sandee Hathaway, *What to Expect When You're Expecting* (New York: Workman, 1991), p. 111.

36. *Shemot Rabbah* 46.

37. Genesis 30:3.

38. Genesis 16:2.

39. Targum on Genesis 30:3.

FOR FURTHER READING

DeCherney, Alan, and Pernoll, Martin, eds. *Gynecologic Diagnosis and Treatment.* East Norwalk, CT: Appleton and Lange, 1994.

Friedman, Rochelle, and Gradstein, Bonnie. *Surviving Pregnancy Loss.* Boston: Little, Brown, 1982.

Grazi, Richard. *Be Fruitful and Multiply: Fertility Therapy and the Jewish Tradition.* Jerusalem: Genesis Press, 1994.

An excellent, informative, and practical guide for infertile Jewish couples.

Gross, Mindy. *How Long the Night?* Southfield, MI: Targum Press, 1991.

An observant Jewish woman's account of her experiences with infertility.

Mason, M. M. *The Miracle Seekers: An Anthology of Infertility.* Indianapolis, IN: Perspectives Press, 1990.

A collection of short stories about infertility and its impact on couples.

Robin, Peggy. *How to Be a Successful Fertility Patient: Your Guide to Getting the Best Possible Medical Help to Have a Baby.* New York: Morrow, 1993.

Silber, Sherman. *How to Get Pregnant.* New York: Warner, 1990.

Adoption

Hallenbeck, C. *Our Child.* Indianapolis, IN: Perspectives Press, 1990.

A guide for expectant adoptive parents.

The Independent Adoption Manual. Lakewood, NJ: Advocate Press, 1993.

This is a 400-page how-to book. It is the most comprehensive, up-to-date book on independent adoption. It covers finding an attorney and a birth mother, the adoption process, medical issues, and prenatal exposure to alcohol and drugs. It includes extensive references, including names of newspapers that run adoption ads. To order, call (908) 363-7600.

RESOURCES

Adoptive Parents' Committee, Inc., 210 Fifth Avenue, New York, NY 10010.

One of the oldest parents' groups in existence.

Adoption Resource Exchange of North America, 67 Irving Place, New York, NY 10003
  Gives information about local programs and referral services.
Infertility Help Line, (800) 435-4220
  Twenty-four-hour-a-day phone line that gives information about common causes of male
  and female infertility, therapy options, adoption, and insurance reimbursement.
Jewish Children's Adoption Network, P.O. Box 16544, Denver, CO 80216-0544, (303)
  573-8113
  Maintains a computer registry of adoptable Jewish children and couples interested in
  adopting. Approximately 15-20 percent of these children are healthy newborns; the
  others have special needs, are older children or groups of siblings, and so forth. This
  network is an exchange that is contacted by social workers, rabbis, lawyers, and birth
  families.
National Adoption Center, (800) TO-ADOPT
New York Hospital–Cornell Medical Center Infertility and In Vitro Fertilization Pro-
  grams, (212) 746-1762
Brooklyn In Vitro Fertilization (affiliated with Maimonides Hospital), 909 49th Street,
  Brooklyn, NY 11219, (718) 283-8600
  This infertility treatment center is especially sensitive to the needs of observant Jews.
  (There are hundreds of infertility clinics throughout the United States. The above two are
  frequented by Jewish patients in the New York City area.)
RESOLVE, 5 Water Street, Arlington, MA 02174, (617) 643-2424
  One of the best support organizations for infertile couples. Gives medical information,
  refers for support groups, and gives counseling. Has chapters and hosts infertility
  seminars throughout the United States.
Stars of David.
  National support network for Jewish adoptive families. For information from the Baltimore chapter, call (410) 466-9200, ext. 234.

6

Understanding and Coping with Emotional Problems

S ee, Lord, that I am in trouble. My insides are embittered, my heart is turned within me. . . . They have heard that I sigh. No one can comfort me. My sighs are many, and my heart is sick."[1]

"No one is as whole as he who has a broken heart."[2]

Emotional problems cause at least as much suffering as physical ones do.[3] They are so widespread that one in four adult Americans has a psychiatric disorder or drug or alcohol problem, and almost half of all Americans will have a mental or addictive disorder sometime during their lives.[4]

Emotional problems and mental illness are not new, although they seem to be more widespread today than years ago. The Bible describes famous people who were depressed, such as Jacob, King Saul, Jeremiah, and Job, as well as people who had anxiety attacks.[5] Insanity was sufficiently common in ancient times that King David feigned psychosis in order to help him escape from the King of Gat.[6] David may also have originated music therapy by playing the harp to soothe King Saul's emotions.[7]

Until recently, people had little contact with those who were mentally ill. But today, emotionally disturbed children are mainstreamed into regular school classes, and many adults with psychiatric problems live fairly normal lives. Mental disorders are so frequent among actors, actresses, writers, and public figures that they openly talk about their suicide attempts, manic-depression, debilitating anxiety, and addictions to alcohol and drugs.

Even so, many people have no idea as to the havoc mental illness can wreak on those affected, their families, and friends. It affects more than bag ladies, homeless people roaming the streets, and vagrants who talk to themselves. It may strike anyone's family, friends, next-door neighbors, and even oneself.

Mark, for example, was a mischievous boy who was bored in school. When he turned eighteen, he volunteered to serve in Vietnam because he thought that it would be fun to be treated like a hero when he came back. What he didn't count on was an experience there that would change his life. Mark was ambushed one night by a nine-year-old Vietcong boy wielding a machine gun. Mark had no choice but to kill the boy, but couldn't live with himself afterward. He ended his tour of duty and came home to a hero's welcome, but it was meaningless. He suffered from frequent nightmares and flashbacks in which the Vietcong attacked him. He was so anxious that he constantly shook like a leaf and needed to stay busy.

When he had a flashback at a shopping center, he pulled a rifle out of his car and "defended" himself by shooting seven people. He was treated in a psychiatric hospital for a month, then discharged. But his anxiety, flashbacks, and nightmares continued for many years.

The world is full of people like Mark. Two years after Anna was raped in her apartment by a burglar, she still slept with the lights on at night and did not trust men. She startled easily, cried over small upsets, and always felt tired.

Frank had yearly manic episodes in which he took his money out of the bank and threw it to passersby on the street. After emptying his account, he drove his car hundreds of miles, without telling his wife or children about it. He reappeared days later, only to find that he was fired from his job, was broke, and had devastated his family.

Leo was an ex-Marine who reflexively dove for cover every time he heard a loud noise. He jumped out of his second-story bedroom twice and instinctively tried to strangle his wife when a backfiring car suddenly roused him from his sleep.

Emotionally ill people are real people who suffer. At one time, most of them had the same hopes, dreams, and feelings that healthy people have. Some of them changed abruptly, others changed gradually for the worse, with terrible repercussions for themselves, their family, and friends.

Why does God make people have emotional disorders, some of which are incurable?

Not surprisingly, we are not the first people to ask these questions. When King David asked God this, God responded when King Saul pursued David in an attempt to kill him. David feigned madness so that Saul would not see him as a threat and would leave him alone. When the ploy worked, David understood that everything was created with a purpose, even insanity.[8] To discover any purpose in mental illness, we must look beyond the havoc that it wreaks.

For instance, the positive effects of Carla's mental illness were not apparent for years. She was a highly successful professional in her twenties, with an extremely lucrative and prestigious job. She spent most of her waking hours trying to advance her career, then indulged in hedonistic pursuits in her spare time.

One day, she became severely depressed for no apparent reason and had several long psychiatric hospitalizations during the next three years. She lost her job, and with it, her self-confidence and self-worth.

Her sudden and unpredictable losses shattered her belief that she could get anything that she wanted by working hard. She lost her arrogance and started to think about what was really important in life. She had done many immoral things in her quest for a "good life," and had hurt some people along the way. Her tribulations sobered her to the damage that she caused by living for herself, and she stopped drinking and having affairs. She learned to respect her body, mind, and other people more.

Carla will probably take medication for the rest of her life. That, together with psychotherapy, have enabled her to live normally. Although her depression turned her life upside down for a while, it made her appreciate that her ability to function is a daily gift that she no longer takes for granted. It is unlikely that she would value life, friends, or family this way had she never lost her mental health.

Marty was also challenged by mental illness. He was afraid of people and could work only at jobs where he was socially isolated. Yet he was kind to animals and fed and cared for the birds and stray cats that frequented his yard. While he could not relate to people, he made an honest living, he behaved morally, and he was compassionate. How many people with fewer emotional limitations do the same?

Sonia was a sixty-five-year-old secretary who was paranoid. While this made it impossible for her to marry, or even make friends, she was self-supporting and did volunteer work for charitable organizations. Everyone has limitations, and Sonia dealt beautifully with hers by finding ways to express her inner goodness.

The Almighty challenges each of us, and we choose how to respond. The Talmud says, "Everything is in the hands of Heaven (i.e., preordained) except for the fear of Heaven."[9] When people are challenged by depression, psychosis, anxiety, and so on, they and their families can choose to react in ways that expand their spirituality and humanity, or contract it.

We are influenced by, but are not entirely scripted by, our traits, genes, temperament, and environment. Contrary to "politically correct" philosophies, *everybody* has some limitations. For example, some people are predisposed to be aggressive, but they can choose what to do with these feelings. One person may become a hunter, while another becomes a ritual slaughterer so that Jews will have kosher meat. A third person becomes a surgeon, while a fourth is a murderer. A fifth person becomes a ritual circumciser (a *mohel*), while a sixth becomes a wife abuser.[10] One temperamentally sensitive person becomes self-absorbed and withdrawn, another uses her sensitivity to help others. Some abandoned or abused children become hateful and sociopathic adults, while others are devoutly religious or heal the wounded.

While psychiatric problems can cause tremendous misery, they can also prompt people to grow spiritually and feel close to God. Millions of people who have gone through twelve-step programs know that.

Even psychotic people are rarely out of touch with reality all of the time. Most mentally ill people make ongoing moral choices, even when they can't control their feelings or thoughts well. It is extremely rare that someone has no control over his or her behavior, contrary to what psychologists, sociologists, and criminologists would have us believe. "Experts" who insist that our families, environments, and genes make us addicted, immoral, or nasty absolve us of responsibility for our choices to act immorally or be morally great. No one is forced to use drugs or alcohol, for example, and religious people typically find meaning and satisfaction in life without using these substances.[11]

Secular society now promotes a "disease" model of mental illness that is often used to absolve people of responsibility for their actions. For example, twelve-step programs like Alcoholics Anonymous insist that alcoholics, drug abusers, overeaters, and the like have diseases over which they are powerless. When people have feelings or cravings that are a result of their environment or biochemistry, how they respond to them is a matter of choice, not predestination. One identical twin may become an alcoholic while the other does not. One woman may be clinically depressed, angry, and nasty while her sister takes medication and works out her feelings in psychotherapy.

Sociologists, biologists, and psychiatrists insist that people have little or no control over their emotions and reactions. They excuse immoral, destructive, and egocentric behavior by diagnosing it as a personality disorder, or resulting from a deprived childhood environment. Legal "insanity" pleas also foster the idea that criminals are mentally ill victims, not responsible for their actions.

We all have emotional limitations, but few of us must remain total victims of the past. A child raised in an abusive home can choose to be a strong, caring, and moral adult, a self-destructive hedonist, or a sociopath. And we can continually reevaluate our paths when we are adults.

Diane was a good example of this. She grew up in the projects in Spanish Harlem and was abandoned by her mother when she was ten years old. Her father came home only once a week when "high," when he beat her and her six younger siblings. Diane was not equipped to raise her family, but she did the best that she could. Still, all of the children wore dirty and torn clothes, their matted hair had lice, and no one helped them with their schoolwork.

Diane dropped out of high school so that she could make money to support her siblings. By the time she was twenty-two, she was a store manager earning a good living. But her boyfriend beat her and introduced her to cocaine, and she soon became an addict.

She finally faced the shambles that she had made of her life after five more years of abusive men and drugs. She decided that believing in God and living a moral life was better than short-lived pleasures. She stopped using drugs, left her boyfriend, and joined a Bible study group.

Diane overcame her terrible upbringing and environment and made choices that are open to everyone. She traded her life of hedonism, abuse, and humiliation for one of delayed gratification, meaning, and self-worth.

Most people who are challenged by emotional disorders can choose to deal with them by learning coping skills, taking medication when necessary, living a healthy lifestyle, and finding meaning in life. Although it may be hard, they can deal with their pain, fears, defeats, and failures and make their suffering redemptive.

Sam and Eta were married for ten years when he became severely depressed after his business went bankrupt. He stayed home for the next year and a half, cried every day, and was very dependent on her. He could not bear his pain and couldn't think about the future. Eta was supportive and loving, despite the fact that she had three young children to raise and little money with which to do it. Thirty years later, she still appreciated this opportunity to love her husband when he was vulnerable and helpless, not only when he was a strong breadwinner. This incident strengthened her ability to deal with adversity, cemented their marriage, and prepared them to weather other crises.

We like to think that we control our lives and our destinies, and we invest ourselves in illusory props. If we lose control of our minds or emotions, we tend to lose our security and self-esteem. But if our self-worth comes from doing the best we can to serve God, we suffer less when adversity limits what we can do.

Many people become depressed or anxious when they don't get a good job, money, a spouse, or children who are healthy and accomplished. Our challenge is to accept not having everything that we want when God has different goals for us than we have for ourselves. A man may have a career that he cherishes but lose it because of debilitating anxiety. A graduate student may have to drop out of school because she can't cope with the stress. A woman may dream of being a wonderful mother but be completely debilitated with postpartum depression.

Emotional illness is easier to deal with if we believe that it happens for a reason. Trusting that God sends these challenges helps us (or our loved ones) find that meaning and gets us back on track as we find inner strength, remember not to take our minds for granted, and help us appreciate how every part of our lives is a divine gift. We can then invite God to be closer to us, develop the faith that He will provide what we need, and accept our dependence on Him.

JEWISH PERSPECTIVES ON MENTAL ILLNESS

Until recently, the non-Jewish world killed, imprisoned, or tortured psychotic people, believing that they were incarnations of the devil. Not long ago, doctors bored holes in their brains to release evil spirits or put them in prisonlike hospitals where patients were often abused. By contrast, Judaism teaches that even severely mentally ill people were created in God's image, and they deserve the same respect that we must give every human being. After prophecy ceased (over 2,000 years ago), the Talmud says that it was given to children and "crazy people." This suggests that God allows some mentally ill people greater sensitivity to His presence. Perhaps this is because the vulnerability caused by mental illness motivates them to draw closer to God as the Source of all stability and meaning.

The talmudic Sages viewed severely depressed people as being in terrible emotional pain, caused by forces outside of their control. Such afflicted people are supposed to observe as many commandments as they can but need not do positive commandments when their illness gets in the way. At the same time, they must do everything possible to improve their situation. If psychotherapy or medication will help, they are obliged to try them.

The Talmud also discusses perpetually psychotic people (*shotim*). Such people wandered around cemeteries at night, slept in graveyards, wore torn clothes, lost everything that they were given, and had no regard for society. Jews who are so out of touch with reality are not required to observe any commandments. Instead, the community is required to care for them since they have no free will and can't make responsible choices.

People who are chronically psychotic still play a vital role in our world.[12] Only God knows why He chose these experiences to refine their souls, but they can encourage us to be grateful for our mental health and to be compassionate and helpful to those who are less fortunate.

Sociologists know that the more people live for themselves and by themselves, the more mental illness there is. Is it merely coincidental that emotional disorders often bring families closer, or bring strangers together into new, caring families? Even at this level, mental illness can serve a purpose.

BEING PRISONERS OF THE PAST

Therapists are in a position to see the best in people, such as patients who overcome the challenges of deprived childhoods by turning misfortune into strength. When life gives them lemons, they make lemonade. Yet we are troubled that God allows vulnerable and helpless children to be mistreated by inadequate or abusive parents. While we don't know why He does this, "science" implies that these children are ruined forever and cannot have healthy or meaningful lives. That is simply not true.

Growing up in an inadequate or abusive home is terrible, yet many who grew up this way develop tremendous inner strength and compassion for others. Most abused children do not become abusive parents, and many people from dysfunctional families have meaningful adult lives. Others choose to stay angry with God or the world and spend their lives futilely trying to get what they missed as children.

Tonya overcame a horrendous past. She was a caring wife and a warm and loving mother to three beautiful children. Her seemingly idyllic present, however, was built from the ashes of a terrible childhood. She was born in Russia and watched soldiers shoot and kill her mother when she was three years old. She and her father escaped by hiding in forests for the next two years, narrowly escaping death many times. Her father died before the war ended, leaving her completely alone. As divine providence had it, she was discovered by a compassionate couple who adopted her and brought her to America.

She was raised in an observant Jewish home and became observant herself. When she was twenty, she married a loving and supportive man. She had a number of good friends, was active in the community, and seemed quite happy. Yet she still had weekly nightmares in which she relived the terrors of her early life. She never got over her personal hell, but she had trained herself not to let it ruin her ability to love.

David also had a heartbreaking childhood. His mother died when he was young, and his father had beaten him almost every day while he was growing up. When he was twelve, he ran away to a *kibbutz* in Israel, where he lived until he got married. He and his wife had two children, but she was unable to care for them or for him. So, David got up at 4:00 A.M. six days a week, readied his store for the day, dashed home at 6:00 to get his children off to school, then went back to work.

Being abandoned by his parents had been so painful for him that he did everything he could to make sure that his children felt nurtured. When he got divorced, he continued to see his children every day and made them feel loved. He said, "People think that I should hate my father, but I don't. I used to, but now I see him as pathetic, and I almost feel sorry for him. He tried his best but he simply didn't know how to be a father. I visit him from time to time now that he's old and mellower. We don't have much in common, but he likes to vicariously enjoy my business success. Unfortunately, he's so limited emotionally that he doesn't appreciate me or my children.

"I also feel sorry for my former wife. She's overwhelmed by life. I had three kids, not two—my son, my daughter, and her. Still, she's my children's mother, and I want them to have a good relationship with her so that they will feel loved and secure. As long as I give them the limits, structure, and direction that they need, I think they'll turn out okay."

Jason should also have been among the "walking wounded." He had been sexually abused by a neighbor and emotionally abused by his parents as a teenager. When I empathized with how emotionally and physically painful his childhood must have been, he replied, "Look, it certainly wasn't something that I would like to repeat, but I learned two things from it: First, as unpleasant as it was, I survived. It didn't kill me, and I'm still here and living a pretty decent life. It taught me that as long as something doesn't kill me, I can survive the most horrible experiences. Second, I will never force myself on a woman as many men do on dates because I know how it feels to be used. I would never want anyone else to go through that."

Jason became an observant Jew in college. Instead of wallowing in pain and bitterness, he was an upbeat, compassionate, and sensitive man who developed a close bond with God.

Psychoanalytic ideas have so pervaded Western society that many people focus only on how destructive poor home environments and mental illness are. They don't notice when people deal with these challenges in growthful ways because they presume that neglect, abuse, or trauma must always leave permanent and irreparable scars. While this is true for some people, it is certainly not true for others. Many people who have been emotionally devastated become stronger and more beautiful as a result. Sometimes their scars even nourish new growth.

Another area in which secularists differ from Judaism is in their views about guilt and shame. Secularists teach that most guilt is bad and that an enormous amount of mental illness is due to shame and guilt. Judaism says that these negative feelings are important for our growth, provided we channel them constructively. Our Creator knows that we are human and expects us to make mistakes, so He gave us these feelings to motivate us to right our wrongs, let go of the past, and be better in the future. By sincerely repenting our mistakes, we can forgive ourselves and not ruin the rest of our lives torturing ourselves for what we did wrong.

Repentance involves regretting and verbalizing to God what we did wrong, making amends, apologizing to people we hurt, and resolving never to repeat our misdeeds. We ask God, not an intermediary, to forgive us, because we are personally responsible to Him for everything that we do. If we use shame and guilt to improve ourselves, they serve an important function.

While many psychological theories say that our behavior is predetermined, Judaism says that we can change at any time. We can't always undo the actual damage that we cause, but we need not be immobilized by guilt. For instance, an abusive parent who later realizes how badly she treated her son cannot make up for the years of pain and suffering she caused. But she can regret and atone for what she did, apologize, and treat the child better in the future.

Bill Wilson decided to turn his life around one day instead of resigning himself to alcoholism. Not only did he stay sober after many years of heavy drinking, he also started Alcoholics Anonymous. A.A. has helped millions of alcoholics achieve sobriety and has become the model for scores of other twelve-step, self-help programs such as Gamblers Anonymous, Overeaters Anonymous, Debtors Anonymous, and the like. Bill overcame his personal challenge and used it to help others, and we can do the same.

Successful, nonprofit, self-help support groups often teach people to take responsibility for their behavior, even if they have no power over their disease. Instead of saying, "Accept me as I am, I don't need to change," members must take an inventory of character flaws and work on them, and make amends to people whom they have hurt. No matter how many mistakes people have made, their pasts don't have to ruin their futures.[13]

Many people prefer not to take responsibility for their emotional problems. Angry people insist that it is others who "make" them this way. Alcoholics and drug abusers blame situations or people who "drive" them to drink or use drugs. Overeaters binge while blaming the fattening foods for being accessible from the pantry, freezer, or grocery store.

Many people like to believe that they could be happy if only God would give them a different life. They fantasize about how idyllic life would be "if only I were married . . . if only I had gotten the job that I wanted . . . if only I'd had better parents . . . if only my children weren't so difficult . . . if only I'd had better opportunities. . . ." Rather than accept what God gives when that can't be changed, some people blame external circumstances to avoid taking control of their lives by changing themselves.

In one town, everyone was so fed up with their respective problems that they decided to exchange them. Each placed his problems in a bundle in the center of a large circle, then proceeded to examine everyone else's pack. After perusing them, everyone decided to reclaim his or her own!

Instead of lamenting our challenges and wishing that we had someone else's life, we can grow best by accepting the challenges that God gives us.

Some people also blame God or the world, yet they are their own worst enemies. Their reactions cause more damage than the events that they lived through. It is bad enough to go through traumas or tragedies once; holding onto hurts and catastrophizing them makes sure that life never gets better.

People with painful childhoods may take out on others what their parents did to them. They attack their bosses, sabotage their careers, hurt people who are close to them, then "prove" that no one can be trusted. They see the worst in others and react defensively rather than see what they do to elicit people's negative reactions.

Some people who were deprived or traumatized feel that God and the world owe them. Others keep themselves enraged at every disappointment. By insisting that life should go their way, they waste their lives waiting for the world to change.

Jerry had an unpleasant childhood and decided that his suffering entitled him to an easy life. He expected women to gratify his every need and make up for all of his past hurts and deprivations. When this did not happen, he felt even more victimized. He stayed single into his forties because he refused to be realistic about life. He could have avoided many years of unhappiness had he accepted that no one could or would want to make up for his decades of deprivation.

Ralph was very hostile at work because he believed that every boss tried to compete with him. When he got fired from four jobs in a row because of his nastiness, he chalked it up to others having it in for him. It was only after months of psychotherapy that Ralph understood that he had caused his problems and the world wasn't going to change for him.

Jodi had no real friends. She was so demanding and needy that no one wanted to talk to her more than once or twice a month. She saw others as ungiving and herself as totally reasonable. Until she realizes that her attitudes are a problem, life won't get better.

God puts us in situations where we suffer, but we choose to make our pain worse by wallowing in it and holding onto destructive attitudes and beliefs. We can medicate our pain by drinking or abusing drugs, running away from responsibility, expecting others to take care of us, or staying enraged. Or we can develop useful ways of coping and heal ourselves instead of pouring salt into our emotional wounds.

We should not blame God for our refusal to accept life as it really is and for expecting life to be "fair." We need to accept our challenges and respond to them constructively. When we stay so angry that we negate everything good in our lives, we make sure that our lives don't get better.

BEING ALL THAT WE CAN BE

Poor self-esteem and feelings of worthlessness are at the root of many forms of mental illness. When this is the case, the more faith we have that God gave us our challenges, the better we feel, and the more our souls grow in the process. People who cannot prevent or control bad feelings, delusions, or hallucinations can act morally whenever possible and discipline themselves to follow a therapeutic protocol that helps them.

For example, John was a twenty-three-year-old homosexual. When he hallucinated, the devil told him that he was bad and that he should kill himself. At those times, he felt so guilty about his homosexual flings that he abstained. John could not prevent his hallucinations or his homosexual feelings. But he could choose to take medication that kept the hallucinations under control and refrain from immoral behavior.

An abusive mother could not initially control her violent feelings toward her daughter. But by seeing a therapist, she learned to recognize her violent feelings before acting on them. She then walked away from her daughter and called a friend for help when she felt that she would lose control. In the space of a few months, she had stopped hitting her child.

Most anxious, depressed, and emotionally disturbed people know the difference between moral and immoral behavior and can choose to do what is right and have a close relationship with their Creator. Emotional illness often prompts them to do this in a way that self-sufficiency and mental health do not.

Many people grow tremendously as they come to terms with their anger, hurt, emptiness, and emotional traumas. Not infrequently, they discover inner strength and become role models and helpers to those who have gone through similar experiences.

Linda's mother hated her. In the days when patients had few rights, Linda's mother committed her to a "snake pit" (an abusive mental hospital) because she did not want to take care of her teenager. After getting electric shocks and drugs for six months, Linda somehow managed to escape and went home. Her mother reincarcerated her for another year of abuse before Linda escaped permanently.

Linda never forgave her mother or the hospital for what they did, yet she didn't let that stop her from repairing her shattered life. She went to college at night and worked full-time to pay for it. She got a good job and eventually married a man whom she loved and supported.

When her mother developed terminal cancer twenty years later, Linda took a leave of absence from work and nursed her mother for a year until she died. Despite her mother's previous abominable treatment, Linda was grateful that her mother had brought her into the world. She felt that the least she could do was to accompany her mother out of it.

Linda suffered terribly, yet she responded by becoming an extraordinarily compassionate woman. She stopped focusing on why she had been subjected to such abuse and instead resolved to make the rest of her life meaningful.

Susan's father physically abused her as a child. He was a minister who excused his sadistic behavior by quoting the verse, "He who spares the rod, spoils the child." He nearly drowned his daughters when he bathed them every night, and beat them at other times until they were black and blue. Susan did not even know that this was unusual or abnormal until she was in her thirties and heard a lecture about child abuse.

Despite this, Susan was a loving, patient, ideal mother to her own children. The horrors that she had been through prompted her to find a better life, and she did so by converting to Judaism. It took her many years to repair the emotional damage that her father caused her, but that did not stop her from realizing her spiritual potentials.

These are but a few people who transcended personal tragedies that are supposedly too damaging to overcome. They used their afflictions of love to lead better lives. Once they stopped feeling bitter, they took comfort in the idea that God wanted them to grow by overcoming their challenges.

RECOMMENDATIONS FOR COPING

We can often feel better by changing our attitudes or situations. Sharing feelings with supportive friends or relatives is also helpful, as is boosting our mood by doing pleasurable things that Judaism permits.

People with poor self-esteem or depression should make sure to take care of themselves. Regular exercise and healthful eating are important, as are meditation, stress management, and/or relaxation techniques to reduce tension and improve sleep.

Consult a counselor or therapist if you have problems that you can't overcome on your own. Bear in mind that some helpers will be better for you than others. A rabbi may help you find spiritual answers along with emotional comfort. A social worker may know governmental or community resources that can help you with financial problems or coping with an illness, an elderly parent, or a disabled child. A psychologist can do psychological or educational testing, vocational counseling, and/or psychotherapy. A psychiatrist can prescribe medication and may also do therapy. The best therapists are usually licensed in their discipline and have at least five years of well-supervised experience. Ask your friends, rabbi, or doctor for a referral.

Various therapies and medications are used to treat anxiety, panic, obsessive-compulsive disorders, insomnia, depression, mania, and psychosis. If possible, learn about your condition and how it is treated before choosing a mental health practitioner.

Your relationship with a therapist is at least as important as the type of therapy that he or she practices. You should feel fairly comfortable with a therapist and sense that he or she understands where you are "coming from." Ask a therapist to clarify before or during your first session how that brand of therapy works, what to expect and how soon, and how much sessions cost.

If money is an issue, ask a therapist if there is a sliding scale. If not, find a clinic that accepts Medicaid or Medicare or has a sliding scale. If you have private insurance, it probably has a provider network whose therapists you can see for little or nothing. Training institutes also have low fees.

Don't stoically shoulder your problems alone, but don't share your problems with anyone and everyone. You don't really want the entire world knowing your personal secrets, and too many people can give you conflicting ideas about how to solve a problem. Many will not even know what they're talking about!

If you can't find a helpful friend or clergy person to talk to, and you don't want individual therapy, try a support group. There are free self-help groups for almost every kind of addiction and psychiatric disorder, such as Alcoholics Anonymous, Adult Children of Alcoholics, Al-Anon, Alateen, Narcotics Anonymous, Gamblers Anonymous, Debtors Anonymous, and Overeaters Anonymous. Ask a local hospital, or find a group near you through the telephone directory. The National Institute of Mental Health in Bethesda, Maryland, or the American Psychological Association in Washington, D.C., can also suggest referrals throughout the United States.

Many self-help groups, especially for alcoholics and drug abusers, are based on nonsectarian Christian beliefs. Few self-help groups are geared to non-Christians, except in large cities. JACS (Jewish Alcoholics, Chemically Dependent, and Significant Others) was founded to address needs of Jewish addicts and their families. It is a lay group that acts as a clearinghouse and resource center for use by rabbis, social workers, educators, addicts, and their families.

Readers need to know that many, if not most, psychotherapists are prejudiced against religion. They view it as an irrational crutch at best and as a neurosis at worst. A therapist should appreciate and respect your religious and cultural beliefs and be willing to help you without "analyzing away" your religious convictions. Religion should be used as a source of strength, not derided as a neurosis that needs to be removed. If a therapist tries to erode your healthy religious beliefs, find another therapist.

Observant Jews should seek therapy from qualified observant therapists when possible, because Jewish beliefs conflict strongly with those of most therapists. For example, secular therapists reject the idea that God has told us how to live and that there are objective, divine standards of morality. Therapists usually use secular standards to decide what it is appropriate to say, do, and feel, then encourage patients to act in ways that are often at odds with Judaism. Despite its name, Jewish Boards of Family and Children's Services rarely offer treatment that is sympathetic to, or knowledgeable about, traditional Jewish beliefs.

Jews who need a treatment referral or short-term crisis counseling can call the Yittie Liebel Helpline at (718) HELP NOW (435-7669). This hotline is staffed from 8 A.M. to 12 P.M. Sunday through Friday, and from 9 to 11 P.M. Sunday through Thursday.

HELPING OTHERS

The best way to comfort and help someone with emotional problems is by giving support and a listening ear. Don't give advice or suggestions unless someone says that he or she wants it. At the same time, people who are capable of solving their own problems should not expect you to do it for them. The best way to help such people is to tell them that you know that they can make the right choices for themselves.

Do not tell someone with emotional problems, "Just snap out of it," or "Just stop thinking about your problems and they'll go away," or "There's nothing wrong with you—you're fine." Some people who are seriously depressed, agoraphobic (afraid of going outside), obsessive-compulsive, or anxious need professional help. Cognitive-behavioral treatments and/or medication often bring relief in a few weeks or months. Delaying treatment can result in some conditions worsening to a point where they become almost intractable.

If you have had a good experience with a therapist or support group, recommend them to others who need help.

Try to encourage people with emotional problems to identify specific issues to deal with, rather than see all of their problems as one big, overwhelming mess. Remind them about which parts of their life are going well. After you empathize with someone's distress, he or she might be receptive to concrete suggestions about how to deal with one or two specific issues.

Reassure emotionally overwhelmed people that they aren't losing their minds. Many of them will feel that they must be going crazy, and that is extremely frightening.

You can't make some people feel better, or live their lives for them; you can only be helpful and supportive. If someone refuses professional help and will not address problems, there's not much you can do (unless the person needs to be prevented from committing suicide or homicide).

You are not helping someone with a drinking or drug problem by minimizing or making excuses for it. If you do not know how to confront him or her about it, ask an expert or go to a self-help meeting. Many sober alcoholics and former addicts turned their lives around because caring friends or family confronted them about their behavior. If someone you live with continues to abuse alcohol or drugs, you might need to move out or insist that they leave. Go to a self-help group such as Alateen or Al-Anon for support.

Local hotlines, hospital psychiatry departments, and clinics can also give you referrals and advice about where to get help for specific problems.

A person does not have to be crazy to see a therapist. Ask if someone deserves therapy, not if he or she can do without it. Sometimes a therapist can be a person's best friend; and these days, that may be hard to find.

NOTES

1. Lamentations 1:20–22.

2. Rabbi Moshe Leib of Sassov.

3. Emotional distress can present as back pain, headaches, abdominal distress, heart palpitations, and other debilitating physical conditions. These are responsible for at least 70 percent of patient visits to doctors.

4. Forty-eight percent of Americans between the ages of fifteen and fifty-four will have at least one psychiatric or addictive disorder at some time. Tens of millions of Americans (23 percent) now abuse alcohol, half as many abuse drugs, and more than 23 percent of Americans between ages fifteen and fifty-four are depressed (Kessler et al. "Lifetime and 12-Month Prevalence of *DSM-III-R* Psychiatric Disorders in the United States: Results from the National Comorbidity Survey." *Archives of General Psychiatry* 51 [January 1994]: 8–19). Fifteen percent of Americans over the age of sixty-five are chronically and severely depressed (Leibowitz, "Special Committee on Aging Senate Testimony," Senate Forum on Mental Health and Aging, July 15, 1993, SH-RG, 103–248). Probably half of all American women have taken psychotropic drugs, and 15 percent of Americans take prescribed antistress pills (Donald Meichenbaum, *Coping with Stress* [New York: Facts on File, 1983]). Twenty-two percent of adult Americans have a diagnosable mental disorder in any given year, and 9 percent will have significantly impaired functioning as a result of a mental illness ("Psychiatry," *JAMA* 271:21 [1993/1994]: 1707).

5. For example, Isaac experienced an anxiety attack when his son Esau challenged him for blessing Jacob. See Genesis 27:33.

6. 1 Samuel 21:14.

7. 1 Samuel 16:23.

8. 1 Samuel 21:14; Psalm 34.

9. *Megillah* 25a.

10. *Shabbat* 156a. The Talmud expresses this idea by saying, "One who is born under the constellation of Mars will be a shedder of blood. . . . Rabbi Ashi observed: Either a surgeon, a thief, a ritual slaughterer, or a circumciser."

11. It has repeatedly been shown that religiosity is the best predictor of nonuse of drugs or alcohol. (L. Aiken, "Hierarchical Use of Alcohol and Drugs in Adolescents of Different Religions, Degrees of Religious Affiliation, and Extroversion-Introversion," *Dissertation Abstracts International,* 1980.) See also Viktor Frankl, *The Unheard Cry for Meaning: Psychotherapy and Humanism* (New York: Simon and Schuster, 1978), pp. 26–27.

12. See, for example, *Genesis Rabbah* 10:7.

13. Despite their stunning success, some of these groups insist that participants not use prescribed medications for mental disorders. It can be dangerous for some individuals to stop their medication for depression, mania, psychosis, anxiety attacks, and the like. Another drawback of these groups is that they often meet in churches, pray, and espouse religious ideas with Christian overtones. Jews can get help from these groups, but they also need to get spiritual direction from authentic Jewish sources.

FOR FURTHER READING

Copeland, Mary Ellen. *The Depression Workbook: A Guide for Living with Depression and Manic Depression.* Oakland, CA: New Harbinger Publications, 1992.

An excellent book giving information about unipolar and bipolar depression, with exercises and suggestions for how to deal with them.

Discover Recovery Communications, Inc., 3201 SW 15th Street, Deerfield Beach, FL 33442-8190.

This firm publishes recovery catalogs for alcohol and drug addictions, and sexual, relationship, self-esteem, and eating disorders.

Duke, Patty. *A Brilliant Madness: Living with Manic-Depressive Illness.* New York: Bantam, 1992.

An excellent book that chronicles Patty Duke's personal ordeals with bipolar disorder. It is especially helpful in describing and enlightening patients about manic episodes.

Hain, M. *Twice Chai: A Jewish Road to Recovery.* Order from (212) 387-3876.

Hazelden Foundation, P.O. Box 176, Center City, MN 55012-0176 (612) 257-4010 (800) 328-9000.

Publishes a catalog of self-help books, including those on addictions.

Mishell, Judith. *Beyond Your Ego.* New York: CIS Publishers, 1991.

A Torah approach to self-knowledge, emotional health, and inner peace.

Tauber, Ezriel. *Self-Esteem.* Monsey, NY: Shalheves, 1992.

Twerski, Abraham. *Growing Each Day.* Brooklyn, NY: Mesorah Publications, 1992.

——. *I Didn't Ask to Be in This Family.* New York: Topper Books, 1992.

How sibling relationships shape adult behavior and dependencies.

——. *Let Us Make Man.* New York: CIS Publishers, 1991.

Developing self-esteem through Judaism.

——. *Seek Sobriety, Find Serenity.* New York: Pharos Books, 1993.

At the time of this writing, Rabbi Dr. Twerski has published almost twenty books. Check your Jewish bookstore for others.

RESOURCES

Addiction Assistance Line, (718) 968-8154

Refers addicted Orthodox Jews to appropriate treatment centers.

Al-Anon/Alateen, (800) 356-9996

Alcohol Abuse Hotline, (800) ALC-OHOL

Alcoholics Anonymous Groups of Greater New York, (212) 683-3900

Bronx Jewish Community Council, (718) 652-5500
  Sponsors groups for drug abusers and alcoholics (not Orthodox).

The Children of Alcoholics Foundation, 200 Park Avenue, New York, NY, (212) 351-2680

Cocaine Abuse Hotline, (800) COC-AINE

Compulsive Gambling Hotline, (800) 332-0402

Counterforce, 601 Ocean Parkway, Brooklyn, NY 11218, (718) 854-7730
  Provides Jewish day-school students in the greater New York area with a full range of
  mental health services administered by Torah-observant professionals.

Depressives Anonymous

National Institute of Mental Health Depression and Panic Disorder Hotline, (800) 421-4211
  Gives a menu of free brochures about depression that one may order. (800) 64-PANIC is
  their information hotline dealing with panic and anxiety disorders.

Drug Information and Treatment Hotline, (800) 662-HELP

Drug Abuse Hotline, (800) 538-4840

Family Violence Resources (Jewish-sponsored)
  Assists battered women by giving shelter, legal or medical aid, and individual or couple
  counseling. The following are contacts for more information:
  Baltimore: Chana Weinberg, (410) 486-0322
  Boston: Jewish Family Service, (617) 227-6641
  Chicago: Project Shalva, (312) 583-HOPE (24-hour hotline)
  Detroit: Jewish Family Service Windows, (313) 559-1500
  Houston: Avda, (713) 520-8620
  Los Angeles: Family Violence Project, (818) 908-5007
    Shiloh, (818) 783-6754
    Ezras Bayis, (213) 896-0981
    L. A. Jewish Family Service, (212) 896-0981
  Minneapolis: Jewish Family Service, (612) 546-0616
  Montreal: Auberge Shalom Pour Femmes, (514) 733-3217
  New York: The Transition Center, (718) 520-8045
    Center for Family Violence, (718) 237-1337
  Rockland County, NY: Rockland Family Center, (914) 425-0112
    Monsey Chai Helpline, (914) 425-2424
  San Francisco: Shalom Bayit, (415) 241-8874
  Seattle: Center for Protection of the Jewish Family, (206) 634-1903
  Toronto: ASTEH, (416) 638-7800
  Jerusalem: Tas Zahav, (02) 223-237
    Maon Horim, (02) 827-805

Helpline (24-hour hotline), (212) 532-2400

JACS Foundation, Inc. (Jewish Association for Alcohol and Chemically Dependent Individuals and Significant Others), 197 East Broadway, New York, NY, (212) 473-4747
  Publishes a list of *havurot* for Jews in recovery, and synagogues (observant and nonobservant) in the metropolitan New York area that offer twelve-step meetings. Also sponsors
  retreats and lectures.

Jewish Board of Family and Children's Services, (718) 435-5700
This branch of JBFCS offers psychotherapy by qualified Orthodox therapists.
Jewish Community Services of Long Island, (718) 896-9090.
Runs support group for parents with children in twelve-step programs.
Jewish Family Service of Los Angeles, 6505 Wilshire Blvd., Los Angeles, CA 90048, (213) 852-7723
Has an Orthodox counseling program staffed by observant Jewish therapists and supervised by rabbis.
Jewish Information and Referral Service of the United Jewish Appeal—Federation, (212) 753-2288
The Jewish Recovery Foundation (JRF), 1170 Broadway, New York, NY 10001, (212) 683-4357
Offers twelve-step programs (AA, OA, ACOA, Alanon, GA, NA, DA, CA) for Jews with addiction problems. Offers Jewish-oriented programs for spiritual fulfillment and recovery.
Kiyum (Self-help groups for Jews)
Manic and Depressive Support Group, Inc., P.O. Box 637, Madison Square Station, New York, NY, (212) 533-6374
National Addictions Hotline, (800) 544-1177
National Depressive Illness Foundation, 245 Seventh Ave., New York, NY, (212) 620-7637
National Depression Hotline, (800) 544-1177
National Eating Disorders Hotline, (800) 544-1177
National Food Addiction Hotline, (800) 872-0088
Narcotics Anonymous
Nassau-Suffolk Jewish Recovery Group, (516) 481-7448
Supplemental monthly programs in four area synagogues (Orthodox and non-Orthodox) to people in twelve-step programs.
Ohel Children's Home and Family Service, 4423 16 Avenue, Brooklyn, NY, (718) 851-6300
Ohr Ki Tov Center for Growth and Transformation, Brooklyn, (718) 253-0090
Offers programs that integrate recovery with Jewish spiritual practice.
Overeaters Anonymous, 243 E. 13 Street, New York, NY, (212) 777-2203, (212) 777-2349
Relapse Prevention Hotline, (800) REL-APSE
Schizophrenia Foundation of New York, (212) 808-4940, (212) 765-0780
Tikvah Clinic (Mental Health Clinic), 2011 Ocean Avenue, Brooklyn, NY, (718) 382-0045
Offers mental health services to (mostly) observant Jews. Under Orthodox auspices. Sliding scale.
Westchester Jewish Community Services, (914) 949-6761
Sponsors therapy groups for drug abusers, gamblers, and alcoholics and their families (not Orthodox).
Yittie Leibel Help Line, 1276 50th Street, Brooklyn, NY 11219, (718) HELP-NOW
Telephone hotline that offers free, anonymous professional help to Jews who have emotional and family problems.

7

Suicide

In my senior year in college, I met a handsome, eligible bachelor named David. Both of us wanted to get into clinical psychology graduate schools, and we forged a friendship based on mutual commiseration and support during those trying times.

David seemed to handle this nerve-wracking situation with the same aplomb that he brought to the rest of his life. He was a very likable young man, calm and soft-spoken, refined and unassuming, bright yet modest. He was also a very gifted singer who performed with a band in his spare time.

I was home the Sunday before the festive holiday of Purim, enjoying a second helping of fresh waffles drenched in maple syrup, when the phone rang.

"Hi, Lisa," a familiar voice greeted me. It was my friend Arthur, who played clarinet with David and who had introduced us a few months earlier.

"Hi, Arthur, how are you?" I mumbled, swallowing a last mouthful of breakfast.

"Uh, I'm okay . . . uh, I have some bad news for you, but I'm not sure how to tell you." A long, tense pause followed.

"Well, what is it?" I wondered. Was he going to say that the youth group's Purim party had been cancelled?

He continued hesitating. "I don't know how to tell you this. . . . It's about David." I waited expectantly for him to continue, but he didn't.

I started feeling annoyed. Why were men his age so awkward around women? Anyway, we were just friends, and he didn't have to ask me out on a date. "What could be so difficult, Arthur?" I encouraged. "You know that you don't have to mince words with me."

Another long pause followed. He then took a deep breath and blurted out, "David's dead."

My heart stopped for an instant, and my hands turned to ice. I started shaking, my mind felt numb, and a wave of nausea came over me. After the initial shock, I assumed that this was some kind of terrible Purim joke. David couldn't be dead. He was going to sing at the upcoming Purim concert, and we had just chatted a couple of weeks before. He had to be fine. I decided to confront Arthur and get him to admit that he was lying.

"Lisa," he said softly, "David *is* dead. He killed himself last night. I called to tell you that his funeral will be tomorrow."

His words struck like a ton of bricks, shattering me and making me shudder. I felt blasted by an Arctic wind. My knees buckled as my world came crashing down, and I grabbed onto the wall to prop myself up. Salty rivulets coursed down my contorted face as I sobbed, "Please, please take it back, Arthur. I'll do anything, just don't let it be true."

Arthur did not retract his words. They were real, and there was no way of undoing what was done.

"I'm sorry, Lisa, I didn't want to be the one to tell you this." I was too numb to listen to more.

I composed myself and reassured Arthur, "I know this wasn't easy for you, and I appreciate your letting me know. Thank you." I was on automatic pilot, and my words had little conviction. But almost as an afterthought I asked the million-dollar question: "Why did he do it?"

Arthur searched for an answer that would be a poultice for our raw wounds, but he could find none. "We all wish that we knew. He didn't leave a note, and he was unconscious by the time his parents found him." A long pause followed, and words seemed superfluous.

"Take care of yourself, Lisa."

"Yeah, you too, Arthur," I said absently as I hung up the phone.

My body felt like lead as my mind raced in circles for days. David's parents were loving, caring, warm, and devoted—everything that parents should be. They encouraged his independence while supporting him. They welcomed his friends, enjoyed his singing, praised and loved him. Children brought up this way weren't supposed to kill themselves. What went wrong?

From time to time, grief gave way to rage. Why didn't David care enough about his parents to spare them this anguish? Why weren't his friends important enough to make him want to live, no matter how he felt? I vacillated between feeling sad and angry, hurt and furious. But most of all, I kept trying to undo the past so that David would magically reappear. My head was like a beehive swarming with unanswerable questions and endless "If only's."

After David's funeral, I went to comfort his parents as they sat *shivah*.[1] When I introduced myself to David's father Jack, he greeted me warmly as tears welled in his eyes.

"It's so nice to meet you after hearing David talk so much about you. You know," he continued, "David always wished that he could have been as bright as you are." His voice cracked with emotion, and I imagined how much he yearned to see the son that he had just buried.

As we shared memories of David, Jack's comment kept reverberating through my mind. I felt terribly guilty. Had I made David feel inadequate? Should I have sounded less hopeful about getting into graduate school when he had such doubts about himself? Should I have said nothing about my qualifications and focused only on how much I cared for him?

My mind felt like a computer scrolling along the same page in an endless loop. The vertical hold in my brain had stopped working. I couldn't stop asking, "What if?" As soon as my mind raced through one list of questions, a new one took its place. What if I'd called last week to see how David was? What if I'd told him how much I liked him and how happy he made me? What if I'd encouraged him to feel more self-confident? I felt at peace only as I slipped into a few hours of fitful sleep in the wee hours of the morning.

Jack's recounting of David's last days helped relieve me of some of my upset about not knowing why and how he had killed himself. His friends and I had not known that David had been increasingly despondent for weeks before his death. His midterm exams were approaching, and he was convinced that he wouldn't do well on them. He had done poorly on his Graduate Record Examinations and had to retake them in two weeks. If he did poorly again, he'd have no chance of getting into graduate school, and there was no career that interested him besides psychology.

When it was suggested that he seek professional help, he refused. Some politicians' careers had been ruined a few months earlier when it became public knowledge that they had received psychiatric care. Psychiatric care at that time carried a heavy stigma that David did not want, and he was afraid to admit on employment papers that he had been treated for emotional problems.

Meanwhile, his increasing obsessiveness and depression alarmed his parents. They worried that their normally stable, sociable son might want to end his life. They spent hours reassuring him about his abilities and tried to show him options for the future. Unfortunately, their frequent talks did not relieve his inner tension and despair.

One night, they went out for dinner in order to get a brief respite from their month-long vigil. They left David contentedly singing in his room as he took a break from studying. When they came home two hours later, they announced that they were back. Alarmed when David did not respond, they raced through the house searching for him. They discovered him lying in a bathtub in a coma, bleeding to death. Minutes earlier, he had found his father's revolver and had blown his brains out.

What David thought or felt that night remains a mystery. Unlike many emotionally disturbed people, he came from a healthy, caring family. His parents had raised him with love and discipline, yet he still took his life because he believed that he was inadequate and a burden to them. His parents could not stop his suffering, nor could they have prevented this tragedy.

If the worst thing that a person can ever experience is a child's death, surely a child's suicide is hell on earth. Some people's guilt can never be assuaged because they won't forgive themselves for leaving the person alone at a fateful time. That is compounded by a loss that is beyond description, accompanied by unfathomable pain. Survivors wish that they could somehow bring the person back to life and keep imagining ways that they could have rewritten the script of the play.

As hard as it is to lose a loved one, some things make it easier. We have time to prepare for the passing when someone is ill for a long time or dies at a ripe old age. We may not like the death, but we can accept it. It is much harder to accept anyone voluntarily giving up the greatest gift that we have, which is life itself.

Suicide is much more common than people realize. Over 30,000 Americans will take their lives in a typical year.[2] Six percent of American teenagers have attempted suicide, and another 15 percent have come very close.[3] It is the third most frequent cause of death for children between ages six and sixteen.[4] Sixty thousand teenagers try to kill themselves every year, and 2,000 succeed.[5]

People wonder why some people choose to die, especially when their entire lives are ahead of them. Teenage suicide attempts are prompted by a variety of causes: problems at home (47 percent), depression (23 percent), problems with friends or with socializing (22 percent), poor self-esteem (18 percent), boy-girl problems (16 percent), and feeling that no one cares about them (13 percent).[6] The best predictor of a teen suicide is abuse of alcohol or drugs.[7]

In at least one study of college students, 85 percent of those who attempted suicide did so because they felt that life was meaningless. An astonishing 93 percent of those who complained about meaninglessness were doing well in college, were on good terms with their families, and had friends![8] This tells us how important it is for people to find meaning in life, not just have external props that show success or satisfaction.

Knowing why some people take their lives does not prepare survivors to cope with their sudden loss of a loved one. They tend to torment themselves about what they could and should have done to prevent the tragedy. "If only I had known he was so unhappy, I would have tried harder to get him out of his rut." "If only I had taken her seriously when she told me how alone she felt." "I would have spent more time with her if she'd only let me know that she needed me." "If only I had not belittled his feelings when he said that he felt stupid. I didn't take him seriously because he was a straight-A student." "If only I had insisted that she get professional help, she wouldn't have done it."

Survivors want to know why someone could have hated himself so much, or felt such despair that he could not see any way out except death. We search for meaning in what seems to be a senseless deed.

Most people commit suicide because they are depressed or are using drugs or alcohol. They have unbearable pain, with no hope that life will get better. Many feel lonely and useless and believe that no one truly cares about them, so they try to end their misery by ending their lives.

Suicidal people are rarely "crazy"; more often, they are simply overwhelmed by life and want their pain to end. Some may want only to escape, while others may want to hurt friends or relatives and make them feel guilty over their death. Others commit suicide to "protect" their loved ones, such as when an elderly parent kills herself so as not to be a burden to a spouse or to caretaking children.

There is a myth that people who talk about killing themselves don't do it, and that those who do it don't talk about it. The truth is that 80 percent of people who commit suicide do warn others of their intentions beforehand.[9] Although most suicide attempts don't succeed, they are not merely pleas for help. Some people are rescued from several lethal attempts before they finally succeed.

Betty was a very bright medical student with terrible self-esteem. Her mother was extremely critical of her and belittled her accomplishments, and her father abandoned the family when she was young. Betty was not especially attractive or popular, and she lived alone. She spent most of her time studying or attending class during her first year of medical school. She was especially despondent as winter exams approached, and she sat in her bathtub one night and slit her wrists. Miraculously, the water leaked through her floor to the superintendent's apartment below. When she did not answer the doorbell, he let himself in with a passkey, found her unconscious, and summoned medics in time to save her life.

Betty went home during winter break, and her mother criticized her without respite. Betty went to bed one night after swallowing a handful of barbiturates. As luck would have it, her sister came into the room to borrow the book that Betty had been reading. When she saw Betty slumped on the floor, she took her to the hospital. Betty came out of her coma the next day.

Betty made two more attempts over the next six months, one by jumping from the roof of her building, and the other by trying to suffocate herself in her gas oven. She was miraculously rescued both times. The following spring, she felt especially lonely and believed that she would never do much good for anyone. She finished her midterms, went home, and tied up her telephone line so that no one could get through. She downed a glass of vodka along with a large handful of barbiturates. A friend happened to call her a few minutes later and got suspicious at hearing the busy signal. By the time she arrived, Betty was dead.

We should always take people seriously when they threaten to kill themselves, especially adolescents and old people.[10] They often worry about feeling useless, inadequate, and burdensome to others in ways that we should, but may not, take seriously. Teens give warnings by talking about or writing that they want to die, withdrawing from friends, giving away their belongings, saying that they feel worthless, or having long-term personal problems. Their reasons for feeling inadequate or hopeless often seem silly or unimportant to adults, but they are very important to teens. They are easily overwhelmed by pressure to do well in school, career uncertainties, and difficulties in growing up.

Most adolescents who kill themselves do so at home (using guns) in reaction to a perceived failure or insolvable problem.[11] Something as "unimportant" as a breakup with a girlfriend or boyfriend, getting poor grades in school, or a series of social humiliations can be straws that break a teenager's psyche.

When people use suicide threats or attempts manipulatively, they need professional help to deal with their helplessness and desperation. We tend not to take some depressed or emotionally needy people seriously. We find that people with many, many problems and poor coping skills are never satisfied by our giving a listening ear or occasional support. When that happens, we should recommend that the person seek other help, such as psychotherapy, medication, self-help groups, support from family or friends, and so on. Such people need to develop the inner strength to make reasonable lives for themselves, deal with their anger, and improve their self-esteem. One person's help can rarely do enough of this.

While God gives us only challenges that we can handle, some people don't want to fight, or feel exhausted and drained from ongoing battles. We can help them by giving support, not by our doing what they can and should do for themselves. Even if they need extra help during a crisis, we should help "with" them, not do everything for them.

When someone does take his or her life, we wonder if we could have prevented it. That depends on whether they let us know about their inner turmoil. Some people appear happy and "normal," yet retreat into a private hell behind closed doors.

Other people might find living tolerable if they believed that anyone cared about them. They feel unimportant, but would not choose to die if they had more reason to live. Their suicide (or attempt) may wake us up to our insensitivities. It reminds us that people may need to talk to us when we don't have time for them. It also reminds us to visit lonely or unhappy people and invite them for family and holiday meals. It is easy to avoid people who are depressed or burdened when we don't want them to ruin our day.

This was demonstrated by a fifty-seven-year-old man who visited a doctor to find out the cause of his headaches. At a follow-up visit two weeks later, the patient mentioned that he had tried to kill himself the week before.

A bit shocked, the doctor asked, "What happened?"

The patient said, "I've been feeling really depressed since my wife divorced me two years ago. I retired then and I live alone. I've never had many friends. I spent my life working and being with my family, but I have no more work and no family now. My children aren't interested in me, and we speak only a few times a year. I have nothing to look forward to from one day to the next, and I feel like a failure. I suffer every day from ulcers, arthritis, and loneliness. 'So,' I asked myself, 'What's there to live for?'

"I kept thinking about how useless I was, and that I had no reason to live. One night last week, I planned to drive seventy miles per hour on the highway and smash my car into the concrete divider. I figured that if the car had a full tank of gas it would explode, and I would be dead in a matter of seconds. So I got into my car and drove to a gas station where I filled up the tank.

"As I left the station, I had to go through two intersections with traffic lights before getting onto the turnpike. The first one had a red light, so I had to wait for it to change. Before it turned green, two female hitchhikers came over and asked me if I wanted to take them to a college party. I know this sounds strange, but I figured that I couldn't be all that bad if they were interested in me. I felt better about myself and realized that I should feel differently about my life. So I dropped them off at their party, turned around, and drove home. It's because of them that I am alive today."

How little it takes to make some people feel worthwhile! We sometimes don't give an inch of our time to others because we are afraid that depressed or needy people will take a mile. We should at least see if showing a small amount of concern and encouragement helps someone get back on his feet before concluding that we shouldn't get involved. Sometimes listening for a few minutes and making a helpful suggestion can give people enough hope to keep on going.

Mary Ellen was a perfect example of this. She became extremely depressed when her husband's company relocated. They moved to a city where she had no support system. Neighbors had more important things to do than to befriend a new woman on the block, and parents in her children's school had lifelong cliques. Six months after moving, she still had no friends; her husband spent most of his time at work and neglected her when he was home. She felt overwhelmed by loneliness and feelings of worthlessness.

One day, she tried to kill herself by sitting in her closed garage while the car engine ran. As she inhaled the fumes, she thought about her two-year-old daughter and how Terry would feel growing up without a mother. The poignancy of her daughter's plight made her put her own pain aside, and she turned off the ignition.

She called her former therapist, and he told her to do two things whenever she felt really depressed: she should remember how much her child needed her, and how Terry would feel if Mary Ellen died. She should then call him or anyone else who could help her get past her pain.

This simple advice has kept this woman going for years. As bad as she feels, she has never again attempted suicide. She has rarely called her therapist, either. Just knowing that he is available and cares about her has been enough to help her past the rough times.

People who feel guilty for not doing enough to prevent a suicide should remember that not all suicides are preventable. Some people are so self-destructive that no one and nothing can stop them. We sometimes cannot know how deep-seated someone else's pain is and how little we might do to ameliorate it. When we give suicidal people our support and love, and encourage them to get appropriate professional help, they might still kill themselves if they are truly intent on doing it.

Manny made four suicide attempts in a very short time. He was then treated by a very dedicated psychiatrist who had him admitted to a locked ward in a psychiatric hospital. Although he was under constant observation, he went to his private bathroom one night to "use the toilet." Within seconds, he had locked the door between himself and his guard, and slashed his wrists with razor blades that he had stolen from another patient. By the time the security guards broke down the door, Manny was dead. He was so determined to kill himself that no one and nothing could stop him.

It can take months or years to get over the guilt, anger, helplessness, and sorrow we feel when we lose a friend or relative to suicide. Grieving is easier when we can share memories of the deceased and support each other. By understanding why someone might have wanted to die, we can lay to rest questions that could otherwise haunt us for a long time. Finding any explanations, even if they are only hypotheses, helps us to get over our loss.

Time may not fully heal all wounds, but it does make them less painful. As with any type of mourning, we tend to slowly but surely let go of our attachment to the person as some memories fade. We find ways to go on with our lives and try to feel comforted by the love and support of friends and family.

SUGGESTIONS FOR COPING

A loved one's suicide can be shattering. Share your grief, pain, and anger with others. If this is not enough, write the deceased an imaginary letter expressing your thoughts and feelings. Try to understand why he or she chose to end life.

As our sorrow about someone's suicide wanes, we typically feel angry. Why didn't he see how much there was to live for? Why couldn't she wait for life to get better, as it almost always does? Why did he hurt us so much by dying? Why wasn't our love enough reason for her to want to live? At some point, we have to stop blaming ourselves for the past. We may never fully understand how intolerable a loved one's pain was.

It is not unusual to have anxiety attacks, nightmares, insomnia, crying spells, and the like after a loved one dies. If these symptoms continue for longer than a month, you might want to ask your doctor about medication to reduce your symptoms, or see a therapist.

SUGGESTIONS FOR PREVENTING SUICIDE

Don't worry about "intruding" on people who are obviously distressed. Mention that you are concerned about them and ask if they would like to talk about what's on their mind. Listen and help them feel understood and cared about. If they have problems that need concrete solutions, don't give advice until they have finished expressing their feelings and indicate that they are receptive to suggestions.

Although everyone's life has a purpose, extremely depressed people may not feel that way. Ask if there is anyone or anything that they find meaningful or enjoyable, and encourage them to think about it or get more involved with it. The fact that you value your health, spouse, children, job, and so forth does not mean that others feel the same way about their lives.

Some people who are overwhelmed by despair may feel rebuffed and angry if you tell them that challenges refine their soul. It is useless or even harmful to tell such people that they should have "faith," that God selects only very special people for difficult trials, and similar "religious" platitudes. These statements tend to make some people who are preoccupied by losses and a sense of inadequacy feel even worse than they already do.

If someone believes in God but is contemplating suicide because he doesn't feel "contributory," suggest that his life task might be as a role model to others on how to live with emotional pain. Perhaps his soul needs to develop simply by going through the challenges of suffering, instead of by accomplishing what he once envisioned for himself.

If a depressed person feels truly overwhelmed by his problems, ask him the following:

How does he see the future? Does he think that life will get better? If it doesn't, how will he cope?

Do others know how he feels, and are they keeping a close eye on him?

What has he done to try to solve his problems? Are there available resources that he should be using? If you suggest reasonable options, is he open to hearing them and following up? Is he getting professional help and following recommendations?

Is he contemplating suicide? Does he have concrete plans about how to do it?

The more realistically optimistic someone is about the future, and the better her support system, the less she is at risk for suicide. Someone with actual plans to commit suicide, without a compelling reason not to, needs psychiatric help immediately. Do not leave the person alone.

If someone is suicidal, alert his personal doctor or therapist, if there is one. If he resists getting professional help, reassure him that treatment is confidential, that there is little stigma to having therapy or taking most medications, and that he is likely to feel a lot better if he gets help.[12] In any case, it is better to be alive and in a hospital or seeing a therapist than to be dead.

If you speak to someone who is seriously depressed and you are not sure what to do, call a professional or your local hospital's psychiatric emergency room. Most cities have hotlines for people with emotional problems, with staff trained to help suicidal people. They can advise concerned friends about what to do.

HELPING YOURSELF

If you feel suicidal, get help. Many medications and therapies are available today that can turn your life around. If you have overwhelming legal, financial, or practical problems, call a local hotline or hospital social work department for help and information.

NOTES

1. Although Jewish law theoretically prohibits honoring people who commit suicide, which precludes sitting *shivah* for them, this is rarely followed today. It is usually assumed that suicidal people were not in their right minds prior to death, were under the influence of alcohol or drugs, regretted their actions just prior to dying, and so on. Thus, most Jews who take their lives are treated as if they had died a normal death, and the family sits *shivah* and recites *Kaddish* for them.

2. "The Mystery of Suicide," *Newsweek,* April 18, 1994, p. 48. The statistics quoted in this article were for 1991.

3. Results of Gallup poll reported in "Suicide in Family, Friends Is Familiar to Too Many Teens," *American Psychological Association Monitor,* July 1991, pp. 36–37.

4. Gallup poll, "Suicide in Family," pp. 36–37.

5. Gallup poll, "Suicide in Family," pp. 36–37.

6. Gallup poll, "Suicide in Family," pp. 36–37.

7. *American Medical News,* September 7, 1992, p. 29.

8. Viktor Frankl, *The Unheard Cry for Meaning: Psychotherapy and Humanism* (New York: Simon and Schuster, 1978), p. 29.

9. Gallup poll, "Suicide in Family," pp. 36–37.

10. The highest suicide rates are among senior citizens. See "The Mystery of Suicide," p. 53.

11. Margaret Usdansky, "Silent but Deadly Statistic in Gun Control Debate: Suicide," *USA Today,* April 4, 1994.

In 1991, 2,164 Americans ages ten to nineteen committed suicide, two-thirds of them by using a gun. In that same year, 18,526 of the nation's 38,317 gun deaths were suicides. Households with a gun are five times more likely to be the scene of a suicide than similar homes without one.

12. Current research shows that a significant number of people who commit suicide or who feel suicidal have a deficit of serotonin in their blood (*Newsweek,* April 18, 1994, p. 53). This is often successfully treated with medication or by nutritional and cognitive-behavioral interventions.

FOR FURTHER READING

Goldstein, Sidney. *Suicide in Rabbinic Literature.* Hoboken, NJ: Ktav, 1989.
Styron, William. *Darkness Visible: A Memoir of Madness.* New York: Random House, 1990.
   The author describes his severe depression and suicide attempt.

RESOURCES

Boys Town National Hotline, (800) 448-3000
   For children or parents with problems.
Helpline, (212) 532-2400
Samaritan (Hotline), (212) 673-3000

National Referral Network for Kids in Crisis, Wiley House Treatment Centers, 5300 KidsPeace Drive, Orefield, PA 18069, (800) KID-SAVE

Referrals for thousands of public and private services for children and adolescents throughout the United States, including emergency shelters, mental health services, and counseling for families, sexual abuse, substance abuse, and so on.

Suicide Hotline, (212) 354-4323

These hotlines offer free, 24-hour-a-day telephone help for people who are troubled or are suicidal. They are staffed by trained volunteers and can recommend free, professional help when necessary.

8

Sick and Handicapped Children

"A ll is in the hands of Heaven except for the fear of Heaven."[1]

It breaks our hearts to see children who are seriously ill or handicapped. So many have leukemia, congenital defects, cerebral palsy, epilepsy, diabetes, or autism that we wonder how a loving God can allow this. We have to look beyond what we see and feel in order to find answers.

As was mentioned earlier, every soul has a mission to accomplish, and many people die without fulfilling it. When that happens, the All-Merciful One may bring the unactualized part of the soul back to this world. He then gives it another chance to fulfill its spiritual potential[2] by prescribing experiences that allow the reincarnated soul to directly or indirectly contribute to the world.[3] This type of reincarnation is so common that almost every Jew alive today has been here before.[4]

According to traditional Judaism, ill or handicapped children did nothing wrong to deserve suffering and are not being punished.[5] Rather, God gives them challenges that can best develop their soul's spiritual potential. This may involve giving their parents an opportunity to model faith and fortitude to others, or giving their caretakers a chance to grow from these challenges. When a child has the intellectual wherewithal, he or she might become a role model and/or actively develop spiritually as well.

God predetermines many of our traits and life circumstances in ways that will help actualize our souls. When we are reincarnated because our souls need rectification, we undergo many experiences that aren't of our doing.[6] We can't prevent these events from happening, but we can decide how to respond to them. It may seem "unfair" to have to go through unpleasant circumstances, but this is one way that the Almighty gives us opportunities to create a better afterlife. Instead of being angry about the way this system works, we may as well do our best to work with what our Creator gives us.

This is how Judaism explains most undeserved and incomprehensible suffering, such as congenital handicaps, childhood illnesses, mental retardation, and living in a "vegetative" state.[7] Even if a child lives for only a few moments, its soul can be rectified for shortcomings from a previous life. For instance, if a baby dies when she is a week old, the parents are faced with enormous emotional and spiritual challenges. If they turn to God in their distress, commit themselves to a religious way of life, or become more sensitive to others, the baby has caused them to make spiritual contributions to the world. Her death makes the parents realize how precious and tenuous life is, and they appreciate people, their health, and their material blessings more. The baby's death might also encourage friends and family to comfort the parents, adding to the amount of loving-kindness in the world.

A baby's soul might once have belonged to someone who did not fully appreciate life, or who was insensitive to others. By inspiring others to live more fully, it can earn a greater reward in the World of Souls.

Knowing this may not stop parents from initially being shocked and horrified to discover that their baby is seriously ill or handicapped. It will take time to stop feeling upset over having an "imperfect" child and give up their prior hopes and dreams. Many of them have to work through feelings of personal failure and help their children do the same when they face ridicule or insensitivity later.

When Eve was in the Garden of Eden, God told her that she and her descendants would raise children in sorrow.[8] This can be interpreted to mean that parents will feel pained when their children do not turn out as the parents had hoped. This reminds parents about how little they can do without their Maker's help and encourages them to feel dependent on Him in ways that motivate them to pray for their children's welfare and survival.

When parents believe that their greatest calling is to fulfill God's will, they wonder why they were chosen to help develop each of their children's souls. They are His partners in developing each soul's greatness, even when a child has serious limitations. Any child's special needs become vehicles for the parents' and child's growth.

After ten years of trying to get pregnant, Maureen was told that she could never have children. She adopted two children, whom she loved dearly. Then, at the age of forty-two she found out that she was pregnant. She and her husband were ecstatic and could not wait for their baby to be born. When he was, they were devastated that he had Down's syndrome. They felt angry and bitter that God had played such a terrible trick on them. Still, they hoped that maybe they could get Him to change His mind. Night after night, the parents stood over the baby's crib and prayed for God to fix him. "We know that you can make miracles, God. Make one for us by healing Bobby," they pleaded.

They did this for weeks, until one day, their prayers were answered. God made a miracle for them. Bobby stayed retarded, but they changed. Maureen explained, "If all this happened to me for only one reason, it was worth it. I was nursing Bobby one night, and I stroked his pudgy little hand. I looked at his funny little eyes, and his funny-looking face, and I realized how much I loved him, despite all of his defects. At that moment, I realized how much God could love me, despite all of my defects."

The challenges of raising special children can help parents draw closer to God. They can ask for His support and guidance as they search for the right schools, physical therapists, doctors, and resources. Families can also grow spiritually as they care for and relate to a handicapped sibling.

Parents' attitudes strongly affect how siblings feel about a handicapped brother or sister. If parents view a child's handicaps as opportunities to do extra *mitzvot* (divine commandments) or *chesed* (kind deeds), children are more accepting than when they are given negative messages.

It is hard for parents to adapt to a special child as long as the parents have unrealistic expectations of the child or feel like failures for having the child. When parents feel constantly angry or disappointed, they convey these feelings to their child, as well as to the rest of the family.

Suzanne's son had a severe attention deficit disorder that made it hard for him to learn in a regular class. She could never appreciate him because she felt so angry and guilty that she had given birth to a defective child, which she assumed was a sign of God's punishment. Acknowledging Mark's neurological problems meant admitting her failure as a mother, so she refused to get him help or set appropriate limits with him. He became a sociopathic teenager, which Suzanne felt was her fault. To compound her guilt, she hated him even more for being difficult and frustrating while his easy-going sister lived up to Suzanne's hopes and dreams.

Suzanne's self-worth depended on her having children who lived up to her expectations. Rather than adapt her hopes to what Mark could accomplish, she saw his handicap as an embarrassment and a sign of her own defects. She could find no meaning in raising him.

Parents cannot raise children without recognizing their strengths and accepting their limitations. Parents' attitudes strongly affect how children feel about their handicaps. Parents who love their children with their limitations encourage children to love themselves the same way. When parents constantly feel disappointed and angry about what their children are not, they set the stage for their children to feel inadequate, ashamed, defective, and incompetent.

Appreciating children's strengths and being realistic about their weaknesses helps children live up to their potentials. Some children are sensitive, caring, and compassionate but are not intellectually gifted. Others have a good memory, or are bright, but are crippled, clumsy, or uncoordinated. Some children who can't read can learn well by hearing information, while others can only make sense of written information or sensory stimulation. Parents help their children enormously by working with their assets.

Norman was born with a crippling neuromuscular disease, had serious speech problems, was confined to a wheelchair, and could not write legibly. Instead of focusing on what he couldn't do, his parents taught him to value himself and to do what he could. They urged him to express his opinions, even though listening to him laboriously form words took a lot of patience. They also encouraged him to read and challenged him intellectually.

Norman did not come from a religious family, but he became an observant Jew as a teen. This was partly because his parents had taught him that physical handicaps don't limit one's ability to live meaningfully. At his bar mitzvah, he gave a beautiful speech from his wheelchair, and he has prayed at the same synagogue almost every day, despite the fact that it takes him an hour and a half to get dressed and be taken there.

It is unfortunate that people often assume that having handicaps makes others less important or contributory. For example, we tend to treat people with muscular handicaps as if they are unintelligent or have less to offer than able-bodied people. There is very little relationship between physical integrity and spiritual development. For example, one of Jacob's righteous grandchildren, Chushim, was born deaf,[9] and Rabbi Yosef, a prominent talmudic Sage, was born blind.[10] Some great Torah scholars in past generations were very sickly as children.

By contrast, some of the world's most evil and destructive people were physically strong or intellectually gifted. For instance, it is well-known that a disproportionate number of SS officers during World War II were medical doctors or held doctorates.

While some parents find it hard to see children's strengths, those like Harry find it impossible to accept their limitations. He was a prominent doctor who lived in an upper-class neighborhood. He and his wife sent their son Seth to a private, religious elementary school where he failed second grade. An evaluation showed that Seth had a serious language and learning disorder, and it was recommended that Seth attend a secular remedial school. His parents insisted that Seth stay where he was and continue learning Hebrew with his classmates. Seth could hardly master English and was completely overwhelmed by a second language. His parents' concern with what their friends would think if Seth got remediation kept them from helping him appropriately. Seth was constantly frustrated by having to do work that he couldn't possibly master, and he became angry and aggressive.

By contrast, Zissi and Chaim were a poor, chasidic couple whose daughter was mildly retarded. They wanted to enroll her in a Jewish school for retarded children, but none would take her. So Mimi went to a secular, special education program where she learned basic English, math, social skills, and skills of daily living. Her parents taught her Judaism at home, at her level of understanding. By encouraging her to learn, make friends, and excel in ways that she could, Mimi became a happy, well-adjusted child and young adult. She has finished high school and is now working at a job that allows her to take care of herself.

Dr. Eliezer Goldstock, a psychologist whose daughter has Down's syndrome, founded a support organization for new parents of disabled children. He calls it Heart to Heart: The Jewish Academy for Distinguished Children. He started it to help parents lose their fear about raising disabled children and to convince them of the importance of raising Jewish children in Jewish homes. Presently, some 3,000 American Jewish babies with special needs are abandoned by their parents every year and are adopted by Gentiles.[11]

Heart to Heart dispels myths about special needs children, such as parents' belief that a child's handicaps are God's way of punishing them. Many parents (especially mothers) feel guilty about causing a child's handicaps. While drinking, smoking, using drugs, having rubella, and being exposed to certain chemicals during pregnancy can cause birth defects, 60–80 percent of birth defects happen for unknown reasons. Mothers used to be "blamed" for a child's disabilities, but research is now beginning to link fetal damage to fathers' exposure to environmental toxins and drugs.

Most parents did not cause their child's handicaps (such as autism, Down's syndrome, spina bifida, etc.) and have no reason to feel guilty. Instead, they should ask why God might have designated them to raise a handicapped child. What might He want them to give, and what special qualities can raising that child draw out in them?

Many parents believe that their other children will not accept a handicapped baby in the family. They also worry about what the neighbors will think. Some religious Jews are convinced that having a handicapped child will ruin their other children's chances of getting a decent *shidduch* (marriage introduction), and they abandon their special children.

Heart to Heart enlightens parents about what really causes infants' problems and what are reasonable expectations for a special child. They reassure parents that every child is created in God's image and that He doesn't make mistakes. Every child is here to serve a purpose in His plan for the world.

While some parents are unable to take care of severely disabled children, some see no purpose in raising mildly handicapped children who will not live up to the parents' dreams. Jonathan was a typical example of what a loving, Jewish home can do for a handicapped child. He was abandoned by his parents as an infant, then was shuttled from one foster home to another until he was six years old. Gentiles were about to adopt him when Emily and Greg adopted him at the eleventh hour. They wanted to share their love with a Down's syndrome child and were delighted to have this opportunity to do it.

A few years later, his parents adopted a Jewish newborn with Down's syndrome. Unfortunately, she had a congenital heart defect and died a few months later.[12] Emily and Greg were devastated, but they became even more upset when they found out that Julie's biological parents refused to mourn her as Jewish law requires. The father, a physician, said, "We told all of our friends that the baby died at birth. We are not mourning her. As far as we are concerned, she never existed."

Jonathan was privileged to find an observant Jewish home where loving adoptive parents and siblings are raising him. As a result, he is happy, well adjusted, and spiritually sensitive. Had Emily and Greg not appreciated the importance of raising retarded Jewish children, Jonathan would be going to church and celebrating Christmas.

OBLIGATIONS OF RAISING A JEWISH CHILD

Many observant Jews believe that mentally deficient children and adults are not "real" Jews and need not observe Jewish laws and rituals. Nothing could be further from the truth. The Chazon Ish was one of the greatest Jewish sages of this century. He once stood in the presence of a mentally retarded young man as a sign of respect that was usually accorded to Torah scholars.

He explained his behavior to his disciples: "Most of our souls have been here before, but they came back because they didn't complete what they were sent here to do. Anyone who is so mentally deficient that he can't make many meaningful choices must have a great soul that doesn't require much more refining. I stood in that boy's presence because his soul must have nearly accomplished everything that it was intended to do in a previous lifetime. If so, his soul must have belonged to a truly great person."[13]

Parents of mentally handicapped children are responsible for preserving the holiness of the souls entrusted to them. If they do not feel equipped to raise a child themselves, they should make sure that he is raised in a Jewish home, eats only kosher food, and lives in a religious environment.

Most mildly, and even moderately, retarded children are intelligent enough to perform many positive commandments. They compensate for their lack of understanding by the excitement and zeal they express in serving their Creator.

A religious man with Down's syndrome looked forward to the Sabbath and Jewish holidays after doing manual labor all week. He lived with relatives who enabled him to share in the *mitzvah* of welcoming guests and serving them food on the Sabbath and holidays. He recited appropriate blessings before and after eating, gave charity with delight, and enjoyed the *mitzvot* of the holidays. He even learned Torah in his social group for developmentally disabled Jews and related some of these ideas at the Sabbath table.

Retarded children should be encouraged to do as many positive commandments as they can and should be prevented from transgressing as many negative commandments as possible. For example, Jonathan's parents take him to the synagogue every Sabbath. He sits quietly (which is often not the case with the adults) until he joins his peers in leading the congregational singing of the concluding prayers. When the weather is too inclement for him to walk the mile and a half to the synagogue, he feels terribly disappointed.

After services, while the congregation is busy eating cake and gefilte fish, his father makes *Kiddush* (sanctifying the day) over a cup of grape juice, and Jonathan repeats each word. When they get home, Jonathan ritually washes his hands and recites the blessings over the handwashing and over eating bread. At the end of the meal, he distributes songbooks to the guests and announces the page on which the grace after meals can be found. He never leaves the table before saying an abridged version of grace and thanking God for his good fortune.

Morris was also retarded and was an excellent caretaker of a synagogue. He took tremendous (and well-deserved) pride in how nicely he kept the facilities and set up tables, chairs, and refreshments for synagogue functions. He welcomed visitors to the synagogue graciously and warmly, and they usually had little idea that he was retarded.

Both Jonathan's and Morris's parents focused on what their sons could do and played to their strengths. They showered them with love and encouragement, structure and loving discipline. They also engineered their sons' lives so that they had frequent opportunities to feel successful, take pride in their accomplishments, and develop self-esteem.

Most Down's syndrome children are exceptionally affectionate, even though they are intellectually limited. They return the love their parents give them many times over. If they are healthy enough to reach adulthood, they can usually be self-sufficient with a minimum of supervision and help.

COPING

Some handicaps are emotionally or physically challenging, while others are potentially lethal. The medical ordeals and expenses that some parents shoulder are simply overwhelming. Some mothers spend three to four hours a day helping clear mucus from their child's lungs. Some parents shuttle their children back and forth for medical treatments for leukemia or other cancers over a period of many months. Some parents visit their children in the hospital for weeks on end as the children have surgery to repair congenital defects, get treatments for infections, and have batteries of diagnostic tests. Meanwhile, these parents wonder how many more surgeries, painful treatments and tests, hospitalizations, and trips for emergency care their child will need. They hope for a brighter future, yet fear that each respite will end in disaster. They can only take one nerve-racking day at a time and can never plan for the future.

Ronna and Jeff had a very premature baby with multiple handicaps. When their blind baby came home from the hospital, he needed to be carefully fed so that he didn't choke to death. He stopped breathing at least once a week, and Ronna had to shake him to get him breathing again. She could not leave him with a caretaker and was exhausted from spending six to eight hours a day simply feeding him and trying to develop his limp muscles.

Ronna and Jeff consulted many specialists in the hope that something could be done to help the baby. They spent thousands of dollars on medical expenses and hundreds of hours reading magazines and books to get practical advice. Shifts of friends helped the baby do special exercises every week, but despite their intensive efforts, the baby died after two years of painstaking care. He never matured beyond the capacities of a two-month-old.

The traumas and day-to-day challenges of caring for children with special needs leave many families physically, emotionally, and financially depleted. Parents with additional children may not have the time or energy to give everyone the attention they need, and they end up feeling guilty and inadequate. Some parents do the best they can, yet always feel that they are shortchanging somebody, including themselves. It is hard to feel like a good parent when doing one's best never feels like it is enough.

Parents of handicapped children need to feel that their efforts are building something meaningful. When children are so sick that they never get better and constantly suffer, or are so limited that they can't even smile, life can feel unbearable.

The stress of raising some special needs children is compounded by the unpredictability of daily life. Parents may never know when a child will be out of control, regress, or need emergency care. Some parents are faced with frequent, unpleasant surprises, or one setback after another. If they could only feel that some part of their life was gratifying, it would be a lot easier to deal with those parts that aren't.

Parents usually feel better if they can adjust their expectations to accommodate their child's needs. When the unknown becomes more familiar, predictable, and manageable, parents feel less anxious and can enjoy difficult children more. Having a routine or structure makes life easier for some, while living one day at a time gives others the fortitude to keep going.

We can be moved and inspired by how some people come to terms with painful and severe handicaps. Their challenges can motivate us to thank God for the daily gifts that we tend to take for granted, such as being able to see, walk, hear, button a shirt, tie our shoes, and dress ourselves. Few able-bodied people can imagine the challenges that some handicapped people face, such as spending thirty to ninety minutes just getting dressed and/or bathing every day. Traveling even a few blocks, especially by public transportation in bad weather, can be a nightmare. Falling down or getting cut or bruised is potentially life threatening for some children and adults.

Jerry grew up with a terrible neuromuscular disease. His mind was intact, but his gnarled, wriggling body was confined to a wheelchair. People didn't like to talk to him because his slurred speech was barely comprehensible. His various disabilities made it impossible for him to find paid employment, so he spent his adult life as a volunteer for an information booth at a hospital.

This gave him a sense of satisfaction, yet he often felt bad that he couldn't do kind deeds for others and did not have enough income to give money to charity.

Since he had not been fortunate enough to marry and raise a family, he was also precluded from that kind of happiness.

One day, he poignantly asked why God had made him so debilitated. His rabbi replied that no one knew why God had chosen him to be so physically challenged, but he had important spiritual contributions to make to the world nevertheless. Perhaps the Almighty wanted him to show others that they could be religious even if their lives were extremely difficult.

That answer helped him. He took comfort in the idea that he was a role model of how to believe in God even when He makes life harsh. He inspired Jews who would not have been moved by the faith of those who had easy lives.

One day, while Jerry wrestled with feelings of inadequacy, a visitor to his hospital had a heart attack, and Jerry summoned doctors who saved the man's life. Jerry understood from this incident that he could help save people's physical lives as well as inspire them to enhance their spirituality.

In retrospect, many handicapped people and their families believe that their challenges led to tremendous growth. For example, Shana had a dozen operations by the time she was a teenager and spent more time inside hospitals than out of them. She developed a vivacious and optimistic personality in reaction to her depressing circumstances. When she was twenty, she went to graduate school, knowing that she might be confined to a wheelchair by the time she finished her doctorate. Her chronic pain and progressive deterioration made her appreciate how precious time was, and she tried to use every minute productively. She finished her Ph.D. just as she could no longer walk, and she put her career on hold while she raised a family. She figured that it was better to have children while she was young and energetic than when she was older. Her optimism was a gift that she gave to her children, and she taught them to appreciate the preciousness of every day as a result of her challenges.

Her mother was instrumental in helping Shana cope so beautifully. As Shana said, "From the time that I was very little, my mother told me how special I was. But when I was old enough to go to school, other kids made fun of me and called me a cripple. When I'd tell my mother, she just picked me up, gave me a big hug and a smile, and told me that they were jealous. She told me that she and I had a secret—that I would always get more attention than other kids because God made me different. And I believed her!

"By the way, don't think that life was easy for me or my mother. I had five brothers, we didn't have much money, and my operations and hospitalizations kept us impoverished. It would have been easy to feel angry about what we went through, but we didn't waste a lot of energy on that. I was originally supposed to have only two operations for a congenital defect, but the surgeons botched the second one. Then I needed many more operations to repair the damage from each previous surgery. Eventually, I had a dozen operations, I was hospitalized or in bed for much of my life, and my parents paid hundreds of thousands of dollars for medical, surgical, and hospital bills.

"That probably would have ruined some people, but not us. No matter what happened, my mother had a wonderful attitude. She never pitied herself or let me pity myself. She lived up to her belief that if God gave us challenges, He also gave us the ability to cope with them. Instead of thinking of my handicap as a liability, she taught me that it was something that made me special. She had high but realistic expectations for me and never stressed my physical or intellectual limitations. She encouraged me to try everything that I wanted, and if I didn't succeed, we sat down together and tried to figure out another approach that might work better. She taught me to set goals for myself and go after them, and to want what able-bodied people want."

Although Shana's mother coped without outside help, most families find that support and information from resource organizations, support groups, caring friends, and health professionals are very important. Raising handicapped children is easier when parents can share their feelings, struggles, and innovative ideas, and support groups offer a good format for doing this.

Most parents of handicapped children need opportunities to recharge their physical and emotional batteries. Some parents find volunteer or low-cost helpers by putting up advertisements on synagogue bulletin boards or by contacting charitable organizations for help. Networking can also enlist volunteers.

When parents realize that there are no support groups or resource organizations to help them deal with their child's handicap, they use their challenge to help others. For instance, mothers in various cities without Jewish schools for their learning disabled children founded them. A mother of two multiply handicapped children started an organization that teaches special needs children and helps the parents by sending volunteers to periodically baby-sit. These weekend helpers give exhausted parents a break from their intense, round-the-clock care.

Thankfully, people are becoming more sensitive to the needs of handicapped children and their parents, but much more needs to be done. Organizations for the handicapped have improved the lives of millions, but a great deal of prejudice and patronizing persists. People think that mentally retarded people don't have feelings and that physically handicapped people have neither feelings nor intelligence!

Lori was beautiful, bright, and talented but had meningitis as a child. She was severely disabled for a year, but rehabilitation helped so that she had only a slight limp and mildly slurred speech. She became an honors student in college and completed a master's degree before becoming a supervisor at a challenging job. Despite her academic and vocational achievements, religious people looked down on her. Matchmakers and "friends" introduced her only to retarded or handicapped men. Instead of seeing her as a sensitive, talented, bright woman who happened to walk slowly, she was perceived as nothing more than a freakish disability.

Sadly, prejudice about handicapped people is rampant among even educated people, as Abby found out the hard way when she was twenty and single. She contracted polio as a child and was largely confined to a wheelchair. Concerned that her disability would make it hard to conceive and have a healthy pregnancy, she asked her gynecologist, "Will I be able to have children?"

The doctor looked at her incredulously and responded, "What makes you think that anyone would even want to marry you?"

A few years later, she was happily married with two healthy children.

RECOMMENDATIONS FOR PARENTS

A child's handicaps affect the entire family, so parents need to consider how to divide their time and energy so that each person gets what he or she needs. When it can be done safely, involve family members in helping a handicapped sibling. Caring for others is a shared responsibility that helps children learn to love, give to, and be concerned about others. Don't disenfranchise them by conveying the attitude that it is a burden to help a brother or sister.

Try to treat physically handicapped children as normally as possible. Develop their strengths, help them work around their limitations, and give them structure and discipline, just as you would other children. Having handicaps doesn't mean that children don't need limits. Parents who feel guilty may overindulge handicapped children, making them feel crippled. Setting healthy limits and boundaries makes them feel responsible, safe, and protected.

Find ways to replenish your emotional and physical batteries. Be realistic about how much time and energy you can, or need to, give a handicapped or sick child. It is common for parents to expend so much energy on their children that their marriages suffer. Try not to let this happen to you. Pay for additional help if you need it, and look for volunteer help if you can't afford paid help.

Share your feelings, and get support and information to help you deal with your special child's condition. Consider starting an organization in your area if adequate resources aren't available.

Ask God for the strength to keep on going. Thank Him when He gives you easy days and appreciate it when He helps you through difficult ones. Share your feelings with Him even when you are angry, frustrated, or hurt, and ask Him to help you find meaning in the challenges that He gives you.

SUGGESTIONS FOR HELPING OTHERS

Don't judge those who are handicapped or who have handicapped children. Some religious people retain lots of myths about special needs children. For example, they think that Down's syndrome is inherited, that retarded people tend to be violent, that handicapped people are not real human beings, or that handicaps are God's way of punishing children or their parents for sinning. These ideas are foreign to Judaism.

It is rare that retardation is inherited. Siblings of most retarded persons have the same chance of giving birth to retarded children as anyone else. Retarded people are not usually unruly or aggressive, unless they are not properly cared for or have a coexisting medical or psychiatric problem. Retarded people are typically less violent than others, not more.

There is no reason to assume that families with handicapped children are being punished. Very pious parents have handicapped children, just as less righteous people do. Instead of being judgmental, we should be exquisitely sensitive never to embarrass or hurt handicapped children or their families. Many of them live up to challenges that we could not.

Not all handicapped children or their parents feel that their disabilities are a "problem," and some rightfully resent people seeing nothing more than their handicaps. It is dehumanizing to summarize the totality of another person as nothing more than "disabled," "retarded," or "crippled." We stop treating people with dignity when we do that.

If a handicapped person needs assistance, ask how you can help instead of assuming that you know what the person wants or needs. For instance, it can be terrifying when an able-bodied person "helps" someone in a wheelchair without knowing how to do it. It is not uncommon for well-meaning "helpers" to injure the person by pitching them out of the wheelchair and onto the ground.

Most people with disabilities want to feel accomplished, to love and be loved, marry, and raise children. They have the same basic desires, feelings, and dreams that able-bodied people have, and most of them achieve similar goals in spite of their limitations.

Most well-intentioned people tend to infantilize handicapped people, such as by ignoring them and talking to their companions. The same thing happens when people pet a guide dog and ignore the blind owner. We tend to act as if blind people can't hear, or as if people who are hard-of-hearing or deaf have no intelligence. These are but a few common situations where able-bodied people lack sensitivity to handicapped ones. We should treat everyone with respect and consideration, regardless of their physical or intellectual limitations.

HELPING THE FAMILY

Most parents whose children require intensive care need periodic relief from their time-consuming and exhausting tasks. One or two volunteers a morning or afternoon every week can give parents a tremendous boost by helping to clean, cook, or baby-sit. Offering to take care of some or all of the children periodically can give parents some badly needed time for themselves. Help out by preparing and delivering extra food to your friends when you cook for your family. Shop or run errands for both families at once. People who can't personally help can encourage their children to do so for an hour or two every week as a *chesed* (kindness) project.

When a child needs hospital care, offer to baby-sit or prepare meals for the rest of the family. This lets parents tend to their hospitalized child without worrying about their other children.

Most people would like to feel like more than "parents of a handicapped child." Invite them for a night out or for a relaxing outing. Sometimes friends can be most helpful by allowing parents to forget their problems for a few hours while they enjoy a "normal" meal, conversation, or evening together. Try to put yourself in someone else's shoes, and do for them what you would like done for you.

NOTES

1. *Brachot* 33b.
2. Moshe Chaim Luzzatto, *The Way of God* (New York: Feldheim, 1983) 2:3:10. See also footnote 39 there. When a person's soul could have grown to a point that we will arbitrarily call "100," and it grew only to "60," God might reincarnate the remaining 40 "parts" into a second person. Since souls are totally spiritual, a fraction of a soul can be a whole entity. When the body and soul are eventually resurrected, the 60 soul "parts" will return to the first body, and the remaining 40 will rejoin the second body. Whichever soul was in a given body will be rejoined to it when they are resurrected.

God challenges us to develop whatever soul potential we are given. Even if "80 percent" of a soul's potential was developed in one lifetime, it may be hard to develop the remaining 20 percent.

3. *The Way of God* 2:3:10. See *Zohar* I:186b; I:94a; 3:215a. Souls normally come back in a human body, but they can also return in other forms of life. For example, they can be reincarnated as edible plants, but it is preferable to come back as a person rather than as a provision for people. *Shnei Luchot HaBrit* on *Parshat Ki Tetze* explains that souls are reincarnated two or three times as people. If they fail to rectify whatever they were sent here to do, they are sent back as a kosher animal. If they again fail to rectify what was needed, they come back as a nonkosher animal.

4. *The Way of God,* part 2, footnote 39.
5. God punishes children in this world for their misdeeds only once they are twenty years old. See Aryeh Kaplan, *Handbook of Jewish Thought,* vol. 2 (New York: Moznaim, 1992), p. 178.
6. *The Way of God* 2:3:10.
7. See *Shvilei Emunah* 9 (86b); *Nishmas Chaim* 4:11, sec. 3; *Shaar HaGilgulim* 28, *Tiferes Israel* (Maharal) 63.
8. Genesis 3:16.
9. *Sotah* 13a.
10. *Kiddushin* 31a.
11. *L'Chaim,* July 31, 1992, p. 2.
12. Forty percent of Down's children have heart problems, and they get leukemia twenty times more often than other children do. T. R. Harrison, ed., *Principles of Internal Medicine,* 8th ed. (New York: McGraw-Hill, 1977), pp. 1220, 1223, 1768.
13. Recounted in *The Jewish Women's Journal,* February 1993, p. 17.

RESOURCES

American Association of Kidney Patients, 1 Davis Blvd., Suite LL1, Tampa, FL, (813) 251-0725

Association for the Help of Retarded Children, 200 Park Avenue, New York, NY, (212) 254-8203

Board of Jewish Education, Special Education Center, 426 West 58th Street, New York, NY 10019, (212) 245-8200 ext. 385

Cystic Fibrosis Foundation, 60 East 42 Street, New York, NY, (212) 986-8783

Diabetes America in New York, 505 Eighth Avenue, New York, NY, (212) 947-9707

Diabetes Care and Information Center of New York, 138-26 58 Avenue, Flushing, NY, (718) 762-7973

Dyslexia International, (800) 222-3123

Epilepsy Foundation of America, (800) EFA-1000
Information and referral service for epileptics, their families, and the public. There is also a training program and placement service (TAPS) in thirteen cities and services for epileptics and their families.

Heart to Heart, 22 Rita Avenue, Monsey, NY 10952, (914) 356-6204 or (914) 356-6206
Resource center for parents of Jewish children with Down's syndrome and other special needs. Provides information about resources available throughout North America, and loans equipment and toys to special needs children free of charge. There are branches in Los Angeles and Toronto.

Help a Special Child, 1311 55th Street, Brooklyn, NY 11219, (718) 851-6100
Preschool and elementary school, workshop and day treatment for developmentally disabled Jewish Children.

Jewish Center for Special Education ("Chush"), 430 Kent Avenue, Brooklyn, NY 11211, (718) 782-0064
Education for learning disabled and speech-impaired Jewish children of normal intelligence. There are similar programs in Montreal, London, Cleveland, and Cincinnati.

March of Dimes, 233 Park Avenue South, New York, NY, (212) 353-8353

March of Dimes Birth Defects Foundation, National Headquarters, 1275 Mamaroneck Avenue, White Plains, NY, (914) 428-7100

National Association for Parents of the Visually Impaired, (800) 562-6265

National Association for the Visually Handicapped, 22 W. 21 Street, New York, NY, (212) 889-3141

National Down Syndrome Society, 666 Broadway, New York, NY, 10012, (800) 221-4602

National Foundation for Jewish Genetic Diseases, 45 Sutton Place South, New York, NY, (212) 371-1030

National Institute for Controlled Epilepsy, (800) 328-3634

National Jewish Center for Immunology and Respiratory Medicine, (800) 222-5864

National Kidney Foundation, (800) 542-4001

National Multiple Sclerosis Hotline, (800) 227-3166

National Multiple Sclerosis Society, (800) 233-7617

Ohel Children's Home and Family Service, 4510 16th Avenue, Brooklyn, NY 11204, (718) 851-6300
Group homes, foster care, and family therapy for retarded Jewish children.

Otsar, 2324 West 13th Street, Brooklyn, NY 11223, (718) 946-7301
Family support services for the retarded and developmentally disabled. Offers evaluations and respite services, preschool and young adult services.

Our Way, 333 Seventh Avenue, New York, NY 10001, (212) 563-4000 (ext. 234)
Social and religious program for Jewish deaf adolescents and young adults.

P'tach–Chaim Berlin High School, 1593 Coney Island Avenue, Brooklyn, NY, (718) 252-3761
School for learning disabled religious Jewish children.

P'tach–Darchei Torah, 257 Beach 17 Street, Far Rockaway, NY, (718) 327-3411

Retarded Infants Services Inc., 386 Park Avenue South, New York, NY, (212) 889-5464

Special Academy for Girls, 1666 51st Street, Brooklyn, NY 11204, (718) 871-1400
Religious school for Jewish girls with learning disabilities. Offers vocational training as well.

Tikvah Layeled–Foundation for Cerebral Palsied Children, 32 Yosef Karo Street, P.O. Box 50044, Jersualem; New York Office: 114-120 Forrest Street, Brooklyn, NY 11206, (718) 596-9755

Tourette Syndrome Association, 42-40 Bell Boulevard, Bayside, NY 11361, (718) 224-2999
Provides literature, support, and information to families of children with Tourette Syndrome.

United Cerebral Palsy Association of New York State, 2324 Forest Avenue, Staten Island, NY, (718) 447-8205; 330 West 34 Street, New York, NY, (212) 947-5770

United Federation of Teachers, 260 Park Avenue South, New York, NY, (212) 777-7500
Can give referrals for secular special education.

World Federation of Hemophilia, 1450 City Councillors Street, STE.830, Montreal, Quebec, Canada H3A 2E6, (514) 848-0315

Yachad, 333 Seventh Avenue, New York, NY 10001, (212) 563-4000 (Ext. 224)
Social and religious programs for Jewish developmentally disabled adolescents and young adults.

9

Coping with Terminal Illness

Our greatest fear about dying is thinking that it is a total separation from our loved ones and the end of our existence. People who know that there is an afterlife where they will meet their loved ones and God are not afraid of death.

Modern physicians such as Elisabeth Kübler-Ross, Melvin Morse, and Raymond Moody have documented countless stories of people who have had near-death experiences (NDEs). NDEers' souls have journeyed into the afterlife, then returned to life here. Not only aren't they afraid to die, they affirm for us that there is a spiritual world beyond.

A 1982 Gallup poll revealed that eight million adult Americans (at least one in twenty) had had near-death experiences (NDEs).[1] NDEs occur after people die suddenly from heart attacks, car or drowning accidents, head trauma, and the like. The person's death is documented by electrocardiogram, lack of brain waves, and loss of vital signs, yet the person comes back to life minutes or hours later.

Although NDEers don't all have exactly the same experience, they typically go through at least some of the following:[2] They feel their souls separate from and hover over their bodies as they watch everything happening to and around them. They initially feel disoriented as they view their lifeless body and the people who are trying to rescue them. They may also see people who are further away, such as relatives in a waiting room or a nurse getting medication down the hallway, as well as machinery that is being used to revive them that is out of their field of vision. When people try to resuscitate them, their souls don't want to return to their bodies. They are happy and peaceful outside their bodies and have no desire to return to the physical world.

Their souls feel utter joy, bliss, and serenity as they travel through a dark tunnel or climb a staircase toward a brilliant light. They enter a world of beauty where the souls of deceased friends, relatives, or religious figures greet them. They feel indescribable pleasure and happiness in this spiritual world where everything is bathed in love and intense vibrancy. They meet a supreme, holy Being of Light who radiates love and total understanding. Once they meet it, their souls want to be with it forever. Time and space cease to exist, and they know that they are confronting eternity.

The Being takes many adults through a life review, showing them everything that they did. Meanwhile, they feel the effects of each of their actions on others.[3] They realize that love and knowledge are two of the most important things that there are.[4]

At some point, the Supreme Being, or the souls that greet the new arrival, explain that it is not yet time for it to stay there. It perceives a barrier between itself and the world beyond. Once that barrier is crossed, it knows that it can no longer return to the physical world. It is either given a choice or told that it must return to its body. Even though NDEers don't want to return, they go back to their bodies anyway. The instant the soul reenters the body, the corpse revives.

People who have had these experiences no longer fear death. They know that they have an eternal soul and a task to fulfill on earth before returning to a world of indescribable goodness.

These modern reports are very consistent with Jewish beliefs about the soul and the afterlife. For example, Judaism symbolically portrays the afterlife as a place where "the righteous sit with crowns on their heads, basking in the glow of the Divine Presence."[5] This is analogous to the light of the Supreme Being that NDEers report.

As NDEers discover, God loves us profoundly and wants us to love His children as if we are all part of one entity.[6] They find out that our every act here has consequences and that we can't hurt God's other children without hurting ourselves.[7] Judaism expresses these same concepts, emphasizing our collective responsibility for one another and the fact that all Jews form one unit. Whenever we hurt another Jew, we hurt ourselves. We do not exist separately from one another.

Judaism teaches that no deeds are ever forgotten and we will suffer negative or positive consequences according to what we do. "The fire of hell" is the shame that a soul feels when it reexperiences its misdeeds, and heaven is the bliss, goodness, and attachment to God that it feels for its good deeds.[8]

NDEers also report that they can take knowledge with them in the afterlife.[9] The type of knowledge that nourishes Jews after death is Torah knowledge. The more we learn it here, the more eternal bliss we will feel studying it and gaining insight into its depths in the next world.

The initial disorientation that NDEers' souls experience when they separate from the body[10] is also discussed in ancient Jewish sources.[11]

Our Sages told us that even though we will die, our souls whisper to us that a spiritual part of us will live forever.[12] This keeps us from becoming immobilized by a sense of futility about life.

Judaism teaches that every soul has senses that allow it to perceive goings-on beyond itself.[13] This is why we are forbidden to observe Jewish precepts, such as studying Torah, in the presence of a corpse. It pains the deceased's soul to see someone observing God's commandments when it no longer can do so. Souls not only see and know what is going on nearby, they even have feelings about it![14]

Our tradition tells us that no one leaves this world without first seeing the "face of God."[15] At the very least, God manifests Himself to us just as our lives end to ease the pain of passing from this world to the next. Death is merely a transition between two stages of existence. When we die, we take off our soul's physical garment (the body) and replace it with a spiritual one (often described as "light"). Who could be a better escort to a higher realm than the Almighty Himself? He personally accompanies each soul to a higher level of existence.

When we go to the next world, each soul confronts the souls of deceased relatives who question it about how moral a life it led while on earth.[16] At least one-third of dying people also see and greet the souls of deceased relatives in the moments, hours, or days before they expire.[17] It is very common for people who are gravely ill to see and talk to the souls of their deceased spouses, parents, grandparents, or children. Unfortunately, doctors and psychologists commonly misattribute this to hallucinations, which they are not.

People who are skeptical regarding Jewish teachings about the soul and the afterlife now have millions of modern descriptions that lend credence to our ideas.[18]

God also made the physical world in a way that it would give us hints about the afterlife. For example, matter can never be destroyed. It can change form or break down into elements, but it can never "disappear." It stands to reason that our inner spiritual force will also live forever.

Nature gives us other hints about the afterlife. For example, a seed sprouts with new life and releases its inner essence only after its outer shell first decomposes. This helps us understand how death breaks our body's shell and allows our true essence (our soul) to emerge.

Imagine growing up in a tropical country, then living through your first winter in a northern country. You would not know that seasons change. You would watch animals become sluggish and hibernate. The greenery would disappear. Everything, including insects, plants, and trees would seem to die permanently. Then you'd wake up one morning and the air would feel warmer. You'd notice blossoms budding on the trees. A few weeks later you'd realize that what you thought was dead was simply in a temporary state of dormancy. The trees and plants that looked dead were simply preparing to thrive with even greater vigor and beauty than before.

We thank God for giving us a sign of the afterlife and resurrection when we see fruit trees' first blossoms in the spring. When we see them coming to life after months of apparent death, we say, "Blessed are You, God, Ruler of the Universe, who did not leave anything out of His world, and created in it good creatures and good trees so that humanity could enjoy them."[19] The Almighty gave us reminders through nature that life and death come in cycles, with life following death.

The caterpillar gives us the same message. It lives for only a few weeks, then spins a cocoon and seems to die. Inside the cocoon is a decomposed creature, but a beautiful, vibrant butterfly soon emerges.

God made life this way to communicate that nothing dies forever. He created nature's life and death cycles and seasons to teach us that physical death and rebirth mirror a spiritual dormancy and rebirth. This keeps us from thinking that death ends our existence. Instead, it marks our transition to a more wonderful life beyond.[20]

FINDING MEANING IN TERMINAL ILLNESS

When we die, our souls go from a physical world to a spiritual one. The less attached we are to a body and to material pleasure, the easier that transition is. Suffering helps detach our soul from the physical world and makes sure that many years of accumulated spiritual toxins don't destroy our essence. That leaves death something to cleanse and bring back to health when we leave this world.

Terminal illnesses can metaphysically prepare our souls to go to the next world. The body's gradual loss of functions and detachment from material and sensual pleasures prepare the soul to enter a wholly spiritual realm. As painful as this deterioration and detachment is, it is better for the soul to go through it here rather than in the next world.

This is one reason why some people become senile or comatose before they die. Losing consciousness is a transition between life and death that causes the soul's detachment from the body. By the time the person dies, the soul has already disconnected from the physical world to a large degree.

People who are terminally ill can hope for God's salvation while preparing for death. They can set their affairs in order and come to terms with unfulfilled dreams and regrets. They can feel good about their meaningful relationships and achievements, make peace with family and friends, ask for forgiveness and repent. Ironically, it is only when many people know they will die that they start living life to the fullest and appreciate the time that they have.

Stephen Hawking was extraordinarily brilliant, yet he was not a very good student. While he was at Oxford, he studied a scant half hour a day and was in danger of failing because he did not apply himself to his work. Soon after he started a doctoral program at Cambridge, he was diagnosed with amyotrophic lateral sclerosis (Lou Gehrig's disease). His doctor told him that he had, at most, two-and-a-half years to live. During that time, his body would steadily deteriorate until he would only be able to move his eyelids, yet his mind would remain intact.

Spurred on by his death sentence, he decided to get serious about living. He got engaged and started to work on a doctorate in physics. He became the Einstein of this generation as he made important discoveries that revolutionized the way scientists understand the universe. The more his body deteriorated, the more he developed novel tools to conceptualize physics in spatial and pictorial terms, rather than in conventional ways. He lost one set of tools along with his ability to write and speak, but this encouraged him to develop another set of tools that no one else had ever thought of. Twenty-two years later, Hawking is still alive and busy revolutionizing the field of physics. All of this despite the fact that he has only minimal use of one hand, with which he presses a computer mouse. The rest of his body is basically immobile.[21]

This is but one example of how people begin to appreciate life only when they are about to lose it. Terminally ill people can achieve in a brief time what others may never do in a lifetime of greater comfort. They do this spiritually by repenting, praying, giving charity, improving themselves, and growing closer to God.

Rebecca became a religious Jew in her twenties and married soon afterward. Her dreadful marriage ended in divorce and she became totally responsible for her two children. Several lonely and difficult years passed, but then she met and married a wonderful man. Soon after they celebrated their first anniversary, Rebecca found herself getting short of breath and was always tired. A series of tests showed that her heart was seriously damaged, and her only hope of recovery was a heart transplant. Despite her prayers and those of her family, no donor was found. She had every reason to be angry with God and bitter, but she was neither. She spent her remaining days growing closer to her Creator, her husband, and her children. She died at the age of forty-two.

Terminal illness not only affects the dying, it also gives survivors a chance to grow. For instance, people who take care of someone who is ill do kind acts that help support the world.[22]

Terminal illness can also be a blessing for survivors who would be terribly shocked if a perfectly healthy loved one dropped dead without warning. Instead, survivors are likely to feel relieved by the time someone dies after a long deterioration.

For example, Estelle became progressively debilitated when her excruciating arthritis prevented her from walking more than a block or two. Although she had been very independent, she had no choice but to rely on others to take her places. When her eyesight failed, she had to give up playing the piano, reading, writing letters, and doing crossword puzzles. Next she lost her sense of taste and, with it, the pleasure of eating. After ten years of slow deterioration, she had two heart attacks and her kidneys stopped working. She felt that she had lived a productive life and was ready to return to her Maker once her daily life became so ungratifying. When she finally died after being in a coma for several weeks, her survivors were ready to accept that it was time for her to leave this world.

Our Sages wanted to convey the idea that God intended aging and illness to be good. They did this by saying that our forefather Abraham prayed for people to develop signs of maturity as they grow old so that others would know whom to respect. God responded by making Abraham's hair turn gray.[23] Isaac prayed for people to suffer in this world so that they would receive greater merit in the World-to-Come.[24] God likewise agreed to his request and responded by making Isaac's eyes dim as he grew older.[25] Jacob prayed that people should not die suddenly so that they would have time to repent and prepare themselves to leave this world. God consented to this, also.[26] King Hezekiah asked the Almighty to send people severe illnesses that weren't necessarily fatal so that they would repent, and God also granted his request.[27]

Given the choice, people would probably like to stay young forever and die suddenly rather than age and have lingering illnesses. These midrashic stories remind us that aging and illness have constructive purposes; they don't only wreak havoc on us. If we contemplate their messages, they can encourage us to review our lives and live meaningfully. They can encourage us to apologize and make amends to those whom we have hurt before it is too late. They can also motivate us to put our affairs in order, give a spiritual testament to children, say goodbye to family and friends, and draw up a will.[28]

Terminal illness also gives survivors time to prepare for a loved one's death. A quick death may sometimes seem like a blessing, but at other times it devastates survivors. For instance, Sam was fifty years old when he died of a sudden heart attack. His widow, Marie, and their two teenage daughters were in a state of shock for weeks.

The reality of his passing didn't set in for a long time. Apart from the indescribable pain of losing a husband and father, they couldn't put "closure" on his death because they didn't have a chance to say goodbye to him. They felt guilty about many things that they had said or done but had no way to redress them.

To add insult to injury, Sam left his family in a financial mess. He had no life insurance or will because he assumed that he would not die for years. Marie was stuck having to pay for a mortgage on the house and a sizable car loan. Not only was she completely in the dark about his financial affairs, she received bills for thousands of dollars that she couldn't pay. Sam had always managed their finances and she didn't even know where to get the money to pay for his funeral. She was on the brink of bankruptcy by the time she began to straighten out their finances. She ended up taking a menial job because she had no marketable skills after being a housewife for twenty years. It was two years before she emerged from the mess that Sam's unexpected death caused.

Philosophical explanations about the benefits of illness are nice, but they don't mean much when we face someone who's dying. It is hard to emotionally reconcile ourselves to a loving God when He is causing us, or someone we love, terrible suffering. The effects of a terminal illness can make us feel that God is absent or uncaring. Because our emotions limit what we can intellectually understand about suffering, it is hard to feel that a tragedy is meaningful while we are in the thick of it.

I experienced this when I was asked to visit a sixty-six-year-old man who was dying of cancer. I had never before seen a dying person, and it was horribly shocking. Mr. Silber's body was ghostly pale and his face was barely distinguishable from his bedsheets. His cheeks were sunken, his fine, white hair was clumped in erratic patches, and his mouth was shriveled. His arms were mottled with black and blue bruises, and hanging bags of murky liquids dripped chemicals through plastic tubes into his forearms. His arms and legs were reduced to flesh-covered bones. His breathing was labored and his chest rattled every time he exhaled. When he opened his once-blue eyes, they were gray and filled with terror.

I timidly stood at the foot of his bed, paralyzed by anxiety. Before I could sneak out unnoticed and steel myself to speak with him, he caught sight of me.

"Doctor," he pleaded weakly, "please give me enough drugs to kill me. I'm ready to die. I don't want to go on like this anymore."

At that moment, all of my religious convictions flew out the window. I was overcome by a panoply of emotions—horror, anger, disgust, sadness, anxiety, and helplessness. I was totally unprepared for my emotional reactions to this near-corpse. Inner screams battled with my intellect. I had learned that man was made in the image of God. Where was His image in this dying skeleton? The Bible says that God is merciful. Where in this tortured human being was a sign of His mercy?

God wasn't supposed to do this to people. He was supposed to be kind, caring, and healing, not a Being who tortured people and made them waste away. As long as this horror confronted me, I could not be soothed or comforted by any explanations of suffering. Had anyone tried to give me rational ideas, I would have dismissed them immediately.

This is a dramatic example of how our overwhelming emotions can block us from receiving information. Intellectual explanations are useless when we are steeped in emotional turmoil. At those times, we need a loving embrace to comfort and soothe us, and caring friends or family to help us feel that we are not alone.

PSYCHOLOGICAL AND SPIRITUAL WAYS OF COPING

"Hope in the Lord, be strong and let your heart be courageous, and hope in the Lord."[29]

"The gates of prayer are sometimes open and sometimes closed, but the gates of repentance are always open."[30]

"Though the gates of prayer are closed, the gates of tears are never closed."[31]

When we discover that we, or someone we love, has a fatal illness, we initially feel shocked, disoriented, and numb. Then we are likely to deny the painful truth by shopping around for other opinions or by convincing ourselves that it is all a mistake. We reassure ourselves that the lab results were in error and a repeat will confirm that everything's fine. We want to believe that because the symptoms have been going on for a long time they must not mean anything.

When the terrible reality sets in, we feel angry with ourselves for not taking better care of ourselves. We feel angry with the doctor. We project our anger onto friends for not saying the right words to comfort us. No matter how nice or compassionate others are, someone whose time is running out can easily displace rage onto them.

Once we stop denying how seriously ill we are, we try to bargain with doctors: "I (or my loved one) will never touch a cigarette again. Just make everything go back to normal." "I (or my loved one) will follow the diet this time. Just give me another chance." "Just take the tumor out, give me radiation, and my cancer will be gone."

We bargain with God: "I'll give a thousand dollars to charity if you just let me (or my loved one) get better." "I'll spend five hours every week doing kind deeds for others, just let me (or my loved one) recover." "I'll never get angry at anyone again. Just let me live long enough to see my children get married."

With time, most terminally ill people work through their feelings and make peace with dying. They usually have a strong desire to live, no matter how debilitating their disease. Many get depressed or withdrawn at some point, but few really want to die. When they do, psychotherapy and/or antidepressant medication usually makes them feel better.

Mark was one of many cancer patients who courageously battled his disease for years without ever considering "throwing in the towel." He was diagnosed with bone cancer at the age of twenty-six. Soon after he got over his initial shock, his leg was amputated. Before his surgery, he joked that he would have to do without being a professional basketball player. Over the next ten years, he had chemotherapy, radiation, and four operations to remove tumors that metastasized to various parts of his body.

Despite the physical pain and emotional devastation of his horrible illness, he remained cheerful and optimistic. He felt that every day of life was a gift and never wallowed in self-pity, although he had every reason to do so. People who met him were amazed that someone so sick could be so happy.

When he became desperately ill for the last time, the doctors wanted him to come to the hospital for more tests. Mark refused. "All you're going to do is to give me bad news," he replied, "and there's nothing more that you can do, anyway. It's depressing being in the hospital and hearing your dismal reports. I'm staying home where I can be with my family until my time is up and God takes me."

Mark died peacefully a month later. It never occurred to him to be depressed. After all, he had loving parents, a wonderful wife, two great kids, and a close relationship with the One Above. From his perspective, why shouldn't he celebrate life?

While many doctors view psychological denial as primitive, denial unquestionably helps sick people live longer. Integrating spirituality with psychological defenses can help people live longer as they grow in their relationship with God.

King Hezekiah experienced this over 2,000 years ago as he lay on his deathbed. He was a righteous man who decided not to have children because divine inspiration told him that they would be wicked. Meanwhile, a prophet revealed that his illness was a punishment for not marrying and having children. Hezekiah defended himself by saying that he did not want to bring unfit offspring into the world.

The prophet told him that his reasons did not justify violating God's command. The Lord had commanded men to marry and procreate, and Hezekiah was supposed to do what he was told. Hezekiah repented and asked the Almighty to take away his illness, which He did. Hezekiah then married, had children, and lived an additional fifteen healthy years.[32]

The Talmud says that we should never stop praying for the Almighty to save us, even when a sharp sword is lying against our necks (i.e., even when we are in a seemingly hopeless situation).[33] When we sincerely cry out to Him, He always hears us, but He sometimes responds, "I hear you, but My answer is 'No.' " We should never belittle the value of prayer, even in seemingly hopeless situations, as the following story suggests:

A Jewish woman had a son who became observant as a teenager. Although she wasn't observant, she supported his getting a religious education, and he attended a *yeshivah* (religious school for men) in another city.

When he came home one summer, he insisted that she see a doctor about her stomach pains. She finally relented and saw her physician, only to be told that there was nothing wrong with her. Meanwhile, the doctor told her son a very different story. She had an inoperable, malignant stomach tumor the size of a grapefruit. The doctor told him that she had no more than six months to live.

The son returned to *yeshivah* and told the rabbis what happened. They asked all of the students and rabbis to pray for her every day for the rest of the year.

Six months later, the mother returned to her doctor, who again told her that there was nothing wrong with her. Only this time it was the truth. The malignant cancer had disappeared without a trace, despite the fact that she had done nothing to treat it. The son told her about the prayers said on her behalf, and they attributed her remarkable recovery to them. Eight years later, she was still in good health with no trace of the tumor.

Giving charity is another way of enlisting divine mercy. When we are merciful to others, God may have mercy on us. Many people who pledge extra money to charity are saved from terminal illness and disasters. There is no guarantee that it will "work," but we still get the merit of giving to charity regardless of the outcome. That is an investment that gives eternal interest.

A well-known woman in Jerusalem was once hospitalized with advanced cancer. The doctors gave her hundreds of pills that they hoped would kill her tumor over a period of months. When her tests miraculously showed no more traces of cancer, the doctors triumphantly announced that their pills had cured her.

"No, they haven't," she countered. "I never took any of your pills." With that, she reached under her bed and displayed a gallon jar filled with thousands of pills that the doctors thought she had taken.

"When I came into this hospital, I made a deal with God. I told Him that if He would cure me, I would devote the rest of my life to collecting and distributing money to charity. He's kept His part of the bargain, and now it's time for me to keep mine."

This woman has devoted herself to fulfilling her promise for the past two decades.

(Even though this woman had faith that God would cure her, we are not allowed to forgo medical treatments that have proven efficacious with serious illnesses. Judaism requires us to do whatever we can to regain our health. We are not supposed to sit back doing nothing while hoping that God will do miracles for us.)

If we follow an appropriate medical regimen, its efficacy is in God's hands. Giving charity (or pledging it when we can't give it), doing good deeds, learning more Torah, teaching others, and being more scrupulous in our observance of commandments may give us the merit to be cured.

A scientist taught Judaism classes one night a week at the request of two students. Several years later, his wife developed a virulent form of cancer that kills 99 percent of its victims within three months. The couple understood her illness as a message to change their lives. She started eating an especially healthy diet and visualized her body conquering her cancer. She changed her name in the hope that the illness that was destined for the former person would not apply to the "new" one.[34] They also decided that he should teach a second Judaism class every week to increase the spirituality in the world.

They attributed his wife's remarkable recovery and remission to their actions. When she relapsed five years later and died, they were grateful for their extra time together and for the extra Torah that her illness brought to hundreds of people who attended his lectures.

While scientists view illness only in biological terms, Judaism sees its emotional and spiritual components as well. At one time, it was known how each of the 613 Torah commandments spiritually nourished a specific part of the Jewish body. Then, transgressions such as gossip or slander could cause illnesses, such as *tzaraat*. These spiritually induced illnesses disappeared when the person repented. When ancient Jews followed a Book of Cures that allowed them to heal illness naturally, King Hezekiah hid it. Jews then were supposed to effect cures by recognizing an illness's spiritual message and improving their moral behavior.[35]

When people lost their spiritual sensitivity, they lost their access to the spiritual reasons that caused specific illnesses. Today, we must use conventional healing techniques in addition to spiritual aids. We are not allowed to expect God to supernaturally take away the damage that we inflict on ourselves by smoking, drinking alcohol, eating junk food and chemicals, and living a sedentary life. We should ask God to heal us, but only after first taking responsibility for our health by eating properly and following good habits.

NONCONVENTIONAL THERAPIES

While most sick people rely on conventional medicine to help them, more and more people are turning to alternative therapies. They are based on the idea that our bodies are designed to be healthy, but only if we give them the tools to function properly. People understand that they can't put sugar syrup or fatty foods in their gas tank and expect their car to run well. Our bodies were not designed to run on fatty, sugared, chemically treated, or refined foods, either. We have to put premium fuel into us if we are to run properly.

Rather than give drugs that destroy the good cells in our body along with the bad, alternative therapies strengthen the body and help it to function properly. These therapies boost the immune system using healthy foods, often with added vitamins or enzymes, and eliminate foods that strip the body of its strength and vitality. Some also use products that remove bodily toxins that interfere with healing and normal functioning.

Many people have had "terminal" cancers killed by conventional medicine while others have been cured by alternative therapies. Most people who try alternative medicine do so only after conventional medicine has failed them or has made them worse. Despite the fact that alternative centers treat only the most debilitated patients, they often have better success rates than conventional medicine does.

Some Mexican clinics are run by American- or European-trained doctors and combine alternative medicine with conventional knowledge. Some have well-controlled data showing their success rates with various kinds of cancer. Both conventional hospitals and doctors as well as alternative ones can be money-hungry or offer treatments with little efficacy. Patients should compare a hospital's or doctor's success rates for their specific kind of cancer with those of alternative centers before choosing a treatment.

Some types of cancer (such as leukemia) have high cure rates using conventional medicine, while patients who have poor prognoses with conventional medicine may get better results with alternative therapies. Alternative therapies work best with patients who have not already been compromised by chemotherapy.

Conventional treatments allow patients to be fairly passive, while alternative methods require patients to take responsibility for their diets and diligently follow treatment protocols. People who are unwilling to scrupulously follow the program should not bother with alternative therapy.

Our emotional states also have a powerful effect on our physical well-being.[36] When Norman Cousins was diagnosed with an "incurable" collagen disease, he discovered that laughter helps improve some people's immune systems. He conquered his disease by watching funny movies like the Marx brothers' *A Night at the*

Opera every day. Laughing for thirty to sixty minutes a day seems to be good medicine. It reduces people's pain and helps them heal.

The usefulness of visualization in treating cancer has also been well researched.[37] There is strong evidence that some cancer patients live longer and/or go into remission if they regularly and vividly visualize their bodies attacking diseased cells. Both children and adults can use these techniques.

To the extent that anxiety worsens pain, parents can do a lot to help terminally ill children. Children find it reassuring and calming for parents to stay with them during painful procedures and hospitalizations. They are cheered by visits from family members and friends, as well as by familiar pictures, dolls, games, and stuffed animals.

Children should be prepared for tests, treatments, and operations. If they are given only vague ideas about what will happen, their imaginations will conjure up terribly scary ideas. Lying to children that painful procedures will not hurt them destroys parents' or doctors' credibility and makes children feel betrayed.

Children should be shown what medical procedures will be like by watching demonstrations on a stuffed animal or doll, then doing the "procedure" themselves. Teaching children relaxation and breathing exercises helps them tolerate painful injections, blood drawing, or intravenous needles. The parent can do the breathing exercise along with the child during these procedures.

While pain medication has its uses, love, attention, and distraction also reduce pain. Giving children TLC and a "security blanket" are good medicine.

MANAGING PAIN

Although many patients with cancer or terminal illness do not have pain, most fear that they will. Since how much pain we feel depends upon our emotional and physical state, it is usually worst when we feel anxious or out of control. It lessens when we feel relaxed and peaceful, or when we know that we can control it.

Few chronically ill patients get painkillers in a predictable way and in adequate doses. This makes patients have much more pain than is inevitable. Patients use much less medication and feel much better when they control how much painkiller they take, and when.

Enlightened doctors now let hospitalized cancer patients administer their own painkillers. They attach patients to a machine with an intravenous line that dispenses as much painkiller as the patient wants, as often as he or she wants, within limits preprogrammed by the doctor. Even though patients could take enormous doses of drugs, they use less medication this way than when they depend on hospital staff to give it to them.

Terminally ill patients with pain should take medications that reduce chronic, not short-term, pain. Short-acting narcotics like codeine wear off after three or four hours and are not meant to be given for pain that goes on for weeks, months, or years.

Patients who have pain from a terminal illness (such as metastatic cancer) should always have enough medication to be comfortable, if they want it. Long-acting narcotics like methadone are good for this purpose and can be given with other drugs that heighten the pain relief.

Many cancer patients refuse to take methadone because they associate it with drug addiction, but it is one of the best drugs for treating the pain of terminal illness. Since these patients will die anyway, they don't have to worry about becoming addicted. They should take whatever they need to be comfortable and/or functional.

Many doctors do not know how to properly help terminally ill patients with pain. Specially trained behavioral psychologists can teach relaxation techniques, use biofeedback, or recommend breathing exercises that help patients decrease their pain and tolerate uncomfortable medical procedures. Physicians with expertise in pain control (dolorologists) can prescribe medications, acupuncture, and trigger-point therapy to help with pain relief.

DYING CHILDREN

Some people naively assume that terminally ill children don't think about dying. Even very young ones do, and they usually know that something is very wrong when they are terribly sick. This is obvious by the way children talk, play with dolls or toys, or draw pictures. Children feel anxious and abandoned when adults do not respond honestly to their questions or hide what is going on.

Many dying children want to talk about death. Unfortunately, they learn not to because visitors avoid them if they ask questions or broach the topic. Likewise, many children find that if they playact a death scene with a doll, or draw "morbid" pictures, their parents or hospital personnel quickly take away their toys and change the subject.

Parents need to address a child's questions about illness and death according to the child's age, capacity to understand, and constitution. This may be done with very young children using puppets, or by direct discussion with older children.

Some professionals who have worked with dying children believe that children may be reluctant to die as long as they have "unfinished business." It is hard for children to tell their parents their fears as long as the parents insist that the child is not dying. Other children want their parents to give them "permission" to die, or feel protective about leaving family members behind. They will not die until they are reassured that a parent or siblings will be okay without them.

For example, one eleven-year-old girl with cancer wrote a will and insisted on speaking to each family member about which of her belongings she wanted each to have. She died a few hours later.[38] Another preteen girl wanted to tell her mother how afraid she was of dying, but the mother kept trying to cheer her up and deny her serious condition. The daughter finally asked a nurse to tell her mother to listen to her. Shortly after the mother held her and allowed her to voice her fears and feelings without interruption, the girl died.[39]

Most terminally ill children initially fear that they will be left alone or will be abandoned by their parents. Many are afraid that death will be painful or that they will be mutilated. It is important to reassure children that death won't hurt, and they won't be alone when they die. If a child wants to know what death is like, explain according to his or her level of understanding.

The following explanation was given by one mother to her young son:

"Larry, you have a wonderful time whenever you go to your friend's house, but it still feels good to come home because that's where you really belong.

"God put us in this world with many wonderful things to enjoy. There are many people who love you here. You have a nice home to live in, you eat delicious food and play with fun toys. But this world is like a friend's house. We have a good time here, but this is not our real home. Our real home is with God. He loves us and waits to bring us home to Him when the time is right. When that happens, we feel a pleasure that is greater than anything we can imagine.

"God made caterpillars to teach us an important lesson. Caterpillars are very happy eating leaves. Then one day they spin a cocoon and seem to die in it. A short while later, they become beautiful butterflies, crawl out of their shells, and fly away.

"God puts each of us here in a cocoon. That cocoon is our body. One day we don't need our bodies anymore, so we leave them behind and we become like butterflies. God lovingly takes us away and carries us with Him to a faraway place that is our real home. It feels so wonderful there that we never want to leave it.

"When Mommy and Daddy and your brothers and sisters are finished with what we need to do in this world, God will take us home to Him, too. Until we get there, you won't be alone. God will keep you company, and you will see your grandmother and grandfather. You will feel safe, happy, and loved, just like you are here."

Many terminally ill children have near-death experiences, encounters with the souls of deceased relatives, or glimpses of the spiritual world beyond. Those who do are unafraid to die, while their parents are the ones who need reassurance. The more comfortable parents are with the afterlife, the more they can reassure children who don't have experience with the world beyond.

Parents of a dying child should also reassure their surviving children that they are healthy and will not die for a long time. They should know that a brother or sister is dying because he or she is sick, not because of sin or because a sibling had bad feelings about the sick child.

Children often feel responsible for killing a deceased relative with their angry or hostile wishes. They need to know that they didn't contribute to that person's death.

Although they may not verbalize it, both adult and child survivors may feel guilty for living when a loved one dies. Reassure children that God took the deceased to be with Him, but the survivors are supposed to live full and long lives.

LIVING AND CONVENTIONAL WILLS

Dying doesn't necessarily frighten terminally ill people. Once they accept that they will die, they are usually most concerned with staying in control of their minds and bodies and not being in pain.

One way that people can control what happens after they die is by writing a will. While a conventional will apportions an estate to heirs or charitable institutions, a living will stipulates what doctors should or should not do to someone who is seriously ill. A health care proxy appoints someone to make decisions on your behalf if you become too ill to make decisions yourself. A proxy should be drafted in consultation with a qualified rabbi, as it directs doctors about what to do regarding organ donation, autopsy, cardiopulmonary resuscitation, invasive or diagnostic tests, surgery, breathing by machine, and so on. Sample documents appear in the Appendix.

People should draw up a living will and appoint a health care proxy if they don't want hospital staff to artificially keep them alive while charging tens of thousands of dollars for unnecessary care and causing anguish to their families. With today's technology, more health care dollars are spent trying to keep people alive during the last year of life than during the rest of their years together.

Since our bodies are on loan from God and only He has the right to take away life, Judaism never permits active euthanasia, such as withholding food or hydration, or "mercy killing." Passive euthanasia, by withholding resuscitation or medication, is sometimes permitted.[40]

Jewish law allows life-saving organs (including corneas) to be donated, provided they are harvested in a Jewishly acceptable, dignified manner.[41] Autopsies are forbidden because they desecrate the body,[42] unless diagnosing a fatal disease may prevent someone else's imminent death. In such rare instances, the autopsy should be done with a rabbi or religious doctor present so that the corpse will be treated respectfully. The examined organs must be buried with the body at the funeral.[43]

Besides a living will, most adults also need an up-to-date conventional will. All too many people avoid this because they don't want to think about dying. When people die intestate, the family's grief is typically compounded by unnecessary fighting and legal problems. If you love your heirs, draw up a proper will, keep it current, and inform your spouse, children, or significant others how to execute the estate according to your wishes.

Terminally ill people should make sure that a spouse (or adult children) know how to take care of financial affairs. Many women whose husbands are breadwinners have no idea as to the savings, investments, life insurance, pension plans, and benefits their husbands have. Discussing these issues ahead of time can prevent much unnecessary grief.

Many Jews don't know that wills should accord with both American and Jewish law. Unfortunately, American tax regulations and inheritance laws are often at odds with Judaism. This is because Jewish law considers property ours to use only while we are alive, and Jewish law regulates how property can be disposed of. For example, biblical law requires a firstborn son to get a double portion of any property that his father doesn't use or give away during his lifetime.[44] Sons always inherit from the deceased, but must first provide for their mother and unmarried sisters out of an estate.[45] If a man has no sons, his daughters inherit from him. If he has no children, his brothers inherit from him. If he has no brothers, his paternal uncles inherit from him. If he has none of these, his closest relative becomes his heir.[46]

These biblical commands sometimes preclude charitable bequests that reduce the amount of money left to heirs. They may also prohibit equal bequests to all of one's children because daughters and a firstborn son must be provided for inequitably.

A theoretical way to get around these problems is to distribute property while we are still alive. Since we rarely know when we will die, and we might want to use what we have until we pass away, this is usually impractical. Also, giving gifts can result in adverse tax consequences, since current federal gift taxes can be as high as 55 percent, and some states add a gift tax to that amount!

A solution is to draw up a secular and "Jewish" will that satisfies Jewish requirements without increasing taxes or sacrificing advantageous estate planning. See the Resources at the end of this chapter for more information about this.

RECOMMENDATIONS FOR COPING

We often appreciate the gifts we have only when we stand to lose them. Realizing how temporary life is helps us to see what is really important and helps us let go of insignificant preoccupations. When we know that time is running out, we are more inclined to invest in our relationships with friends, family, and our Creator. If we try to leave behind a meaningful legacy, we can make the most of whatever time we have.

People with a terminal illness should hope for the best (i.e., recovery or remission) but prepare for the worst. Get a second opinion about your diagnosis, treatment options, and prognosis. Educate yourself about your condition and what can be done. Read relevant literature and talk to other survivors about their experiences.

Don't assume that doctors know or will tell you everything there is to know about your illness and possible treatments. Learn about conventional and alternative therapies before choosing a treatment. After choosing your best option, know that a cure depends upon more than doctors or medicine. Ask God to be the head of your treatment team.

The *Ethics of the Fathers* tells us to repent one day before we die.[47] Since we never know when we will leave this world, we should repent every day and live each day as fully as if it were our last.[48] Contemplating our last moments of life prepares us to face them when they occur. We can then die with equanimity instead of in panic or despair.

The ordeals of a terminal illness help cleanse us of our negative deeds, as can death. But death atones only if we prepare ourselves for that,[49] such as by confessing on our deathbed. The following is one version of confession:

> I admit before you, Lord my God, and God of my forefathers, that my recovery and death are in Your hand. May it be Your will to heal me with a full recovery, but if I die, may my death atone for all of my unintentional sins, intentional sins, and rebellious sins that I have committed before You. And grant me my portion in the Garden of Eden, and let me be worthy of the World-to-Come that is concealed for the righteous.[50]

COPING WITH A LOVED ONE'S TERMINAL ILLNESS

If you are taking care of a person who is likely to be ill for a long time, you will need to reserve time and energy for yourself, your job (if you have one), and your family. Prioritize your time and commitments, and get help if you need it. Learn to ask for support and assistance.

Coping with a short illness is very different from dealing with a long one. Learn about the expected course of the illness and the medical, practical, legal, and religious issues that will arise. Encourage your loved one to write a living will and tell you what he or she wants. Discuss your loved one's wishes with a qualified rabbi, then with treating doctors or hospital administrators.

Find out which medical care (such as experimental procedures or private nurses) will not be covered by insurance, and protect yourself against catastrophic bills. A knowledgeable hospital social worker can help eligible patients apply for Medicaid or Medicare, make suggestions about how to be financially protected, and assist with hospital red tape.

Patients and their families often know better than doctors or nurses when a patient's health is getting better or worse. Family members tend to notice the effects of a hospital environment, visits from friends, gifts, flowers, or home-cooked food on a loved one when hospital personnel do not. You may need to trust your instincts about what is helping or harming your loved one, even if the doctors or nurses believe differently. When hospitals have only bills and invasive procedures to offer, consider bringing your loved one home or to a hospice to die.

If a relative has early Alzheimer's disease or another form of senility, let him or her know the diagnosis in order to plan for the future. Tell only as much as he or she wants to know, but answer questions honestly. Make it clear that you will not abandon the person and that your love remains. Help keep dignity and self-esteem intact.

Families should have a planning meeting about how to take care of and financially support a loved one who is deteriorating. One family member, usually a daughter, typically ends up being the primary caregiver for infirm parents, even when she has a job and a family. This often leaves her little personal time and is totally draining. Responsibilities should be shared more equitably among siblings.

If you are willing to help care for a dying relative, see if he or she prefers to die at home, in a hospice, or in a hospital. Hospices are less expensive and more comfortable and private than hospitals. They also encourage patients' families to be involved and let patients die more peacefully than most hospitals will.

Bereaved parents should never compare living children to their dead sibling, except to say that the dead one was ill through nobody's fault. Surviving children should not have to live in the shadow of a dead brother or sister who is viewed as perfect. Children worry that their parents love a dead child more than they will ever be loved, and feel guilty if they do anything that meets with their grieving parents' disapproval. They often fear losing their parents' love if they don't act like model children, and need reassurance that they can be themselves.

A child's (or spouse's) terminal illness can take up most of your time. It is important to spend time with your other children and make them feel valued, special, and loved. If you are married, don't neglect your spouse. You may need to make appointments or dates to be alone together, but you'll both benefit from the mutual support and the respite from living with death.

Get periodic breaks from the constant tension and sadness of hospital visits, medical regimens, and so forth. Otherwise, you will burn out. Take a walk, see a movie, read a magazine, take a class, go on a vacation, and leave your guilt behind. Even a devoted parent, child, or spouse is entitled to some time away from a desperately sick relative.

There are countless relatives who feel guilty that their child, parent, or other loved one died while they were away. While some people prefer to die in the company of a loved one, and Judaism recommends that we not leave a dying person alone,[51] Risa told the following story:

"My grandfather loved his family more than anything in the world, and we loved him, too. When he was sick, I spent every day by his bedside, while other relatives visited him in the hospital. One evening around dinner time, I was the only one there. Grandpa looked very tired and he told me to get a snack from the cafeteria while he took a nap. On my way back to his room, I found a quiet lounge where I said some prayers. By the time I came back, he was dead.

"Grandpa was a very private man. Some people would kick themselves for not being there when he died, but I think that he knew that he was dying soon and wanted me not to be there when it happened. I have no doubt that he waited to die until he could do it in private. I have worked with a lot of dying children in hospitals, and I think some of them do the same."

HELPING THE TERMINALLY ILL

Many dying people would like to talk about death but don't because it makes most listeners uncomfortable. While you can't prevent people from dying, you can be enormously helpful by letting them share their regrets, fears, unrealized dreams, and so on. It is very comforting to know that they don't have to face their fears alone.

Ask if there's anything they'd like to talk about, then listen. If you feel uncomfortable seeing them cry, discuss their fears, or talk about death, don't say things like, "I see this is upsetting you. Let's talk about something else," or, "You're a good person, you have nothing to be scared about. You'll go straight to heaven," or "Don't get yourself upset by thinking about this," or, "Why are you talking about nonsense like death? Of course you'll get better." It's not your responsibility to take away people's fears; they'll feel comforted just sharing their feelings and getting support to work things out themselves.

Let the person know how much you appreciate their sharing feelings and how willing you are to listen whenever they want to talk. Don't try to "fix" their feelings and cheer them up with superficial responses or philosophical platitudes. If they regret their mistakes, suggest that they redress them as best they can with God or with the appropriate people.

Some sick people dislike it when visitors talk only about morbid topics like illness, hospitals, people's problems, and so on. While some dying people want to talk about death, others want to be cheered up. Let the person be your guide. One woman who was dying of cancer said that her favorite visitor was a friend who used to tell her jokes and make her laugh.

The Bible obligates us to visit sick people and do what we can to help them recover.[52] We are told that "visiting the sick takes away one-sixtieth of their illness."[53] We are supposed to cheer up the sick, bring them tasty kosher food and beverages, and give them religious items for the Sabbath and Jewish holidays if they need them. We should make sure that their room is clean, that they have clean clothes and linens, and that they have easy access to a telephone, books, a radio, or whatever else they need to feel at ease.

We are also supposed to pray for them.[54] Prayers in their presence should be short and inaudible so that we don't alarm them about the seriousness of their condition. Two verses that are customarily said are: "God will remove all sickness from you, and all of the bad afflictions of the Egyptians He shall not put on you, but He will put on all of your enemies,"[55] and "Heal us, Lord, and we will be healed, save us and we will be saved, because You are our salvation."[56]

The following is a longer prayer that is traditionally said for the recovery of someone who is very ill (with appropriate changes for a woman):

"Lord, Lord, a God who is merciful and compassionate, slow to anger and abundant in kindness and truth. He guards kindness for thousands of generations and carries over iniquity, rebellious sins, errors and exonerates them."

"Yours, Lord, is greatness, strength, splendor, victory, and glory, because everything in heaven and on earth is Yours. Yours, Lord, is the kingdom and You are uplifted over all leaders." In Your hand is the soul of all life and the spirit of all human flesh. In Your hand is the strength and might to make great, to strengthen and heal a person, even if he is crushed to the last drop of his soul. Nothing is too wondrous for You and the soul of all life is in Your hand. Therefore, may it be Your will, trustworthy God, Father of mercy, Healer of all illnesses of Your people Israel, even to those who are near the gates of death, the One who binds healing bandages on His loved ones, and redeems His scrupulous ones from destruction, and who saves the soul of the miserable one from death: You, trustworthy Healer, send a healing, a cure, and a remedy with Your tremendous kindness, grace, and compassion to the unfortunate soul and spirit of [person's Hebrew name] the son of [his mother's Hebrew name], that he not go down to the grave. Have much compassion on him and restore, heal, strengthen, and make him live, as all his friends and relatives wish. May his merits and righteous deeds appear before You, and may You throw all of his sins into the depths of the sea.

May Your mercy conquer Your anger at him, and may You send him a complete healing, a healing of the soul and body. And renew his youth like an eagle's, and send him and all of the sick people in Israel a long, blessed, healing cure, a cure of mercy and compassion, a cure that is known and revealed, a cure of kindness, peace, life, of long days and good years.

May it be fulfilled in him, and for all of the sick people in Israel, the scriptural verse that Moses, Your servant who was trusted in Your house, wrote: "If you will surely listen to the voice of the Lord your God, and do what is proper in His eyes, and listen to His commandments, and keep all of His decrees, I will not put upon you any of the diseases that I brought upon Egypt, because I am the Lord your Healer." And you shall serve the Lord your God, and He will bless your bread and your water, and I will remove disease from your midst. You will not have a miscarrying or barren woman in your land, and I will fulfill the number of your days. And the Lord will remove from you all sickness and all of the Egyptian afflictions that you experienced. He will not put them on you, but will put them on all your enemies.

And by the hands of Your servants, the prophets, it was written, "And you shall eat to satiety, and you will praise the Name of the Lord your God who did wonders with you, and My people will never be ashamed." I saw his ways and I will heal, guide, and give him and his mourners comfort. I will create a new expression of the lips, "Peace, peace to the far and to the near," said God, "and I will heal him." A sun of righteousness that will heal with its wings will shine for those who fear My Name. Then your light will break forth like the dawn, and your length of days will sprout quickly.

"Heal us, Lord, and we will be healed, save us and we will be saved, because You are our praise." Raise a complete recovery for all of Your people Israel who are stricken, and especially to [name], bring a complete healing to his 248 organs and 365 sinews. Cure him as You cured Hezekiah, king of Judea, from his illness, and Miriam the prophetess from her leprosy.

Please, God, heal [name] to raise him from his sickbed, and further lengthen the days of his life so that he may serve you with love and in fear. And give him a life of compassion, health, peace, and blessing as it is written, "Because length of days, years of life, and peace shall be added to you. Amen, Selah."[57]

Upon leaving sick people, we traditionally say to them, "May the All-Present have mercy on you among all the other sick people of Israel." It is also customary for individuals or groups of people to recite Psalms as a merit for a person's recovery.[58]

HELPING THE FAMILY

Many families have financial problems when a breadwinner is too ill to work or when medical expenses mount. When a mother is sick for a long time, children may quickly outgrow their clothes and shoes and have no one to replace them. It may be hard for one parent to manage day-to-day chores alone. Concerned friends or relatives can help clean the house, baby-sit, cook or send prepared food, do laundry, run errands, or simply show up and offer whatever help is needed. Sometimes the greatest help is to attend a homebound sick person so that caretakers can get rest, leave the house for a few hours, and take care of their needs.

Some communities have an organization that lends crutches, wheelchairs, walkers, and medical equipment for people who cannot afford to buy them. Some organizations give loans or gifts to help families pay their bills, and concerned friends may set up tax-deductible funds for families in dire straits.

Let the time soon come when all sickness will be removed from the world!

NOTES

1. Raymond Moody, *The Light Beyond* (New York: Bantam, 1988), p. 5.

2. *The Light Beyond,* pp. 5–15.

3. Aryeh Kaplan, *The Aryeh Kaplan Reader.* (New York: Mesorah, 1985), pp. 178–180. See also *The Light Beyond,* p. 11.

4. *The Light Beyond,* pp. 11 and 33.

By loving others, both Jews and Gentiles fulfill many of the commandments that pertain to them. For example, the Noahide commandments include not stealing, not murdering (including medically unnecessary abortion), not committing adultery, and setting up courts of law. People who truly love others automatically uphold these commandments.

Rabbi Akiva once said, "You should love your fellow Jew as yourself. This is a major foundation of the Torah." Hillel once told a potential convert, "The essence of Judaism is that you should not do to your neighbor what is hateful to you. The rest is commentary. Now go and learn the commentary."

NDEers are taught the importance of loving others. That doesn't mean that Gentiles won't be punished for having forbidden sexual relations or for worshiping idols, or that knowledgeable Jews won't be punished for eschewing *mitzvot* (not loving God) or for not learning Torah (accumulating knowledge). The NDE simply gives a shorthand lesson that loving others is a foundation for living properly.

The Jewish prophets repeatedly admonished the Jews for oppressing and hating each other and stressed the importance of loving one another. They did not suggest that if Jews are loving, they can violate the rest of the Torah.

The Second Temple was destroyed because of causeless hatred between Jews. Rabbi Avraham Kook, *zt"l,* said that the Temple will not be rebuilt and the Messiah will not come until there is causeless *love* between Jews. It stands to reason that NDEs should stress this same idea.

5. *Brachot* 17a.

6. Leviticus 19:18. *Brachot* 17a states, "One should always strive to be on the best terms with his brethren, his relatives, with all Jews, and even with the heathen on the street, so that he may be beloved Above and well-liked below. . . . It was related of Rabbi Yochanan ben Zakkai that no one ever greeted him first, even a heathen in the street."

7. This phenomenon has frequently been experienced by NDEers, as quoted in *The Light Beyond,* pp. 33–34.

8. This concept is discussed more fully in *The Aryeh Kaplan Reader,* pp. 178–180.

9. *The Light Beyond,* pp. 11 and 35.

10. *The Light Beyond,* p. 67.

11. See Aryeh Kaplan, *Handbook of Jewish Thought,* vol. 2 (New York: Moznaim, 1992), p. 357.

12. *Pirkei D'Rabbi Eliezer* 34.

13. *Brachot* 18b discusses some very interesting conversations between souls and their awareness of what goes on in our world. See also *Handbook of Jewish Thought,* pp. 356–358, and *The Aryeh Kaplan Reader,* pp. 180–182.

14. *Pirkei D'Rabbi Eliezer* 32.

15. *Pirkei D'Rabbi Eliezer* 34. See also *Handbook of Jewish Thought,* pp. 356.

16. *Zohar, Vayechi* 281b.

17. Interview with Raymond Moody, *Visions Magazine,* October 1994, p. 14.

18. While people of all religions have NDEs, as do many nonreligious people, they interpret the details of their experience according to their culture and their perceptions. For example, a religious person will call the Being of Light "God," while a nonreligious person will describe it as a "Being of Light." Their interpretations sometimes differ with what Judaism teaches. For example, NDEers conclude that loving others and gaining knowledge are of primary importance, as was discussed in note 4. Some conclude that God cares little about religious dogma, which is true concerning Gentiles, as long as they are monotheistic and observe the Seven Noahide Laws. Jews have a different calling.

Near-death experiences are not the same as the totality of the afterlife. NDEs cannot take away a person's free choice. They can encourage people to be "good" but not stop them from making immoral choices.

19. Based on *Brachot* 43b.

20. Discussed in Aryeh Kaplan, *Immortality, Resurrection, and the Age of the Universe* (Hoboken, NJ: KTAV), pp. 86–91.

21. "A Brief History of Time," televised on The Discovery Channel, December 19, 1994 at 9 P.M.

22. *Pirkei Avot* 1:2.

23. *Genesis Rabbah* 65:9.

24. *Genesis Rabbah* 65:9.

25. Genesis 27:1.

26. *Genesis Rabbah* 65:9.

27. *Genesis Rabbah* 65:9.

28. *Me'am Lo'ez* on Genesis 24:1 and 48:1.

29. Psalms 27:14.

30. *Deuteronomy Rabbah* 2:12.

31. *Brachot* 32b.

32. *Brachot* 10a.

33. *Brachot* 10a.

34. This is an ancient Jewish custom that reflects the idea that we can change our identity by changing our name (*Rosh HaShanah* 16b).

35. *Pesachim* 56b.

36. Norman Cousins cites research and anecdotes about this in his book *Anatomy of an Illness as Perceived by the Patient: Reflections on Healing and Regeneration* (New York: Norton, 1979).

37. Some of this data appears in O. Carl Simonton, Stephanie Simonton, and James Creighton, *Getting Well Again: A Step-by-Step, Self-Help Guide to Overcoming Cancer for Patients and Their Families* (New York: St. Martin's, 1978), and in Stephanie Simonton, *The Simonton Approach for Families Facing Illness* (New York: Bantam, 1984).

38. Marilyn Webb, "The Art of Dying," *New York Magazine,* November 23, 1992, p. 52.

39. "The Art of Dying," p. 52.

40. From "A Torah Perspective Regarding the Health Care Proxy," developed and published by the Commission on Medical Ethics of the Rabbinical Council of America. For more information, contact the RCA, 275 Seventh Avenue, New York, NY 10001, (212) 807-7888.

41. From "A Torah Perspective."

42. See Maurice Lamm, *The Jewish Way in Death and Mourning* (New York: Jonathan David, 1981), p. 8.

43. Extenuating circumstances under which autopsies are allowed are cited in *The Jewish Way in Death and Mourning,* pp. 8–12.

44. Deuteronomy 21:15–17.

45. Jewish law states that a man's heirs may not claim their inheritance until all creditors have been satisfied. The law tried to ensure that a widow and her daughters would be guaranteed continuing support from the deceased's estate, so it made relatives creditors, not heirs. They have a lien on the decedent's property that has priority over all heirs and precedes any claim that arose subsequent to the marriage. Maimonides, *Hilchot Ishut* 17:1–8; *Bava Batra* 175b and 176a. Cited in *Aish HaTorah, The Eye of a Needle* (New York: Feldheim, 1993), p. 103.

46. Numbers 27:8–11.

47. *Pirkei Avot* 2:15.

48. *Shabbat* 153a.

49. From Rabbi Kirzner's tape on Suffering.

50. A longer version appears in the *Shulchan Aruch, Yoreh De'ah,* 337:2: "I admit to You, Lord my God, and God of my fathers, God of Abraham, Isaac, and Jacob, the God of gods and the Lord of lords, in the heaven above and on the earth below there is none other, the Maker of heaven and earth, who does kindness, justice, and righteousness on earth, who was, is, and will be, who gives life to all, in whose hand are my recovery and my death. May it be Your will, Lord my God, and God of my fathers, that You heal me with a complete healing, because You are the God who is a merciful Healer. And if, far be it from me, I die, let my death be an atonement for all of my errors, intentional sins, and rebellious sins that I mistakenly, intentionally, and rebelliously did before You, and give me a portion in Your

Torah and in Paradise. And let me be worthy of the World-to-Come that is hidden for the righteous.

"I admit and believe that You are the absolute and total existence, that You are One and not like individuals, and [that You are] the head of all beings that exist. You have no body and no bodily strength, and You are not subject to bodily events and forces, and no part of You can be described in physical terms. You are the precedent for all existence. It is appropriate to serve and exalt You. You put prophecy in the mouths of all of the prophets, and the prophecy of Your servant and prophet Moses is above all prophets. You gave us a complete Torah that restores life through him, from heaven. This is the holy Torah that is found among us, and reached him [Moses] from the "mouth" of the Almighty. This Torah has nothing missing and will not be changed. You know the thoughts of human beings, and will not overlook them. Your way is to bestow goodness on the righteous and punish the wicked, and bring our beloved Messiah and revive our dead. May the words of my mouth and the thoughts of my heart be pleasing before You, my Rock and my Redeemer."

51. See *Handbook of Jewish Thought*, p. 356.

52. Bahag, Positive Mitzvot 36; Ramban's commentary to *Sefer Hamitzvot*, shoresh 1, response 3.

53. *Yoreh De'ah* 335.

54. *Yoreh De'ah* 335.

55. Deuteronomy 7:15.

56. Based on the prayer from the *Shemoneh Esrai*, which itself is based on Jeremiah 17:14.

57. This prayer, in Hebrew and in English, may be found in Chaim B. Goldberg, *Mourning in Halacha*, (Brooklyn, NY: Mesorah, 1991), pp. 436–437.

58. For a comprehensive list of prayers and Psalms that are said for sick people, see Aaron Levine, *How to Perform the Great Mitzvah of Bikur Cholim, Visiting the Sick* (Toronto: Zichron Meir, 1987), pp. 89–126.

FOR FURTHER READING

AHCPR Publications Clearinghouse, P.O. Box 8547, Silver Spring, MD 20907, 800-358-9295
    Offers free reference guides for pain management for children and adults, and free reference guides for medical treatment.

Boteach, Shmuel. *Wrestling with the Divine: A Jewish Response to Suffering.* Northvale, NJ: Jason Aronson, 1995.

Cohen, Donna, and Eisdorfer, Carl. *The Loss of Self: A Family Resource for the Care of Alzheimer's Disease and Related Disorders.* New York: Norton, 1986.

Cousins, Norman. *Anatomy of an Illness as Perceived by the Patient: Reflections on Healing and Regeneration.* New York: Norton, 1979.

Daly, Eugene. *Thy Will Be Done: A Guide to Wills, Taxation, and Estate Planning for Older Persons.* New York: Prometheus Books, 1990.
    People who are doing estate planning and drafting wills should not rely solely on information in books. Tax laws change frequently, and vary from state to state. Consult a qualified attorney or estate planner about particular circumstances once you are familiar with the basics.

Duda, Deborah. *Coming Home*. Santa Fe, NM: John Muir, 1984, pp. 61–117; 124–136; 146–168; 194–201.

A guide to home care for the terminally ill. Recommended for its practical information on pain control, and emotional, medical, and legal aspects of dying. Her philosophies about life and spirituality are not Jewish.

Gerson, Max. *A Cancer Therapy*. Bonita, CA: Gerson Institute, 1990.

A scientific presentation of Gerson's philosophy and experience with alternative therapy for cancer.

Harpham, Wendy. *Diagnosis: Cancer. Your Guide Through the First Few Months*. New York: Norton, 1992.

A young doctor relates her personal experience with cancer and offers advice on how to cope while getting treatment and adapting to a different life.

Kaplan, Aryeh. *The Handbook of Jewish Thought*. Vol. 2. Brooklyn, NY: Moznaim, 1992, pp. 354–359.

Rabbi Kaplan gives fascinating Jewish insights about immortality and the soul.

Kübler-Ross, Elisabeth. *On Death and Dying*. New York: Macmillan, 1969.

One of the earliest books to address the process of dying. Dr. Kübler-Ross is considered one of the world's experts on this topic.

——. *On Children and Death*. New York: Macmillan, 1983.

This book relates difficulties faced by parents of dying children and how to cope with them. Her philosophies about the purpose of life and what happens after death are sometimes at odds with Jewish beliefs.

Levine, Aaron. *How to Perform the Great Mitzvah of Bikur Cholim, Visiting the Sick*. Willowdale, Ontario: Zichron Meir, 1987.

One of the few books in English about visiting the sick.

Ozarowski, Joseph. *To Walk in God's Ways: Jewish Perspectives on Illness and Bereavement*. Northvale, NJ: Jason Aronson, 1995.

Reingold, C. *The Lifelong Anti-Cancer Diet*. New York: New American Library, Plume Books, 1982.

Sander, Seryl. *Times of Challenge*. Brooklyn, NY: Mesorah, 1988.

The author chronicles the challenges and coping techniques of Orthodox Jewish individuals and families with terminally ill or severely handicapped relatives.

Simonton, O. Carl, Simonton, Stephanie, and Creighton, James. *Getting Well Again: A Step-by-Step, Self-Help Guide to Overcoming Cancer for Patients and Their Families*. New York: St. Martin's, 1978.

Simonton, Stephanie. *The Simonton Approach for Families Facing Illness*. New York: Bantam, 1984.

Weiss, Avner. *Halakhic Ways of Coping with Mourning and Death*. New York: Ktav, 1991.

RESOURCES

AIDS Information Clearinghouse, (800) 458-5231

Alzheimer's Association, P.O. Box 5675-NADM, Chicago, IL 60680-5675

Supplies information about Alzheimer's disease, including a free booklet, "When the Diagnosis is Alzheimer's." Also sponsors national support groups for families of people with Alzheimer's.

Alzheimer's Disease and Related Disorders Association, New York City Chapter, 551 Fifth Avenue, New York, NY, (212) 983-0700, (800) 621-0379
Offers support groups, information, telephone helpline, and referral services for families of people with Alzheimer's disease.
Alzheimer's Disease Education and Referral Center, (800) 438-4380
Camp Simcha, (The only kosher camp for children with cancer.) 48 West 25 Street, New York, NY 10010, (212) 255-1160
Cancer Care/ The National Cancer Care Foundation, Executive Offices, (212) 221-3300
Assistance for Cancer Patients and Their Families, (212) 302-2400
Cancer Control Society, 2043 North Berendo Street, Los Angeles, CA 90027, (213) 663-7801
Connects cancer survivors with those who want information about the alternative and conventional treatments they received. Ask to speak to survivors with your specific kind of cancer.
Cancer Counseling and Research Center, P.O. Box 1055, Azle, TX 76020, (814) 444-4073
The Simontons pioneered the use of visual imagery to help combat cancer. They provide taped materials that combine imagery, progressive relaxation, and meditative techniques for use by cancer victims.
Cancer Information Service–Memorial Sloan Kettering Cancer Center, 1275 York Avenue, New York, NY, (800) 422-6237
Cancervive, Inc., 6500 Wilshire Blvd., Suite 500, Los Angeles, CA 90048, (213) 203-9232
Offers support groups to help cancer survivors with common challenges, from finding a job to making new friends.
Chai Lifeline, (718) 255-1160
Offers support services for Jewish children with cancer and other life-threatening illnesses.
Children's Hospice International, (800) 24-CHILD
CHIPSA–Max Gerson Clinic, Administrative Offices, Bonita, CA, (619) 267-1150
This is the Mexican treatment center that follows the methods of Max Gerson. It is currently run by his daughter. They have been very successful using alternative methods to treat cancer.
ECHO–National Jewish Institute For Health, 32 Alturas Road, Spring Valley, NY 10977, (914) 425-9750
Gives information and referral for all types of medical and emotional illnesses. Specializes in referrals for conventional medical treatments for cancer, and for catastrophic and serious illnesses in children.
Atlanta, GA, (404) 636-5010
Cleveland, OH, (216) 321-6669
Los Angeles, CA, (213) 934-7099
New York, NY, (212) 796-0555
Passaic, NJ, (201) 473-0424
Toronto, Canada, (416) 633-2525
Geneva, Switzerland, 460-961
Jerusalem, Israel, (02) 537783
Mathew E. Hoffman, Esq., c/o Rosen and Reade, 757 Third Avenue, New York, NY 10017, (212) 303-9029

Mr. Hoffman has developed a novel dual will (secular and Jewish) that has been approved by rabbis and experienced attorneys. Contact him for more information.

Jewish Association for Services for the Aged (JASA) Nachas Healthnet, 1310 48th Street, Brooklyn, NY 11219, (718) 436-7373
Offers medical referrals and advocacy; child life and support services for Jewish patients and their families.

National Coalition for Cancer Survivorship, Albuquerque, NM, (505) 764-9956
Coordinates a network of groups, services, and events for cancer survivors.

National Institute for Jewish Hospice, (800) 446-4448
Provides contacts for support programs for the dying, with names and locations of hospices, information about services provided, and so on. Offices in Los Angeles and New York City. Sensitive to the specific needs of Jewish patients.

Rofeh International, 1710 Beacon Street, Brookline, MA 02146, (617) 734-5100
Rofeh is an international medical referral center. It provides up to six months' housing for patients receiving medical care in Boston and their families. Also assists Jewish patients with their religious needs. Under the auspices of the Bostoner rebbe.

Ronald McDonald Houses: In New York, 419 East 86 Street, New York, NY 10128, (212) 876-1590
Offers pleasant, very cheap accommodations in over 200 cities for families of patients undergoing out-of-town medical treatments. A 22-page listing of facilities is available.

Y-ME National Breast Cancer Hotline, (800) 221-2141

Bikur Cholim Organizations

These are a few of the organizations whose volunteers visit the sick and help their families with concrete financial and support services.

Bikur Cholim of Baltimore, 401 Yeshiva Lane, Pikesville, MD 21208, (301) 358-0680, (301) 358-8024

Bikur Cholim Bnos Chayil, 2318 Avenue P, Brooklyn, NY 11229, (718) 253-8014

Bikur Cholim of the State of New York, 260 Broadway, Brooklyn, NY 11228, (718) 387-3876

Nshei Ahavas Chesed (Boro Park), 1680 47 Street, Brooklyn, NY 11204, (718) 438-0211, 435-1508
There is a confidential hotline for people who have a catastrophic illness or whose families need help. (718) 851-0050 or (718) 435-0088

Bikur Cholim of Rockland County, 1 Acer Court, Monsey, NY 10952, (914) 425-4567

Bikur Cholim of Toronto, 12 Reddick Court, Toronto, Ontario, M6N 2S1, (416) 783-7983, 782-6365, 783-8321

The Elke Silberstein Bikur Cholim Group of Miami Beach, 4101 Pinetree Drive, #914, Miami Beach, FL 33140, (305) 531-5351

10

Coping with Death

A plague may last for seven years, but no one dies before his appointed hour."[1]

Americans as a whole are obsessed with denying death. Youth is revered to a point where older people are treated as if they are useless, and they are hidden away in retirement communities or old-age homes. People are so concerned with looking youthful that even men have cosmetic surgery to remove signs of aging. Death is not discussed by polite people and is too frightening for most people to think about. Doctors are so terrified of death that they use extraordinary means to keep people alive, long after patients are ready to leave this world.

Gentiles deny death by embalming people to look like they are still alive. They create an atmosphere at funerals that is more appropriate for a cocktail party than for a gathering of grief. Not long ago, family members even posed for portraits with made-up and dressed-up deceased relatives before they were buried![2]

Some people confront their fears of death by having midlife crises or frantically chasing every pleasure they can. But we don't have to be afraid of death. We can anticipate our last moments with equanimity as long as we don't make the physical world more than it really is. Anyone who uses this world for spiritual ends simply disrobes from the soul's physical "garment" at death, then enters an eternal, spiritual world of bliss.

This idea is expressed by the Hebrew term *niftar*. It refers to a deceased person and means "released from service." We work hard in this world to serve God, then death releases us from this service. When our time of toil is over, we go to a world of reward for our labors.

While most people think of death as the worst possible calamity, this is only true if there is no better life beyond. Death is actually extraordinarily pleasant for people who have near-death experiences. They experience serenity, love, and a closeness to God that is so delightful they have no desire to come back to our world. They return here only because they must.

Life is good only insofar as we use its opportunities and challenges to perfect our souls and the world. If we do that, death is good because it releases us into a world where we are rewarded with pleasures that are more enjoyable than anything we can experience here.

People often wonder if anyone has real knowledge of what happens after we die. While no one knows precisely what the afterlife is like, there are many biblical, talmudic, and contemporary anecdotes about it. For instance, as many as 66 percent of widows see or feel their dead husband's presence shortly after his death, and 75 percent of bereaved parents have contact with their child's soul within a year of his or her passing.[3] Survivors find these encounters very comforting because the soul usually communicates that it is happy and aware of what happens to loved ones on earth. The following is but one of many such stories:

A secular Israeli family drove to the Catskill Mountains one torrid summer day. The weather suddenly turned nasty and an unexpected downpour flooded the road. The husband lost control of the steering wheel, the car jumped a guard rail, and it then hurtled down a ravine. He was killed when he, his wife, and two of their three children were thrown from the car. When his wife regained consciousness, she saw that the two young boys were battered and bruised but not seriously injured. Then she saw that her screaming baby was still strapped in his car seat in the overturned, crushed vehicle. Despite all of her desperate efforts, she couldn't pull him out. No matter how hard she tried, her reach stopped a few inches short. Feeling utterly helpless, she realized that she might as well pray, even though she had never believed in God before.

"Please, God," she pleaded, hoping that Someone was listening, "help me get my child out of the car." Just then, her arm extended a tad further, and she managed to pry her baby out. A short while later, the family was taken to a hospital where they were treated and released.

Since they had been in America only for her husband's job, they returned to Israel. Even though he had died in the accident, she believed that God had made a miracle that enabled her to rescue her baby. She acknowledged this by enrolling her sons in a *yeshivah* (religious school) where they could get a good Jewish education.

A few weeks later, her ten-year-old son Avi came home from school. His class was having a Talmud test the next day and he was very agitated because he lacked the background to learn the material on the study sheet. His mother tried to reassure him that he would soon catch up, but he could not be consoled. He went to bed very upset.

The next morning he woke up happy and calm. His mother was pleased that he was feeling better, but his improved mood piqued her curiosity. She asked what had made him so exuberant.

He explained, "After I went to sleep last night, Daddy appeared to me in a dream. I told him how happy I was to see him, and he was glad to see me, too. We started to chat, and I told him that I was going to a *yeshivah*."

"Daddy said, 'I know.' "

"I asked how he knew, and he said, 'The day that you started *yeshivah* down there, they allowed me to enter *yeshivah* in Heaven.' "

"Then I told Daddy what chapter of the Talmud I was studying, and he replied, 'I know that, too.' "

"I asked him, How do you know?"

"He said, 'What you learn in your *yeshivah*, I learn in *yeshivah* in Heaven.' "

"So, since he and I were studying the same material, I asked him all of the questions that were on my study sheet and he gave me all of the answers. Now I feel much better."

When the mother related this story, she concluded, "Three days later, Avi came home with his graded test paper. He had received a 100."[4]

Death neither makes us disappear nor severs our ties to our loved ones. It merely frees our souls to go to another realm where our essential self lives on.

Each of our souls is so linked with past, present, and future generations that our spiritual accomplishments can even elevate the souls of deceased people.[5] We do this by studying Torah and observing God's commandments (*mitzvot*) in their memory. Our immortality encompasses the effects of everything that we do for ourselves and for others.

Knowing this, the loss of a loved one still feels like a terrible tragedy. We believe intellectually that death can lead to a beautiful afterlife, but it's hard to relate to that emotionally. That being the case, we often feel that our world has shattered into little pieces when a loved one dies. We feel angry, guilty, and confused, and don't know how to make sense of our lives. A tidal wave of disorienting feelings crashes over us and carries us into darkness before dropping us on uncharted shores. What we feel is so strong that we don't know where to turn.

We first want to deny that a beloved friend or relative is gone. We insist, "He can't be dead. I just spoke to him yesterday." We hope to wake up from our bad dream and hear that everything is okay. In our state of shock or denial, we want others to sit with us, listen to us, and hold us. We don't want to hear the voice of reason, we only want a comforting presence to stay by our side and give us a shoulder to cry on.

Parents often feel destroyed by a child's death, and their pain is unimaginable. They wish that they could have died and feel guilty that they couldn't save their loved one. Their future feels irreparable and they don't want to go on.

A boy begged his father from the time he was eleven to take him flying in a small plane. George surprised Joey on his seventeenth birthday by taking him on an hour-long sunset flight. Joey was ecstatic as the seven-seater soared above the Atlantic shoreline. He could see the magnificent fall colors, and the scenery glowed in the golden and red sunlight.

As they returned to the airport at twilight, their dream turned into a nightmare. The engines died before they got near the landing strip and the plane crashed into the ocean. The boy lost consciousness on impact and stayed strapped into his seat as the plane sank into the turbulent, icy, pitch-black water. The father nearly drowned as he repeatedly dove in desperate and herculean efforts to rescue his son. An hour and a half later, the Coast Guard retrieved the waterlogged, shivering survivors. But the father didn't care about being rescued. He could think only about his son's remains that went down with the wrecked plane.

This tormented man relived the horror of his son's last moments hundreds of times every day. Each time, he imagined how he could have rewritten the script. He tortured himself for almost a year before he reluctantly accepted that he could have done nothing more to save his beloved child. But he never stopped blaming himself for the tragedy.

We expect older people, not children, to die. Just a hundred years ago, though, 30–50 percent of Americans died before the age of 10.[6] Thanks to medical advances, relatively few children die today, but it is extremely traumatic when it does happen. In the United States, approximately one in three women loses a child through miscarriage,[7] and one in 200 deliveries ends in stillbirth.[8] Approximately 10,000 American infants die every year from Sudden Infant Death Syndrome (SIDS),[9] and another 40,000 die from other causes during the first six months of life.[10] Parents are devastated when they lose children of any age, and they often feel responsible for the death.

Judaism helps us grieve and mourn the loss of any loved one as we find comfort with God and a community. The detailed Jewish mourning rituals help us work through our feelings and make wise decisions when we are vulnerable and least capable of making good choices.

The importance of grieving cannot be overestimated. Unresolved grief over a loved one's death brings 30 percent of psychologists' patients to them.[11] Neglecting Jewish rituals and trying to cut short the grieving process is a serious mistake. It deprives us of the chance to mourn fully and get emotional support.

One poll of nonreligious psychologists showed that two-thirds believed that religious rituals play a major role in helping people cope with a loved one's death.[12] One in four therapists believed that not following religious traditions is a primary cause of long-term problems.[13] They also said that turning to religious traditions when someone dies is important even for Jews who do not normally practice Judaism.[14]

JEWISH FUNERAL, BURIAL, AND MOURNING PRACTICES

Judaism has a comprehensive system for helping mourners come to terms with their loss by integrating their emotions with their spirituality. It recognizes that the recently bereaved are totally preoccupied with a loved one's death. Since they can't do much more than think about their pain, close relatives are absolved from performing religious rituals until the deceased is buried.[15] This validates survivors' emotional turmoil at an overwhelming and confusing time.

The *Chevrah Kadisha* (a nonprofit communal burial society) takes responsibility for preparing Jewish bodies for burial. Members ritually wash the corpse, then dress it in white linen shrouds without pockets. This purifies the body before it appears for judgment in front of the King of Kings. The lack of pockets symbolizes that we can't take anything material with us when we leave this world.

The *Chevrah Kadisha* also makes sure that a corpse is not left alone from the time of death until burial. It is disrespectful to abandon the former house of the image of God, and it pains the soul to be left alone before burial. This is why a Jewish "guard" keeps it company by reciting Psalms in its presence until the funeral.

Survivors are especially vulnerable when someone dies, and funeral directors do their best to play on their emotions. They try to coerce the bereaved into spending a lot of money on a Cadillac of coffins, on embalming, on an expensive funeral and a large monument, all of which are forbidden by Jewish law, in part because we are not allowed to waste money on the dead.[16] Judaism requires rich and poor to be buried in an unadorned pine box (with wooden pegs) in the ground, clothed in plain linen shrouds. (In Israel, Jews are buried directly in the ground without coffins.) This ensures that the body and the coffin will decompose quickly. Cremation or above-ground burial is forbidden.

Jewish law requires a corpse to be buried as soon as possible, preferably by nightfall of the day of death.[17] The bereaved are not extended condolences before the burial, and the corpse is not viewed. The funeral normally honors the deceased by eulogizing him or her.[18]

The Torah goes to great lengths to describe the difficulties that our forefather Abraham had when he bought his wife Sarah a burial plot. He ended up paying a fortune for the Cave of Machpelah and the surrounding field in Hebron because it was unthinkable that a Jew would not bury his relatives.[19]

One of the hallmarks of Judaism is that we do kind deeds for others, but the only time that our actions can be completely altruistic is when the recipient cannot pay us back. We have many opportunities to do this for the deceased. For instance, it is a tremendous *mitzvah* to escort the deceased to the grave. As the pallbearers carry the coffin from the hearse to the grave, they stop several times. This symbolizes the various stages of life. Meanwhile, Psalm 91 is said:

He who dwells in the shelter of the High One will stay in the shadow of the Almighty. I will say of the Lord, "He is my refuge and fortress, my God in whom I trust." He will save you from the ensnaring trap, from terrible pestilence. He will cover you with His pinion, and hide you under His wings. His truth is a shield and armor. You shall not fear the terror of night, nor the arrow that flies by day, the pestilence that walks in the dark, nor the plague that lays waste at noon. A thousand will fall by your side, and ten thousand by your right side—they won't approach you. You will only take it in with your eyes and see the punishment of the wicked. Because the Lord is your shelter, you made the Most High your refuge, no evil will befall you, a plague will not go near your tent. He will command His messengers to guard you in all of your ways. They will carry you in their palms lest you strike your foot on a stone. You'll tread on lion and snake, and trample young cubs and serpent.

Because he yearns for Me, I will help him escape, I will elevate him because he knows My name. He will call to Me and I will answer him, I am with him in his trouble and I will release him and honor him. I will satisfy him with long life and show him My salvation. I will satisfy him with long life and show him My salvation.

We have the privilege and obligation to personally bury the deceased and not give this important *mitzvah* to gravediggers.[20] Those in attendance customarily do this by throwing the first spadeful of dirt into the grave using the back of the shovel. This poignant custom symbolizes how difficult it is to part with the deceased. As we slowly fill the grave and cover the coffin with earth, we feel the reality and permanence of our loss.

At the burial, mourners often feel angry with God for taking their loved one away, and/or feel that life is meaningless. They begin working through their feelings by saying the *tzidduk hadin.* This prayer acknowledges God's justice in ruling the world, and reminds us that there is a purpose to life and an eternal world beyond. The next-of-kin say this (paraphrased) after the grave is filled:

The Rock, whose work is perfect, whose ways are all just, is a God of faith without iniquity. He is righteous and fair.

The Rock who is perfect in every action—who will say to You, "What have You done?" You rule below and above, kill and bring to life, bring people to the grave and raise them up.

The Rock who is perfect in every act, who will say to You, "What did You do?" You are the One who says and does. Do undeserved kindness with us, and in the merit of the one who was bound like a lamb [Isaac], listen and act.

Righteous in all of His ways, the perfect Rock who is slow to anger and full of mercy, please have pity and spare parents and children, because You, Master, are forgiving and merciful.

You are righteous, Lord, to kill and revive. In Your hand is the safekeeping of all spirits. Far be it from You to erase our memories. And may You regard us with compassion because You are the Master of compassion and forgiveness.

It is no better for a man to be one year old or live a thousand years. Each will be as if he had never been. Blessed is the true Judge who kills and revives. You are blessed, because Your judgment is true. You oversee everything, and reward man according to Your accounting and judgment. All must acknowledge Your name.

We know, Lord, that Your judgment is righteous. You are righteous when You speak and meritorious when You judge, and we can't question Your attribute of judgment. Lord, You are righteous, and Your judgments are honest.

True Judge, righteous and true Judge, blessed is the true Judge whose judgments are all righteous and true.

The soul of all living is in Your hand. Your right hand is full of righteousness. Have mercy on the remnant of your flock, and say to the angel [of death], "Hold back your hand."

Great in advice, and abundant in actions, who knows all of man's ways—He will reward him according to his deeds.

I state that God is honest, my Rock, who has no flaw in Him. The Lord gave, and the Lord took, may God's name be blessed. He is merciful, forgives iniquity, and does not destroy. He often takes His anger away, and does not arouse all of His wrath.

Afterward, the comforting Psalm 23 is read:

A Psalm of David: The Lord is my shepherd, I shall not lack. He makes me lie down in lush pastures, He leads me beside restful waters. He restores my soul, He leads me on paths of righteousness for His name's sake. Even though I walk in the valley of death, I will not fear evil because You are with me. Your rod and staff comfort me. You prepare a table before me in front of my tormentors. You put oil on my head, my cup overflows. Only goodness and kindness will pursue me all the days of my life, and I will sit in the Lord's house for my length of days.

It is easy to think that death ends all existence when we stand in the midst of a cemetery, surrounded by graves. That is why mourners say a prayer that sanctifies God's name and affirms their belief in the future resurrection of the dead. This is known as the *Kaddish HaGadol* (the "Great *Kaddish*") and is said after the grave is filled:

May God's name be made great and sanctified in the world which will be renewed in the future, where He will bring the dead back to life and raise them to eternal life. He will build the city of Jerusalem, complete His Temple in it, uproot idol worship from the earth, and return worship of Heaven to its place. There the Holy One, blessed is He, will rule in His Kingship and splendor. [May this happen] in our lifetimes and in our days, and in the lifetimes of the entire house of Israel, quickly and soon, and say "Amen."

May His great name be blessed forever and for all eternity.

May the name of the Holy One, blessed is He, be blessed, praised, glorified, exalted, uplifted, adorned, raised, and extolled higher than any blessing, song, praise, and consolation that are said in this world. And say "Amen."

Let there be much peace from Heaven and life upon us and on all Israel. And say, "Amen."

He who makes peace in the high places, let Him make peace for us and for all Israel. And say, "Amen."

Finally, a last prayer is said (with respective changes for a woman):

God, full of mercy, who is present on high, give proper rest on the wings of the Divine Presence—in the heights of the holy and pure ones who shine like the splendor of the sky—to the soul of [person's name] that went to his world. In the merit of my giving charity for his soul's memory, may his resting place be in the Garden of Eden. Therefore, Master of mercy, shelter him under the protection of Your wings forever, and bind his soul in the bundle of life. The Lord is his inheritance, and let him rest peacefully in his resting place. And say, "Amen."

These prayers help survivors deal with the terrible pain, hurt, confusion, and anger that we feel when a loved one dies.

Close relatives then vent their destructive anger by ripping an outer garment that is never repaired.[21] They do this right before the funeral, or just after burial. At the same time they say, "Blessed are You, Lord our God, Ruler of the Universe, the true Judge." If a parent has died, children tear the clothing next to their heart. This symbolically tells the world that the person's heart has been torn irreparably and will never feel whole again.

Many survivors want to join the deceased, or at least express their grief by harming themselves. Ripping one's clothes is a 3,000-year-old custom that expresses how painful someone's loss is.[22] (Wearing a torn ribbon is a cheap symbol that defeats the purpose of tearing one's own garment.) Mourners wear the torn garment during *shiva* (the week of formal mourning) as a visible expression of their broken heart.

When death steals a loved one away, mourners often feel helpless and victimized, and life seems insignificant. By accepting God's verdict and sanctifying Him by saying *Kaddish,* we affirm that life has meaning and that our Heavenly Father is running the world according to a plan. This sanctification of God also brings tremendous merit to the deceased's soul.

After the burial, next-of-kin sit *shivah* (literally, "seven" days), where they formally mourn at home for a week.[23] They return home from the cemetery, and friends feed them a solemn meal and keep them company. Mourners may be too depressed to take care of themselves, so others do it for them. They do not leave the house for the entire week, except on the Sabbath.

This week of *shivah* gives mourners a chance to indulge their depression, despair, and even self-loathing in ways that promote healing. They sit on the floor or on low boxes to symbolize their sense of "lowness." They neglect their appearance and do not wear leather shoes, bathe, or shave. They look disheveled and unkempt, which expresses outwardly how they feel inside.

Visitors to a *shivah* house don't greet mourners, nor vice versa. We comfort mourners by keeping them company, giving a listening ear and a shoulder to cry on. We don't talk to them unless they initiate conversation. We give them a chance to tell us about their guilt, confusion, sadness, outrage, and other feelings in an atmosphere of total acceptance. This intense catharsis normally lasts for a full week and is extremely important for proper grieving, feeling comforted, and coming to terms with an overwhelming loss. By the time the week ends, mourners are ready to begin a long journey back to "normalcy."

Lay people often expect mourners to overcome their devastation in a few days or weeks, and get impatient when mourning continues much longer. The Reform shortcut of observing only three days of *shivah* is a good example of this. Torah Judaism teaches that people go through stages of mourning that last an entire year, and this process should not be hurried.

Mourners continue grieving after *shivah* ends, but the religious restrictions diminish as time passes. During the first thirty days after burial (known as *sheloshim,* meaning "thirty"), mourners are not allowed to attend joyous activities such as concerts, weddings, bar mitzvahs, or ritual circumcision meals. They reflect on their loss instead of trying to block out their pain.

For the next eleven months, surviving children continue some mourning practices. They may not attend joyous events like parties, musical events, or public entertainment during the year. That gives them time to fully work out their feelings and reminds the community that the bereaved still need consolation and comfort.

Survivors slowly reintegrate into life. They start their painful journey wondering how anyone can laugh and enjoy themselves, and wonder if they will ever be happy again. They constantly think about their loved one during their dark days and sleepless nights. They even have bodily pains that express their emotional hurts.

Survivors find it hard to imagine, during the darkest days of their lives, that they will ever find pleasure and meaning in life again. Yet they do start sleeping and eating better, resume socializing, and think about topics besides their loved one. Over time, most survivors do feel happy again, and may be comforted through remarriage or the birth of a baby, even if they reexperience their loss on holidays, anniversaries, special occasions, or behind closed doors.

Whenever survivors say *Kaddish,* they automatically find themselves among supportive Jews. Communal memorial prayers (known as *Yizkor*) are said four times a year in the synagogue. Close relatives also say *Kaddish* and light a *yahrzeit* candle every year on the anniversary of a loved one's death. Some fast on a parent's *yahrzeit,* give extra charity, and/or learn Mishnah in their memory. Loved ones are never forgotten.

HOW TO COMFORT

Survivors need to share their feelings and memories with others, but listeners often feel uncomfortable seeing people who are in so much pain that they lose interest in life and may even want to die.

We spend years learning academic subjects such as history or math, yet we're rarely taught how to respond appropriately to others' pain and loss. We should not be upset or worried when bereaved people sob, "fall apart," feel anguished, or want to die. That is exactly how they are supposed to feel, and they can feel this way for many months. We need to support and listen to them without telling them not to grieve. It is therapeutic for them if we simply acknowledge their loss and pain. It is counterproductive to "cheer" them up or give religious platitudes and useless advice.

There are no "right words" that can magically take away the pain of a loved one's death. The best we can do is to let survivors say what they feel, make it safe to cry, and let them know that they are not alone. Without saying anything, our presence alone can be very comforting.

A woman gave a bereaved friend exactly what she needed by saying but a few choice words: "I've thought about you so often during these past few days. I have no words to comfort you, other than to say, 'I'm so sorry.' I can't possibly imagine what you are going through." This is a most appropriate response under most circumstances. No one wants to hear pat reassurances, stories about someone else's loss, or explanations about why their tragedy occurred.

A six-year-old boy spent the afternoon with his grandfather soon after his grandmother passed away. When he came home, his mother asked what they had talked about for four hours.

"I didn't say anything," the boy replied.

"So what did you and grandpa do all day?" the mother persisted.

"Grandpa needed to talk, so I listened. Then he needed to cry, so I hugged him while he did," the boy said nonchalantly.

If only adults could do the same!

It is normal for mourners to obsess about the deceased, ask rhetorical questions about why they died, and feel immobilized. They will reconstitute themselves much, much later. In the meantime, we should not dissuade them from doing this because we think that they are "too emotional," or insist that they take medication to "calm down." Most grieving people will resent this as soon as they realize that they were stripped of the opportunity to mourn.

One of the most harmful things that people do to mourners is to try to make them "get over" their loss too quickly or minimize their loss. One woman said, "My father died after being senile for five years. I felt sad, but not because I would never see him again. I had so many unresolved feelings about him. He was a very critical and cold man. My whole life, I had desperately wanted him to approve of me, but he never once told me that he loved me or was proud of me. I wanted him to know that I became a lawyer, which is what he had wanted me to be. I wanted him to have a relationship with my children. I wanted him to know that I loved him even though he hurt me terribly. By the time I told him these things, he no longer recognized me. Our relationship was one of so many missed opportunities.

"At his funeral, people kept offering condolences that made me feel worse than if they'd said nothing at all. They made idiotic comments like, 'You should be grateful that he died so peacefully. He's better off this way,' or 'He's in heaven now. It's good that he's out of his suffering.' What is wrong with people? Why can't they simply say that they are sorry that he died and that it must be painful for me to have lost my father?"

We can never feel "comfortable" responding properly to people who are in emotional pain. Unfortunately, this prompts some people to offer "condolences" that minimize their loss or make them feel worse. Visitors to *shivah* homes often say extremely inappropriate things. For example, they tell the bereaved about someone else's problems. They focus on themselves, get chatty, or try to cheer the person up. It would be much more comforting just to say, "I'm so sorry."

It is normal and healthy for mourners to be extremely sad and preoccupied with their loss for at least a month, and sometimes for as long as a year or two. We should offer a listening ear without giving suggestions or advice, changing the topic, or minimizing their loss. Never tell people that a loved one's death was "God's will" or that everyone is better off now that the person is out of his or her misery. Such comments are harmful and trivializing.

A friend wanted to comfort a widow whose husband died of Alzheimer's disease. The couple had been married for forty-eight years, and the wife had been his round-the-clock nurse at home during his last three years. He had not been lucid during those years, then she had to feed him and he wore diapers.

The friend was about to say, "His death must have been such a relief for you. Now you can get on with your life." But before she had a chance to say anything, the widow lamented, "I miss my husband so much. It's so hard getting used to living without him."

This woman had not felt burdened taking care of her husband, even though it had required all of her time. She did this as a labor of love and would gladly have done it for many more years. Her friend learned not to assume how anyone else feels. She now asks instead.

People who have never lost a loved one can say, "Thank God, I don't know what it's like to go through such a loss. What has it been like for you?" Those who know what it is like should share a brief comment of support and let the mourner respond.

A businesswoman's father died of cancer. When she came back to work, her normally gruff and aloof boss came to her office and asked how she was. She replied that it was still hard to concentrate. She felt like someone had punched a hole in her stomach, and she cried every day.

Much to her surprise, he replied, "I lost my father ten years ago, and it was the worst experience of my life. I know how you feel. The world is a different place once you've lost a parent. . . . If you ever want to talk about it, my door is open." His brief comment made her feel supported and understood, and she never felt the need to take him up on his offer.

Men and women tend to grieve differently, with women usually verbalizing feelings more than men. Our society expects men to be "strong" and not "fall apart," cry, or be vulnerable. Unfortunately, this strips them of the chance to grieve their loss with our support. The process of saying *Kaddish* with at least ten men every day is one way of joining a male support group, but this alone is not enough. Men still need to share their feelings with others. Those who try to "put the past behind them" as quickly as possible pay a high price for not allowing themselves to mourn. They may bury their sadness, anger, and resentment inside for years, but it eventually catches up with them.

Paul was a fifty-six-year-old man who was raised with WASP values. He had to keep a stiff upper lip no matter what. His mother died of cancer when he was in his early thirties, and he was denied the chance to grieve. He shed a tear or two at her funeral but was expected not to share his feelings of devastation and sorrow with anyone. He returned to a "normal" life three weeks after her funeral.

After being in therapy for a year, Paul had said almost nothing about his mother. When the therapist mentioned this, his eyes filled with tears and he buried his face in his hands. He sobbed for the next twenty minutes. His raw wound was unbandaged for the first time in two decades and the dam that had kept his feelings in check finally collapsed.

How he had wanted to say goodbye to his mother, but he had been denied the chance! How he had ached when he saw her dying in the hospital, so frail amid a mass of tubes and needles! How he had yearned for her to put her arms around him and comfort him!

Unfortunately, his feelings were not acceptable for a grown man. "Real men" were supposed to stuff down their feelings and not feel pain. What a price Paul, and others like him, pay for living by these ridiculous rules!

Men often grieve as deeply as women but are rarely as adept at expressing their feelings. If they can't share their hurt, sadness, and vulnerability, men can carry unresolved feelings with them much longer than is necessary.

Some therapists believe that most patients have problems as a result of never fully mourning a loved one's death. The more a bereaved person shares his grief and memories, the more he dissipates his pain, and the easier it is to accept the loss. It is almost impossible to mourn alone, and we should help mourners regain their emotional equilibrium and reintegrate among us at their own pace.

People have individual styles and paces for coping with a loved one's death, but some do it much more successfully than others. For example, widowers usually cope worse than widows, and young people initially cope worse than older people, but usually recover more quickly.[24] Our beliefs and expectations strongly affect how well we cope with tragedy. Surprisingly, people with the highest self-esteem, who believe that they can handle anything, cope the worst. Their arrogance leaves them unprepared for a loss that they couldn't prevent or control.[25]

People cope best if they find meaning in a loved one's death, or if they believe that it fits into God's plan for the world.[26] The Jewish belief that God controls the world gives us a wonderful foundation for coping. Since the general population doesn't accept Jewish ideas about life and death, 70–80 percent of them can't make sense of tragedies, and coping is very difficult for them.[27]

Besides feeling sad and pained about a loss, most survivors also feel guilty. They berate themselves for what they said or didn't say, for what they did or didn't do. They worry that they hurt their loved one or made decisions that hastened the death.

It was only after a man lost his wife of forty years that he realized what a wonderful wife she had been and how he had mistreated her. He kept asking all of his friends and relatives if she knew how much he had loved her. They all said that she did, but he didn't believe them. He knew that he hadn't told her in years that he loved her and couldn't remember the last time that he had bought her a gift, complimented her, or thanked her for taking care of him. For the rest of his life, he never forgave himself for taking her so for granted.

Unlike this man, some people don't feel bad when a close relative dies. For instance, spouses who had a bad marriage typically feel relieved when their partner dies, as do children who lose a hated parent. Some widows have mixed feelings after a spouse is murdered or dies. When their initial shock wears off, they may feel relieved that they can start a new life. If they don't think that their friends will be sympathetic, they keep their feelings to themselves.

Some survivors feel guilty for not being sad when a debilitated relative passes away. Some even feel relieved that the deceased is no longer a burden to them. They feel guilty, though, if they hoped or prayed that God would take their loved one away.

It is normal to want an ill person's suffering to end, or to want the strain of taking care of a deteriorating loved one to stop. The Talmud beautifully describes the ambivalence that we feel when someone is terminally ill and suffering:

Rabbi Judah the Prince (who compiled the Mishnah) was deathly ill and in terrible agony, yet his disciples prayed fervently that he would live. His maidservant, a woman known for her piety, went to the roof and prayed, "The angels want Rabbi to join them, and humans want him to stay with them. May it be God's will that the mortals overpower the immortals." As he lingered on, she realized that he was terribly debilitated by his loss of bodily control and its disruption of his religious practices. She then changed her prayer and asked, "May it be God's will that the immortals overpower the mortals." But the Sages' ongoing prayers for heavenly mercy rendered her prayers ineffective. Finally, she threw a pottery jar from the roof. When it shattered on the ground, it so startled the rabbis that they stopped praying momentarily, and Rabbi's soul went to its eternal rest.[28]

Just as this righteous woman did not have to regret her actions, we needn't feel guilty for wanting a loved one to be out of agony. However, we need to be clear whose agony we are praying to end—the person who is sick, or our own.

DEATH OF CHILDREN

Hundreds of thousands of American children die every year, many of them after long illnesses. Parents with terminally ill children feel tortured as they watch their children go through painful medical procedures and horrible treatments, sometimes for years. Their helpless youngsters turn black and blue from hypodermic needles and intravenous lines. They get sick from radiation, infections, and cancer. Some struggle to breathe, others' muscles waste away. Their parents mourn as their children slowly slip away and lose their beautiful color, their energy, their weight, and perhaps their hair. They suffer as they watch their children make extraordinary efforts to breathe or move. Parents are tortured by having to make medical decisions, and most feel torn and inadequate trying to divide their time and energy between several children and a spouse.

Many bereaved parents are comforted by talking to others who have suffered a similar loss. The talmudic Sage Rabbi Yochanan had ten sons who died when they were very young. (He regarded these tragedies as afflictions of love.) He always wore a necklace from which hung a tooth of the last child that he had buried. When he comforted other bereaved parents, they saw his poignant, nonverbal message of empathy and knew that he understood how they felt.[29] Simply sharing his sense of profound and irreplaceable loss was more helpful than any words. At the same time, his presence implied that he had found a way to overcome his grief and find meaning in life.

A religious couple whose infant died were consoled by the following story:

A Gentile governor ruled an Eastern European town where many Jews lived. He treated them well for years, then called in their rabbi one day and gave the following ultimatum: "I have noticed that you Jews have a special connection to God. When you pray for things, even miracles, I know that you are answered.

"My wife and I have been married for many years, and we have not been blessed with a child. I want all of you Jews to pray for us. If we don't have a baby by this time next year, I will know that you didn't take me seriously, and I will tax you very heavily and treat you badly. Go relay this message to your people."

The rabbi convened all of the town's Jews and told them the governor's ominous words. "We must pray with all of our strength that they have a child," the rabbi announced. "Otherwise, it will be a desecration of God's name and the governor will make us miserable."

The Jews did as they were told, and each beseeched the One Above to give the governor and his wife a child. The couple was delighted when they had a baby boy eleven months later. But the parents died soon afterward in an accident, and the child had no one to raise him.

The Jews had prayed for this child to be born, so they felt a special responsibility to take care of him. A righteous couple adopted him, converted him to Judaism, and raised him as their own.

In a very short time, it was apparent that he was very special. He loved people and had an exceptional intellect. By the time he was eighteen, people came to him from far and wide. He became a rebbe who was known for his kindness and pearls of wisdom. He died in his nineties after living a very full life, and his soul went to the sixth level of heavenly reward. The angels wanted to take him to the seventh (and highest) level, but God did not allow it. He said that his soul needed a small rectification in order to go to the highest heights because the child had spent the first part of his life in a non-Jewish home. God asked the soul if it wanted to remain at the sixth level of reward or be reincarnated so that it might fully rectify itself. The soul asked to be reincarnated.

God sent it back to the world at a time when it could fully actualize itself. It was put into the body of a baby boy who was born to a religious Jewish couple. By the time the baby was nine months old, his soul was perfected and ready to enter the highest level of Paradise.

That morning, the mother came to take the baby out of his crib. She softly hummed to herself as she reached over to wake up the little boy. Then, to her horror, she saw that the baby was dead. His soul had just gone to its eternal reward because she and her husband had done such a good job taking care of him. As she grieved, her baby's soul was in a place of indescribable pleasure.

Children who die or who are sickly usually have reincarnated souls that are here to complete a mission from a previous life. When they die after doing this, God takes them to the next world to enjoy their eternal reward.[30] In these cases, parents did nothing to contribute to their child's death. To the contrary, God chose them to enable their child's soul to become perfected.

Many of our pious ancestors had to come to terms with the death of their children. The Talmud relates a poignant story about a famous Sage, Rabbi Meir, and his extraordinary wife Bruria. One Sabbath, she discovered that their two young sons had died. Meanwhile, their father was lecturing in the study hall. Not wanting to disturb his serenity on the Sabbath, she kept the tragic news to herself. When he came home, he asked where his sons were.

"They went to the study hall," she said.

"I didn't see them there," he responded.

When the Sabbath was over, she gave him the wine cup and he said the blessings that end the Sabbath and start the weekday. He then asked again, "Where are my sons?"

"They went elsewhere, and now they've come home."

She then fed him the Saturday night meal that escorts the Sabbath queen on her way. After he blessed God for the meal, she said, "I have a question for you."

"Ask," he said.

"Earlier, someone gave me some precious gems to keep for him. Now he is asking for them back. Must we return them?"

The rabbi replied, "But of course. Someone who gets a deposit must return it to the owner."

She replied, "I would not return it without your knowledge." With that, Bruria led her husband to the bedroom. She pulled back the sheet and he saw his sons' corpses on the bed. As he cried out in anguish, she gently told him, "Did you not tell me that we must return a deposit to the owner? The Lord loaned us two precious gems, and today He came to reclaim them."[31]

Rabbi Meir felt somewhat comforted knowing that his tragedy was no "accident" and was not caused by "random forces." Knowing that God must have had a good reason for taking back His precious children made the experience meaningful.

The rabbi took solace in having been God's partner in raising these gems and preparing them to return to their Heavenly Father.

There is no greater pain than losing children. Rabbi Nachman of Breslov lost most of his to typhus, and only one son survived childhood. He dealt with his tremendous anguish by composing many prayers asking God to help him cope with his tragedies. In one of these he pleaded (paraphrased):

> Awesome, Holy One, please keep me from trouble and suffering, and be with me constantly. If Your divine justice and goodness ever require me to suffer, help me by giving me the strength and understanding to fathom its ultimate good purpose. Let me become completely and genuinely merged with You in my moment of pain. Let me make myself into nothing, and completely shut my eyes to this world and its desires, until I can look into the distance and catch sight of the true, eternal goal. Let my suffering bring me to this vision, and with it, let my suffering completely disappear.

Besides praying at home or in the synagogue, we also pray at the graves of pious Jews. Their souls are aware of our existence and can ask God to be merciful to us and help us.[32] Among other things, they can take our prayers before God's "Heavenly Throne."[33]

Besides the obvious pain that parents feel when a child dies, there are other subtle, destructive consequences. For example, a young child's death often shatters the mother's self-esteem and the couple's closeness. Some couples are afraid to have more children lest they also die, while others obsess about replacing their loss. Couples often miscommunicate and feel tense with one another after they lose a child. An empathic obstetrician or couple's therapist may need to intervene.

Michael and Lynn were in their late thirties when Ezra was born. He had serious neurological problems and died a few weeks later. Concerned friends gave Michael and Lynn food, comfort, and consolation during their week of *shivah*. Their rabbi shared with them how painful it had been when his wife had had a stillborn baby. He also gave them practical advice, such as suggesting that they reassure their two surviving sons that they were healthy and would not die, and that they didn't cause Ezra's death. God had taken him because he was very sick.

Six months later, Lynn's obstetrician had a frank talk with her and asked how she and Michael were doing. Lynn lied and said that they were doing well, having reconciled themselves to the fact that they would have no more children. Yet Lynn was very sad, and her doctor got her to admit that she and Michael were devastated that they could raise only two children. Lynn didn't like to talk to Michael about Ezra or having children because it made her feel so sad.

The doctor confronted Lynn about her avoidance of marital relations. Lynn admitted, "We're both afraid that if we have more children, they will die like Ezra did."

Lynn's doctor reassured her that she and Michael had no more chance of having a defective child than any other healthy couple and encouraged them to try again.

When their healthy and vigorous son was born, they finally put their fears behind them. It was fortuitous that Lynn's doctor had been so perceptive.

While it is devastating to watch a sick child die, some parents don't have that "luxury." One hundred thousand American children end up in morgues every year after disappearing. Many have undergone foul play or died under mysterious circumstances. Their parents have no clue as to what the children felt between the time they left home and died, and they may never even know how or when they died.[34] These parents feel especially guilty that they didn't adequately protect their children.

To compound their suffering, few people want to listen to their gory stories of what happened. These unfortunate parents often have no one to listen to their despair, self-blame, anger, and pain, and their presence makes others so uncomfortable that they are avoided socially.

When people are murdered, or die under suspicious circumstances, their next-of-kin must go through ordeals that other survivors do not. For example, parents may be suspects in their child's death. If there is a murder trial, they must go to multiple interrogations, depositions, and visits to police stations and courts. These can keep parents reliving a nightmare for years and prevent them from putting closure on a child's death. Their frustration and pain is then compounded by knowing that the legal system will never do justice to their child's killer.

When we turn to God in our pain and suffering, at least we don't suffer alone. We can ask Him to help us find meaning in our tragedies and give us the strength to live productively despite our losses.

Bereaved parents find it easier to go on living if they can only know that their child was taken away for a reason, and that he or she is now in a better place. It can be so comforting to meet or read about people who have had near-death experiences. They can reassure parents that God took their loved one to a safe place where he or she is happy. Senseless tragedies are always hard to accept, and NDEers can tell them that death is never arbitrary. Parents whose children's souls have communicated with them report that their children feel loved and wonderful in the next world and look healthy and happy, even if their bodies were ravaged by disease or mutilated when they died. (Don't let unenlightened doctors and therapists dismiss these phenomena as being unreal or imaginary.)

Some souls do more good from the next world than from this one.[35] One woman told the following story:

"Our daughter-in-law Helen died suddenly for no apparent reason. My son Robert and his daughter were extremely distraught, especially since Helen died so unexpectedly. They never had a chance to say goodbye and this bothered them tremendously.

"A few weeks after her death, Helen appeared to Robert in a dream and apologized for dying so abruptly. She told him not to worry about her, that she loved him very much, and that she was taken from this world because she could do more good from the next world than she was doing here.

"She informed Robert, a dentist, that he would soon get a new patient who would need a lot of expensive dental work in a short period of time. She told him to use the money to take their daughter to Israel as they had planned before Helen died.

"Later that week, Robert received a phone call from a woman whom he had never met. She told him that she urgently needed dental care and wondered if he could treat her. When he saw her, her mouth was in such a terrible state that she needed nine thousand dollars of dental work. She insisted that he complete the job in the next few weeks.

"He agreed, but was curious as to how she had found him. She said that she had looked in the yellow pages for a dentist, and his name suddenly jumped off the page.

"Needless to say, Robert was not happy that his wife had died, but he felt very comforted that death did not sever their emotional and spiritual bonds. By the way, he and his daughter had a very meaningful trip in Israel."

Survivors frequently get signs that a deceased relative is watching out for them in the next world, as Masha related:

"My husband and I had tried unsuccessfully to have a baby for seven years. During that time, I lost two babies through miscarriage. My father then died, and my husband and I made one last effort to get pregnant before adopting. Two months after my father died, I conceived, and I had a baby boy just before my father's *yahrzeit*. Of course, we named the baby for his grandfather, and they look just like each other. I have no doubt my father's merit helped us have this child."

RESPONDING TO LOSS

We can't prevent a loved one from dying, but we can decide how our tragedy will affect us. We can stay paralyzed with grief, or channel our loss into personal growth. We can stay bitter and self-absorbed, or intensify our spirituality and help others.

We might think that a child's death would make most parents abandon their faith in God, yet just the opposite usually happens. Most bereaved parents seek a more intense relationship with God than they did while their child was alive. The death of a loved one often motivates people to seek, and find, greater meaning in life.

Eva's son and daughter-in-law died in a tragic car crash. Her husband then died of a heart attack after he heard the terrible news. She was bitter, inconsolable, and angry with God, and she lost all interest in life.

A year later, Eva met Sarah, a young widow with nine children. As Sarah's husband lay dying, she brought all of their children to his hospital bed to say good-bye. They sadly accepted his death without turning against God, even though they were orphaned and left penniless. Sarah had to assume enormous responsibilities, but she accepted her painful destiny with an inner calm that stemmed from a deep faith in God's ways of running the world.

Eva met Sarah a number of times and slowly adopted Sarah's perspective about life. Eva carried a well-worn book of Psalms with her and read from it every day. It gave her solace to know that others had suffered as she had. She felt comforted knowing that the Jews' greatest king, David, came to terms with two of his sons' deaths by deepening his relationship with God. She didn't have to think that we live in an arbitrary world. David had so many tribulations that he was a good model for Eva of how to cope with tragedy.

Three years after her husband's death, Eva said, "I have no complaints against God. All in all, He gave me a very good life. I'll never understand why He took away my family as He did, but I've learned to let Him run the show."

Death can help us truly appreciate life and jar us into living as we ideally should. Most Jews, whether they are Reform, Conservative, or Orthodox, turn to Jewish traditions when a relative dies.[36] They can use this time to learn more about Judaism, to deepen their commitment to it, and to forge a closer relationship with the Almighty.

Many people discover true meaning in life only after a loved one dies, as happened in the following story:

A young man was raised in a nonobservant Jewish home and had never met an Orthodox lay person or rabbi whom he respected. When he was in his twenties, his mother underwent a prolonged, nightmarish bout with breast cancer, radiation, and chemotherapy, to which she eventually succumbed.

Even though he wasn't observant, he sought out a synagogue where he could say *Kaddish.* The observant rabbi was completely different from any Jew whom he had ever known. During the man's time saying *Kaddish,* the rabbi taught him and his wife about authentic Judaism. They started keeping kosher, observed Jewish rituals, and transferred their children into traditional Jewish schools. Eventually, both parents and their five children became observant as an indirect result of his mother's death.

This story is especially meaningful to me because I am one of those five children.

SUGGESTIONS FOR COPING WITH DEATH

People need time to grieve when a loved one dies, and they will grieve in different ways and at different paces. Some couples find that sharing a tragedy, making joint decisions about the future, and supporting each other creates a tremendous bonding, while others need to get support from friends, relatives, a spiritual adviser, a Jewish support group for the bereaved, and/or a professional.

Talk to people who knew your loved one. Ask them to share memories, photographs, mementos, and stories.

If you must dispose of possessions, give them to people who appreciate their emotional value, or donate them to charity.

If you hurt the deceased, you can make amends by going to the person's grave and asking for forgiveness in the presence of ten Jewish men. The person's soul will be aware of what you are doing and forgive you.

You can bring merit to a loved one's soul by doing good deeds, giving extra charity, and studying Torah in their memory. You can also encourage others to do the same. One family asked friends to memorialize their mother by doing one or more of the following:

For children:

- Thank your parents for doing things for you.
- Be careful to say only nice things for one hour every day.
- Say something nice about friends, relatives, or neighbors once a day.
- Be polite and share your toys and food when you play with friends.
- Do an additional chore that helps your parents, such as taking out the garbage or caring for a younger sibling.
- Help a handicapped child.
- Befriend someone who seems lonely.

For adults:

- Pray with concentration for at least five minutes a day.
- Visit sick people in a hospital or nursing home once a week.
- Help a bedridden pregnant woman or a new mother.
- Cook extra food and bring it to someone who is homebound.
- Give charity before lighting the Sabbath candles on Friday afternoon.
- Baby-sit for the children of a woman in labor or one who is in the hospital.
- Take care of a handicapped child for a day or a weekend so that the parents can have time for themselves.
- Read to a blind person.
- Go to a weekly class in Judaism, or listen to a Torah tape every week.
- Study Judaism from a book or with your spouse for an extra forty-five minutes a week.
- Learn with your children or spouse how to properly do a *mitzvah*. The Sabbath table is a good place to do this.
- Help a large family once a week.
- Donate old clothes, toys, or baby furniture to a charity.
- Drive a disabled person or immigrant to a doctor's appointment, or help run errands and shop.
- Donate time to a charitable organization.
- Say two positive things to your spouse and each child every day.
- Invite guests to your house for the Sabbath and/or holidays.
- Work on controlling your temper.
- Remind yourself not to speak negatively about others when you talk on the telephone.
- Develop an area of your spiritual life that needs work.
- Ask your spouse and children if you have a negative behavior that they would like you to change, and try to do it.

If a loved one's death makes you question your faith in God, talk to a spiritual adviser. Don't talk to people who think that you should be unshakable in your religious convictions.

You are not faithless for finding it hard to believe in God when tragedy strikes. Even very righteous people have serious questions as a healthy part of religious growth. Instead of battling your feelings alone, find someone who can listen to your misgivings and help you rebuild your faith.

Read about people's near-death experiences. Several references are listed in For Further Reading.

BEING HELPFUL

Only a *very* close friend or relative should go to a house of mourning before the funeral. Call and ask the family if there's anything you can do. They may need you to make phone calls to inform people about the death, prepare food for the week of *shivah,* coordinate people to visit during the week, make sure that there will be a quorum of men for daily services, or bring over chairs and prayer books.

Help mourners by sitting with them and allowing them to cry, be angry, or say nothing. There are times when nothing we say will erase their pain and we shouldn't try. Being a good listener is much more helpful than saying "correct" or inspiring words.

Don't give philosophical explanations to people who are suffering. No one in pain wants to hear that he brought his problems on himself or is being punished because of God's love. Explanations help only when our pain subsides enough to find emotional comfort in ideas.

If you aren't comfortable listening to someone's pain, anger, and depression, don't give pat "explanations," cheery encouragements, or advice. Never tell the bereaved that it's good the deceased is out of his suffering or is in heaven, or that life must go on. Don't tell survivors to be strong or not get "too upset," that everything will be okay, or that their beloved didn't suffer. Just listen and say how hard the loss must be for him or her.

Imagine someone losing his wife of thirty-six years. He cries, "Why did she have to die?"

A sensitive friend would say, "It must be so painful for you to live without her."

An unthinking person says, "Come on, Lou, your wife died because she was old and sick. You're lucky that she lived five years after her first heart attack. You can't expect her to have lived forever. Think about how many good, long years you had together."

These words might be true, but they are not comforting. We need to acknowledge and empathize with someone's anguish and loneliness, not tell them what to be grateful for.

Pay a *shivah* call to the family, but not late at night. If you aren't a close friend or relative, or don't have much to say to the mourners, don't stay longer than ten or fifteen minutes. Go to console them and listen to their feelings, not distract them from mourning. If you knew the deceased, share your pleasant memories. Don't think that focusing on the deceased will cause the survivors more pain. Their pain is already indescribable, and it is consoling to know that their loved one brought happiness or meaning to others.

If you didn't know the deceased, let survivors share their feelings and memories with you. Holding someone's hand or putting your arm around a person while he or she cries can be more comforting than words. Saying "I'm sorry" is usually more helpful than long-winded words of intended solace. Even if you or the survivors don't have much to say, your company will be appreciated.

When a child dies, encourage classmates to visit the family and share their memories. (This also helps the classmates mourn.) When a teacher dies, it means a lot to the family to see his or her students and hear the impact that the deceased had on their lives.

It is very painful for people to have to grieve alone. We can't take their pain away, but we can help them grieve in the company of people who love them. All grief ends, except that which is never faced.

A mourner's loss can feel worst when support vanishes soon after the funeral. Call every few days to chat, and invite the bereaved for a weekly cup of coffee or a meal. Be mindful of their concrete and emotional needs. Ask what you can do to help, and offer to baby-sit, cook, help children with homework, and so on.

Many widows don't know much about finances, including how to pay bills, balance a checkbook, keep tax records, or manage money. Refer them to an attorney and/or an accountant if they have no family to help them and cannot take care of things on their own.

Some older people have poor eyesight and cannot read their bills or letters, drive, or shop without assistance. Offer to help them sort through mail, read letters, and run errands.

Some widows need help with home repairs or keeping up the house and grounds. Either offer help or refer them to reliable and honest help. Call during severe weather to make sure that they have electricity and heat and can get into and out of their home.

Many widows have never conducted a Passover *seder* and don't feel comfortable doing it. Most have never bought a *lulav* (palm branch) and *etrog* (citron) for the holiday of Sukkot (Tabernacles) or put up a *sukkah* (ritual booth) for the family. Offer to help do these.

Some widowers have no idea how to run a home or cook. Invite them for meals and recommend a housekeeper if they need one.

Widowers with children may need a lot of help arranging play dates, carpooling children, and buying clothes, furniture, and birthday presents. Give recommendations or offer to help until the father learns the ropes.

Many widows with young children cannot afford baby-sitters, yet they must go to school and/or work to support the family. Some need help disciplining children. Some older widows need housekeeping help or someone to drive them places.

People are more apt to help a widower with children than a widow. They expect widows to somehow run the family unaided, although they may offer financial help. They don't think to invite a widow for meals because they assume that she can cook for herself, while they readily invite a widower.

Some survivors are loathe to burden others with their problems. A young widow with sons aged six and eight lamented, "I am so disappointed by my neighbors. When my husband was murdered, everyone came and extended their condolences, but their concern lasted for about three weeks. Then they avoided me as if I had the plague. People asked if I needed money, and that was one thing that I didn't need. My sons needed a father, and no one seemed interested in hearing that. Every Friday night, my male neighbors filed past my house on their way to the synagogue. They all had their kids in tow as they greeted me, but it never occurred to them to take my sons with them. At first, I asked them to take my kids with them, and they reluctantly did it. When they never volunteered, I felt like I was imposing by asking, so I stopped.

"It's been three years since my husband died, and my boys want to feel that some man cares about them. I feel so bad for them. I still ask my neighbors to take my sons to the synagogue on occasion. At best, they do it once, then 'forget.' I'm not asking them to play father, I just want my sons to be able to feel like normal kids by going to the synagogue with a man."

Some bereaved people are too disoriented even to know what they need. For example, a widower did not know where to turn when his ten-year-old daughter had a high fever the day of an important meeting at work. Another widower was greeted by wails when he forgot his child's birthday. Another was so overwhelmed that he constantly ran out of diapers, baby food, and clean clothes for the children.

Some children in large families never have a chance to talk to anyone about how they feel when they lose a parent. The parent is too busy shouldering burdens for everybody, and all of the children have so many emotional needs that some get lost in the shuffle.

Survivors have needs that continue long after *shivah* is over. Treat bereaved people the way you would want to be treated if you were in their shoes. Call once a week and say, "I was thinking about you and just wondered how you were." Invite survivors for *Shabbat* and holiday meals, but don't feel miffed if they decline. People appreciate being remembered.

Once *shivah* ends, don't worry that sharing memories of the deceased with family members will pain them. Survivors constantly think about their loved one for months or years anyway, and it is comforting to reminisce with someone who cares.

Don't encourage or force mourners to get rid of a loved one's clothing or belongings prematurely. Keepsakes can be tremendously comforting, and mourners may not be ready to part with them for a long time after their loved one dies.

Even though feelings of loss are much stronger around the time of death, they often continue for years. Don't assume that bereaved people stop appreciating concern and support when the year of mourning ends. Some people need companionship most afterward, as they try to repair their shattered lives and start socializing again.

Adults often try to shield children from death in unhealthy ways. This is due to adults' anxiety about death, not because children can't deal with it. How and what to tell children about death depends upon their intellectual and emotional maturity. Interested readers can learn more about this in Judy Tatelbaum's *The Courage to Grieve,* chapter 8 (Children's Grief).

NOTES

1. *Sanhedrin* 29a.

2. "Remains to be Seen," *New York Times Book Review,* July 28, 1991, p. 12.

3. Raymond Moody, *Reunions: Visionary Encounters with Departed Loved Ones* (New York: Villard, 1993), p. x.

4. Told by the mother at an Arachim weekend.

5. Aryeh Kaplan, *Handbook of Jewish Thought,* vol. 2 (New York: Moznaim, 1992), p. 283.

6. "Remains to be Seen," p. 12.

7. Boston Women's Health Book Collective, *The New Our Bodies, Ourselves* (New York: Simon and Schuster, 1992), p. 506.

8. Richard Jones, *Human Reproductive Biology* (New York: Academic Press, 1991), p. 259.

9. *Human Reproductive Biology,* p. 259. A Swiss study documented that parents of children who die of crib death often had premonitions of the event. Quoted in Melvin Morse, *Closer to the Light* (New York: Villard, 1990), p. 74. It is now known that at least half of SIDS deaths can be prevented by putting infants to sleep on their backs or sides instead of on their stomachs.

10. Quoted in Robert Kavanaugh, *Facing Death* (Baltimore, MD: Penguin, 1974).

11. "Therapists Say Ignoring Traditional Funeral Rites a Mistake," *Dade Jewish Journal,* June 2, 1994, p. 17.

12. "Therapists Say," p. 17.

13. "Therapists Say," p. 17.

14. "Therapists Say," p. 17.

15. *Shulchan Aruch, Yoreh De'ah* 341:1.

16. Based on Deuteronomy 20:19.

17. *Shulchan Aruch, Yoreh De'ah* 357:1, based on Deuteronomy 21:23; *Sefer Ha-Chinuch, mitzvah* 537.

18. Jewish babies who die before they are a month old are buried, but without a formal funeral. For more information about specific circumstances, consult a qualified rabbi. Guidelines can be found in Maurice Lamm, *The Jewish Way in Death and Mourning* (New York: Jonathan David, 1969).

19. Genesis, chapter 23.

20. *Maavar Yabok* 45, chapter 18.

21. *Shulchan Aruch, Yoreh De'ah* 340:1 and 374:4.

22. *Menachem Aveilim os kuf,* section 6, quoting responsa *Halachos Ketanos* section 116.

23. Mourning is suspended on the Sabbath. When a Jewish holiday occurs during *shivah, shivah* ends.

24. T. Adler, "World View Shapes Bereavement Pattern." *American Psychological Association Monitor,* October, 1991, pp. 20–21.

25. "World View," pp. 20–21.

26. "World View," pp. 20–21.

27. "World View," pp. 20–21.

28. *Ketuvot* 104a.

29. *Brachot* 5b.

30. *Shnei Luchot HaBrit* on *Parshat Ki Tetze* discusses some concepts of reincarnation. For example, reincarnation can occur because a person lacked the opportunity to do certain *mitzvot* in a previous lifetime; because someone had an opportunity to do a certain *mitzvah* but didn't; because God wants that soul to perform acts of kindness for its generation; or because it needs spiritual rehabilitation for sins in a prior lifetime that can't be atoned for in a purely spiritual realm.

31. *Midrash Rabbah* to Proverbs 31:1.

32. *Brachot* 5b.

33. *Taanit* 16a. This was also the reason that Caleb prayed at the Patriarchs' graves. He asked them to pray that he be delivered from the spies' wicked plan (*Sotah* 34b).

34. Elisabeth Kübler-Ross, *On Children and Death* (New York: Macmillan, 1983), p. 33. Fifty thousand children disappear each year without a trace, p. 98.

35. For example, the soul of a righteous person in the next world can save souls from suffering in purgatory. (*Song of Songs Rabbah* 8; *Zohar* 3, 22) See also 2 Kings 13:21, where the Prophet Elisha gave someone life long after Elisha died.

36. "Jews Turn to Tradition at Times of Mourning, Poll Says," *The Jewish Week,* June 11, 1993, p. 27.

FOR FURTHER READING

Goldberg, Chaim B. *Mourning in Halacha.* Brooklyn, NY: Mesorah, 1991.
  A comprehensive listing of the Jewish laws and customs of mourning. This book is too detailed for people who are not interested in the minutia of these laws.
Kastenbaum, Robert. *Is There Life After Death?* New York: Prentice Hall Press, 1986.
  Gives accounts of near-death experiences.
Kavanaugh, Robert. *Facing Death.* Baltimore, MD: Penguin, 1974.
Kübler-Ross, Elisabeth. *On Children and Death.* New York: Macmillan, 1983.
Lamm, Maurice. *The Jewish Way in Death and Mourning.* New York: Jonathan David, 1969.
  A comprehensive guide to the Jewish laws and customs about mourning, funerals, burial, and the grieving process.
Levine, Aaron. *To Comfort the Bereaved: A Guide for Mourners and Those Who Visit Them.* Northvale, NJ: Jason Aronson, 1994.
Moody, Raymond. *Life After Life.* Harrisburg, PA: Stackpole, 1976.
  Moody discusses people's near-death experiences and their souls' encounters with a spiritual afterlife.
——. *The Light Beyond.* New York: Bantam, 1988.

——. *Reunions: Visionary Encounters with Departed Loved Ones.* New York: Villard Books, 1993.

Morse, Melvin. *Closer to the Light.* New York: Villard, 1990.

Dr. Morse's collected children's reports of their near-death experiences. Required reading for parents who have lost a child.

——. *Transformed by the Light.* New York: Villard, 1992.

A compilation of reports of near-death experiences and how they changed people's lives.

Ozarowski, Joseph. *To Walk in God's Ways: Jewish Pastoral Perspectives on Illness and Bereavement.* Northvale, NJ: Jason Aronson, 1995.

Peppers, Larry G., and Knapp, Ronald J. *Motherhood and Mourning.* New York: Praeger, 1980.

A description of mothers' reactions to miscarriage, stillbirth, and infant death with suggestions for coping.

Rabinowicz, Tzvi. *A Guide to Life: Jewish Laws and Customs of Mourning.* Northvale, NJ: Jason Aronson, 1989.

Tatelbaum, Judy. *The Courage to Grieve.* New York: Lippincott and Crowell, 1980.

An excellent intellectual and emotional description of the grieving process and how to grow through it.

RESOURCES

AMEND (Aiding a Mother Experiencing Neonatal Death), Los Angeles Chapter, 4032 Towhee Drive, Calabasas, CA, or 4324 Berrywick Terrace, St. Louis, MO 63128

Helps bereaved parents grieve perinatal death.

Chai Lifeline, (212) 255-1160

Offers parent bereavement workshops under observant Jewish auspices.

Chazack Ve'ematz–Jewish support organization for bereaved parents (Contact Elie Kranzler, M.D., and Michal Frank, C.S.W., in New York City)

Compassionate Friends, P.O. Box 1347, Oakbrook, IL 60521, (312) 323-5010

Clearinghouse of self-help groups for bereaved parents and siblings, founded by an Anglican priest. See if they have nonsectarian groups in your area.

HOPE (Help Other Parents Endure), P.O. Box 153, Florrisant, MO 63032

Offers six-session course for grieving parents.

Parents of Murdered Children, 1739 Bella Vista, Cincinnati, OH 45237, (513) 242-8025 or (513) 721-LOVE

Support organization for survivors of murdered people.

11

National Suffering and the Holocaust

Now if you obey Me and keep My covenant, you will be My special treasure among all of the nations. . . . And you shall be a kingdom of priests and a holy nation to Me."[1]

"God made the rectification and elevation of all creation totally dependent on the Jews. . . . By their deeds, they can cause His light to shine forth and have influence, or hold it back and conceal it."[2]

Nothing is a greater barrier to the faith of some modern Jews than the Holocaust. Many older Jews lived through torture and saw the brutal slaughter of their families and communities in a carnage that was unparalleled in history. Millions of others have read about these atrocities or seen them on film. They ask, "Where was God during the Holocaust? How could He have allowed six million innocent Jews to be slaughtered?" How can God care about His people if the Holocaust made them into whipping boys?

We should not decide that God couldn't exist based on our emotional revulsion to Jewish suffering. We must know if the God who chose the Jews to be bearers of His morality abdicated His relationship and responsibility to us during the Holocaust. The only way to answer this question is to take a journey through 3,300 years of Jewish history through the eyes of the Torah.

As we previously discussed, the Almighty created people only so that we would worship Him as the sole Creator and Director of the world and obey His moral principles.[3] Until Abraham's time, few people were willing to do this. When he and his descendants showed their willingness to do God's will, the Almighty gave Jews the Torah on Mount Sinai 3,300 years ago. At that time, He made a covenant with every Jewish soul that was in the earthly world, as well as with all those that were yet to come here. Every Jewish soul became part of one spiritual entity,[4] whose deeds would reveal God's presence to the world at large. With the giving of the Torah, Jews were given the power to bring holiness or unholiness into the world with their every thought, word, and action. Each of us can metaphysically affect all other Jews and the world for better or for worse. This ability is an integral part of every Jewish soul, and we can't make our behavior irrelevant to God's plan for the universe. We are required to show our absolute commitment to God even when it is not pleasurable, and even when it means dying in order to sanctify His Name.

Once God made His covenant with us at Sinai, He guaranteed that we would have comfortable lives as a nation if we followed the Torah and that we would go into exile and suffer national tragedies if we didn't. There are dire consequences to not living as He commanded us, because when we don't observe the Torah, God loses His emissaries for bringing spiritual light and divine morality into the world. When that happens, the world loses its purpose.

One brief period when the Jews fully lived up to their magnificent calling was during King Solomon's reign. At that time, people of all nations heard about the Jews' wisdom to a point where even the Queen of Sheba visited Solomon because of his renown. Gentiles came from far and wide to see the miracles in the Temple and the utopian society that living by the Torah created. The Jews' sanctification of God at that time earned them the economic bounty and the security that the Torah had predicted:

> If you carefully listen to the Lord your God, by observing and doing all of the commandments that I command you today, He will raise you above all of the nations of the earth. All of these blessings will come upon and overtake you, as long as you listen to Him. You will be blessed in the city and in the field. Your children will be blessed, as well as your land's fruit, your beasts' offspring, your cattle's young, and your sheep's flocks. Your basket and kneading trough will be blessed. You will be blessed when you come in and when you go out. The Lord will cause your attacking enemies to be beaten in front of you. They shall come against you from one direction and flee from you in seven directions. The Lord will command His blessing upon you in your storehouses, in all of your handiwork, and will bless you in the land that He gives you. The Lord will elevate you as a holy nation, as He swore to you, if you will keep His commandments and walk in His ways.
>
> All of the world's nations will see that the Lord's name is upon you, and they will fear you. God will give you abundance of good, children, offspring of beasts, and produce in the land that He swore to your forefathers to give you. He will open His storehouse of good for you. The heavens will give your land rain in its season, and all of your handiwork will be blessed. You shall lend to many nations, but not borrow. The Lord will make you the head and not the tail, and you will be elevated and never

lowered if you listen to the Lord your God's commandments that I command you today to observe and do. Don't turn away from anything that I command you today to the right or left, to go after other gods to serve them.[5]

Just as the Jews' bounty in the land of Israel was Providential, and not due to military prowess or quirks of history, neither were their national suffering and exiles accidental.

The first time that the Jews were severely persecuted, God wanted them to be enslaved so that they would accrue spiritual benefits that they couldn't get any other way. But He did not direct any particular group to enslave them, nor did He direct that the slavery be inhumane.

ATTEMPTED GENOCIDE IN JEWISH HISTORY

Many people think that the Holocaust was the only time when Jews were subjected to unspeakable horrors and attempted genocide. In fact, the Holocaust was a culmination of centuries of European hatred against Jews and attempts to exterminate them. But the first "Final Solution" really occurred 3,500 years earlier, before the Jews even formally became a nation. It happened at the hands of the Egyptians.

Abraham's great-grandson Joseph saved the ancient Egyptians from starvation and economic ruin by predicting that they would have seven years of severe famine. He then devised a system for stockpiling grain before the famine started and thereby allowed them to survive.[6] Yet a subsequent pharaoh had the audacity to "forget" what Joseph had done and how the pharaoh in Joseph's time had shown gratitude by inviting Jacob and his descendants to live in Egypt.

The later ruler proclaimed, "Let us deal wisely with [the Israelites], lest they become too numerous."[7] He set up slave work camps for Jewish men. He forced them to build pyramids and storage cities under atrocious working conditions. When their numbers miraculously increased, he decreed that all Jewish male babies be drowned in the Nile.[8]

As the Nazis repeated millennia later, the Egyptians selected Jewish overseers to ensure that the Israelites met their daily work quotas. The Egyptians then beat Jewish officers whose workers failed to meet the unrealistic standards.[9] Sharing the Nazi penchant for child-killing, the Egyptians slaughtered 300 Jewish babies a day and Pharaoh bathed in their blood.[10]

In all, the Jews were in Egypt for 210 years, and suffered harsh slavery for 86 of those years. Miraculously, the Jews not only survived but grew from 70 people to almost three million during their years in Egypt.[11] When the Almighty fulfilled His promise to Abraham to take His descendants out of Egypt, it was the only time in the ancient world that any enslaved people escaped from there.[12]

Finally, when it was time for the Jews' redemption, God identified Himself to Moses as "I will be what I will be."[13] This expressed the idea that our Heavenly

Father never abandoned His children in Egypt ("I will be with them in this time of trouble"), just as He would never abandon them in future exiles.[14]

Throughout history, nations attempted to annihilate us, but this never happened as a random event or a sign that God stopped caring about us. Each instance was either a response to the Jews' misdeeds or part of a divine plan to improve the world spiritually.

The Torah predicted what would happen to the Jews throughout history if they acted contrary to God's will:

> But if you won't listen to Me, and don't do all of My commandments, and you abhor My seemingly irrational laws, and detest My laws of justice . . . I will cause terror, consumption, and a burning affliction to consume your eyes and cause you sorrow. You will sow your seed in vain because your enemies will eat it. I will set My face against you, and your enemies will slay you. People who hate you will rule over you, and you will flee when no one pursues you. . . .
>
> If you . . . [insist that these calamities are coincidences and not divine reactions to your behavior] I will add seven times more plagues, according to your sins. I will send wild animals against you, and your children will be taken from you. Your cattle will be destroyed, you'll be few in numbers, and your highways will be desolate. . . . I will bring a sword to avenge My covenant, and you will be gathered into your cities. I will put a plague on you and give you into enemy hands. . . . Ten women will bake bread in one oven, but remove bread of meager weight. You will eat and not be satisfied. I will give over your cities for destruction, destroy your Temple, and not smell the pleasing fragrance of your sacrifices. I will make the land desolate, and your enemies who live there will be astonished. I will scatter you among the nations and pursue you with the sword. Your land will be desolate and your cities will be destroyed.
>
> To those who remain, I will bring a faintness into your hearts in your enemies' lands. . . . You will be lost among the nations, and the land of your enemies will devour you. Those of you who remain will pine away in your enemies' lands because of yours' and your ancestors' deliberate sins.
>
> You will [finally] confess your's and your parents' sins, and acknowledge your misappropriations against Me and how you walked contrary to Me. . . . If you humble your uncircumcised hearts and accept punishment for your sins, then I will remember My covenants. . . . And you will accept punishment for your sins of spurning my laws of justice and for your souls' loathing of My [seemingly] irrational laws.
>
> Despite it all, when you are in your enemies' land, I will not cast you away, and won't despise you to utterly destroy you, and break My covenant with you, because I am the Lord your God.[15]

This warned the Jews that once God gave them material comfort, they would be tempted to spurn Him and live like Gentiles. But if they assimilated, that would scuttle His plan for the world. He would then send anti-Semitism to preserve the Jews' unique spiritual identity.[16]

While the All-Merciful One usually tempers punishment with kindness, He is not always so lenient when Jews as a nation don't live up to their mission. Whenever we forget that our only purpose is to serve God, other nations remind us. Gentiles keep us from deluding ourselves into thinking that we are just like them and can become permanent citizens who meld into our host countries. National tragedies are terrible, but they are one way that God continually reminds us of our separateness and uniqueness and warns us not to assimilate.

When many Jews get spiritually off track, God doesn't only remove them in order to protect the healthy ones. He often causes the healthy ones to suffer so as to improve the spiritually diseased segment, just as a doctor heals a diseased organ by doing something unpleasant to the whole body. Jewish children and righteous people often suffer for this reason when they help cleanse the Jewish people's collective soul.

Being ministers in God's cabinet confers tremendous responsibilities on us. We are judged by very high standards and are chastised when we shirk even small duties because we play such an indispensable role in the divine plan for all of humanity.[17]

God's covenant with us requires Him to grant us special providence and closeness if we live properly. But it also means that He will discipline and cleanse us whenever we violate our covenant with Him. Historically, He has often let us go against His will for scores of years until our actions can no longer be ignored. When we think that violating His will really hurts no one, God shows us how terrible it really is.

We can learn from our experience, as well as from good advice. But sometimes we are willing to learn only from the school of hard knocks. *How* we learn is our choice. God prefers us to learn from His teachings, but we sometimes refuse to act properly unless we see how destructive our beliefs and behavior are. God's commitment to our having free will gives us opportunities to learn from unpleasant experiences. We can understand this better from the following analogy:

A teenager wanted his parents to get him a motorcycle, but they refused because motorcycles are dangerous and they didn't want him to get hurt. He got furious, threw some tantrums, and wouldn't give them a moment's peace until he got his way. His parents decided that the only way for him to learn an important lesson was to give him what he wanted. After he had an accident and broke his arm, he finally appreciated his parents' point of view.

God sometimes withholds justice so that we will appreciate the full impact of our choices. When He "sits out" and lets us learn the hard way, we pay a terrible price for continuing our spiritual misdeeds. But *we* determine our willingness to pay that price, not God. He would like us to learn our lessons in an easier way.

We tend to think of God as a Being totally detached from our world. We reinforce this idea whenever we use the world without considering how He wants us to use it. When we disconnect Him from the world, we pay the price of having a Godless world.

We sometimes wonder where God is when we suffer as He corrects or cleanses us of our negative choices. But divine punishment and justice can never be bad since they rectify negativity. Truly bad situations occur when God lets people make negative choices without correcting them.

People think that the Lord is wonderful when He does pleasant miracles, but He is no less wonderful when He brings the world closer to its spiritual destiny using painful events. The fact that we don't like unpleasant things doesn't invalidate their importance. Rather than insist that the Master of the World do what we like before believing in Him, we should be mature enough to accept that He has many valid ways of bringing the world to where it needs to be.

God sends the Jewish people national calamities as divine messages. In ancient times, they were a punishment for worshiping idols and/or infighting. They happened to Diaspora Jews for many reasons, including as a response to Jews imitating Gentiles, viewing their host country as their true home, and/or fomenting causeless hatred between one another. (The Jews' dispersal among the nations was also intended to bring spiritual light to the nations of the world.) Several illustrations follow:

NATIONAL SUFFERING IN ANCIENT TIMES

"Why was the first Temple destroyed? Because of three things: idolatry, immorality, and bloodshed."[18]

"Why was the second Temple destroyed, seeing that in its time the Jews occupied themselves with Torah, observing commandments, and giving charity? Because people hated each other for no reason. This shows that groundless hatred is an even graver sin than the cardinal sins of idolatry, immorality, and bloodshed together."[19]

God gave us the land of Israel as a holy place where we would live according to the Torah and become "a light unto the nations."[20] Soon after Solomon's reign ended, Jews started worshiping idols. Over a period of hundreds of years, God sent the Jews many prophets who warned them to stop their idolatry, illicit sex, and murder. Sadly, the Jews ignored these spiritual mentors and refused to improve their ways. As a result, the Assyrians exiled the Ten Lost Tribes. Instead of listening to the prophet Jeremiah during the next forty years, the remaining Jews threatened to kill him for his gloomy predictions. After these many warnings went unheeded, God finally gave the Babylonians license to destroy the First Temple, massacre many Jews, and exile those who were spared.

This exile occurred because Jews did not live up to their moral mission, and the land of Israel can't tolerate persistent rejection of Godliness. The Jews' terrible punishments occurred as God used the forces of justice to get the Jews on the right spiritual track. By exiling them, He hoped that they would improve their ways and live morally in the Diaspora. They could then influence the world to recognize God and live by the Noahide laws.

Not long after the Babylonian exile, the Jews were threatened with extermination again. This happened under the reign of Ahasuerus (Xerxes) because the Jews started to assimilate and rejected the rabbis' authority to tell them what to do. One of the king's ministers, Haman, paid a huge sum of money for the privilege of engineering the Jews' genocide. In response, the entire Jewish people repented, fasted for three days, and resolved to respect the Sages and observe the Oral Law properly. At the eleventh hour, the king miraculously rescinded his decree, and we commemorate this every year on the holiday of Purim.

Once the biblical predictions about the Jews' first exile came true,[21] it was time that God's predictions of their return to the land be fulfilled. Darius, the son of the Jewish queen Esther and King Ahasuerus, gave the Jews permission to return to Israel. Only a tiny minority (42,000) chose to do so,[22] because the others were very comfortable in their new land. These returnees built the Second Temple and reestablished centralized Jewish courts in Jerusalem.

The Second Jewish Commonwealth lasted 420 years.[23] Unfortunately, many wealthy, "intellectual," and priestly Jews became enamored of Hellenistic body-worship, hedonism, and Greek philosophy during the 180-year Syrian-Greek reign. The Jewish children went to Greek *gymnasia,* and the adults saw Hellenization as a passport to first-class citizenship. (Sadly, this theme repeated itself in more modern times among Western European Jews.) Some Jewish men even had a painful operation to reverse their circumcisions so that they would look as "perfect" as the Greeks when they competed in naked athletic competitions such as the Olympics.

Some Jews then tried to "reform" the traditional Jews. The reformers allied with the Greeks and soon replaced the Temple's observant high priests with Hellenized ones. Next, decrees forbade Jews to practice their religion. These were probably promulgated by the reformers in the name of the Greek rulers, and they made observing, teaching, or studying Torah a capital crime. They transformed the Temple into a pagan house of worship.

The observant Jews, instigated by their women and led by the Hasmonean priests, finally rebelled against the Greeks. God granted them a military victory so that they could resume living authentic Jewish lives. The Hasmoneans removed the idols that the Greeks had put in the holy Temple, purified its altars from pagan sacrifices, and rededicated the Second Temple to the Almighty. We commemorate this every year during the holiday of Chanukah.

Some time after the Hasmonean revolt, God let the Romans conquer the land of Israel. This gave the Jews a tremendous opportunity to teach monotheism and divine morality to most of the world. At that time, Jews constituted up to 10 percent of the Roman empire, and their way of life influenced over three million Romans to convert to Judaism![24]

Unfortunately, the Jews did not maintain their idyllic behavior, and God allowed the Romans to become hostile to them and lay siege to Jerusalem. Rather than heed the warning to repent, the Jews did not improve.

The city's inhabitants had enough provisions to withstand a siege for many years, but the rabbis (the Pharisees) urged the Jews to let the Romans rule them. The rabbis knew that God did not want the Jews to fight the Romans, but a group of arrogant Jewish zealots thought they knew better. The zealots burned the city's food stores in an attempt to force the Jews into battle. The result was mass starvation and death.[25] (As we will repeatedly see, some of our worst national suffering throughout history was caused by apostate, secular, and arrogant Jews.)

The Jews suffered terribly as they scavenged for grain in animal dung and ate their children's corpses. Many of the thousands who died could not be buried, and the Romans captured most of those who escaped through the city walls, and killed or enslaved them.[26]

The Romans were so incensed by the Jews' rebellion that they lost interest in negotiating. They breached Jerusalem's walls after a lengthy siege, burned the city and the Temple to the ground, slaughtered many of the remaining Jews, and plowed the city under. They captured countless Jewish boys and girls to use as prostitutes in Roman brothels. Four hundred of these children committed suicide by jumping into the sea rather than be used as Roman sex slaves. Captive adults were sold as slaves in Greece and Egypt, and sometimes glutted the market so that purchasers paid more for a horse than for a Jewish slave. Other Jews were taken to Rome for public execution in the Forum or were killed in sports arenas by animals.

Despite the masses of Jews who perished and the hundreds of towns that were destroyed, one large remnant of Jews remained in a fortified city named Betar. Fifty-two years after the Romans destroyed Jerusalem, they slaughtered Betar's Jews during the Bar Kochba revolt. The killings were so ruthless that Gentiles fertilized their fields with Jewish blood for years.[27]

To add insult to injury, the Roman officer who organized the massacre refused to let Jews bury Jewish corpses for years. Hadrian was so enraged at the Jews' rejection of Roman rule and paganism that he stacked their corpses around his vineyard as a protective wall. The bodies covered its perimeter for miles.[28]

The Torah foretold the Roman destruction of the Jews with chilling accuracy some 1,500 years earlier:

And if you don't listen to the Lord your God's voice by observing all of His commandments . . . including the laws that seem illogical, then all of the following curses will befall you and overtake you. You will be cursed in the city and cursed in the field. Your produce and dough will be cursed. Your children, the fruit of your land, your cattle and your flocks will be cursed. You shall be cursed when you come in and when you go out. The Lord will afflict you with curses, confusion, and rebuke in everything that you do until you are exterminated quickly, because of the evil way by which you abandoned God. The Lord will strike you with pestilence until you are wiped off the face of the land of Israel. . . . The heavens above you shall become copper and the earth beneath you iron. The Lord will make the rain of the land powder and dust that will come down on you until you are exterminated.

The Lord will give you over to be beaten by your enemies. You shall go out to them by one path and flee before them by seven paths, and you shall be an apparition to all of the kingdoms of the earth. Your corpses will be food for all the fowl of the heavens and for the beasts of the earth, and no one will frighten them away. The Lord will afflict you with the boils of Egypt . . . from which you can't be healed. The Lord will strike you with madness, blindness, and abject panic. . . . You shall build a house and not live in it. You will plant a vineyard and not harvest the grapes. Your ox will be slaughtered in front of your eyes, and you shall not eat of it. Your donkey will be stolen in front of you. . . . Your flocks will be given to your enemies, and you will have no one to save them. Your sons and daughters will be given to another nation. Your eyes will see it and long for them all day long, but you will have no strength. The fruit of your ground and all of your labors will be devoured by a nation whom you don't know, and you will only be oppressed and crushed all day long. You will go insane because of what your eyes see. . . .

The Lord will bring you, and the king that you have set over yourselves, to a nation that neither you nor your ancestors have known. You will serve other gods there, of wood and rock. You will be an astonishment, a proverb, and a topic of conversation to all of the nations where the Lord will lead you. . . . You shall give birth to sons and daughters, but they shall not be yours, because they will go into captivity. The locust will denude all of the trees and fruit of your land. The stranger in your midst shall rise higher and higher and you shall go lower and lower. He will lend to you, but not borrow. He will be the head, and you will be the tail.

All of this will happen . . . because you did not listen to the Lord your God's voice, to observe His commandments and ordinances. These events will be a sign . . . upon your seed forever that you did not serve the Lord your god with happiness and a joyful heart when you had great abundance. Instead, famished, thirsty, naked, and lacking everything, you will serve enemies whom the Lord will send against you. . . .

The Lord will bring a nation from afar . . . as the eagle soars [swiftly] – a nation whose language you will not understand. A brazen nation, who will show no deference to the elderly, and will have no compassion for the young.

They will eat your animals and produce until you are annihilated. They will leave you no corn, wine, oil, cattle, or flocks, and they will destroy you.

They will besiege you in all of your gates until your high and fortified walls, where you placed your trust, come down throughout your land. . . . You will eat your children, the flesh of your sons and daughters whom the Lord your God gave you, because of the siege and the straits that you will be in.

The most tender and delicate man among you . . . won't give others the flesh of the children he eats because there will be nothing else to eat. The tender and delicate woman among you . . . will secretly eat the placenta . . . and the children that she bears, due to lack of everything, caused by the siege and straits that the enemy will inflict upon you.

[This will all happen] if you don't carefully observe all of the words of the teaching that are written in this book, to fear the honored and awesome name of the Lord your God . . . .

And you shall remain few in number, whereas you had been as numerous as the stars of the heavens, because you did not listen to the Lord your God. Just as the Lord once rejoiced over you to do you good, and to multiply you, so will He rejoice to make you perish and exterminate you. You will be plucked off your land and . . . He will scatter you among all of the nations, from one end of the earth to the other. You will worship other gods of wood and rock there, which neither you nor your ancestors knew.

You will not have peace of mind among these nations, and the sole of your foot will have no rest. The Lord will make your heart panic, your eyes fail, and your mind faint. Your lives shall hang in doubt before you, you shall feel dread day and night, and there will be no security. In the morning you will say, "I wish that it were evening," and in the evening you will say, "I wish that it were morning," because of your fear and what you will witness.

The Lord will send you back to Egypt in ships by the path that I said you would never again see. You will be sold there as male and female slaves for your enemies but no one will buy you.[29]

These predictions all came true during the Roman conquest of Israel in the first century and during the subsequent exile. The Romans were the nation that came from afar, whose Latin language the Jews did not understand and whose symbol was the eagle. They had no respect for the young or the old and were ruthless. The Romans destroyed every fruit-bearing tree near Jewish settlements so that the Jews would die of starvation. They were so enraged over the Jews' rebellion that they plowed under Jerusalem and laid waste to much of the country by plowing salt into the soil. The formerly lush land of Israel was so desolate after the Roman exile that it barely grew anything for the next 1,900 years.

During the Romans' three-year siege of Jerusalem, the Jews suffered terribly from disease and starvation. They and their animals died. They suffered insanity, terror, and despair. A mother cooked and served her young son to the leader of the Jewish zealots to show him how ruinous his misguided efforts were. People died from diseases contracted through the unavoidable filth on the streets. The carnage that followed the Romans' breach of Jerusalem's and Betar's walls was horrific.[30]

As the Torah predicted, the Romans sent captured Jews to Egypt to sell as slaves. The market was so glutted that, at times, no one bought them. They exiled the Jews to the four corners of the earth—to Babylonia, Egypt, and Rome, and from there to many other countries. Agrippas, the king whom the Jews set upon themselves, was exiled to Rome. The Jews eventually came under Christian and Moslem rule. Some adopted Christianity (symbolized by the wooden crucifix) and Islam (symbolized by the rock), while millions were forcibly baptized, forced to worship Christian idols, or made to accept Islam.

These gods were unknown to our ancestors because these religions began after the Jews were exiled from their land.

The Torah also predicted that the Jews in exile would become small in number. Before the Roman exile, Jews numbered at least 8 million, and possibly much more. By the tenth century, there were no more than 1.5 million Jews worldwide.[31]

Had God not directed the Jews' destiny, even the few who remained should have disappeared into the great melting pot of the Roman empire. Never before in history did any people maintain their unique identity for many generations after leaving their homeland. Other exiled nations died, or assimilated beyond recognition into their host cultures. It defies history that the Jews are still a distinct group after 1,900 years in exile.

Even though God preserved us as a people for so many years, we wonder what the Jews could have done to warrant such terrible suffering, slaughter, and exiles. The Talmud sheds some light on this by saying the primary reason that God let the Romans conquer us is that Jews hated each other for no reason.[32] There was also tremendous disdain for the authority of the rabbis at the time. As a result, splinter sects such as the Sadducees and the Essenes developed, and Jews had little regard for each other.

Two talmudic stories illustrate the kind of causeless hatred that pervaded the Jews before the Roman conquest:

Jerusalem was destroyed because of an incident between Kamtza and Bar Kamtza: A man had a friend named Kamtza, and an enemy named Bar Kamtza. The man made a party and told his servant, "Invite Kamtza to my party." The servant brought Bar Kamtza by mistake.

When the host arrived, he found Bar Kamtza there. The host said, "You are my enemy. What are you doing here? Get up and leave."

Bar Kamtza said, "Since I'm here already, let me stay and I'll pay you the cost of what I eat and drink."

The host replied, "No."

Bar Kamtza offered, "I'll pay half of the cost of the party."

The host said, "No."

He said to the host, "If you let me stay, I'll pay the cost of the entire party."

The host said, "No," took Bar Kamtza by the hand, and made him get up and leave.

Bar Kamtza said, "The rabbis were sitting there and didn't rebuke him for embarrassing me. That shows that they agree with what he did. I'll take revenge by slandering them to the Roman authorities."

Bar Kamtza went to the Roman emperor and said, "The Jews are revolting against you."

The emperor asked, "How do you know?"

Bar Kamtza continued, "I'll prove it if you send them an animal sacrifice. It will prove my point if they refuse to offer it."

The emperor sent a three-year-old calf with Bar Kamtza, and Bar Kamtza maimed it on his trip home. . . . He gave it a blemish that disqualified it for Jewish sacrifices, but not for Roman sacrifices.

The rabbis decided not to offer the animal and the Romans responded by conquering them for revolting.[33]

A second story involved an apprentice carpenter who desired his master's wife. When the master needed to borrow money from his apprentice, the apprentice said, "Send your wife for the money and I'll lend it to her."

The master sent his wife, and she stayed with the apprentice for three days. The master then went to him and asked, "Where is my wife?"

The apprentice replied, "I sent her back to you immediately after she got here, but I heard that youngsters played with her on the road."

"What shall I do?" the master inquired.

"I think that you should divorce her," the apprentice advised.

"But I can't afford that," the master continued. "I contracted to pay her a large amount of money in the event of divorce."

The apprentice offered, "I'll lend you the money for her divorce settlement."

So the master divorced her and the apprentice married her. When the time came for the master to pay back the loan, the apprentice said, "Come and work off your debt with me."

So the apprentice and his wife used to sit, eat, and drink while the master waited on them, as tears fell from his eyes and dripped into their cups. When that happened, the fate of the Jewish people was sealed.[34]

Causeless hatred has been such a consistent failing among Jews that it has caused us to stay in exile until now and has brought us countless calamities. It is said that the Temple will not be rebuilt, nor will the Messiah come, until Jews show causeless love for one another.

MEDIEVAL CALAMITIES

"Behold, I have refined you, but not as silver. I have chosen for you the crucible of affliction."[35]

The Jews' plight was especially bleak during medieval times, when they lived in Europe and Russia. Gentiles frequently plundered and confiscated their possessions and extorted their money. Christians repeatedly expelled the Jews from their countries. (Moslems occasionally did the same, but they generally had good relations with Jews until modern times.) Christians gleefully promulgated countless blood libels, massacres, and pogroms to a point where they became an annual event in some towns.[36]

The following is just one of many thousand acts of Christian cruelty to the Jews, and a typical Jewish response to it:

Almost a thousand years ago, a prominent Jewish scholar named Rabbi Amnon lived in Mainz, Germany. The archbishop repeatedly tried to get him to convert to Christianity, but the rabbi always refused. Shortly before Rosh HaShanah (the Jewish New Year) one year, the archbishop again asked the rabbi to convert. The rabbi asked the archbishop to let him think about it for three days, hoping that this would give him a short respite from the harassment. The archbishop wishfully assumed that Rabbi Amnon would "see the light" and finally be a feather in the cap of the Catholic Church, and he invited Christian nobles to the expected baptism.

Three days later, the nobles and archbishop waited, but the rabbi did not appear. Furious, the archbishop forcibly brought the rabbi to explain himself.

Rabbi Amnon responded, "I committed a grievous sin by giving the impression that I might even consider Christianity. You should cut off my tongue for its deceit in suggesting that I would ever abandon Judaism."

The archbishop replied, "We won't cut off your tongue. We will cut off your hands and feet for not coming here as you promised." He then did exactly that with a sword.

The next day, Rosh HaShanah, Rabbi Amnon asked to be carried to the synagogue and placed before the holy ark. As he lay dying from his wounds, he composed the following (paraphrased) prayer:

> We will give an account of the holiness of this day, because it is a frightening and awesome time. On this day Your kingdom is exalted, and Your throne is established in mercy, and You sit upon it in truth. You are truly the Judge, Prosecutor, Knower, and Witness, the One who records and seals. You remember all that is forgotten and You open the book of memories that tell each's story. Each person's deeds seal his record. . . .
>
> Even the angels tremble . . . [as You] write the decree of destiny of every living person. . . . But repentance, prayer, and charity can remove the evil decree!

Rabbi Amnon expired as he finished reciting this beautiful and moving prayer. The Christians killed him for refusing their false beliefs, yet they could not silence him. He died testifying to the truth of Judaism and God's justice. To this day, his dying words sanctify God's name to the millions of Jews who recite his *Unetaneh Tokef* prayer every year on the High Holidays.

As we will soon see, the Jewish suffering that began in Europe during the Middle Ages culminated in the Holocaust centuries later. Almost all of the Jews' suffering from the eleventh century until modern times was caused by Christians punishing them for rejecting the "truth" of Christianity, and/or as a pretext to confiscate Jewish wealth or wipe out debts from borrowing money from Jews. The Nazis' use of special yellow badges, enforced ghettoes, exclusion of Jews from trades and professions, confiscation of Jewish property and wealth, and torture and murder of Jews was invented by the Church centuries earlier.

By the year 1500, Solomon Ibn Verga described sixty-four major, devastating persecutions of European Jews in his book *Shevut Yehudah*. The following is but a partial, representative list of Jewish persecution during the eleventh to the mid-sixteenth centuries:

1012	Jews were expelled from the Rhineland.
1095	Pope Urban II ordered the First Crusade.
1096	Christian crusaders exterminated the Jews in Speyer, Worms, and Mainz, Germany. They slaughtered more than 5,000 European Jews after torturing them and raping the women. Jews who were forcibly converted committed suicide.
1099	Crusaders burned alive the few hundred Jews of Jerusalem in their synagogue and beheaded the survivors.
1121	Baghdad Jews had to wear two yellow badges, a lead necklace, and humiliating clothes.
1144	The first blood libel in England took place in Norwich.
1147	Arabs fomented pogroms against Jews in Spain.
1146–49	The Second Christian Crusade murdered German Jews. The Church promised, "Whoever kills a Jew who refuses baptism is forgiven for all of his sins."
1171	All of the Jews in Blois, France, were massacred in a blood libel.
1181	Austrians rioted against Jews in Vienna.
1182	The King of France expelled all French Jews and confiscated their property.
1189–92	The Third Crusade fomented a special slaughter of English Jews. Christians besieged the Jews in York, who committed suicide rather than let themselves be baptized.
1198	Jews in Yemen were forcibly converted to Islam. Those who defected were beheaded.
1209	The French crusaded against the Jews.
1211	Germans rioted against the Jews in Frankfurt-am-Main.
1212	Spanish Christians staged a bloodbath against the Jews of Toledo, Spain.
1215	The Lateran Council of Rome declared that Jews must wear a badge of shame in all Christian countries. (The Nazis followed the Catholics' example nine centuries later.) The Church forbade Jews to hold civic positions and ordered them to pay taxes to the Church.
1221	Christians staged pogroms against the Jews of Erfurt, Germany.
1225	Germans rioted against the Jews of Miklonberg.
1227	Christians made a blood libel against the Jews in Miklonberg and in Breslau.
1231	Christians rioted against the Jews of Leon, Spain, and forced them to convert.

1233	The Church confiscated Maimonides' books in France, then publicly burned them after prominent Jews publicly slandered his works.
1235–36	There were blood libels, torture, and murder of more than 3,000 European Jews; many Jews were forcibly converted.
1239	Christians banned Jewish learning and talmudic study in Paris.
1240	Austrian Jews were imprisoned, burned, converted, and expelled. Louis IX said, "The best way to argue with a Jew is to plunge a sword into him."
1242	King Louis IX staged a public burning of the Talmud in Paris. (The Church canonized him as a saint for persecuting Jews.)
1242–47	There were blood libels in Western Europe against the Jews. There was a pogrom against the Jews of Valreas.
1248	Three hundred Jewish communities in Germany, Austria, Spain, and France were destroyed. Charles IV pardoned anyone who murdered a Jew.
1255	The Jews in Lincoln, England, were tortured and burned in a blood libel.
1260	There were blood libels in England and Italy. Jews were murdered and the survivors were expelled from Toureno.
1264	Germans murdered thousands of Jews. The Council of Vienna required Jews to wear dunce caps and badges of shame.
1267	Jews in Bada were murdered in a blood libel.
1270	All English Jews were imprisoned and hundreds were hanged.
1276	The Bavarian Jews were expelled and forcibly converted in Mainz.
1278	Edward I had British Jews arrested and hanged, then appropriated their money.
1279	Hungarian and Polish Jews were forbidden to hold civic positions and were ordered to wear badges of shame. Hundreds of Jews were murdered in an English blood libel.
1280	Castillian Jews were imprisoned and their property was seized.
1283–88	Numerous blood libels occurred. Jews were massacred in Troyes, France. English Jews were imprisoned in order to extort astronomical ransom fees from them.
1289	Edward I confiscated the property of Gascony Jews after hanging dozens of Jews in Norwich.
1290	English Jews were expelled by Edward I and drowned. Jews weren't allowed back in England until 1656.
1290–93	Italians rioted against Italian Jews.
1291	English Jewish refugees were expelled from France; thousands of Jews were slaughtered in Iran and Iraq.
1292	Italian Jews were forcibly converted and expelled.
1294	Spanish Jews were forced to wear "Jewish patches."

1298	The Jews in over a hundred communities were forced to convert to Christianity. More than 100,000 Jews were murdered in German and Austrian riots. Bavaria and the Rhine Valley were "Judenrein" for the next fifty years. By the end of the thirteenth century, persecution of Jews led to a mass migration to Eastern Europe.
1306	French Jews were expelled and their property was confiscated.
1318–19	European Christians rioted against the Jews, insisting that they caused the bubonic plague.
1320	Christian shepherds and swineherds massacred thousands of Jews throughout Europe.
1322	The Jews who remained in France were expelled.
1328	Spaniards rioted against the Jews.
1348–51	Christians massacred the Jews, especially in two hundred German communities and in Poland. There were mass burnings of Jews, with German Jewry nearly exterminated.
1355	The Spaniards massacred 12,000 Jews in Toledo.
1360	Hungarian Jews were expelled.
1378	There were riots against the Jews of Seville, Spain; the Jews there were expelled in 1391. The Church canonized the Dominican preacher who fomented the riots.
1380–82	There were riots against Parisian Jews.
1381	The Jews of Strasbourg were expelled.
1391	The Italians murdered 50,000 Jews in Palma. Pogroms in Spain and Portugal massacred 50,000 Jews in seventy Jewish communities. Twenty years of pogroms followed. (Many of these pogroms were instigated by apostate Jews.)
1399, 1407, and 1494	There were Polish blood libels and riots against the Jews.
1421	Castillian Jews were evicted and their homes were given to Catholics. Jews had to live in restricted areas, wear specific garb, and stay out of professions and business. Jews were also expelled from Linz and Vienna.
1424–53	Jews were expelled from many German cities.
1474–82	There were continuous riots against Spanish Jews.
1475	The Jews of Trent were tortured, executed, and/or expelled.
1480	The Spanish Inquisition began. Catholics forced thousands of Jews to convert, then tortured and burned them at the stake. (Those who "converted" were treated the worst.) Their property was confiscated by the Church.[37] Ultimately, the Inquisition punished 341,000 victims, mostly Jews, included 32,000 who were burned at the stake.
1485–94	Jews were expelled from Perugia, Vicenza, Parma, Milan, Lucca, Florence, and Tuscany.

1492	Hundreds of thousands of Spanish Jews and 40,000 Sardinian Jews were expelled after refusing to convert to Catholicism. Their property was confiscated by the Church.[38]
1495	The Jews in Lithuania and Cracow were expelled.
1496	The Inquisition and expulsion of Portuguese Jews occurred.
1498	All Jews were expelled from Provence.
1500	Jews in Venice were forced to pay high taxes in order to live in mandated ghettoes and were disqualified from being citizens.
1511	The Inquisition of Jews in the West Indies took place.
1516	The Inquisition of South American Jews took place.
1541	The Jews of Prague were expelled.
1550	Ivan the Terrible ordered Jews to convert to Christianity or be drowned. Jews were excluded from Russia until the late 1700s.
1565	The Church ordered Jews to stay confined in ghettoes. (This was the origin of the Jewish ghetto.) Jews had to wear badges of shame. The Church confiscated Jewish possessions.
1569	Pope Pius expelled the Jews from all papal territories except for Rome and Ancona.[39]

Gentiles have oppressed and slaughtered us for thousands of years in the hope that we will stop testifying that God expects people to live by divine standards of morality. Our martyrs have repeatedly shown the world that dying for the sanctification of God's name is better than living physically without spiritual integrity. In generation after generation, Jews have shown that a life without absolute obedience to God is meaningless. As painful as our persecutions have been, each time a Jew refused to adopt expedient beliefs, he or she brought intense spiritual light into the world. The events of Jewish history have shown how evil people can be when they reject Torah and the Noahide laws.[40]

WHERE WAS GOD?

Some people ask where God was during these Jewish national horrors. Other people ask, "Where was man?" God didn't force Christians to relentlessly murder, rape, and plunder Jews. He didn't tell them to forbid Jews to earn a livelihood, to burn us in synagogues, or to grant sainthood to barbarians who killed us. Nor did He command the Babylonians, Romans, or Arabs to be cruel to us. Their monstrous behavior was due to choices they made by rejecting God's system of morality (the Noahide laws).

When God needed to punish the Jews by exiling or conquering them, other conquerors could have been kind. The barbarism shown to Jews by pagans, Christians, and Moslems demonstrates how evil people become when they make up their own rules of morality instead of following God's laws.

While it is better to be monotheistic Christians or Moslems than pagans, the former's barbarism toward Jews has exposed their moral bankruptcy for over 1,000 years. Their religion espouses beautiful rhetoric about love and charity that Christians have consistently failed to put into practice. Christians caused untold suffering and butchery to Jews during the Crusades. To this day, the Catholic Church maintains as saints the murderers and torturers of innocent and saintly Jews! Only recently did the Church admit any responsibility for humiliating, terrorizing, and slaughtering Jews in the basest of ways for centuries. The Church historically maintained that their violent, humiliating, and confiscatory actions were good and were deserved by the Jews for rejecting the divinity of Jesus. While Jews believe that Gentile monotheists can be righteous, the Church refuses to legitimize Jewish beliefs to this day.

Our history has bred a people who were willing to live and die for their beliefs. Our predecessors' actions continually showed that poverty, expulsion, and death were better than a life of affluence living by false values.

People establish their scale of values by how they live, not by what they preach. Jews who refused to "convert" to Christianity, even on pain of death, demonstrated that the highest value in life is living for God and His system of morality.[41] People who devoted themselves to torturing, raping, burning, killing, or expelling Jews showed the scale of values by which they lived regardless of the beliefs they professed.

Our history has been terribly painful, but we have revealed Godliness to anyone willing to see it. Not uncommonly, Gentiles in every generation saw our martyrs and persecutions and decided to become Jews.

One case in point involved Onkelos, the nephew of the Roman emperor, Hadrian. Onkelos wanted a pretext to leave Rome and go out into the world, so he asked his uncle for advice. Hadrian hated the Jews, and was persecuting those under Roman rule, especially in Israel. He told his nephew, "Keep an eye on commodities. Invest in them as much as possible when they're low because they're bound to rise." Onkelos then went to Jerusalem, where he asked the rabbis to teach him Torah. They wouldn't because it is forbidden to teach the Oral Law to a Gentile. So he got circumcised and learned Torah with Rabbis Eliezer and Yehoshua for many years.

When he went back to Hadrian and told his uncle that he had converted, Hadrian slapped him. "How dare you?" the furious emperor charged.

Onkelos replied, "I only followed your advice. You told me to invest in the lowliest commodities because their lot is bound to improve, so I joined the Jews." Onkelos then returned to Jerusalem and wrote a Torah translation and commentary (*Targum Onkelos*) that Jews study to this day.[42]

One of the many reasons that Jews were exiled among the nations is so that Gentiles with reincarnated Jewish souls would become righteous converts.[43] Our ancestors revealed God's truth through suffering and sacrifice, as well as through the beauty of a Jewish way of life.

Some of the Jews' worst oppressors even converted to Judaism when they saw how the Jews lived and died. For example, the Romans sentenced Rabbi Chaninah ben Tradion to death for teaching Torah. His cruel executioner wrapped him in the Torah scroll from which the Sage taught, then inserted wet wool between the parchment and the rabbi's skin. When he set the Sage on fire, the wool prolonged the rabbi's agony instead of allowing him to die quickly. The rabbi's students urged him to hasten his death by opening his mouth, yet the rabbi insisted, "Let the One who gave me life take it away when it pleases Him."

When the executioner saw this religious devotion, he repented for his evil deeds. He hastened the rabbi's death by removing the wool, then jumped into the pyre and also died. A heavenly voice proclaimed, "[The souls of] Rabbi Chaninah and his executioner are now entering Paradise."[44]

Around that same time, Onkelos converted to Judaism.[45] The Roman emperor wanted to bring him back to Rome and to paganism, so he sent a delegation of soldiers to capture Onkelos. Onkelos engaged the men in a theological conversation that convinced them of the truth of Judaism, and they all decided to stay and convert. The emperor sent a second delegation with similar results. After he sent a third group who also converted, the emperor left Onkelos alone rather than lose more soldiers.

Nebuzaradan was a Babylonian officer who slaughtered hundreds of thousands of Jews, including tens of thousands of rabbis, priests, and children. He repented after committing his horrific crimes and converted to Judaism.[46] His act proclaimed his acceptance of God and truth to the entire Babylonian empire.

Rome wanted Nero to wage war against the Jews, but he realized that God would hold him accountable if he harmed them. He fled from Rome and converted to Judaism. Rabbi Meir, one of the greatest Talmudic Sages, descended from him.[47]

Even today, past Jewish suffering continues to shine forth with the truth of Judaism. For example, a woman named Mary had a grandfather who was a minister. He baptized her, and her parents and grandparents were missionaries. In her second year at university, she took a course in comparative religion. Among other things, Mary learned that European Christian leaders forced the Jews to publicly debate them, hoping to expose the fallacy of Judaism and the legitimacy of Christianity. Instead, in every forced debate, the Jews argued so persuasively for the truth of Judaism and Christianity's lack of validity that the Jews won. The rulers then punished and/or expelled the Jews.[48] Most Christians were too threatened by the truth of Judaism to embrace or even tolerate it, but the Jews continually revealed it to them. (Ironically, Christian scholars often consulted rabbis, such as the Rashba, to learn how to authentically translate and understand "Old Testament" verses, yet then ignored the implications of this!)

When Mary discovered the "historic arrogance of the Church, particularly vis-à-vis the Jews," she continued studying and realized that the Christian Church had totally distorted Hebrew texts in order to bolster their indefensible beliefs. She had the courage to become a Jew a few years later.[49]

Every Jew who suffered as a result of showing truth to the world helped God bring the world one step closer to its rectification and redemption. God gave everyone the ability to seek truth, reject evil, and live spiritually fulfilled lives. This was expressed so beautifully by Prince Rudolph of Austria in his memoirs when he visited Hebron at the turn of the century:

> Upon reaching Hebron, I immediately went to the cave of Machpelah. There I was overwhelmed by the realization that my feet stood at the sepulchre of the saintly Hebrew Patriarchs. Involuntarily, I knelt down, lifted my hands toward Heaven, and with tears streaming down my eyes I said,
>
> "Holy Patriarch Abraham . . . open your eyes and observe the lot of your ten million children dispersed and scattered among all lands, persecuted and oppressed by tyrants and murderers, hated and hounded by cruel foes. . . . Your children can find no resting place. . . .
>
> "I will endeavor with all my power to help your unfortunate children when I ascend the throne of Austria."[50]

Despite the many attempts by the nations of the world to silence us, we have quietly borne witness to anyone who was willing to listen to our message about what God wants for the peoples of the world.

We can't know why, in each instance of communal suffering, God saw fit to bring it upon us, but we can know that our national suffering has brought truth to the world and preserved us as a unique people for over 3,000 years. No other nation can make this claim.

EVIL AND FREE WILL

"The light of God's presence is the true cause of everything good. The cause of all evil is the hiddenness of this light."[51]

Every Day of Atonement, we recite a chilling account of the cruel murder of ten righteous Jewish Sages during the Hadrianic persecutions. The following is excerpted from these enigmatic prayers:

> The Ten Martyrs were shown no mercy by the Roman emperor. He wanted to contrive an excuse to kill them, so he searched the Torah until he discovered a commandment that requires executing a kidnapper who has witnessed selling a person.[52] The emperor was elated, and decreed that his palace be filled with shoes. He then summoned ten of the greatest Jewish Sages . . . and asked them, "What is the law if a Jew kidnaps a fellow Jew, enslaves and sells him?"
>
> The rabbis replied, "The thief must die."
>
> The emperor said, "These kidnappers were your ancestors [ten sons of our forefather Jacob]. They sold their brother [Joseph] to a caravan of Ishmaelites for the price of a pair of shoes. And you must accept the heavenly [death] decree upon yourselves because no Jews have been as great and as pious as you since your

ancestors died. Were your ancestors still alive, I would sentence them. [Since that isn't possible], you must bear your forefathers' sin."

The rabbis requested, "Give us three days so that we can find out if this was decreed upon us by God. If we are guilty and culpable, we will suffer the consequences of the All-Merciful One's decree. . . ."

The Sages turned their eyes to Rabbi Ishmael, the high priest. . . . He purified himself, pronounced the Ineffable Name of God, and ascended to Heaven to know if this decree had come from God Himself. When he ascended, he asked [his question of] the angel Gabriel. Gabriel said, "Accept the decree upon yourselves, beloved and righteous ones. I heard from behind the heavenly curtain that this is your destiny."

The rabbi descended and relayed God's word to his comrades. The base emperor then commanded the ten righteous men to be brutally slaughtered. Two of the greatest Sages were brought out first—Rabbi Ishmael, the high priest, and Rabbi Shimon ben Gamliel, the prince of Israel.

Rabbi Shimon begged to be killed first, so as not to see the high priest's death. The despot ordered that lots be cast, and the lot fell upon Rabbi Shimon. The ruler hurried to spill Rabbi Shimon's blood as if he were an ox. When he was decapitated, Rabbi Ishmael took the head and wept over it with a bitter, *shofar*-like voice: "Ay! The tongue that rushed to teach words of beauty now licks the dust due to Israel's sins."

Rabbi Ishmael sobbed and trembled over Rabbi Shimon's head. The daughter of the base tyrant stood up when she heard Rabbi Ishmael weeping, and desired him because he was an extraordinarily attractive man. She asked her father to let him live. The base one refused her wish, so she asked that his skin be flayed while he was still alive [so that she could stuff it and look at his preserved features]. The tyrant did as she wished, and when he reached the place of Rabbi Ishmael's *tefillin,* the rabbi shrieked bitterly to the One who formed his soul [and he expired].

The celestial angels screamed out, "Is this the reward for those who study Torah? The One who spreads out light like a garment, allows the enemy to insult Your great and awesome Name, and revile and blaspheme the words of Torah?"

A heavenly voice answered, "If I hear another sound I will turn the world to water, the earth to formlessness and void. These goings-on are a decree from Me. Accept it, those of you who delight in Torah."

Jewish officers were killed together with scholars who studied late in houses of study. They observed as many commandments as a pomegranate is full of seeds.

They removed Rabbi Akiva, who interpreted the meanings of the crowns of the Torah's letters, and tore his skin off with sharp combs. [As they flayed him alive], the time to say the morning *Shema* prayer arrived. His executioner and students were astonished that he recited this prayer with joy, as blood flowed from his many wounds. As he died, he explained, "My whole life I was troubled when I said in the *Shema* that I should love God with all my heart and with all my soul and with all my might. I wondered how I could ever fulfill the commandment to love God with all of my soul. Now that I have the opportunity to do it, should I not take advantage of it?"

With that, Rabbi Akiva recited the first verse of the *Shema,* "Hear, Israel, the [merciful] Lord is our God [of justice], the Lord is One." He died as he finished saying the word "One." A heavenly voice then called out, "Happy are you, Rabbi

Akiva, that your soul left you as you reached a state of oneness with Me. You realized that everything that happens—the painful and the pleasant—emanate from one and the same God. You fully prepared yourself in the earthly world to enter the World-to-Come."

The ruler commanded that they bring out Rabbi Chaninah ben Teradion from the study hall. [He had violated the Roman prohibition against teaching Torah publicly. They wrapped him in the Torah scroll that he always kept with him.] They burned him alive by placing him on top of burning twigs. In order to prolong his agony and delay his death, the executioner had inserted wet wool between the Torah scroll and his chest. His students urged him to hasten his death by removing the wet sponges. He replied that it was up to the One who gave him life to take it back.

The executioner was so moved by the rabbi's piety that he asked, "If I hasten your death by removing the wet sponges, will I have a share in the World-to-Come?" When the rabbi assured him that he would, the executioner took away the wool and intensified the flames so that the rabbi died quickly. The executioner then threw himself on the pyre and also died. A heavenly voice declared, "Rabbi Chaninah and his executioner are about to enter the World-to-Come."

While some people are moved or inspired by the piety and poignancy portrayed in these incidents, others are outraged. How could God let pious people suffer so terribly? How could a merciful God not intervene and stop these unjust massacres?

Before we go on, we must realize that no intellectual explanations are meaningful unless we can distance ourselves from the emotional horror of Jewish history. To put it differently, we can never accept that God has good reasons for letting Jews suffer as long as we feel pain of such magnitude. Once we are able to accept intellectual answers, however, they give a beautiful explanation as to why God allows apparent, wide-scale injustice to happen with impunity.

God determined that our world would have a purpose only if we have free choice. If He intervened every time that we violated His will, it would defeat His purpose in having created us. He wants us to perfect the world by freely choosing to be good, but that can happen only if He simultaneously lets us build a world of evil.

Imagine that our Creator always punished wrongdoing immediately and blatantly, such as by killing the Romans who tortured righteous Jews. That would take away people's free will. It is no challenge to be righteous and believe in God when He does manifest miracles. We must have a much more sincere commitment to Him when life is "unfair" and He seems to be hidden or uncaring.

Nor could we live in an evil world if the Almighty always meted out justice as soon as people sinned. His withholding justice lets us learn that people inevitably create a world of evil when they detach Him from daily life. We inevitably do selfish and harmful things when we can do whatever we please.

In the short run, the One Above wants us to make the world everything that we so stubbornly want it to be. He lets us live with false values so that we will realize that living without Him builds a world of nonsense and self-destruction. He lets evil intensify for a long time because that is how we eventually recognize its ugliness and seek truth.[53]

We would never appreciate the importance of doing God's will if we never saw how much evil people created by spurning His rules and ethics. He lets evil intensify so that we will eventually get rid of it.

The Martyrology prayers on Yom Kippur remind us that God lets evil prosper as part of a divine plan. Were He to prevent people from doing evil, the world would lose its purpose. This is what the Martyrology prayers convey when God tells the angels not to interfere with the Roman evildoers, else the world will return to nothingness. The world was purposeless and void before it had people who could choose to do right or wrong. It will be so again if God interferes with man's free will.

Despite being tortured, Rabbi Akiva's last words expressed his understanding that his suffering was allowed by a benevolent God, and he died proclaiming God's Oneness. That is, he realized that both pleasant and apparently evil events are part of the same divine plan. Heavenly voices from the World of Truth congratulated Rabbis Akiva and Chaninah for their magnificent sanctification of God and reassured the survivors that martyrs are fully rewarded in the next world for their steadfast faith here.

Some people try to escape the national suffering of the Jews by assimilating or "converting" to other religions. We annihilate ourselves spiritually if we try to make life easier in the short run by forsaking our magnificent role in this world. Not only do we deprive ourselves of true meaning here and in an eternal afterlife, we can't run away from God's mission for us, anyway. For example, the Nazis traced genealogies back three generations in order to decide who was a Jew worth persecuting. Ultimately, we can run, but we can't hide from God or our soul's Jewish identity.

Rabbi Akiva expressed this by continuing to teach Torah after the Romans made it a capital crime to do so. After he was caught and sentenced to death, he explained his suicidal behavior using the following parable:

A fox walked on a river bank and watched fish swimming in a panicked frenzy. He asked why they were doing this.

"The fishermen are trying to catch us," they replied.

The fox suggested, "Why don't you come onto dry land? We'll live together as our ancestors did!"

The fish refused. They said, "We're afraid to live in water, which keeps us alive. We'd be so much worse off living on dry land! We'd surely die there."

Rabbi Akiva continued, "We are afraid of being caught by the Romans, but at least we study Torah, which is described as 'your life and your length of days.'[54] How much more should we be afraid to abandon our Torah studies?!"[55]

While our millions of martyrs suffered physically, they magnificently sanctified God's name to the world. Their souls are now receiving rewards in the next world that are beyond description. It is said that God has a "scarlet garment" dyed with their blood, and that He will avenge their deaths in the future.[56]

These martyrs left an everlasting spiritual legacy that we benefit from to-day. Jews who assimilate or adopt other religions leave no spiritual legacy at all and have no spiritual afterlife. They exchange their immortal and eternal lifeline to God for dubiously better physical lives that end after sixty or seventy years.

It is hard for us to live by spiritual and moral convictions when the hedonists and immoral people around us seem to have easier lives than pious and upright people. We wonder if living by the Torah is really worth the sacrifices that we must make and the suffering that we endure as a result. Our greatest Sages were troubled by the desecration of God's name that occurs with our suffering. It took Rabbi Akiva to console them that this is part of a divine plan that is a prelude to a future, ultimate sanctification of God's name, as the following story recounts:

Four Sages were walking along a road when they heard Romans partying far away. The first three rabbis wept, while Rabbi Akiva laughed. The rabbis asked, "Akiva, why are you laughing?"

Akiva countered, "Why are you crying?"

They said, "These heathens who worship and burn incense to idols live in safety and comfort while our Temple, God's 'footstool,' is burnt [and we Jews suffer and are downtrodden]. Shouldn't we weep?"

Akiva replied, "That is why I'm laughing. If those who transgress God's will fare this way, how much better will be the lot [in the eternal world] of those who obey Him?"[57]

With this background, we can now discuss the Holocaust.

THE HOLOCAUST

"And the Lord said to Moses, 'Behold, you will sleep with your fathers, and this nation will rise up and go astray after the strange gods of the lands they are entering. They will abandon Me and abrogate the covenant that I made with them. And My anger will burn against them on that day, and I will abandon them, and hide My face from them, and they will be devoured, and many evils and troubles will find them. And they will say on that day, "Have these evils not found us because God is not in our midst?" And I will completely hide My face on that day because of all the evil that they have done in turning to other gods.' "[58]

The terrible pain and suffering of the Jews during the Holocaust convinced many people that God has no special relationship with us, and He certainly doesn't care if we live according to the Torah. But the Torah not only predicted the Holocaust, it says that it was meaningful!

The Holocaust showed the world how monstrous people become when they divorce themselves from God and His morality. It exposed the untenability of secular humanism, which insists that the human conscience is perfectly adequate to determine moral rules. The Holocaust showed that the human conscience is totally self-serving. Left to our own devices, people create evil by degrading others, by promoting persecution, theft, torture, and even murder, and by setting barbaric standards of morality.

Pre-Nazi Germany was considered to be one of the most civilized, cultured, and wise nations. But their intellectual and scientific development went hand-in-glove with such moral bankruptcy that they gassed, shot, and burned one and a half million Jewish children. Despite the Germans' merciless persecutions and killings of hundreds of thousands of Jews during the previous millenium, it took the Holocaust to make the world (and German Jews!) see how depraved the Germans really were.

Many civilized people believe that sophisticated people don't need to believe in God. Science, technology, and culture replaced God after the Emancipation and the Industrial Revolution. The Nazis and European anti-Semites showed the world that scientific advances can never substitute for morality. No matter how smart, "cultured," and technologically advanced people are, they create absolute evil when they reject God's laws for humanity and substitute their own. The banality of evil worldwide, even by "sophisticated" and educated people, was apparent to all as the Nazis murdered six million Jews and almost no one minded.

Until the Holocaust, few people believed that average and intelligent people would be evil if they only had the chance. It took the horrors of the Holocaust to convince people that without believing that God cares how we act in the most mundane parts of our lives, a next-door neighbor could happily kill for the right price. People do greedy and cruel things unless they believe that God watches over them and expects them to live up to His code of morality.

The Holocaust showed that the richest countries in the world preferred to let starving, homeless refugees die, rather than enter. The world saw the SS, at least one-third of whose officers were professionals and academics, delight in torturing, shooting, and gassing to death millions of children, old people, and naked women and men. This same "elite" intelligentsia enjoyed Jew-hair-stuffed mattresses, soap made from body fat, Jew-skin lampshades, and gold from Jewish corpses. Millions of Germans, Frenchmen, Poles, Hungarians, and others still enjoy stolen Jewish possessions to this day, as they sleep peacefully in Jewish homes whose owners they murdered or gleefully watched being deported.

The Holocaust showed the world that people who reject God's Noahide laws are capable of doing anything. While Jewish suffering and persecution stripped some people of their faith in God, seeing what people can do by rejecting divinely given morality has also caused many people to grow closer to Him.[59]

For example, a woman was raised in the Roman Catholic Church and attended Catholic schools until law school. At that time, she picked up a copy of *Mila 18* and learned about the Holocaust for the first time.

"I wanted to know what it was about the Jews and their beliefs that made others want to exterminate them," she explained. When she found out after studying for four years, she converted to Judaism.[60]

Jane was schooled in a convent. Her Catholic family was so religious that one sister became a nun and a brother became a priest. She grew up during World War

II and was startled to discover that the Catholics refused to help the Jews. They justified this by their belief that Jews were supposed to suffer unless they accepted Christianity. Jane began to study Judaism, converted, and moved to Israel.[61]

Sally was a non-Jewish woman who spent a summer traveling through Europe with her secular Jewish fiancé. Many of their friends joined them for a while, then went to visit Israel. Sally and Dan decided to see for themselves what Israel was all about. At the end of their tour, they visited Yad Vashem, the Holocaust Museum in Jerusalem. They were horrified and nauseated, but also very moved and unsettled by the shocking and graphic photographs and exhibits. When they emerged in the bright daylight, Dan was as white as a sheet.

Sally asked, "What's the matter?"

He didn't know how to respond to the woman whom he dearly loved, and with whom he had planned to spend the rest of his life. After thinking for a few moments, he said, "Sally, if I marry you, I will do to my people what Hitler tried, but failed to do. I will end 3,300 years of Jewish continuity, and exterminate all future generations of Jews that were destined to come from me."

Instead of being angry, Sally replied, "If your God made you come all this way to have this realization, I want to learn more about your God."

They both found their ways to *yeshivot*. A year later, Sally converted, and Dan became an observant Jew. They were married in a traditional wedding ceremony and now live in Israel.

THE SUFFERING OF THE RIGHTEOUS

We are especially troubled that many Holocaust victims seemed to be innocent or pious people. In ancient times, God's seeming injustice to the righteous troubled even Moses. He asked, "Master of the World, why do some righteous people prosper while other pious people have it bad, and some wicked people have it good while other wicked people have it bad?"

God responded with a cryptic statement that meant that only He knows why, in any given situation, certain good people suffer or wicked people prosper. We can know only general reasons.[62]

God brings suffering to most righteous people, in part so that they will serve Him more intensively than most people can. Like a farmer who has a weak and a strong ox with which to plow a field, he gives the strong one most of the work and the weaker one much less.[63] The "field" is the world, and it needs to be sowed with spirituality. Since people can't attain equal amounts of spiritual devotion, God benefits the rest of humanity by giving righteous people the yeoman's share of work to do.

When innocent people suffered during the Holocaust, it may have been because God knew that He could rely on them to sanctify His name and not renounce their faith during times of unspeakable atrocities. He couldn't necessarily rely on assimilated Jews to do the same.

Traditional Judaism believes in collective responsibility.[64] When one Jew draws down blessing or causes spiritual damage, he benefits or hurts everyone connected to him.[65] When righteous people suffer, their merit spiritually cleanses everyone connected to them. Their suffering may even save their entire generation from annihilation.[66]

Righteous people can also suffer if they keep silent when they could have changed the world by decrying certain actions.[67] According to some Jewish commentators, this is why Job suffered so terribly.[68]

Some people think that they are not accountable for wrongs that they don't personally commit. But Jews are all responsible for each other, so righteous people are held accountable when they don't try to stop the failings of their generation.[69] This is why God may even punish righteous people first when He responds to an immoral community.[70] Good people could have made a difference.

Sometimes when the Master of the World lets evil prosper, good people who don't deserve it are exploited and hurt. They usually have very great souls, and they earn the highest possible spiritual reward for helping God bring the world to its ultimate destination.

For example, the Roman emperor Trajan framed the Jews when his daughter was found murdered, and he ordered their extermination. Two innocent Jewish brothers confessed to the crime in order to exonerate the other Jews. The Romans immediately executed them and left the rest of the Jews alone. The brothers' place in Paradise is so great that even the greatest saints cannot enter there.[71]

Jews who died during the Holocaust are all enjoying a portion in the World-to-Come now, even if they would not otherwise have deserved it.[72]

Even though both can occur simultaneously, the reasons that Jews suffer as a nation are different than the reasons that individuals suffer. Jews suffer as a people when God needs to redirect or rectify the Jews as a whole. While each person will be able to fully serve God according to his soul's destiny,[73] God responds to our collective choices in a way that simultaneously allows the world to reach its spiritual destiny.

THE TRAGIC EFFECTS OF ASSIMILATION

The terrible events of the Holocaust cannot be understood without appreciating the pervasive effects that the "Enlightenment" had. Many German Jews promoted the Enlightenment, or secularization of Judaism, to Western European and Russian Jews. The goal of this movement was to destroy belief in the authenticity of traditional Judaism and in the divine authorship of the Torah. For the first time in 3,200 years, a large group of Jews had the audacity to deny that God gave the Torah and proclaimed that Jews did not need to observe its commandments.[74] "Enlightened" German Jews in the 1800s spawned modern Reform and Reconstructionist movements that abolished adherence to authentic Judaism and ridiculed its divine origin and traditions.

Until a few hundred years ago, large numbers of Jews almost never denied the divinity of Torah and Jewish law. Its undeniable authenticity had been passed down in an unbroken chain from parent to child for over 3,000 years. That is why the Torah repeatedly exhorts us to *remember* our leaving the enslavement in Egypt.[75] It tells us to *remember* our receiving the Torah[76] and the covenant that we made with God at Mount Sinai.[77] We are required to *remember* how He protected, fed, and clothed us during our wanderings in the wilderness.[78] Because our history began with real events and a real revelation of God and Torah to at least two and a half million Jews (something no other religion can claim), it was only recently that large numbers of Jews dared deny it.[79]

Josephus Flavius wrote some 1,900 years ago:

> Despite the many [1,400] years that have already passed [since the giving of the Torah], no Jew has been so bold as to either add to our holy books nor take anything from them, nor make any changes in them. All Jews drink in, with their mother's milk, the belief that these books are of divine origin; the determination to remain faithful to them; and the willingness to die for them if required. It is not new for numerous Jewish captives, time and time again, to endure tortures and deaths in all kinds of arenas, rather than say one word against our laws and the books that contain them.[80]

Some people believe that the Holocaust was a divine response to huge numbers of Jews spreading the belief that God and the Torah were products of un-enlightened imagination. These assimilated Jews flocked into cultural circles of "enlightened" Gentiles and extolled the virtues of leaving behind archaic Jewish beliefs and practices. A few generations later, similarly "enlightened" Gentiles took great pleasure in murdering millions of innocent people. Some prominent, "enlightened" Jews were also responsible for the death of millions of "old-fashioned" European Jews whom they regarded as fossils from a backward world. The Holocaust showed the world the lack of morality that these "enlightened" philosophies breed.

By the time of the Holocaust, the majority of Western European, Hungarian, German, Austrian, and Russian Jews were no longer observant, and assimilation was occurring at a frightening rate.[81] So many Jews had "converted" to Christianity or intermarried within the past two generations that Hitler defined a Jew as someone with a Jewish grandparent. Jews who thought that they could melt into German society and make Berlin their Jerusalem were painfully reminded that Jews have a different calling.

Two decades before World War II, assimilated Russian Jews like Karl Marx and Leon Trotsky, and their Jewish followers established an atheistic country and persecuted those who believed in God. Jews were at the forefront of building a godless world where belief in man, culture, and/or money had replaced spirituality.

Apart from the fact that every Jew who survived the Holocaust did so only by a miracle, millions of other Jews had miraculous opportunities to be saved but were tragically doomed by the irresponsible behavior of assimilated Jews and secular Zionist leaders. For example, secular Jews in America put enormous political pressure on the president and State Department *not* to allow Holocaust refugees into the United States. They vigorously opposed religious Jews' efforts to send European Jews food, medical supplies, money, and visas. Rabbi Michael Weissmandel sent secular Jewish leaders in the United States detailed maps of Auschwitz and timetables of the death trains to the camp. He pleaded for these leaders to persuade Roosevelt and Churchill to bomb the camps and the railroads leading to them. His pleas fell on deaf ears. [82]

The Reform rabbi Stephen Wise was the head of the America Jewish Congress when Nazis were willing to free 70,000 Romanian Jews for $50 apiece. He replied, ". . . no collection of funds would seem justified." The Jewish Agency in London also denied the offer. Secular Jews pressured the U.S. State Department not to release information about the proposal to the public. The result was that the Romanian Jews were herded into barns, hosed with gasoline, ignited, and then shot as they ran out of their infernoes.

Assimilated Jews often did unconscionable acts to sabotage rescue attempts by religious Jews to smuggle European Jews into safe havens. [83] The secular Jewish Agency and secular Jewish leaders in Israel also played a shameful role in the Holocaust, turning a deaf ear to millions of Jews who could have been saved and brought to Israel. [84] Instead, these Jews died on ships or at the hands of the Nazis.

Rabbi Weissmandel and other Jewish leaders of Bratislava paid a senior SS officer $50,000 in a deal to stop the deportation of Slovakian Jews in 1942. Meanwhile, nonobservant and secular Zionist officials refused Weissmandel's pleas to send money to save additional European Jews. One secular Jewish official told Weissmandel that the Eastern European Jews exaggerated reports of Nazi atrocities, and refused to help. Thanks to these "leaders," the deportations of Slovakian Jews were resumed in 1944 with tragic consequences. [85]

Jews were given at least two opportunities to save approximately 800,000 Hungarian Jews from extermination. One was when Rudolf Kastner, a secular Jew, had an opportunity to warn Hungarian Jews about their impending extermination in time for many of them to avoid their terrible fate. His spectacular and self-serving failure to do this prevented them from escaping and resulted in their mass annihilation.

The second was when Adolf Eichmann was willing to free one million Hungarian Jews in exchange for 10,000 trucks. He offered to free 100,000 Jews in advance as a show of good will and proof of his intentions. After he presented his proposal to Joel Brand, Brand was betrayed by the secular Zionist leaders of Palestine who did not want religious Hungarian Jews swamping their country. The secular Zionist leaders got Brand arrested and imprisoned by the British until most of the Hungarian Jews were murdered. To their eternal shame, David Ben-Gurion,

Moshe Sharett, and Chaim Weizmann were more concerned about preserving "Zionism" and "elite Jews" than in helping these masses.[86] The result was that millions of Jews perished.

A bitter lesson of the Holocaust is that we have two choices in life: to live as Jews, or to live as Gentiles. When we think that this world is all there is, some trade a life of spiritual meaning and holiness in order to be "sophisticated" and accepted by the nations of the world. But it never works. We are either spiritually annihilated, or spiritually *and* physically annihilated. As lamentable as it is that six million Jews died during the Holocaust, many more have been lost in America alone since the turn of the century. In the past two decades, over two million American Jews have been spiritually exterminated through assimilation and intermarriage. Like the fish in Rabbi Akiva's parable, we can survive only by maintaining our religious integrity and relying on God's protection, not by assimilating to gain security, wealth, and comfort. People who are upset by the Nazis' destruction should ask themselves what they are doing to stem the Jewish spiritual Holocaust that continues worldwide today. It has claimed more than ten million Jewish souls since World War I.

The Holocaust taught us that there is no such thing as moral neutrality. We either live for truth and righteousness every day, or contribute, actively or passively, to evil in a godless world.

BUILDING FROM THE ASHES OF DESTRUCTION

"Because God loves Israel, He punishes them in this world with pain and exiles to cleanse them of their sins."[87]

In the final analysis, we don't fully know why God saw fit to allow the extermination of a third of our people at the time, and in the way that it happened during World War II. But we do know that the Bible predicted the Holocaust and many of its horrors:

[The Jews] will rise up and go whoring after the strange gods of the lands in whose midst they will be. They will leave Me and abrogate My covenant which I made with them. My wrath will be against them that day, and I will leave them, and hide My face from them. They will be devoured, and many evil calamities will befall them. And they will say in that day, "Isn't it because God is not among us that all of these evils have befallen us?" And I will completely conceal My face on that day because of all of the evil that they have done, in turning to other gods.[88] (Gods here refer to non-Jewish ideologies and pursuits.)

One of the worst aspects of the Holocaust was that God totally "concealed [His] face on that day." This does not mean that He left the world for a while so that anything could happen. Rather, it means that we cannot comprehend more than general reasons why He might have allowed these atrocities.

The Holocaust was not simply a quirk of history. Its magnitude and intensity were unique in world history, even though suffering is far from unknown to us. We cannot yet fathom the Holocaust's meaning as a divine response to us, partly because we are still so close to it. We simply have to trust that God had His reasons for allowing it to happen, and like everything else, it somehow furthered His plans for the world.

Some readers undoubtedly want an appealing explanation as to why the Holocaust occurred. But the anger, horror, sadness, and outrage that we feel about it is still so fresh that no explanations can possibly feel good. This is like looking at a beautiful mosaic hanging on a distant wall. When we look at the whole picture from afar, we see clearly that every single piece is in its proper place. But if we stand right next to it, or are part of the mosaic ourselves, the pieces look like a jumbled mess! It will take many years for us to have enough distance to fully understand the Holocaust.

An older woman once asked, "Why did the Holocaust happen?" She was an observant Jew, despite having spent three years in a concentration camp and having seen unspeakable horrors. She had watched the Nazis torture and murder her parents and siblings. Forty years later, she still bore the physical and emotional scars of her ordeal. A question like hers did not stem from a desire to hear a philosophical explanation of tragedy. It came from a much deeper place, from a heart that could not comprehend how an all-merciful God could have allowed the barbarity that she had witnessed and undergone. It emanated from a sensitive woman who was still haunted by dreams of unimaginable butchery that took place in a hell on earth.

Had her question reflected a desire for knowledge, an intellectual explanation might have satisfied. In her case, a response had to address her emotions.

"Mrs. Goldberg," I replied, "I can't give you a reason. Sometimes the best that we can do is to accept that God had His reasons for allowing the Holocaust, but we can't know exactly what they were. The best that we can do is to make sure that we live meaningfully just the same."

We can know that God runs the world, even without fully knowing why He acts as He does at any given time. We can even be immensely troubled by His actions during the Holocaust and still believe in Him.

Even though we want to relate to a God who is always giving and nurturing, He must sometimes allow evil, mete out justice, or act harshly with us for other reasons in order for the world to fulfill its mission. One of our greatest challenges is to learn about and accept the Almighty as He is, not as we would like Him to be.

Rather than dismiss belief in a God who could allow a Holocaust, we should recognize that the Torah predicted it, in addition to our other national Jewish calamities. These tragedies are proof of God's existence and His involvement in our lives as much as miracles are.

After the Second Temple was destroyed, Rabbi Akiva and three other Sages were walking to Jerusalem. As they came to Mount Scopus, they saw where the

Temple had stood in its splendor but a few years earlier. Now it lay in ruins, and they ripped their garments in grief. As they approached the Temple Mount, they saw a fox scampering out of the Holy of Holies.

They still remembered the daily miracles in the Temple that once testified to God's presence in their daily lives, and they now felt His "absence."

The three Sages began to weep, while Rabbi Akiva laughed. The Sages asked him, "Why do you laugh?"

He replied, "Why do you cry?"

The Sages answered, "[This place was once so holy and awe-inspiring.] It was said about this place, 'And the nonpriest who draws close shall be killed [for profaning its holiness].'[89] Foxes now walk there. Shouldn't we grieve?"

Akiva responded, "That is why I am laughing. It is written, 'And my faithful witnesses will testify about Me, namely Uriah the priest and Zechariah the son of Yeverachiah.'[90] What does Uriah have to do with Zechariah? Uriah lived during the First Temple period, and Zechariah lived during the Second Temple era.

"Scripture tells us that the fulfillment of Zechariah's prophecy depends upon the fulfillment of the prophecy from Uriah's time. Uriah's prophecy says, 'For your sakes shall Zion be plowed like a field.'[91] Zechariah's prophecy states, 'In the future, old men and old women will sit in the streets of Jerusalem.'[92]

"Until I saw Uriah's prophecy come true, I was afraid that Zechariah's prophecy would not come true. Now that I see Uriah's prophecy fulfilled, it is certain that Zechariah's prophecy [of redemption] will also come true."

The other rabbis replied, "Akiva, you have comforted us, Akiva, you have comforted us."[93]

Every Tisha B'Av (the ninth of Av), we mourn the totality of our national calamities, from the time of the ancient Israelites until the present. On each of the three Sabbaths before Tisha B'Av, we read prophetic verses (called *haftarot*) that foretold the terrible punishments that God would send the Jews if they did not repent and stop sinning. On the seven Sabbaths after Tisha B'Av, we read prophetic consolations that God conveyed to the Jews. The following Sabbath, which falls between the Jewish New Year and the Day of Atonement, we read prophetic exhortations to repent for our sins.[94]

This order of prophetic readings expresses a beautiful idea. The Jews were first warned, then punished on Tisha B'Av with the destruction of both Temples and exile from Israel for not improving their behavior. God consoled them, and only afterward did He urge them to repent. We would think that they should have been (1) warned, (2) punished, (3) exhorted to repent, and then (4) consoled after repenting.

This "out-of-order" sequence teaches us that we have to feel God's Presence before we feel ready to repent. Our Heavenly Father has to console and convince us that He still wants to have a relationship with us before we will want to repent and rebuild His world that we destroyed through misuse.[95]

When Isaiah tried to comfort the Jews after their punishment during the First Commonwealth, they initially wanted to kill him. They were so devastated that they were inconsolable. People who have been punished are open to emotional soothing only if they believe that the punisher still cares about them. Some Jews believe that God deserted them during the Holocaust (or after other tragedies), so they can't be comforted. To keep us from thinking that God no longer cares about us when we undergo terrible tragedies, we read consoling words on the Sabbath immediately after Tisha B'Av: " 'You will be comforted, you will be comforted My people,' says your God."[96]

These words can also be read, " 'You will be comforted, you will be comforted *with Me,'* says your God."[97] The One Above reassures us that His punishment does not mean that He has stopped loving us. He wanted our ancestors, and He wants us, to take down the barriers that we erect between us and Him so that we can be close again.

Some Jews in Isaiah's era thought that God's promise applied only to that generation. They wanted future generations of Jews to know that God would also be with them during their calamities. This is why the verse in Isaiah can also be ᵣead, " 'You will be comforted, you will be comforted My people,' your God *will say* in the future."[98]

"Be comforted" is repeated for a very poignant reason. When we suffer, we sometimes can't believe that a loving God is doing this to us. Nor can we believe that He yearns for us to come to Him for consolation. We instinctively feel that our pain is a sign that He no longer cares about us and has rejected us.

The first "Be comforted" tells us that we must consider the idea that tragedy happens in the Almighty's Presence and may be caused by His providential hand. Once we formulate that thought, the second "Be comforted" teaches us that we must internalize and relate to that idea.

This concept is reinforced by the verse that follows, "Speak to the heart of Jerusalem, and call to her . . . for her iniquity has been appeased. . . ."[99] Isaiah had to convince the Jews that God was with them during their worst suffering. He could do this only by first reviving them emotionally ("call to her"). Otherwise, they could not see the Almighty's love for them in the ashes of their destruction.

This is why the rabbis who lived during the Roman conquest said, "Akiva, you have comforted us, Akiva, you have comforted us." Their emotional pain overwhelmed them when they saw a ruined world from which God seemed totally removed. Rabbi Akiva's words first told them not to let their momentary despair devastate them (the first "You have comforted us"). Then he encouraged them to reconnect to God from their depths (the second "You have comforted us").

When the Sanctuary and the Temples stood, two angelic figures (cherubim) stood atop the Holy Ark. One represented God and the other represented the Jews. These were spiritual barometers of the relationship between the Lord and His beloved people. When the Jews related properly to their Creator, the cherubim hugged each other. When the Jews did not, the cherubim faced away from one another.

When the Romans destroyed the Temple, they saw the cherubim embracing. This was God's way of telling the Jews that He had to destroy the holy Temple and exile them from their land because of His love for them. That is, they had to be cleansed of their sins, so He did it by destroying their cities and buildings instead of them.[100]

Our commentaries explain that the Divine Presence, as it were, is terribly pained when we live in a world from which we exclude Him. It's as if our Provider invites us to a scrumptuous feast where we gorge ourselves, then don't bother to acknowledge the Host.

God made the physical world a place where we would look for, find, and connect to Him. It only makes sense that He walk out on us or ask us to leave the party if we are so callous as to ignore Him and desecrate the place where He "wants" to dwell.

We suffer most when we divorce ourselves from our Creator and His constant supervision of us. Doing this creates a lonely world where God isn't real to us. We find it burdensome to sanctify every moment of life by acting as if we are always in the Almighty's presence and by trying to live up to His expectations of us. We want to relegate our religiosity to the synagogue, or to the Sabbath and holidays, or to a few religious rituals, and do what we want at other times. We don't want a heavenly eye to monitor our every deed, word, and thought. But the more we disconnect ourselves from God, the more we suffer the consequences. Whatever emotional or physical pain we suffer because of our circumstances is infinitely worse when we feel alone and subject to fate's whims and random forces.

We feel consoled when we put God back into the world and let ourselves feel comforted by His presence. We can do this only by inviting Him back into our lives with our minds, hearts, and senses. Studying Torah teaches us how to live so that we can feel our Heavenly Father constantly holding us. Praying every day and properly observing His commandments are ways that we embrace Him.

There is an expression, "Woe unto children who were chased away from their Father's table, and woe unto a Father who doesn't have His children at His table."[101] In Isaiah, God turns to us and says, "You comfort Me, and I'll comfort you." Once our relationship has been damaged, comforting each other is a step toward rebuilding it.

One final interpretation of Isaiah's words, "Be comforted, be comforted," speaks to our hearts as we await our final redemption. The first expression means that God will comfort us when the Messiah comes by showing us why all of our personal and national suffering was necessary. The second "Be comforted" tells us that at that time, He will also say how sorry He is that we had to go through such terrible pain.[102]

NOTES

1. Exodus 19:5–6.
2. Moshe Chaim Luzzatto, *The Way of God* (New York: Feldheim, 1983) 2:4:9.

3. The first ten generations of mankind (Adam until Noah) misused the world and corrupted themselves. God gave them approximately 1,600 years to repent, but they didn't, so He annihilated humanity during the Great Flood. Then He gave Noah and his family another chance to start over. He reiterated the moral code that they and their descendants were to uphold forever (known as the Seven Noahide laws). These laws still apply to all humanity and encompass seven principles of morality (Genesis 2:24; 9:3–7; *Sanhedrin* 56b). The practical details of these laws can be found in Aaron Lichtenstein, *The Seven Laws of Noah* (New York: Rabbi Jacob Joseph School Press, 1981).

God patiently waited for the next sixteen generations to live up to their divine mission, but they chose to worship idols and act immorally instead. Since the world served no purpose as long as things continued that way, God offered His Torah to the nations of the world. The Torah reveals God's will for how He wants us to act so that we can have an intimate relationship with Him and spiritually perfect the world. No Gentile nations were willing to give up their hedonistic and immoral pursuits to live by the Torah's restrictions. See Rabbi Moshe Chaim Luzzatto, *Maamar HaIkkarim*, "About the Torah and the Commandments."

4. *Shevuot* 39a.
5. Deuteronomy 28:1–14.
6. Genesis 41:25–57.
7. Exodus 1:10.
8. Exodus 1:11–16.
9. Exodus 5:5–19.
10. *Exodus Rabbah* 1:34.
11. *Iggerot Moshe,* vol. 7, p. 168.
12. *Zohar Chadash* Yitro. See also Maimonides, *Mishneh Torah, Hilchot Teshuvah,* 3:5.
13. Exodus 3:14.
14. *Brachot* 9b.
15. Freely translated from Leviticus 26:14–45.
16. *Meshech Chochmah* on Leviticus 26:14–45.
17. Much of the above material is detailed in *The Way of God* 2:4.
18. *Yoma* 9b.
19. *Yoma* 9b.
20. Isaiah 42:6.
21. These included the fact that few Jews would remain in Israel during the Babylonian exile, that the land would be desolate in their absence, and that Jews would return there seventy years later, rectifying the exact number of Sabbatical and Jubilee years that the Jews did not properly observe during their first Commonwealth. The Jews were supposed to let the land lie fallow every seventh year in a forty-nine-year cycle, as well as during the fiftieth, or Jubilee year. In the hundreds of years that Jews lived in Israel before the Babylonian exile, they planted and/or commercially harvested crops during seventy of these Sabbatical and Jubilee years.
22. By contrast, at least three million Jews entered the land of Israel after they left Egypt hundreds of years earlier.
23. *Yoma* 9a.
24. Aryeh Kaplan, *Facets and Faces* (Brooklyn, NY: Moznaim, 1993), pp. 43–44.

25. *Gittin* 56a.

26. The many horrors of this period are related in both *Gittin* 55b–58a and *The War of the Jews* by Josephus Flavius. See also *Me'am Lo'ez* on Deuteronomy 4:26.

27. *Gittin* 57a. Paul Johnson wrote that 985 towns, villages, and agricultural settlements were destroyed; 580,000 Jews died in the fighting and countless more starved to death or died by fire and sword. *A History of the Jews* (New York: Harper and Row, 1987), p. 142.

28. Quoted in Eliyahu Kitov, *The Book of Our Heritage,* vol. 3 (Jerusalem: Feldheim, 1968), p. 313.

29. Paraphrased from Deuteronomy 28:15–68.

30. *Gittin* 56a.

31. *A History of the Jews,* p. 171.

32. This is illustrated by the stories told in *Gittin* 55b and *Yoma* 9b. It is interesting that one Midrash (*Shemot Rabbah* 1) says that the Jews had to remain enslaved in Egypt because they told tales about each other. Causeless hatred of one Jew for another has been a distressingly recurrent theme throughout our history.

33. Paraphrased from *Gittin* 55b–56a.

34. Paraphrased from *Gittin* 58a.

35. Radak on Isaiah 48:10.

36. Blood libels were accusations by Christians that Jews killed Christian children and used their blood to make matzos for Passover, or drank it at the *seder.* These outrageous claims were pretexts for local Christians to kill Jews and plunder their possessions.

Christian hatred of Jews originated in Christianity itself. See Matthew 23, John 8:44, and the writings of the early Church fathers, Origen, John Chrysostom, Thomas Aquinas, and others. Many were canonized for their works. Martin Luther was representative of many other Christian leaders when he wrote: ". . . their synagogues should be set on fire, and whatever does not burn up should be covered with dirt, so that no one may be able to see a cinder or a stone of it. And this ought to be done for the honor of God and of Christianity, so that God may see that we are Christians, and that we have not wittingly tolerated blaspheming of His son and His Christians . . ." (in *Concerning the Jews and Their Lies,* 1543.)

37. Torquemada, the chief Inquisitor, is likely to have been of Jewish descent.

38. Jewish preachers in the sixteenth century attributed the persecution of Spanish Jewry to God's retribution for their love of secular philosophy.

39. Readers interested in Jewish history can read Eliyahu Kitov, *The Book of Our Heritage,* vol. 3 (Jerusalem: Feldheim, 1968), pp. 245–302; Shlomo Rotenberg, *Am Olam: The History of the Eternal Nation* (Jerusalem: Feldheim, 1988); Johnson, *A History of the Jews;* and Berel Wein, *Triumph of Survival* (New York: Shaar, 1990), and *Herald of Destiny* (New York: Shaar, 1993). Jewish history during the past 350 years, including the Chmelnitzski massacre of half a million Jews in 1648, is discussed in *Triumph of Survival.*

40. *The Way of God* 4:4:5.

41. This happened when people like Torquemada tortured Marranos in order to convince them to relinquish their belief in Judaism.

42. *Daat Zekanim* on Exodus 21:1. In the time of Queen Esther, the Jews were threatened with extinction. After God saved them when they rededicated their lives to serving Him properly, many Gentiles converted to Judaism (Esther 8:17).

43. See the *Or HaChaim* on Genesis 28:5, 49:9, and on Deuteronomy 21:10–11. Some Gentiles have souls whose sparks of holiness are held captive. They are released from their spiritual prison only when the person converts to Judaism. Kabbalistic reasons for the exile are discussed in *Herald of Destiny,* pp. 236–237.

44. Yom Kippur Martyrology prayers.

45. *Gittin* 56b.

46. *Gittin* 57b.

47. *Gittin* 56a. This Nero may not be the same one that historians identify as the emperor Nero.

48. In one instance, the ruler of the Khazars asked a Jew, a Christian, and a Moslem to argue the merits of their respective religions. The truth of Judaism was so clear that he and his subjects converted to Judaism.

49. Maurice Lamm, *Becoming a Jew* (New York: Jonathan David, 1991), pp. 53–54.

50. Quoted in Aharon Soloveitchik, *The Warmth and the Light* (Jerusalem: Genesis Press, 1992), pp. 47–48.

51. *The Way of God* 1:5:8.

52. Exodus 21:16.

53. The nature and importance of evil is discussed at length in Rabbi Moshe Chaim Luzzatto, *The Knowing Heart* (Jerusalem: Feldheim, 1982), pp. 143–179. God created evil only so that it will be eradicated. Evil intensifies to a point where it ultimately reveals God's oneness: "Whereas evil in itself is nothing but defect, and loss, and destruction, still, in conjunction with other mechanisms . . . it is the source of man's good itself. For upon it hinges all merit and possibility of Divine service . . . by its being intended to be conquered. . . . It exists only to be hewn down by man . . . [it] was created to be destroyed." When it asserts itself it is a precursor of good: "For this is the darkness through which the light of the Supreme perfection will be recognized when it reveals itself in time to come. . . . The darker it grows, the greater will be the truth of His oneness when He destroys this evil. And what is more, this evil affords gain to the one who is tested by it. . . . [It also] creates for man the opportunity for true service and action; for he perfects the creation with his own hands . . . and becomes a partner . . . with the Holy One, Blessed be He."

54. Deuteronomy 30:20.

55. Quoted by the *Me'am Lo'ez* commentary on Genesis 39:21.

56. *Kohelet Rabbah,* quoted in *Me'am Lo'ez* on Genesis 39:21.

57. *Makkot* 24a–b.

58. Deuteronomy 31:16–19.

59. The more religious Holocaust survivors were before the war, the more they stayed that way. One study showed that 61 percent of "ultra-Orthodox" survivors stayed religious, while only 9 percent of moderately religious Jews did so after the war (Reeve Robert Brenner, *The Faith and Doubt of Holocaust Survivors* [New York: Free Press, 1990], p. 46). Many survivors realized that the only reason they survived was because God miraculously saved them from the jaws of death.

60. *Becoming a Jew,* p. 8.

61. *Becoming a Jew,* p. 51.

62. *Brachot* 7a, based on Exodus 33:13, 19; *Yevamot* 121b.

63. *Genesis Rabbah* 32:3; *Kiddushin* 40b.

64. *Shevuot* 39a.

65. *The Way of God* 2:3:9.

66. *The Way of God* 2:3:9; *Mo'ed Katan* 25a.

There are many other reasons that pious people suffer as individuals: One is because God's yardstick for measuring their guilt or innocence is different from ours, and righteous people are judged more stringently. The more people are connected to God, the more damage they cause by their misdeeds. The ripple effects of a righteous person's sins on everyone around are much greater than those of people who are less spiritually developed (see *The Way of God* 2:2:5 and 1:3:9).

God takes away some righteous people because we take them for granted. We then contemplate what they should have meant to us and adopt their values.

Some pious people also die so that we won't be punished on their account. If they are good role models but we don't live properly, their piety subjects us to punishment. Since the entire raison d'etre of righteous Jewish leaders is to serve their generation, they have no desire to live when they can't improve the lot of the Jews.

67. *Shabbat* 54b. See also Alshich on Psalms 5:7.

68. *Shemot Rabbah* 1:9; *Sotah* 11. Job was one of Pharaoh's three advisers. When Pharaoh asked what to do about the "Jewish problem," Bilaam recommended annihilating the Jews, Job kept silent, and Jethro fled the country. Pharaoh heeded Bilaam's advice by enslaving and murdering the Jews. Even though Job was righteous, he was punished for being remiss at a critical time.

69. *Shevuot* 39a; *Zohar* 1:68a.

70. *Bava Kamma* 60a.

71. *Bava Batra* 10b.

72. All of a Jew's sins are atoned for, even without repentance and confession, if he or she is murdered or executed by the government for being a Jew (*Kohelet Rabbah* 4:2).

73. *The Way of God* 2:3:2. We can conceptualize having free choice in the context of God's directing history by imagining that we are in a river flowing toward a destination. We each have free will to respond to the water's flow. Some of us will try to swim upstream, others will traverse the current and reach the river banks; still others will drown because they waste all of their energy trying to stay in the same place; a small number will stay afloat and let the water carry them to its destination. We can't stop the river (the divinely guided course of world history) from flowing. We can only decide how we will respond to it.

74. Though there were Jewish splinter sects even in ancient times, none prior to the eighteenth century even entertained the idea that God did not give the Torah. Karaites denied the divinity of the Oral Law but steadfastly maintained that God gave the Five Books of Moses and observed their laws literally. Even Christians believe that God gave the Torah, and the early ones observed Jewish rituals until Paul tried to make Christianity more appealing to the masses by discarding the commandments.

75. Deuteronomy 16:3.

76. Deuteronomy 4:9–10.

77. Deuteronomy 4:23.

78. Deuteronomy 8:2–4.

79. At best, other religions claim to have been "revealed" to only one or two select people under unobservable circumstances.

80. Josephus Flavius, *Against Apion* 1:8.

81. Ben Hecht refutes the commonly held notion that most Hungarian Jews were observant. See *Perfidy* (New York: Julian Messner, 1961), p. 98. Large numbers of Polish Jews were also assimilated.

82. Michael Dov Weissmandel, *Min HaMetzar* (Jerusalem: Zeirei Agudat Yisrael, 1960). Quoted in David Landau, *Piety and Power* (New York: Hill and Wang, 1993), p. 140.

83. Much of this is described in Joseph Friedensen, *Heroine of Rescue* (New York: ArtScroll, 1984).

84. The truth about how leaders of the state of Israel, secular Zionists, and their organizations betrayed European Jews is described in *Perfidy*.

85. *Min HaMetzar,* quoted in *Piety and Power,* p. 140.

86. See *Perfidy,* especially p. 192.

87. *Midrash Mishlei* 12.

88. Deuteronomy 31:16–18.

89. Numbers 1:51.

90. Isaiah 8:2.

91. Micah 3:12.

92. Zechariah 8:4.

93. *Makkot* 24b.

94. There are two *haftarot* of repentance because we can repent out of love for God or out of fear of divine punishment. Both are valid, but repentance out of love can bring us to higher spiritual heights than fear of punishment.

95. Vilna Gaon on *Mishlei,* brought down by Rabbi Shlomo Brevda in *Yibaneh HaMikdash* (p. 130 or 132).

96. Isaiah 40:1.

97. *Yalkut Shimoni* on "*Nachamu, nachamu ami.*"

98. *Brachot* 3a, quoted by Rabbi Yitzchok Kirzner in his tape on the Holocaust.

99. Isaiah 40:2.

100. *The Book of Our Heritage,* pp. 257–258.

101. Rabbi Kirzner quotes this on his Holocaust tape.

102. Rabbi Moshe Kobriner in *Torat Avot* on Shabbat Nachamu.

FOR FURTHER READING

Berkovitz, Eliezer. *Faith after the Holocaust.* New York: Ktav, 1973.

——. *With God in Hell.* Brooklyn, NY: Sanhedrin Press, 1979.

Dawidowicz, Lucy. *The War Against the Jews 1933–1945.* New York: Holt, Rinehart and Winston, 1975.

Flannery, Edward. *The Anguish of the Jews.* New York: Macmillan, 1965.
A comprehensive history of anti-Semitism, written by a Catholic priest.

Friedensen, Joseph. *Heroine of Rescue: The Incredible Story of Recha Sternbuch.* New York: ArtScroll, 1984.
Describes the heroism of an observant Swiss Jewish woman in saving Jews during World War II.

Hecht, Ben. *Perfidy.* New York: Julian Messner, 1961.
Details the shameful behavior of the secular Zionist leaders, the Haganah, Ben-Gurion, Weizmann, and others during the Holocaust and the creation of the state of Israel.

Kahn, Ari, ed. *Discovery.* Jerusalem: Rothman Foundation, 1991.
   A textbook for use in Aish HaTorah Discovery seminars. One of the best sources to show
   the authenticity of the Torah and traditional Judaism.
Rosenberg, Bernhard H., and Heuman, Fred, eds. *Theological and Halakhic Reflections on
   the Holocaust.* Hoboken, NJ: Ktav, 1992.
Tauber, Ezriel. *Darkness Before Dawn: The Holocaust and Growth Through Suffering.*
   Monsey, NY: Shalheves, 1992.

Epilogue

T he Messiah will not come until people despair of redemption, and say Israel has neither a Supporter nor a Helper."[1]

Not only did the Torah predict the Jews' destructions, exiles, and Holocaust, it also predicted our final redemption. Moses told the Jews before he died:

> And it shall come to pass, when all of these things have happened to you, the blessing and the curse . . . and you take them to heart . . . among . . . the nations where the Lord your God has scattered you. You will return to Him and . . . listen to . . . everything that I command you today—you, and your children—with all your heart and . . . soul. And the Lord your God will return you from your captivity, and will have compassion on you, and will . . . gather you from all of the nations where He has scattered you. And if your scattered ones shall be at the ends of the earth, from there the Lord your God will gather you and . . . fetch you. And He will bring you to the land which your forefathers inherited, and you shall inherit it, and He will do good to you, and will multiply you more than your ancestors. And He will circumcise your hearts, and the hearts of your children, to love the Lord your God with all your heart, and with all of your soul, in order that you might live. . . . And the Lord will again rejoice over you for good . . . because you will listen to Him, to keep His commandments and seemingly irrational laws that are written in the Torah.[2]

Everything that happens to the Jewish people is scripted by a divine Author with a purpose in mind, and this is especially obvious in the events of this century. Our prophets predicted that God would "turn Jerusalem into a heap of ruins, a haunt of jackals."[3] The Almighty promised that during our long and dark exile, "I will devastate your land, and it will stay desolate for your enemies who live there."[4] That is, the land of Israel would be infertile for inhabitants other than the Jews until the time of our redemption. We were promised that once we returned to our land, it would flourish as it once did.[5]

Our Sages foretold hundreds of years ago how we would know that our time of redemption was near: "When the land of Israel will yield its produce in superabundance, it will signal the approach of the end of the exile. There is no clearer 'end' than this."[6]

These same words were echoed by a sixteenth-century Jewish commentator, at a time when the land of Israel was swampland and arid wilderness: "As long as Israel does not dwell in her land, the land won't produce as it used to. When the land begins to reflourish, and gives fruit in superabundance, this is a clear sign that the end, the time of Redemption, is close, when all Jews will return to their land."[7]

The Zohar, an ancient Kabbalistic work, predicted hundreds of years ago:

In the future, the descendants of Ishmael [the Arabs] will rule the Holy Land for a long period of time, while the land is empty. . . . They shall prevent the children of Israel from returning to their place until the Arabs' right to the land expires. . . .

Ishmael's descendants will stir up great wars in the world, and Edom's descendants [Christians] will gather against them and wage war against them on the sea, on land, and near Jerusalem, but the Holy Land will not be surrendered at that time.[8]

"All the nations will unite together against Jerusalem and make a peace treaty among themselves to turn against Israel and annihilate her, because Israel will establish a sovereign state for herself. It will be a time of crisis for the Jews, but they won't be broken. Rather, they will be saved from it."[9]

We have seen these prophecies fulfilled: there is now a large Jewish presence in the land of Israel for the first time in 1,900 years.

The United Nations, representing the peoples of the world, passed numerous resolutions condemning Israel. It has repeatedly tried to force us to give our land to the Arabs since the 1960s.

The land has become so productive that Israel now exports fruits and vegetables to Europe and America.

The Arabs have started six wars against Israel since 1948, and in the 1956 and Gulf Wars, the Western powers fought against the Arabs. Despite outnumbering the Jews by more than 100:1, the Arabs never won a war against the Israelis because God miraculously protected us.

We are now living on the "heels of the Messiah."[10] We have no more than a few hundred years before the world must reach its intended spiritual goals.[11] God is now accelerating history to get the world back on its spiritual track. He must make sure that the world will soon be ready for the Messianic era and world peace. At this time, He is not meting out visible justice to the nations of the world.[12]

During the twentieth century, we have witnessed countless seemingly unrelated events whose purpose is to move the world to its final destination. To name a few: two world wars and the use of nuclear weapons (both predicted in the Book of Joel); the rise and fall of Communism; the reunification of Germany and the destruction of the Berlin Wall; the establishment of the European Common Market; the resurgence of Jewish observance throughout the world.

God fulfilled His promise to disperse Jews to the four corners of the earth, and we are now privileged to see Him fulfill His promise to bring us home to Israel. Terrible famine and civil war in Ethiopia spurred Jews to abandon their country and move to Israel overnight. Jewish persecutions in Yemen, North Africa, Middle Eastern Arab countries, the former Soviet Union, and Yugoslavia likewise spurred Jews to move to Israel. Civil wars in Lebanon, Iran, Yugoslavia, the former Soviet Union, and other countries motivated many Jews who remained there to leave. Khomeini came to power and made Iranian Jews realize that Iran is not their real home. World War II convinced German and Austrian Jews that their primary identity is as Jews, not as Europeans, professionals, or intellectuals. Terrible persecutions of Iraqi and Syrian Jews reminded them that their only security comes from God, not from their host countries.

In recent years, we have seen the rise and fall of many "isms." Communism, socialism, ethical humanism, and liberalism all promised to create utopias, but each was a spectacular failure. Americans are finally realizing how secular morality and liberalism have ruined their country by creating a society with one of the highest crime rates in the world, rampant poverty among children, a society of single mothers, third-generation welfare recipients, millions of out-of-wedlock and teen pregnancies every year, and an epidemic of AIDS and other sexually transmitted diseases. People who grew up rejecting authority and conservative values are finally turning to belief in God and religion. They realize that unbridled freedom ultimately breeds violence, lack of respect for human life, and disintegration of family and society. The world is slowly but surely recognizing the evils inherent in man-made political, moral, and economic systems that are not linked to how God wants us to live.

We are also seeing thousands of estranged Jews return to their traditional heritage (the *baal teshuvah* movement). Hundreds of *yeshivot* (Jewish religious schools) have opened in Israel during the past two decades, as well as in the United States, Canada, South America, the former Soviet Union, and Europe. There are now more *yeshivot* in Israel than at any former time in history. Jews are thirsting to return to their heritage and are bringing their parents with them, just as the prophets predicted.[13]

We can know that just as the Torah accurately predicted our national calamities, it also predicted our future redemption, whose indications we now see on an almost daily basis.

Instead of being consumed by our past tragedies, we should do our best to guarantee that our national suffering and martyrdom have served worthwhile purposes. We bear a tremendous responsibility for ensuring that our martyrs did not die in vain. We do this by learning Torah and living according to it, by sanctifying our daily lives.

All of us will suffer at some time. Rather than expecting to have easy lives, we should try to find redemptive meaning in our suffering. We can also take solace in the fact that in the not-too-distant future, God will show us why all of our suffering was necessary and worthwhile.

NOTES

1. *Sanhedrin* 97a.
2. Paraphrased from Deuteronomy 30:1–6, 9–10.
3. Jeremiah 9:10.
4. Leviticus 26:32.
5. Nachmanides on Leviticus 26:32.
6. Rashi on *Sanhedrin* 98a.
7. Maharsha on *Sanhedrin* 98a.
8. *Zohar, Shemot, VaEra* 32a.
9. Rabbi Moshe Cordovero's commentary on the Zohar in the year 1522.
10. This term comes from *Sanhedrin* 98b.
11. Rabbi Moshe Chaim Luzzatto, *Maamar HaIkkarim,* "The Redemption."
12. During the first 6,000 years of human existence, God does not constrain evil. Rabbi Moshe Chaim Luzzatto, *The Knowing Heart* (Jerusalem: Feldheim, 1982), p. 47.
13. Malachi 3:24.

RESOURCES

Discovery seminars, given by Aish HaTorah throughout the world, introduce Jews of all backgrounds to the history of Judaism with scientific, historical, and archeological validation of its beliefs and divine origins. Contact your local Aish HaTorah office, or New York offices at (718) 377-8819; (212) 643-8802; or (914) 425-8255 for more information.

Arachim seminars and lectures, (800) 722-3191 or (914) 356-2766.
Similar to Discovery Seminars, they have lectures in English for Americans and in Hebrew for Israelis throughout the United States and Israel.

Appendix

A TORAH PERSPECTIVE REGARDING
The Health Care Proxy

QUALITY OF LIFE . . .

Life is a sacred trust over which we have stewardship. We have a halachic obligation to preserve this life and do nothing to endanger it. Active Euthanasia is never a permissible option. Withdrawing hydration and/or nutrition, since it must inevitably lead to the death of the patient, is considered to be active Euthanasia.

A quality of life that is burdensome to the patient may justify passive Euthanasia such as withholding resuscitation, blood pressure raising medication, or antibiotics. Only the patient and his/her proxy can declare a quality of life unacceptable.

ORGAN DONATION . . .

The saving of a life takes precedence over all but three halachic imperatives— murder, idolatry and adultery. Therefore, no halachic barriers exist to donation of the organs of the deceased if they are harvested in accord with the highest standards of dignity and propriety. Vital organs such as heart and liver may be donated after the patient has been declared dead by a competent neurologist based upon the clinical and/or radiological evidence. In accord with the ruling of the Rav, Reb Joseph Dov Soloveitchik, Shlita and Hagaon Harav Moshe Feinstein, z'tl and of the Chief Rabbis of Israel, death as determined by neurological criteria fully meets the highest standards of halacha.

Since organs that can be life saving *may be* donated, the family is urged to do so. When human life *can* be saved, it *must* be saved. Cornea transplants that can restore sight to the blind are treated in halacha as life-saving surgery. The *halacha* therefore looks with great favor on those who facilitate the procurement of life-saving organ donations.

PROCUREMENT . . .

It is important that the Health Care Proxy you appoint either be personally knowledgeable in both the medical and halachic considerations in making critical health care decisions or that you specify the persons your health care proxy is to consult or if you prefer, you may state at the discretion of my health care proxy.

Developed and published by The Commission on Medical Ethics of the Rabbinical Council of America, 275 Seventh Avenue, New York, N. Y. 10001, Tel. (212) 807-7888, Fax (212) 727-8452.

Health Care Proxy—A

GENERAL

(1) I,_____

hereby appoint _____

      (name, home address & telephone number)

as my health care agent to make any and all health care decisions for me, except to the extent that I state otherwise. This proxy shall take effect when and if I become unable to make my own health care decisions.

(2) *Optional instructions: I direct my agent to consult with Orthodox halachic authority prior to making his/her decisions.

    *(Your agent will not be allowed to make decisions about artificial nutrition and hydration.)

(3) Name of substitute or fill-in agent if the person I appoint above is unable, unwilling or unavailable to act as my health care agent

_____

      (name, home address & telephone number)

(4) Unless I revoke it, this proxy shall remain in effect indefinitely, or until the date stated below. This proxy shall expire (specific date or conditions, if desired):

_____

(5) Signature _____

Address _____

Date _____

Statement by Witnesses (must be 18 or older)

I declare that the person who signed this document is personally known to me and appears to be of sound mind and acting of his or her own free will. He or she signed (or asked another to sign for him or her) this document in my presence.

Witness 1 _____

Address _____

Witness 2 _____

Address _____

Health Care Proxy—B

(DETAILED DIRECTIVE)

MY MEDICAL DIRECTIVE

This Medical Directive expresses, and shall stand for, my wishes regarding medical treatments in the event that illness should make me unable to communicate them directly. I make this Directive, being 18 years or more of age, of sound mind, and appreciating the consequences of my decisions.

	SITUATION A		SITUATION B	
	If I am in a coma or a persistent vegetative state and, in the opinion of my physician and several consultants, have no known hope of regaining awareness and higher mental functions no matter what is done, then my wishes regarding use of the following, if considered medically reasonable, would be:		If I am in a coma and, in the opinion of my physician and several consultants, have a small likelihood of recovering fully, a slightly larger likelihood of surviving with permanent brain damage, and a much larger likelihood of dying, then my wishes regarding use of the following, if considered medically reasonable, would be:	
	I Want	I Do Not Want	I Want	I Do Not Want
Cardiopulmonary Resuscitation: if at the point of death, using drugs and electric shock to keep the heart beating; artificial breathing.				
Mechanical Breathing: breathing by machine.				
Major Surgery: such as removing the gall bladder or part of the intestines.				
Kidney Dialysis: cleaning the blood by machine or by fluid passed through the belly.				
Chemotherapy: using drugs to fight cancer.				
Invasive Diagnostic Tests: such as using a flexible tube to look into the stomach.				
Blood or Blood Products: such as giving transfusions.				
Antibiotics: using drugs to fight infection.				
Simple Diagnostic Tests: such as performing blood tests or x-rays.				
Pain Medications, even if they dull consciousness and indirectly shorten my life.				

	SITUATION C		SITUATION D	
	If I have brain damage or some brain disease that in the opinion of my physician and several consultants cannot be reversed and that makes me unable to recognize people or to communicate in any fashion, *and I also have a terminal illness,* such as incurable cancer, that will likely be the cause of my death, then my wishes regarding use of the following, if considered medically reasonable, would be:		If I have brain damage or some brain disease that in the opinion of my physician and several consultants cannot be reversed and that makes me unable to recognize people or to communicate in any fashion, *but I have no terminal illness,* and I can live in this condition for a long time, then my wishes regarding use of the following, if considered medically reasonable, would be:	
	I Want	I Do Not Want	I Want	I Do Not Want
Cardiopulmonary Resuscitation: if at the point of death, using drugs and electric shock to keep the heart beating; artificial breathing.				
Mechanical Breathing: breathing by machine.				
Major Surgery: such as removing the gall bladder or part of the intestines.				
Kidney Dialysis: cleaning the blood by machine or by fluid passed through the belly.				
Chemotherapy: using drugs to fight cancer.				
Invasive Diagnostic Tests: such as using a flexible tube to look into the stomach.				
Blood or Blood Products: such as giving transfusions.				
Antibiotics: using drugs to fight infection.				
Simple Diagnostic Tests: such as performing blood tests or x-rays.				
Pain Medications, even if they dull consciousness and indirectly shorten my life.				

Health Care Proxy—B (CONTINUED)

DURABLE POWER OF ATTORNEY

I understand that my wishes expressed in these four cases may not cover all possible aspects of my care if I become incompetent. I also may be undecided about whether I want a particular treatment or not. Consequently, there may be a need for someone to accept or refuse medical interventions for me in consultation with my physician. I authorize

_____

_____

as my proxy(s) to make the decision for me whenever my wishes expressed in this document are insufficient or undecided.

Should there be any disagreement between the wishes I have indicated in this document and the decision favored by my above-name proxy(s),

(Please delete one of the following two lines.)
I wish my proxy(s) to have authority over my Medical Directive.
(or)
I wish my Medical Directive to have authority over my proxy(s).

In matters concerning halacha, should there be any disagreement between the wishes of my proxies, a prominent orthodox halachic authority must be consulted and shall have final authority. Halachic authorities I would prefer to be consulted are:

1. _____

2. _____

3. _____

or

4. If above not available, my proxy may choose anyone he prefers.

ORGAN DONATIONS

I hereby make this anatomical gift to take effect upon my death for the sole purpose of transplantation of life saving organs such as: cornea, kidney, heart, lung, liver, pancreas. An orthodox halachic authority must be consulted as to proper protocol to follow.

MY MEDICAL DIRECTIVE

This Medical Directive expresses, and shall stand for, my wishes regarding medical treatments in the event that illness should make me unable to communicate them directly. I make this Directive, being 18 years or more of age, of sound mind, and appreciating the consequences of my decisions.

Signed _____ Date _____

Witness _____ Date _____

Witness _____ Date _____

The Halachic Living Will

PROXY AND DIRECTIVE WITH RESPECT TO HEALTH CARE DECISIONS AND POST-MORTEM DECISIONS

FOR USE IN NEW YORK STATE

The "Halachic Living Will" is designed to help ensure that all medical and post-death decisions made by others on your behalf will be made in accordance with Jewish law and custom (*halacha*). This document, the "Proxy and Directive with Respect to Health Care Decisions and Post-Mortem Decisions," is the basic form that provides such protection.

INSTRUCTIONS

(a) Please print your name on the first line of the form.

(b) In section 1, print the name, address, and day and evening telephone numbers of the person you wish to designate as your *agent* to make medical decisions on your behalf it, G-d forbid, you ever become incapable of making them on your own.

You may also insert the name, address, and telephone numbers of an *alternate agent* to make such decisions if your main agent is unable, unwilling, or unavailable to make such decisions.

It is recommended that before appointing anyone to serve as your agent or alternate agent you should ascertain that person's willingness to serve in such capacity. In addition, if you have made arrangements with a burial society (*Chevra Kadisha*) for the handling and disposition of your body after death, you may wish to advise your agents of such arrangements.

Note: *New York law allows virtually any competent adult* (an adult is a person 18 years of age or older, or anyone who has married) *to serve as a health care agent.* Thus, you may appoint as your agent (or alternate agent) your spouse, adult child, parent or other adult relative.

You may also appoint a non-relative to serve as your agent (or alternate agent), unless that individual has already been appointed by 10 other persons to serve as a health care agent; or unless that individual is a non-physician employee of a health care facility in which you are a patient or resident. (*continued*)

Developed and published by: Agudath Israel of America • 84 William Street • New York, NY 10038 • 212-797-9000

Underwritten in part by a grant from Elderplan, Inc. • 1276 50th Street • Brooklyn, NY 11219 • 718-438-2600

(c) **In section 3, please print the name, address, and telephone numbers of the Orthodox Rabbi whose guidance you want your agent to follow,** should any questions arise as to the requirements of *halacha*.

You should then print the name, address, and telephone numbers of the Orthodox Jewish institution or organization you want your agent to contact for a referral to *another* Orthodox Rabbi *if* the rabbi you have identified is unable, unwilling or unavailable to provide the appropriate consultation and guidance.

You are of course free to insert the name of any Orthodox Rabbi or institution/organization you would like, but before doing so it is advisable to discuss the matter with the rabbi or institution/organization to ascertain their competency and willingness to serve in such capacity.

(d) **At the conclusion of the form, print the date, sign your name, and print your address.** If you are not physically able to do these things, New York law allows another person to sign and date the form on your behalf, as long as he or she does so *at your direction, in your presence,* and *in the presence of two adult witnesses*.

(e) **Two witnesses should sign their names and insert their addresses beneath your signature.** These two witnesses must be competent adults. *Neither of them should be the person you have appointed as your health care agent (or alternate agent).* They may, however, be your relatives.

(f) It is recommended that you keep the original of this form among your valuable papers; and that you **distribute copies to the health care agent (and alternate agent)** you have designated in section 1, **to the rabbi and institution/organization** you have designated in section 3, as well as to **your doctors, your lawyer,** and anyone else who is likely to be contacted in times of emergency.

(g) **If at any time you wish to revoke this Proxy and Directive, you may do so by executing a new one; or by notifying your agent or health care provider, orally or in writing, of your intent to revoke it.**

If you do not revoke the Proxy and Directive, New York law provides that it remains in effect indefinitely. Obviously, if any of the persons whose names you have inserted in the Proxy and Directive dies or becomes otherwise incapable of serving in the role you have assigned, it would be wise to execute a new Proxy and Directive.

(h) It is recommended that you also complete the second component of the Halachic Living Will, the **"Emergency Instructions Card,"** and carry it with you in your wallet or billfold.

(i) If, upon consultation with your rabbi, you would like to add to this standardized Proxy and Directive any additional expression of your wishes with respect to medical and/or post-mortem decisions, you may do so by attaching a "rider" to the standardized form. If you choose to do so, or if you have any other questions concerning this form, please consult an attorney.

Halachic Living Will

PROXY AND DIRECTIVE WITH RESPECT TO HEALTH CARE DECISIONS AND POST-MORTEM DECISIONS

I, _____, hereby declare as follows:

1. Appointment of Agent: In recognition of the fact that there may come a time when I will become unable to make my own health care decisions because of illness, injury or other circumstances, I hereby appoint

Name of Agent: _____

Agent Address: _____

Telephone: Day _____ Evening: _____

as my health care agent to make any and all health care decisions for me, consistent with my wishes as set forth in this directive.

If the person named above is unable, unwilling or unavailable to act as my agent, I hereby appoint

Name of Alternate Agent: _____

Alternate Address: _____

Agent Telephone: Day _____ Evening _____

to serve in such capacity.

This appointment shall take effect in the event I become unable, because of illness, injury or other circumstances, to make my own health care decisions.

2. Jewish Law to Govern Health Care Decisions: I am Jewish. It is my desire, and I hereby direct, that all health care decisions made for me be made pursuant to Jewish law and custom as determined in accordance with strict Orthodox interpretation and tradition. By way of example, and without limiting in any way the generality of the foregoing, it is my wish that Jewish law and custom should dictate the course of my health care with respect to such matters as the performance or non-performance of cardio-pulmonary resuscitation if I suffer cardiac or respiratory arrest; the initiation or discontinuance of any particular course of medical treatment or other form of life-support maintenance, including tube-delivered nutrition and hydration; and the method and timing of determination of death.

3. Ascertaining the Requirements of Jewish Law: In order to effectuate my wishes, if any question arises as to the requirements of Jewish law and custom in connection with this declaration, I direct my agent to consult with and follow the guidance of the following Orthodox Rabbi:

Name of Rabbi: _____

Rabbi   Address: _____

Telephone: Day _____ Evening _____

If such rabbi is unable, unwilling or unavailable to provide such consultation and guidance, then I direct my agent to consult with and follow the guidance of an Orthodox Rabbi referred by the following Orthodox Jewish institution or organization:

Name of Institution/Organization: _____

Organization   Address: _____

Telephone: Day _____ Evening _____

If such institution or organization is unable, unwilling or unavailable to make such a reference, or if the rabbi referred by such institution or organization is unable, unwilling or unavailable to provide such guidance, then I direct my agent to consult with and follow the guidance of an Orthodox Rabbi whose guidance on issues of Jewish law and custom my agent in good faith believes I would respect and follow.

4. Direction to Health Care Providers: Any health care provider shall rely upon and carry out the decisions of my agent, and may assume that such decisions reflect my wishes and were arrived at in accordance with the procedures set forth in this directive, unless such health care provider shall have good cause to believe that my agent has not acted in good faith in accordance with my wishes as expressed in this directive.

If the persons designated in section 1 above as my agent and alternate agent are unable, unwilling or unavailable to serve in such capacity, it is my desire, and I hereby direct, that any health care provider or other person who will be making health care decisions on my behalf follow the procedures outlined in section 3 above if any questions of Jewish law and custom should arise.

Pending contact with the agent and/or rabbi described above, it is my desire, and I hereby direct, that all health care providers undertake all essential emergency and/ or life sustaining measures on my behalf.

5. Post-Mortem Decisions: It is also my desire, and I hereby direct, that after my death, all decisions concerning the handling and disposition of my body be made pursuant to Jewish law and custom as determined in accordance with strict Orthodox interpretation and tradition. By way of example, and without limiting in any way the generality of the foregoing, it is my wish that there be conformance with Jewish law and custom with respect to such matters and questions as whether there exist exceptional circumstances that would permit an exception to the general prohibition under Jewish law against the performance of an autopsy or dissection of my body; the permissibility or non-permissibility of the removal and usage of any of my body organs or tissue for transplantation purposes; and the expeditious burial of my body and all preparations leading to burial.

Time is of the essence with regard to these questions. I therefore direct that any health care provider in attendance at my death notify the agent and/or rabbi described above immediately upon my death, in addition to any other person whose consent by law must be solicited and obtained prior to the use of any part of my body as an anatomical gift, so that appropriate decisions and arrangements can be made in accordance with my wishes. Pending such notification, it is my desire, and I hereby direct, that no autopsy, dissection or other post-mortem procedure be performed on my body.

6. Incontrovertible Evidence of My Wishes: If, for any reason, this document is deemed not legally effective as a health care proxy, or if the persons designated in section 1 above as my agent and alternate agent are unable, unwilling or unavailable to serve in such capacity, I declare to my family, my doctor and anyone else whom it may concern that the wishes I have expressed herein with regard to compliance with Jewish law and custom should be treated as incontrovertible evidence of my intent and desire with respect to all health care measures and post-mortem procedures; and that it is my wish that the procedure outlined in section 3 above should be followed if any questions of Jewish law and custom should arise.

7. Duration and Revocation: It is my understanding and intention that unless I revoke this proxy and directive, it will remain in effect indefinitely. My signature on this document shall be deemed to constitute a revocation of any prior health care proxy, directive or other similar document I may have executed prior to today's date.

Date: _____

    Signature _____

Signature [Your signature: or, if you are not physically capable of signing, the signature of another person signing your name on your behalf]

    Residing at _____ [address]

DECLARATION OF WITNESSES

I declare that the person who signed (or asked another to sign) this document is personally known to me and appears to be of sound mind and acting willingly and free from duress. He (or she) signed (or asked another to sign for him or her) this document in my presence (and that person signed in my presence). I am not the person appointed as agent by this document.

Witness No. 1 _____

Residing at _____ [address]

Witnesses

Witness No. 2 _____

Residing at _____ [address]

Agudath Israel of America - 1990

Index

About the Author

Lisa Aiken received her Ph.D. in clinical psychology from Loyola University of Chicago. She was the chief psychologist at Lenox Hill Hospital in New York City and clinical assistant professor at New York Medical College, Long Island University, and St. John's University. She currently does psychotherapy with individuals and couples in Manhattan and Great Neck, New York.

Dr. Aiken coauthored the *The Art of Jewish Prayer* with Rabbi Yitzchok Kirzner and is the author of *To Be a Jewish Woman*. She gives lectures throughout the United States, Canada, and Israel on diverse Jewish and psychological topics and has appeared on radio and television.